The Secretary's Complete Self-Training Manual

Printed in the United States of America

Library of Congress Cataloging-in-Publication Data
The secretary's complete self-training manual / Bureau of Business
    Practice editorial staff.
        p.   cm.
    Includes index.
    ISBN 0-13-799529-6 : $15.95
    1. Office practice—Handbooks, manuals, etc. 2. Secretaries—
Handbooks, manuals, etc.   I. Bureau of Business Practice.
HF5547.5.S422   1992
651.3'741--dc20

                                                    92-19850
                                                    CIP

ISBN 0-13-799529-6

Introduction

What is it that makes that secretary so exceptional? Why is it that the clerical worker down the hall always seems to tackle tasks so easily? And why does the administrative assistant sitting at the desk next to you seem able to juggle countless assignments without ever missing a deadline? In other words, what exactly do these employees have in common? Just what is it that makes them the best?

Today's office-support professional must not only have the ability to communicate politely and intelligently (whether it's in person, over the telephone, or in any kind of writing) but also have exceptional organizational skills and a working knowledge of various types of business math. In addition, he or she is faced with the extra challenges (and advantages) of the automated office. Combine these skills with a desire for professional growth and pride in performance and you have the beginnings of what makes the best and most talented office-support professionals.

In truth, these employees are *committed* to being the best and doing the best that they can at all times. It's a commitment that they have made to themselves—and it's one that *you* can easily make. You must simply ask yourself the question, *Am I doing all I can to improve myself professionally?* and you must answer honestly.

Once you've answered that question, you must find out where you need improvement and *how* you can improve yourself. You have to look for the ways and the tools that will help you achieve your goal of becoming the best office-support worker you can be. *The Secretary's Complete Self-Training Manual* is one of those tools.

You'll find that this manual covers several topics in detail. They include:

- Professional PR Skills: Effective Office Communication

- Organization and Time Management: Discipline Your Daily Plan

- Communicating Clearly: Making Words Work

- Writing for Results: Better Letters and Reports

- Word Processors and Computers: Tackling Office Technology

- Figures and Finance: Mastery of Office Math

Each of these sections will provide you with basic and detailed information concerning the topic in question, easy-to-use suggestions and hints, examples or charts to illustrate particular points, and quizzes to help you determine how well you've understood the information that has been presented.

The purpose of this manual is to help you pinpoint any weaknesses you exhibit on the job, boost your knowledge about those particular areas, and help you turn those weaknesses into *strengths*. It is meant to inform you about areas you may not have known about, to point out misconceptions you may have had and replace them with accurate information, and to increase your knowledge about areas you may be particularly interested in. In short, this manual will help you examine several subjects you need to understand if you want to perform your job in the best manner you can. It will also help you take a good look at exactly how you go about performing your job—and provide you with ways to complete your tasks in a more organized and efficient manner.

But this manual will also do a bit more. It will get you thinking not only about *how* you are performing your job but also what exactly your performance *means*. For instance, we all know that it's important to spell words correctly when we're writing a business letter. But do we know exactly *why* it's so important? Do we think about the fact that a misspelling may cause our reader to misunderstand the letter's message? that it may cause him or her to form a negative impression not only of the letter-writer but of our *entire* company? that there's a good chance that bad impression may cause our reader to choose to do business with another company? In other words, we need to think about what our performance is telling others about ourself and about our company as a whole.

In short, this book will allow you to examine the role your job plays within your company. It will help you understand the value of the tasks you perform every day, the effect those tasks have on other people within and outside your company, and the goals your company is working toward. Simply understanding the importance your work has in helping your company achieve those goals will make your job that much more enjoyable. And the more enjoyable your work, the more motivated you'll become to gather additional knowledge and to improve your job skills as much as possible. And that's what this manual is all about.

For information on how to use this manual, please turn to page 11.

Table of Contents

Section One: Professional PR Skills: Effective Office Communication

Table of Contents

Section Two: Organization and Time Management: Discipline Your Daily Plan

Table of Contents

Section Three: Communicating Clearly: Making Words Work

Table of Contents

Section Four: Writing for Results: Better Letters and Reports

Table of Contents

Section Five: Word Processors and Computers: Tackling Office Technology

Table of Contents

Section Six: Figures and Finance: Mastery of Office Math

How to Use This Manual

You're about to see that this manual is unlike others of its type. Although on the surface it may not seem all that unusual, you'll find that its contents contain several surprises. You see, *The Secretary's Complete Self-Training Manual* can be used in a number of different ways; how you choose to use it is strictly up to you. For example, you may decide to treat it as:

- **A WORKBOOK:** If you choose to read this manual from start to finish, you can treat each new chapter as a lesson. Each lesson will build on the previous one, and you'll be given several opportunities to test and apply your knowledge. Some sections will even provide you with a "final exam" that will show just how much information you have retained after completing all the lessons in those sections. You'll be able to work at your own pace, go through lessons again if you didn't quite understand them the first time around, or even skip lessons if you feel you already have a good understanding of that topic. You may decide to go through all six "courses" that are provided, or you may choose to skip one altogether, feeling that you're already strong in that area. Or you may want to randomly browse through a particular "course" for a quick review of the subject or to brush up your skills a bit. In short, you can use this workbook in any way you want; just be sure you use it in the manner that will be the most helpful to you.

- **A REFERENCE BOOK:** This manual can also serve as a desk reference that you can turn to whenever you need some help with an office problem or the answer to a particular question. You'll find that locating the topic you're interested in can be accomplished in several ways. If you're interested in locating information about filing, for example, you can simply flip to the index at the back of the book. There you'll find that the book contains information about filing systems and fundamentals along with a chapter concerning computer files. But there is another way to locate the information you need. If you know that the topic you're interested in will appear in a particular section of the book, simply go to the beginning of that section. If you only want to read about *computer* files, for instance, rather than turning to the large index at the end of the book, flip to the beginning of the section entitled "Word Processors and Computers: Tackling Office Technology." There you'll find a smaller, more specific index that will pinpoint exactly where you can find the information within that particular section.

You'll find that each of the six sections within this book begins with such an index.

The small indexes at the beginning of each section can also serve another purpose. Let's say that you want to locate a particular rule concerning capitalization. You find the page number you need when looking through the index beginning the section called "Communicating Clearly: Making Words Work." Yet as you're skimming through that index, you also spot the headings "Verbals," "Word Division," and "Pronouns," other topics that you feel you need to look into. The point? When you're looking for a particular topic, these indexes can also help you pinpoint other areas that you should probably read up on.

But you'll find that *The Secretary's Complete Self-Training Manual* will do even more for you than build your office skills or serve as a handy desk reference: It will help you discover a new self-confidence and reliability within yourself that you may not have known existed. And once you've discovered this, nothing can stand in the way of your success.

PROFESSIONAL PR SKILLS
Effective Office Communication

INTRODUCTION

When you're on the job, you probably spend a great deal of time working and dealing with people. That's why you always need to be conscious of the impression you're making, know how to develop a cooperative, professional relationship with customers, co-workers, and supervisors alike, and understand how to handle awkward situations both tactfully and effectively. In short, you need to become a public relations expert. In this section, you'll learn several important PR skills that will allow you to work better with those around you—and to get the results you need from others to get the job done in as efficient a manner as possible.

Would you like some tips to help you improve your technique over the telephone? Perhaps you need some information on how to defuse an angry customer? If you'd like to research a particular aspect of public relations, you can locate the subject you want simply by glancing at the index below.

- How do you create a positive company image? Let us show you the ways.

- Good interpersonal skills: an important must for your job.

- Tips on greeting customers, answering questions, and making introductions.

PUBLIC RELATIONS IS AN ESSENTIAL SKILL

In today's fast-paced marketplace, businesses must be highly competitive just to exist. But the company that *succeeds* does so because of an intangible factor—the attitude of the customer toward it.

What does this customer attitude have to do with you? Well, as an office-support professional, you play a crucial role in influencing customer opinion. It may not seem so at first, but public relations is a very important part of your job. In fact, you represent your company every time you greet a customer, answer the telephone, or write a letter. If, for example, you dress carelessly for work or speak poorly of your job, other people certainly won't think much of the organization that employs you. And your firm could end up losing valuable customers.

What Can an Office Employee Do?

Obviously, you want to be a good company booster since doing so means boosting business. But if you're not sure of exactly *how* to be a good company representative, the following guidelines can help. They'll show you how to create a positive image for your company.

Public Relations Guidelines

Find out as much about your company as you can. Read the publications it distributes, ask questions whenever you're unsure about a change in policy, and learn the company's viewpoints on important issues you may have to discuss with outsiders.

Listen to what others have to say about your company. If you hear false information or rumors about your company, be sure to correct them. These public misperceptions, if left uncorrected, could damage business. You can prevent these misunderstandings from occurring in the future by letting your boss or a member of your personnel department know about them.

Take pride in your company's products and in the services that it offers. Then don't hesitate to let others know about them. Be a good company booster.

Remember that you represent your company. So speak favorably about it wherever you go.

Make an effort to get people interested in working for or doing business with your company. If you have business cards or samples of your company's products, give them out. Stand behind your company's goods or services, and let others know that you do.

If appropriate, encourage those outside your company to make visits to your firm for further explanations of what it does or to see how it operates. Promote community interest and involvement.

Questions to Ask Yourself

Following is a list of questions and explanations that should help you assess your personal value to your company in the area of public relations.

1. How Do You Greet People?

Chances are, you're responsible for welcoming others into the office. When you greet visitors, show them the same warmth and genuine concern that you would show to visitors in your own home. A chilly smile and mechanical attitude won't encourage repeat visits. Instead, greet office visitors with a smile that says, "I'm a competent professional here to assist you."

2. Can You Answer Questions Authoritatively?

In order to answer the various questions the public might ask, it's important that you know your company well. You must also be able to answer "why" questions— why something has to be done or why it can't be done; why something happened or why it didn't happen. So learn as much as you can about the production, procedures, and policies of your company. Keep abreast of policy changes, ask questions, and learn the company rules in case you're asked to explain the company's actions. When you answer questions for your company, you should be able to do so in a confident, informed manner.

3. How Do You Handle Introductions?

When there's a new customer or client or a new employee at your company, it's up to you to make the proper introductions. Start by being friendly when the new person introduces himself or herself to you. Make the caller feel welcome. And remember to make sure that you have understood his or her name correctly. Then as soon as possible, introduce the new employee, customer, or client to the appropriate company executives, and explain either the new employee's role within the company or the purpose of the caller's visit to your boss.

4. What Impression of Your Company Do You Create Outside the Office?

Because of your position in the company, your actions or your words can affect public opinion. So always act in the best interest of your firm. Handle confidential matters discreetly. Speak well of your firm. Don't try to impress people with your knowledge or position by discussing business outside the office. Remember, you are your employer's representative—a public relations expert!

HOW TO HANDLE OFFICE VISITORS

■ A tactful approach to office visitors can smooth the way to a good business relationship.

■ Screening office visitors for your boss.

■ What to do when a customer doesn't have an appointment.

Good business relations are vital to a company's success. That's why it's so important that you make a good impression for your company right from the start, especially for those hard-to-please customers.

As you know, dealing with difficult customers is never easy. But it's your job to see that office visits go as smoothly as possible.

To help, here are some guidelines for greeting every office visitor in a professional and confident manner:

1. Introduce yourself to a new visitor. For example, you might say: "Good morning, Mr. Roberts. I'm Judy Allen, Ms. Weston's secretary."

2. Find out the name of the caller, his or her company, and the purpose of the visit. When a visitor doesn't hand you a business card—and if it seems likely he or she would have one—don't hesitate to ask for it. These cards will come in handy later for introductions and for your files.

3. If your boss isn't immediately available, make the caller comfortable while he or she waits. Never look upon visitors as interruptions to your work—no matter how many letters, memos, and reports you have to type. You're never so busy that you can't give visitors a few minutes of your undivided attention.

4. Maintain a businesslike atmosphere. When a visitor is near your desk, make an extra effort not to carry on personal conversations with office co-workers or over the phone. Also, take precautions with confidential information.

5. After a visitor has seen your boss, send him or her off with a smile and some pleasantry, such as "It was good to see you." If you're busy when a visitor is leaving—or if the visitor is involved in a conversation—a friendly smile is enough.

Screening Office Visitors

Even the most efficient method won't take all the guesswork out of the screening procedure, but there is a way to make the screening process a lot easier:

To help judge which callers would be welcomed by your employer and which should be avoided, ask your boss for a list of people he or she will see under *any and all* circumstances. This would include family members and especially important business contacts. Know which visitors can be seen by someone else and which you can take care of yourself. And be tactful in your explanations to those callers your employer will not see.

Fortunately, most callers don't object to telling you the purpose of their visit. But, occasionally, you do run into these problems:

SITUATION

A visitor walks into your office without an appointment and asks to see your employer. He gives you his name but says that the purpose of his call is personal. Which of the following three approaches would you use?

Approach #1

"I'm sorry, but I'm not able to make an appointment for you unless I can tell Ms. Weston what you want to discuss with her. If you can take it up with me, perhaps I can save you time by discussing it with Ms. Weston for you."

Approach #2

"I'm sorry, but Ms. Weston sees people only by appointment. I make all her appointments, and I have to ask you what you want. You'll understand, I'm sure, that I'm merely following instructions."

Approach #3

"I'm sorry, but Ms. Weston has a busy schedule today and she told me not to disturb her. But I would interrupt her if I knew why you wanted to see her. Then maybe she could squeeze you in or make an appointment for another time."

Which approach did you select? Number *three* is the most tactful. It should get you the information you want without offending the visitor. Number *one* is acceptable, but *two* should be avoided.

SITUATION

You have tactfully tried to find out the reason for the call, but this visitor stubbornly refuses to tell you. Which one of the following approaches do you think is best?

Approach #1

"I'm sorry that I can't be of help to you, but office rules are office rules—they are made by Ms. Weston herself and not by me, and Ms. Weston expects me to abide by them. So if you cannot give me even a hint as to what business you wish to take up with her, I'm afraid that I cannot help you."

Approach #2

"In that case, perhaps you will write Ms. Weston a note that I can take in to her. Just tell Ms. Weston briefly what you want to see her about, and ask for an appointment. Then she can make her own decision."

Approach #3

"That is unfortunate, for until I know what you wish to discuss with Ms. Weston, I can't very well make an appointment for you."

Approach *two* is the most discreet. Your employer will be able to find out what the visitor wants, and then she can decide whether or not she wants to see this caller. Approaches *one* and *three* are tactless and should be avoided.

SPEAKING TIPS FOR THE TELEPHONE

- Are your telephone skills up to par? Find out with these helpful telephone tips.

- Test your telephone pronunciation skills with this telephone quiz.

- Learn the key to effective telephone deliveries.

In this age of high technology, the telephone remains one of the most powerful and influential tools at your company's disposal. In the right hands, the telephone can dramatically improve sales and public relations. In fact, it's doubtful whether a business could survive without one.

As an office-support professional, it's up to you to make the most of this powerful tool. When you talk on the telephone, your voice represents your company. The key to productive telephone use is your delivery. When you're on the phone, your voice has to carry your message. You can't use body language and facial expressions to make your point clear.

Training Your Telephone Voice

Since your own personality as well as your company's is reflected over the telephone, you should work to make your telephone voice as effective as possible. Here are a few simple rules to follow for cultivating a pleasant telephone voice:

1. Speak directly into the telephone transmitter. Don't let the telephone drift from its proper position; your voice will become difficult to understand.

2. Try to convey a friendly and intelligent interest in the caller. When someone calls, you want to sound alert and helpful.

3. Visualize the person on the other end of the line. Speak directly to that person, not to the telephone.

4. Use simple, nontechnical language and avoid slang. For example, at the end of the telephone conversation, don't say "bye-bye." Slang can leave a very bad impression.

Pronunciation

The most important telephone skill is pronunciation. Every syllable of every word must be pronounced properly. Otherwise your listener will have trouble understanding you.

How sure are you of your pronunciation? See if you can underline the correct pronunciation of each of the words in the following quiz.

▼ ▼ TAKE A TEST ▼ ▼

QUIZ

1. infamous	a) in' fuh mus	b) in fay' mus
2. vanilla	a) vuh nel' uh	b) vuh nil' uh
3. genuine	a) jen' u ine	b) jen' u in
4. irreparable	a) ir re pair' a ble	b) ir rep' ar a ble
5. psychiatrist	a) sye kye' a trist	b) sye' ke a' trist

6. remuneration	a) re new' mer ay' shun	b) re mew' ner ay' shun
7. preferable	a) pref' er a ble	b) pre fer' a ble
8. hospitable	a) hos' pit a ble	b) ha spit' a ble
9. alumnae	a) a lum' nee	b) a lum' nia
10. municipal	a) mu nis' i pal	b) mu' ni sip' al

ANSWERS

1. a) in' fuh mus—accent the first syllable and pronounce the second syllable *fuh*.

2. b) vuh nil' uh—let the second syllable rhyme with pill.

3. b) jen' u in—the last syllable should rhyme with pin.

4. b) ir rep' ar a ble—accent the second syllable, not the third.

5. a) sye kye' a trist—focus your attention on the second syllable for accent and pronunciation.

6. b) re mew' ner ay' shun—the second syllable is *mu*, not *nu*.

7. a) pref' er a ble—the first syllable should be accented.

8. a) hos' pit a ble—accent the first syllable.

9. a) a lum' nee—the last syllable should rhyme with glee. It can also be pronounced *a lum' nye* as in cry.

10. a) mu nis' i pal—the accent is on the second syllable.

When you are doubtful about a pronunciation, say the word slowly, concentrating on each syllable, to make sure you get it right. Don't be afraid to use your jaw, your tongue, and your lips to form sounds properly.

Speaking Tips

✓ Don't talk too fast or too slowly. A person speaking at the average rate says about 126 words a minute. Suggestion: Why don't you time yourself to find out how fast you talk? If you're very far off the average, you can practice slowing down or speeding up your delivery. But keep a natural pace. You don't *have* to say 126 words *every* minute.

✓ Watch out for monotonous delivery. Your voice is capable of more than 1,000 inflections. Try using some of them. You can emphasize words by saying them at a higher pitch, just as you can emphasize words by pausing after them.

✓ Don't vary your volume. While you want to have some variation in the pitch of your voice, you should not vary the volume too much. Shouting into the phone will only annoy the caller, and speaking too quietly will make it difficult for you to be understood. Your aim: to speak in a normal conversational tone with plenty of inflections, but not too much variation in voice level.

✓ Strike a happy medium. Of course you want to sound pleasant and friendly on the phone, but you don't want to seem too familiar. Overfriendliness will jar the person at the other end of the line just as quickly as a cold tone.

- In this chapter, you'll find twenty great tips for a pleasing telephone personality.

- Pointers for carrying on a professional conversation with customers.

- Guidelines for placing, answering and transferring calls.

DEVELOPING GOOD TELEPHONE TECHNIQUES

Think about how frequently you use the telephone to contact customers and clients, to order goods and services, or just to communicate with the people within your organization. Without the telephone, your company wouldn't be able to keep in touch with the people who are most important to it.

But the telephone is only a tool. How effective a tool it is depends on how well you use it.

Here are 20 tips on telephone techniques. They're a condensation of hints published by telephone companies. Study this list, and practice the suggestions daily.

1. When the phone rings, answer promptly. Otherwise your caller may hang up and take his or her business elsewhere.

2. Identify yourself and your company or department. Examples: "This is Ms. Jones." "Brown Brothers, Ms. Jones speaking." "Editorial Department. This is Ms. Jones." "This is Mr. Brown's office, Ms. Jones speaking."

3. Speak distinctly and pleasantly. As we mentioned in the last chapter, your voice may be the first impression of your company a caller receives. Remember, a friendly voice makes friends.

4. If you must put your caller on hold to get information, explain how long you'll be gone and offer to call him or her back.

5. Screen calls tactfully. A polite way of asking who's calling is "May I ask who is calling?" or "May I tell Ms. Smith who is calling?" If the caller still refuses to identify himself or herself, you can politely say, "May I suggest you write to Ms. Smith and mark your letter 'Personal'? I'll be glad to see that she gets it at once."

6. Know where your employer is. If he or she is out of town, make sure you know the expected date of return and the phone numbers of the places where he or she can be reached in an emergency. However, don't give out this kind of information unless it's absolutely necessary. *Never* give out a home phone number unless you have permission to do so.

7. Take messages willingly. Note the caller's name, the name of his or her company if appropriate, the telephone number, the date and time of the call, and whether the caller wants to be called back. Repeat the information to make sure it's correct. Don't forget to initial the message or put your name on it. Then deliver the message promptly.

8. If you must transfer a call, ask the caller's permission before doing so, and explain why he or she is being connected to someone else. Transfer only when you definitely know the correct person with whom the caller should be in touch.

9. When placing a call, be sure of the number. Wrong numbers can be embarrassing. If you're in doubt, you'll find it pays to look up the number *before* you call.

10. Allow enough time for your call to be answered. After you call a number, give the person you're calling at least a minute to reach the telephone.

11. Be ready to talk as soon as the person you called answers the phone. Because most calls go through without delay, doing this is not only courteous but also timesaving.

12. Ask whether it's a convenient time for the other person to talk. You wouldn't break into a conference to talk to someone in person, and you should try to observe this same rule of etiquette when you're on the phone. It's a matter of courtesy to inquire of the person you call whether it's a convenient time for him or her to talk.

13. Don't raise your voice. Shouting distorts your voice over the telephone. The instrument is tuned to normal voice level, and loudness causes the sound to blur. A loud voice also sounds gruff and unpleasant.

14. Identify yourself immediately to the first person answering your call.

15. Be attentive. If you need to ask the other person to repeat information he or she has already given you, that person will surely become frustrated or angry.

16. Use your caller's name frequently. There's no sweeter music to another person than the sound of his or her own name.

17. Plan an effective conversation. Get your thoughts in order before you call. Try to complete your business in one call by securing the information you want or by leaving a message.

18. Apologize for mistakes. When you dial a wrong number, don't bang down the receiver. Instead, apologize for your mistake. It's equally courteous to be pleasant when someone calls you by mistake.

19. Who should end the call? The person who originates the call usually ends the conversation.

20. Hang up gently. Slamming the receiver may cause an unpleasant noise for your caller. It's as discourteous as slamming the door.

- The high-tech office still needs the human touch. Find out what *you* can do to improve your people skills.

- Answer customer questions with confidence.

- Find out what you know and what you *need* to know about your company.

THE HUMAN FACTOR

In this age of high technology, the office-support professional has become an information specialist. This means that whether you work on a typewriter, a dedicated word processor, or a personal computer, your basic function is still the same—to communicate information. If you aren't compatible with the people you work with, communication suffers.

The emergence of the high-tech office doesn't mean that the human touch is no longer necessary. In fact, as office systems and equipment become more complex, the volume of information generated continues to expand. This makes it imperative for the office worker to be able to communicate effectively with others. You are a professional communicator—and your communication skills deserve special attention. Here are some basic communication pointers to keep in mind:

Communicating the Right Way

Is this the right time? To avoid problems in communication, you must pick the appropriate time to discuss an issue with someone. For example, when you call a customer, ask whether it's a convenient time to talk. If the time is convenient, the individual is bound to be more receptive to what you have to say. Or if you want to talk with a co-worker, first ask yourself whether he or she may be too busy right now. Is your co-worker involved with preparations for an upcoming meeting? Is he or she waiting for an important phone call? Remember that if someone is preoccupied when you start talking, you won't get his or her full attention. What you're more likely to get is a gruff response.

Is this the right way? Generally, it's a good idea to be forthright. However, there are two ways to broach any matter—a right way and a wrong way. Whenever you talk to someone, keep the other person's point of view in mind. Try to understand how he or she feels and why. By doing so, you'll be much more tactful in your approach. Also remember to keep your conversations private. The whole office shouldn't hear your discussion. Besides, if there's a conflict with a customer or a co-worker, you don't want every ear in the office directed your way.

Is this the right information? You won't be able to answer customer questions or follow company directions if you don't know enough about the organization you work for. Find out how familiar you are with your company by taking this short test.

▼ ▼ TAKE A TEST ▼ ▼

Write out the answers to each of the following questions in the blank spaces provided.
  1. What is your company's official name?

2. Who founded your company? Where? When?

_____

3. Does your company have a slogan or a logo?

_____

4. Approximately how many people does your company employ?

_____

5. What are the major departments in your firm, and, generally, what does each do?

_____

6. What role does your department or division play in your firm's operations?

_____

7. Does your company own subsidiaries or run branch offices? If so, what are their names and locations?

_____

8. Who are your company's leading competitors?

_____

9. Does your company advertise? Can you recall the themes of its advertisements?

_____

10. What media does your company use to promote its products or services?

_____

11. If you work for a manufacturing firm, what products are made and what are their purposes?

_____

12. If your company offers services rather than products, what are they?

_____

13. Finally, draw a simple organizational chart of your company, showing the major officers and executives and the chain of command.

_____

How did you do? Make sure you learn the answer to any question that you missed. Start by contacting your advertising or public relations department for the information. Take the time to really get to know your company. Not only will customers appreciate your ready answers, but your boss will be impressed by your wealth of knowledge too.

- Building rapport with your boss depends in part on how well you do your job.

- Learn how to do your best work for your boss.

- Develop professional employee-boss communication skills.

STRENGTHENING THE EMPLOYEE-BOSS BOND

An important aspect of your job is cultivating a good relationship with your boss. That means anticipating his or her needs, heading off office difficulties, and being a reliable company representative when your boss isn't available. Clear communication between you and your boss is the key here. Remember, no other individual has such a profound effect on your level of job satisfaction or your chances for professional advancement.

Don't expect true rapport with your boss to happen overnight, however. People who work well together have *learned* to understand and respect each other's strengths and weaknesses. Building and maintaining rapport takes time. But the benefits will be well worth the effort.

To ensure that you're doing your best to strengthen the employee-boss bond, consider the following suggestions.

Creating a Superior Relationship

Improving your working relationship with your boss is simply a matter of give-and-take. After all, you can't be impatient and rude to your boss and then expect him or her to be kind and understanding when you're in a hurry, need a question answered, or have made a mistake. Always treat your boss the way you would like to be treated.

✓ Don't keep your boss in the dark. Be sure that you keep your boss informed about the status of all your assignments, and always report any work that you have received from other supervisors.

✓ Follow established channels or lines of communication when discussing job matters with your superiors. In short, don't go over your boss's head when you encounter difficulties.

✓ If you're forced to disagree with a decision or a direction from your boss, be sure to do so tactfully—and only if you have a positive alternative to offer. When a disagreement is resolved—one way or the other—give your wholehearted support to the final decision.

✓ Be understanding. If a conflict should arise with your boss, remember that supervisors are only human. They, too, have personal and professional problems and an occasional bad day.

✓ Recognize your boss's basic nature—both the good and the bad points. It's counterproductive and inadvisable to attempt to change these basic traits.

When You're the Bearer of Bad News

How do you tell your boss that you've made a mistake? It's never easy to bring bad news to someone—especially to your boss—but there are a few things you can do to make the chore less difficult:

☛ Choose the right time. Don't give bad news when your boss is extremely busy. Try to tell him or her in private and, remember, remain calm and straightforward. Ranting and raving won't accomplish anything.

☛ Get right to the point. To do otherwise would only cause unnecessary tension. And don't try to soften the blow by discussing unrelated matters first. People prefer to hear bad news up front so that they don't waste time making wild guesses.

☛ Accept responsibility. Even if you delegated some of the tasks that went astray, you should assume the blame. But don't overdo it—just accept the responsibility and move on.

☛ Offer a solution to the problem. This will let your boss know that, although you goofed, you're thinking about ways to remedy the situation.

How Do You Keep Your Image Spotless?

Even when you're not dealing directly with your boss, you can still keep him or her happy by doing your best in the office. Your professionalism will ultimately be a reflection of your boss's good judgment.

→ Don't worry about getting sufficient credit for things that you do. In any organization, it's unlikely that outstanding performance will go unrecognized for long.

→ Beat deadlines. Whenever possible, do a task as soon as it's assigned. Getting things done quickly usually leaves a favorable and lasting impression.

→ Anticipate problems that may arise, and develop possible solutions. This could prevent a minor difficulty from turning into a catastrophe.

→ Be conscious of timing when presenting requests or proposals. For example, don't interrupt your boss when he or she is grappling with a major problem just to ask if you may take a late lunch.

→ Use your strengths to complement those of your boss to increase the efficiency of your department. For instance, it may be advantageous for you to do most of the letter writing if you are skilled in doing so and your boss dislikes this particular task.

→ Remember to thank your boss for any special favors, privileges, or commendations that come your way. And when you see your boss do a superb job at something, say so! Bosses like recognition, too, and often they get less of it than others.

Keep in mind that it takes time and effort to develop a strong and successful working relationship with your boss. But the rewards are great. And when you make your boss look good, you look good, too!

ADJUSTING TO A NEW BOSS

- Does the thought of working for a new boss make you a little nervous? It doesn't have to.

- Let us show you how to establish a working partnership with the new boss.

- Discover what you can do to make the transition smoother for you and your new boss.

Making a switch to a new boss can be difficult. But it can also be an exciting experience for you. It can give you the chance to grow and to really show your organizational and cooperative skills. But you have to make this experience work for you.

What's the key to adjusting to a new boss? The minute he or she takes over, think of yourself as starting a brand-new job somewhere else. Aim to build a team of two—a working partnership between you and your boss. You'll need to adapt to your new boss's goals and objectives by making communication a priority.

➤ **Keep an open mind.**
You must remember above all that your job is to make things run smoothly for the boss. So when a new boss comes in, your cooperation and understanding are of primary importance.

➤ **Don't live in the past.**
As any employee knows, it's upsetting to have your ideas dismissed with comments like "This is how we've always done it." So even if you feel that your way of doing something is best, remember that there's more than one effective way to accomplish a task.

➤ **Use a little empathy.**
Even bosses have moments of insecurity—and this can be especially true for new bosses in their first few days on the job. Try to make your new boss feel comfortable and accepted. It's important to acknowledge your respect for his or her position. A sincere offer of assistance in getting him or her settled will make a nice welcome.

➤ **Keep the lines of communication open.**
Ask for approval of or instruction about procedures or tasks that you normally handle independently. Chances are that your new boss won't want to change a system that's running smoothly, but it's common courtesy to give him or her the opportunity to make that decision.

➤ **Offer suggestions.**
Failing to quickly adapt to a new boss's work style can trigger problems. You might try suggesting that you and your boss meet for a few minutes every morning to discuss the agenda for the day. That will alert you to your new boss's priorities and help show you how to best handle them.

➤ **Have patience.**
Adjusting to a new boss isn't always easy. In fact, life may become quite chaotic for a while, especially if the new boss decides to shake things up a bit. But "different" isn't necessarily "bad." And your steadfast support during this period of adjustment will provide a firm foundation for a suc-

cessful working relationship in the future.

Breaking the Age Barrier

What happens when the new boss is young enough to be your son or daughter? This situation can be very uncomfortable for some people. It's often assumed that age is synonymous with wisdom and maturity. And often, along with that assumption, comes the feeling that the younger boss is being patronizing or disrespectful when complimenting or reprimanding the older employee.

Maintaining a professional attitude will be difficult if you allow yourself to regard your supervisor in this way. You must look at the situation realistically. Your boss wouldn't have been promoted to this position if he or she weren't competent. Try these suggestions to help you break the age barrier:

⇨ **Separate your feelings of parent-child from those of employer-employee.** Your boss doesn't criticize or give you advice to lord it over you. He or she wants you to do your best.

⇨ **Recognize that your boss may have more knowledge** than you do, even though he or she hasn't put in as many years on the job.

⇨ **Don't take everything your boss says personally.** For example, if your supervisor speaks to your group about too many personal telephone calls, don't think the lecture is directed only at you.

⇨ **Reverse roles.** How would you feel if you were in your boss's shoes? Sometimes role reversal can give you a whole new perspective. When you realize that your boss is only human and has faults like everyone else, it'll help you to overcome any negative feelings you might experience at first.

Getting Off on the Right Foot

Regardless of your new boss's age, it's important that you do everything in your power to help out and make the transition a smooth one. An office should run like a finely tuned machine—everyone doing his or her part to make the whole run efficiently.

If you were suddenly faced with a new boss, would you act appropriately? To find out, try answering the following questions:

1. Am I optimistic about facing a potentially challenging situation? If so, do I spread my optimism to other co-workers?
2. Do I give the boss a chance to settle in before I form an opinion about him or her?
3. Do I do whatever I can to make the new boss feel welcome?
4. Do I make myself available when the new boss is looking for help?
5. Do I welcome change in my office routine?

If you answered No to any of these questions, it's time you examined your attitude and its effects on your office relationships. Resolve to start out on the right foot with a new boss. If you stay open-minded and maintain a professional manner, you will find this new situation to be one in which the benefits and the growth potential far outweigh possible disadvantages.

COPING WITH CRITICISM

- By becoming more assertive, you'll be able to face office conflicts with confidence.

- Learn how to distinguish negative criticism from constructive criticism.

- Instead of getting steamed by criticism, learn to profit from it.

Every office employee faces a certain amount of criticism on the job. How you handle that criticism can affect your relationships with your co-workers and supervisor, as well as your feelings about yourself and about your work environment.

How should you deal with criticism? Some experts say that when communicating with people in the workplace, being assertive is the answer. The idea is that you should learn how to listen as well as how to talk, maintaining a balance between empathy for others and respect for yourself and your thoughts, feelings, and behaviors. Assertiveness also means accepting that others have their own feelings, thoughts, and ideas that are valid for them even if you don't agree. In other words, if you want people to respect your position, you have to respect theirs as well.

There are two styles of assertiveness. One style is appropriate when you're dealing with people who are peripheral in your work or personal life—those who have no real power over you. With this style, you stand up for your own rights without making yourself vulnerable. Basically, what you do is acknowledge whatever these people are saying to you, but at the same time you don't give a defensive response or disclose anything personal.

The second style is used when you really want to assert what you think and feel. This type of assertiveness is generally used with intimates and close associates. Here, personal disclosures may well be appropriate. Yet both styles, the more open as well as the more closed, can be used with intimates and nonintimates, depending upon the situation.

In order to better understand how to communicate assertively, imagine a typical office conflict, with two different ways of handling it:

Sheila is eating her lunch at her desk 15 minutes before the designated lunch break. She has an appointment and must leave early to keep it. Unknown to anyone but her supervisor, Sheila came in early to make up her time. As she is eating, one of the workers from the next department comes into the office to make a delivery. While still within Sheila's hearing, he comments to another co-worker: "It must be nice to come and go whenever you please."

The nonassertive way of dealing with this situation would be for Sheila to become defensive, apologize for eating early, and explain that she had made up her time in the morning. But why should Sheila even have to explain all this to someone she barely knows, who is criticizing her just to get a rise out of her? This is an example of negative and unwarranted criticism.

To be assertive, Sheila should not apologize but should simply acknowledge, in a very neutral tone, that the worker is correct. Yes, she is eating lunch early. Yes, it would be nice to come and go whenever you please. This way, Sheila does not apologize for herself. She does not get hooked by her associate's criticism, nor does she make any unnecessary personal disclosures.

Being assertive can help you stick to your point and hang on to your goals.

Coping With Criticism From the Boss

Criticism from the boss can be more difficult to deal with than criticism from a co-worker. You should keep in mind that criticism from the boss is usually constructive. Unlike negative criticism, constructive criticism usually has a positive side to it. Your boss's aim in criticizing you is not to cut you or your achievements down or to rile you—but to help you improve some area of your work. You should respond calmly to this kind of criticism. If you have a negative reaction every time your boss tries to give you some advice, eventually he or she may give up trying to correct those areas of your skills that could use some improvement. If this happens, you may soon notice your boss becoming increasingly displeased with your overall job performance.

Here are some tips to help you make the most of a supervisor's criticism:

→ **Don't take it personally.** If your boss criticizes your handling of your work, don't conclude that he or she is also finding fault with you as a person. Your boss is merely pointing out an area of your office work that could stand some improvement. Learn to separate your job performance from your personal self-image. In other words, your boss's criticism of your office skills relates to your professional self, not to your personal self.

→ **Don't let offhand criticism like "You can't type a decent letter" slide by**—even if it comes late in the afternoon of a particularly hard day and you suspect your boss is just blowing off steam. There is probably some legitimate problem underlying the outburst. If you think this is a good time, ask that the criticism be made specific. For instance, you could respond with a positive statement such as: "It would help me a lot to know exactly what I'm doing wrong so that I can take steps to correct the problem right away." Sometimes, however, it might be wiser to pursue the matter the next day so that both you and your boss have time to relax and put things into perspective.

→ **Don't blow criticism out of proportion.** If your boss says something like "Well, we all make dumb mistakes," don't translate that to mean that your boss thinks you are dumb. Take statements like this in stride. After all, you're entitled to make occasional mistakes. We all do.

→ **Do listen attentively to what your supervisors have to say.** Even if you believe that the criticism is unwarranted, your critic may be able to suggest some legitimate ways to increase your efficiency and improve your office skills. No matter how long you've been on the job or how experienced you are, there's always room for improvement. If you listen in that spirit, criticism won't be so hard to take.

→ **Do react to criticism in a way that encourages the critic to offer real advice.** If your boss is discussing your writing skills with you, for example, look him or her right in the eye to show that you're listening. Looking away from a person who is criticizing your performance might imply a number of things, including anger, fear, or indifference—any of which might lead to a misunderstanding.

→ **Do let your boss finish what he or she is saying** before you begin to explain your point of view or defend your performance. When your boss has finished criticizing you, repeat what he or she has said in your own words. This shows, in effect, that you have listened to the criticism, that you understand it, and that you'll consider it. If you haven't fully understood your boss's point, ask questions to clarify the criticism and to avoid potential misunderstandings.

Even constructive criticism can be hard to take. But it is possible for us to begin to change our perception of critical remarks. By learning to examine critical comments objectively, we can be our own best friend—and best critic.

- Use these suggestions to get your message across in a clear and concise manner.

- Let us show you how to communicate effectively so that you can respond to problems like a true professional.

- Discover the nonverbal messages that your associates may be sending you.

SUCCESSFUL COMMUNICATION MEANS SUCCESS FOR YOU

Twenty minutes after a brief meeting with your employer, she calls to ask you a few questions—questions that you thought you had answered during your meeting. Are you sure that you stated your message clearly?

Effectively communicating your thoughts and ideas is a skill that, once mastered, can bring you success in interpersonal relations. By delivering your message in a clear and organized manner, listening to the thoughts and feelings of others, and reading nonverbal messages to detect hidden feelings, you can achieve effective communication. These techniques can help you eliminate common communication problems, such as answering the same question twice and asking questions that may have already been answered. Information will be exchanged correctly the first time—and you'll find your job easier and your performance more efficient as a result.

Getting Your Message Across

Effective communication is vital to your success and to the smooth operation of your office. You can gain credibility with your co-workers and associates by communicating policies and procedures in a simple and straightforward way. Clear communication also helps to prevent misunderstandings and head off problems. Here's what you can do to get your message across in a clear and concise manner:

➤ **Be courteous.** Your associates will be more receptive to your suggestions, ideas, and requests when you flavor your phrases with simple courtesies like "please" and "thank you."

➤ **Organize your thoughts.** State the purpose of your message right up front to prepare your listener for what is to follow. For example, saying "I'm going to show Nancy how to do the mail because I'll be on vacation next week and she can do it while I'm gone" is not as effective as "Nancy will be handling the mail while I'm on vacation next week; I'll show her what to do."

➤ **Be direct.** Try a direct but tactful approach when you are trying to communicate. Don't confuse directness with rudeness, however. For example, instead of saying "Don't be late coming back from lunch again!" you could say "We need you here to help cover the phones promptly at 12:30. I hope that won't be a problem." To get your message across efficiently and professionally, be direct in a positive way.

➤ **Enunciate.** One of the most frequently identified communication problems is poor articulation—especially when you're on the telephone. Think about it: "ABC Company" and "XYZ Company" do sound similar enough to confuse a caller. Pronounce your words clearly and correctly to avoid misunderstandings.

Sharpen Listening Skills

Getting your message across to others is only one half of effective communication. Listening carefully and being able to evaluate a situation is the other half. To do this, you must be receptive to the thoughts and feelings of your boss, co-workers, and other associates. With first-rate listening skills, you can weigh sensitive situations and respond appropriately. Here's what you can do:

✓ Mentally block out distractions.
✓ Maintain eye contact with the speaker.
✓ Be patient while your speaker makes his or her point.
✓ Focus your attention on what the speaker is saying.
✓ Look for the intent and feeling behind the message.

Listen to Body Language

Whereas improving your listening skills and learning how to send clear messages can help you achieve the kind of first-rate communication you are striving for, how can you communicate with employers or associates who don't speak their mind? Pay attention to the nonverbal signals people send to find out what they *really* think. Here's an example:

A customer whose account is delinquent has an appointment with your employer. The customer arrives late, clears his throat several times, and chooses a chair that is farthest from your employer's office. He sits with his arms folded and his legs crossed. As he greets your employer, he comments, "I'm happy to be able to meet with you. . ."

Some experts believe that body language says it all. In the situation given above, tardiness, tight vocal cords, and choice of seating all suggest that the customer is anxious. His closed body position suggests a defensive attitude. In this case, the customer's body language speaks more clearly than his courteous comment.

While a person's nonverbal expressions can clue you in to his or her real feelings, keep the concept of body language in perspective—one gesture doesn't translate into a specific thought or feeling. You can get a more accurate idea of the person's feelings by interpreting a gesture within the context of other gestures, facial expressions, and conversation. Take this test to see how proficient you are at deciphering a person's body language:

1. You're telling a co-worker about a course on grammatical skills you've started taking at a local college. Your co-worker looks at the clock, then rests her chin in her hand and nods when you pause. She is:
   A. Uninterested.
   B. Considering taking the course herself.
   C. Jealous that you are improving your skills.
2. You suggest to your boss that she use pie charts and bar graphs in a report that she's been working on. As you speak, your boss leans forward on her desk and nods slowly. Then she walks around the desk and sits in the chair beside you. She is:
   A. Angry that you commented on the report.
   B. Interested in your ideas.
   C. Not in agreement with your suggestions.

The answer to the first situation is A. Distracted eye movements and untimely nods can signal that your listener is not paying attention.

The answer to the second situation is B. Your boss is pleased with your ideas and, by coming around the desk to sit beside you, has used physical position to encourage you to communicate your ideas!

DEALING WITH OFFICE DISPUTES

- When conflicts arise and
  the going gets rough,
  use these suggestions to
  keep your office running
  smoothly.

- You can turn conflicting
  points of view into successful problem-solving.

- Are you a good winner
  and a good loser? Find
  out why being both is
  useful in the office.

The people you work with undoubtedly have their own opinions and their own ways of doing things. And while a little give-and-take (and a lot of tolerance) can go a long way toward avoiding office disputes, disagreements are an unavoidable fact of business life. But if you know how to handle conflict effectively, you can turn disagreements into opportunities to search for solutions while maintaining the rapport you worked so hard to establish.

Because people take disagreements personally, they often adopt either a domineering or defensive attitude. These attitudes, however, act as emotional barriers to resolving their differences. To avoid personal conflicts with your co-workers, step back from the problem and look at it objectively. By approaching office disputes this way, you'll win more than the argument; you'll improve your professional image and your high level of productivity as well.

Maintain your high professional standards during a disagreement by showing respect for your co-workers and associates. Make every effort to be magnanimous—that is, generous of mind and spirit—despite the outcome of the disagreement. If you can be magnanimous toward your co-workers and associates in all situations, you'll prove that your priority is to find feasible solutions—not to indulge your ego. By showing respect for others, you'll win their respect, too, and what you say will carry more credibility. When you find yourself engaged in conflict, try these helpful suggestions:

⇨ **Focus on the issue.** Don't let your personal opinion of the co-worker or associate you are arguing with influence the outcome. For example, if this is a co-worker you like and respect, you may be inclined to give in just to avoid a confrontation. In order to arrive at the best solution, however, put your feelings aside for the moment and focus on the facts of the problem at hand.

⇨ **Argue effectively.** You can argue in a way that is both productive and professional by being as diplomatic as possible. When you feel your temperature start to increase, your stomach start to knot up, and your voice start to rise, regain control of your emotions and remember to show respect for your co-worker or associate. Rephrase what you want to say to take the harsh emotion out of the argument. By stating flatly, "You're wrong," you are attacking your co-worker on a personal level, disregarding his or her feelings, and putting yourself in an adamantly opposed position. You could get the same point across, however, by saying, "I understand the point you're making, but I can't quite go along with you on that…" Or instead of "There's no possible way that will work," use an alternative: "I can see why you'd want to do it this way, but I just don't see that it's feasible because…"

Win Gracefully

Winning an argument can be a positive experience for everyone involved if you handle the triumph modestly. By being magnanimous, you can win the argument and the respect of your co-workers as well—you can turn a tense situation into a successful problem-solving session. Remember to be generous and respectful to your co-worker by allowing him or her to "save face." Here's what you can do:

⇨ **Forgo any temptation to gloat to other people in the office.** Don't dwell on your triumph, retelling the circumstances over and over. Take pride in your success quietly to yourself, and if co-workers or your boss asks you about the outcome, show your true colors. Respond by saying something like this: "Kathy and I talked about the alternative solutions, and we both decided that the best way to go is..." rather than "Well, you know I was right—and she finally admitted it!"

⇨ **Use amicable phrases.** Deferring to your co-worker's expertise once you've won an argument can go a long way toward preserving an amiable work relationship. To show your co-worker that you value his or her point of view despite the outcome of the disagreement, use phrases like these: "You've made several good points that I think would be useful on another system..." and "I think you've got some good ideas and I'd like you to continue to work with me on this..." You'll help your co-worker feel that he or she has contributed to finding a workable solution.

Be a Good Sport

Whenever you admit that your co-worker is right, you also admit that you are wrong. Keep an open mind so that if your co-worker's point of view is more logical, you can easily recognize that fact and say, "I'm glad we explored all avenues, and at this point, I have to agree with you." While such an admission can be difficult, put your ego aside and concede your co-worker's point gracefully.

You can maintain your credibility in the office by accepting your co-worker's hard-won victory with integrity. Say something to show that you don't have any hard feelings. By offering a comment like "You've certainly made a good case. I'll back it 100 percent and help you in any way I can," you can preserve a productive working relationship and your professional integrity.

There may be times, of course, when you may not be able to give in gracefully. In cases like these, try removing yourself from the conflict for a brief period of time to let things cool down a bit. Just tell your co-worker that you have another pressing deadline to meet and that you will get back to him or her in a day or two. Take the time to think the problem over objectively. Remember that your priority is to find a feasible solution—not to win an argument. Put your emotions aside and, whatever the outcome is, be magnanimous.

■ Do you have a personality that promotes productivity? A good rapport with others can make a difference!

■ Let us show you how meeting social needs in the office can result in a higher level of productivity.

■ Do your co-workers work together or compete in the office? Find out what you can do to promote teamwork.

"ALL FOR ONE—ONE FOR ALL"

Think about your typical workday—have you ever gone beyond the boundaries of your job description to help a customer or associate? Do you pitch in and lend a hand when there is a close deadline to meet? Can you always count on your co-workers to cover your telephone while you are at a meeting? This kind of give-and-take is an important part of achieving top-notch productivity in your office.

You can help establish a sense of camaraderie in your office by developing rapport with your co-workers. With a strong relationship as a base, you and your co-workers will be able to work well together even through incidents that hinder teamwork, such as those driven by competition and cliquishness. When you foster productive camaraderie, your co-workers will all share the responsibility of achieving your company's goals.

Working with your co-workers and your boss toward a common goal is what teamwork is all about. Consider this scenario:

You and your co-workers went to eat at a busy restaurant on your lunch break. After waiting several minutes to be waited on, you signaled to a passing waitress and asked to see a menu. The waitress turned to you and politely replied, "I'm sorry, but this is not my section," and walked away.

The employee at this restaurant obviously lacks that important sense of teamwork. The result? Poor service and dissatisfied customers—problems that can be solved or avoided by working together. If this waitress had shared a sense of teamwork with her co-workers, perhaps her response would have been, "Certainly! Here are our luncheon specials—I'll send your waitress right over."

Being able to get along with your co-workers can go a long way toward maintaining a high level of productivity in your office. In fact, your office will run more smoothly and efficiently when you are easy to get along with and are respected by your co-workers. For example, say your company's annual report is due to the print shop on Friday. Thursday afternoon you have to make last-minute corrections and then photocopy and collate this 130-page manuscript. If you don't have rapport with your co-workers, you may not feel comfortable asking anyone to lend a hand. But if you have demonstrated that you're easy to get along with, it will be easier for you to ask another employee for help with this job. This would be especially true if you had pitched in to help that employee when he or she was swamped. This kind of "all for one" attitude can make everyone's job a little easier.

Make Others Feel Valued

Teamwork requires dedication and cooperation. It is the job of all team members to bring out the best in themselves and also to help others toward this goal. For teamwork to "work," everyone involved—co-workers, customers, and associates—must feel valued. And to feel valued, certain needs must be met. Members of the team must:

☞ feel confident and secure in their positions

☞ utilize their skills to their full potentials

☞ be recognized and appreciated by others

When you address these basic needs, you can make the people you work with feel good about themselves and the jobs they do. Here's how:

→ **Bolster confidence.** Your co-workers are flooded with doubts about their jobs and their responsibilities just as you are about your own at times. When co-workers seem unsure about certain aspects of their jobs, do what you can to provide the support and reassurance they need. This supportive attitude will catch on, and the next time you find yourself doubting your own abilities, chances are a co-worker will reassure you as well.

→ **Build on strengths.** Since people take pride in the skills they develop, show your respect by acknowledging their expertise. For example, if your new office aide just mastered the new computer software and you need to use the system, why not ask for her help? A comment like "Kathy, you seem to know a lot about this new system. Would you mind showing me how to call up a customer's account history?" will not only bring forth a helpful response, but it will also reward Kathy for her diligent effort in learning the software. Or, if you have a co-worker who has top-notch writing skills, why not voice your observation: "You always get positive responses, Mark. I think it must be those effective letters you write!" Comments like these will make your co-workers feel good about the work they do, and they'll feel free to make similar positive comments to one another.

→ **Be accepting.** Beyond economic necessity, most people admit that they work for social reasons and that they are happiest with their jobs when they are accepted for who they are personally as well as for who they are professionally. Make it a point to accept your co-workers and to let them know that you value them as individuals. Ask your co-workers about their interests. Remember and celebrate birthdays. Show concern or happiness as situations develop. They'll appreciate your sentiments and you'll reap the benefits on both a personal and a professional level. When you care about the people you work with, your interest and concern will help carry you and your co-workers through more difficult times.

Teamwork or Competition?

You may look around your office one day and, seeing your co-workers working side by side, you may think that your office operates amiably and efficiently. Take a closer look, however, and ask yourself these questions:

✓ Is there an informal leader in the group who has a good amount of influence over office activities?

✓ Are there social cliques that work against one another—or against an individual?

✓ Is there an individual or a group of staff members who do not participate in group projects or share available resource material?

✓ Are there occasional defensive outbursts by co-workers?

✓ Is communication throughout my office somewhat limited?

✓ Do employees often vie for my boss's attention?

If you've answered yes to one or more of these questions, then your office is not working as a team. Rather, employees are competing for either professional or social status in the workplace. To encourage teamwork in a situation like this, do what you can to disseminate information to all members of the group. Discourage any gossip you hear being passed around the office, and don't take sides in any disputes. Let your co-workers know that you are striving to work with them toward your company's goals.

AN AGE OF OBJECTIVITY

- Do you find working with people of different age groups frustrating? It doesn't need to be.

- Find out how to overcome preconceived ideas about people of all ages to reach a higher level of productivity.

- Learn what you can do to make working with others easier and more effective.

In school, students learn basic skills, such as math and English, that are needed to be successful in today's work force. They also learn less tangible skills, such as how to work with others. But that lesson is usually limited to working with those of their own age. As a result, most office employees feel comfortable with peers in their age group—but they also need to know how to work effectively with people of different ages to be really successful.

Consider your own ideas about people older or younger than yourself. Do you think of young professionals as naive and inexperienced? Do you consider older workers to be slow and past their prime? If so, try to focus on the benefits that these people contribute to your office, and envision how efficient your office can become if you work *with* them *effectively*. Think about the fresh enthusiasm and innovative ideas that young co-workers bring to a workplace and the mature, stable attitudes and meticulous work habits that older co-workers contribute. By reassessing your ideas, overcoming prejudices, and learning to treat your co-workers with the respect they deserve, you can work together harmoniously to achieve top-notch productivity in your office.

Is Age an Issue?

Recent social trends have wiped out most expectations and restrictions traditionally attached to a person's age. For example, many retired people are active in recreational sports and earn advanced academic degrees. Fifteen- and sixteen-year-old students enter colleges for more sophisticated studies. In other words, people are no longer pressured to earn a degree, get married, and start a family or a career at a certain age. But in spite of the barriers that have been broken, prejudices still exist. To find out if you harbor any of these prejudices, ask yourself these questions:

✓ Are all of my close friends in my own age group?
✓ Am I more comfortable in social situations with a group of predominately older or younger people?
✓ Do I make assumptions about people's competence based on their age? For example, do I assume that older people are less informed or that younger people are less skilled?
✓ Do I gravitate toward people who are closer to me in age?

Honest answers to these questions will probably indicate at least some prejudices about people of different ages. How can you overcome these ideas? Spend some time getting to know people older or younger than you are. Once you learn to appreciate the differences between you and your co-workers, you'll find a new respect for each of them. You may learn that a co-worker nearing retirement age is a World War II veteran who has traveled all over Europe. Or you may find that a younger employee new to your company has had previous work experience that your office can benefit from. By appreciating your co-workers as individuals and respecting their differences, employees of all ages can work together to establish high standards for quality work.

Maintain Professional Objectivity

The different outlooks on life that people of diverse age groups usually have can sometimes become the cornerstone of conflict. For example, an employee who remembers rationing during World War II may have values very different from those of someone whose childhood memories were of bell-bottom jeans and the Vietnam Era. Such distinct value systems may surface in office procedures or in work ethics. In this case, the older employee may have strong feelings about the conservative use of office supplies, whereas the younger employee may be more concerned about company policies. Carol Sapin Gold, author of *Solid Gold Customer Relations,* says that you should relate to people as *they are,* rather than as *you are,* to appreciate and work with people's differences. Here are some of Gold's suggestions to help you achieve this kind of objectivity and understanding with co-workers:

➢ **Regard them as professionals.** You may work with someone who is young enough to be your son or daughter or old enough to be your parent. But don't fall into the trap of treating a co-worker as you would a family member. For example, if you are training a co-worker who is your son's age to use the new software, don't slip into a parental role with this employee. Maintain an objective frame of mind and pay him or her the professional respect that you would give any peer. Your co-worker will undoubtedly learn how to do the job effectively and you'll have won his or her respect in return.

➢ **Be able to adapt to different kinds of people.** You need to be flexible to understand the shifting priorities and concerns of the people you work with. Take the initiative to approach others, and try to understand problems from their point of view. For example, if an older worker is taking a long time opening the mail, why not mention the problem? This employee may be concerned about screening the mail when such screening isn't necessary, or he or she may have a problem with arthritis that you weren't aware of. Adapting to situations like these can give you a broader understanding of what motivates the people you work with, and it can help improve communication as well.

➢ **Be consistent with your job performance and your attitude.** A difference in values and priorities in the workplace may also signal differences in work habits and quality. Set the standard for a productive office by being consistent in your own work ethic. You can close generation gaps when your co-workers know what they can expect from you and what is expected of them.

➢ **Channel your energy into meeting goals.** A productive day at the office means expending energy—be sure that you do so in a positive way by working toward your goals in an upbeat, productive manner. Despite the differences of ages in your office, a positive and consistent work ethic is one that is understood and respected by people of all generations.

THE ESSENTIALS OF ETIQUETTE

- Do you respect the rules of office etiquette? Following protocol can make a lasting impression on others.

- Striving for a higher level of productivity? Let us show you how common courtesy and a productive work ethic go hand in hand.

- Do you "fit in" with your office culture? Find out about the unwritten code of conduct in your office.

It's Friday morning, and you've decided to don your favorite jeans and take your time getting to work. "After all, Friday is a day to wind down from a hectic week," you may rationalize to yourself. "And last week, Diane wore jeans…"

As you take your place at your desk several minutes late, you notice the glances that your co-workers cast your way. Self-consciously you think, What's the big deal?

Breaching office etiquette is a big deal, even in a less-than-formal work environment where it seems that the boundaries of professional propriety can be stretched. Why is it so important to respect the unwritten code of office conduct? There are two main reasons: First, these rules reflect and define appropriate office behavior. People know what sort of conduct is expected from them and they know how to react to other people's conduct. If you do something—either consciously or unconsciously—that doesn't fall within the boundaries of accepted behavior, people may not know how to react and therefore will feel uncomfortable. The second reason to respect office etiquette is that you represent your company. No matter where you are on the corporate ladder, you must always put on your most professional face. By doing so, you contribute to your company's success.

In many offices, etiquette is not as formal or as meticulous today as it was in the past. But that doesn't mean you can "just let it all hang out" and flout what rules there are. The people who advance in their careers are usually those who work within the boundaries of propriety. By adhering to an appropriate dress code, remembering basic courtesies, and conforming to office culture, you'll work well with others and earn the reputation of a true professional.

Make Courtesy More Common

Respect and consideration toward others are key elements in your productivity and in nurturing your professional relationships. By showing others deference and courtesy, you will let your co-workers know you respect them, and they will be more inclined to work with you to achieve your company's goals. Remembering basic courtesies goes beyond saying *please* and *thank you*. It involves your commitment to a productive work ethic—one that will encourage you to respect the time and space of your co-workers. Here are some tips:

- **Be punctual.** Always assume that your co-workers' time is just as valuable as your own. Be conscientious about meeting deadlines, attending meetings on time, and returning calls promptly.

- **Don't interrupt.** If what you have to discuss is important, simply signal to your co-worker that you'd like to speak with him or her as soon as it's convenient. And if your conversation is interrupted by what appears to be a confidential telephone call from your boss or co-worker, bow out as quickly as possible.

- **Return materials promptly** after borrowing them—and make sure that they are in top-notch condition when you return them. For example, don't return a stapler empty or a disk that cannot be used.
- **Respect the chain of command.** The most efficient way to get things done is to follow the proper channels; this means respecting the authority of others.
- **Acknowledge the work done by others.** If you make a suggestion that you heard at the water cooler and your boss responds in a positive way, simply say, "Actually, it was Stewart's idea—and I thought it was a good one!"

Professional Protocol

Just like technology in the workplace, some rules of office etiquette have become obsolete and some have evolved to complement a more fast-paced, efficient workplace. While the specifics of office etiquette vary from one office to the next, the areas generally covered are:

→ **Appropriate dress.** A professional appearance can bolster your credibility in the office. How? Your manner of dress reflects your attitude, and a neat, coordinated appearance lets your supervisor, your co-workers, and customers know that you care about the job you do. Your company may not enforce a dress code, and jeans may be more comfortable than a suit, but successful professionals say that indulging in informal dress can work against your image in most professional offices.

What constitutes professional office attire? Most companies agree that suits, slacks with a matching blazer, skirts, or dresses are best. Do everything you need to to create a well-groomed, conservative appearance.

→ **Greeting visitors.** This is an opportunity for you to make a great impression and cement good relations with customers and associates. When someone comes into your office, extend a warm, friendly greeting that will make your visitor feel valued and put him or her at ease. Follow these suggestions:

- ✓ Acknowledge visitors as soon as they enter your office area. If you are on the telephone or busy with another client—or if your boss cannot be seen immediately—be sure to smile and say something like "We'll be right with you, Ms. Preston. Please have a seat while you wait."
- ✓ Make official introductions properly. When introducing clients and associates to your boss or to co-workers, you must know your visitors' correct names and titles—and their correct pronunciations. The protocol for introductions is logical and easy enough to remember: Introduce a person with lesser status to a person with greater status. This general principle translates into four specific rules. First, introduce a member of your company to a client. Second, introduce a junior employee to a senior employee. Third, introduce a younger person to an older person. And fourth, introduce a man to a woman. Always keep in mind, however, that rank or someone's relationship to the company—specifically a customer's or client's—takes precedence over someone's age or sex.

→ **Office culture.** Each office has its own level of formality and professionalism, and most employees know what is expected of them. But offices also have a more subtle realm of etiquette—codes of behavior that are not quite as obvious as, say, a dress code. They involve practices like washing out the coffee pots and bringing in a birthday cake for a co-worker. Generally, customs that surround topics like coffee, birthday celebrations, the office telephone, and lunchtime activities are all elements that make up your office culture. Try to gauge what your involvement should be by watching your co-workers and asking plenty of questions. For example, if there is a "coffee fund" in your office but you don't drink coffee, why not ask, "Is there tea provided with the coffee fund?" Though protocol on this level may seem trivial, respecting office culture is proper etiquette—and it can strengthen your work relationships and create a pleasant and productive environment.

CONTEND WITH COMPLAINTS

- Do you handle complaints professionally? Do you know how to get consistently positive results? Your company's success depends on your skills.

- You can retain valuable customers by welcoming their complaints. Let us show you how to handle complaints effectively.

- Are you uncomfortable with or intimidated by emotional outbursts? Find out how you can communicate with dissatisfied or irate clients for a favorable outcome.

In nearly every industry, companies are doing all they can—from publicizing toll-free numbers to setting up videotaping booths—to allow and encourage customers and clients to air their complaints. Companies have found that by allaying complaints, they can develop long-term relationships with customers and associates to secure their future success in business. Efforts to respond to complaints are not unfounded: Statistics indicate that companies can retain *more than half* of their dissatisfied customers as loyal patrons if complaints are handled correctly.

While an employee's level of client or customer contact varies from one office to the next, you can contribute to your company's success by learning to handle complaints and getting positive results. After all, you hold a key position in your organization, and you are usually the person people turn to when something goes wrong; patrons look to you to give them information and to solve problems. In this chapter, we will examine the nature of complaining customers and offer suggestions on how to resolve their grievances while preserving your company's rapport with them. By communicating in a courteous, professional manner and by showing others the respect they deserve, you'll successfully turn dissatisfied customers into loyal, satisfied patrons.

Show Customers You Care

Service experts concur that there is no *easy* way to cope with a complaining client. How should you respond when someone comes to you with a complaint or a problem? Be positive and *welcome* complaints. After all, it's your chance to reconcile relations with a client—and that's good business. Think about it: If dissatisfied customers *didn't* complain, or if you *didn't* respond appropriately, their recourse would be to simply stop doing business with your company. Look at complaints as an opportunity to assist valued clients. There may be problems that you can help with, and there may be problems that are beyond your control. Regardless of the actual outcome, however, receiving complaints with a positive attitude shows customers that you care about their problems and their business. Consider this problem:

Mr. Murdock, a longtime loyal customer, placed an order with your company stipulating that his company must receive the order by the end of the month. Since the sales representative failed to make a note of this stipulation on the order form, the order was shipped late. When Mr. Murdock finally received the shipment, he promptly called your office to complain.

Customer complaints come in many shapes and sizes and are caused by a variety of problems or misunderstandings. No matter what the problem is, however, it's your company's priority to keep patrons like Mr. Murdock satisfied. Your skillful handling of a situation like this one can maintain the good relations and the professional rapport you already have with your patrons. Here's what you can do:

→ **Show concern.** Let Mr. Murdock know that you care about his company's problem and that you are committed to directing him toward a solution.

→ **Maintain objectivity.** Since you don't know all the details, be wary of exaggerations and misrepresentations. Keep an open mind regarding the source of the problem until you have researched all the facts.

→ **Focus on the client** and the problem at hand. If possible, don't allow other calls, customers, or co-workers to interrupt. For example, ask a co-worker to answer incoming calls while you work with Mr. Murdock on finding a solution to his problem. If you must answer calls that interrupt your conversation with a client, take a quick message and be sure to apologize for the interruption.

→ **Listen to the explanation** of the problem and take notes, if necessary. Clue in to pertinent facts that may lend insight to the problem. For example, make a note of the sales representative Mr. Murdock spoke to and when the order was placed.

→ **Ask plenty of questions** to be sure that you have all the information you need. Questions like "What is your account number?" or "When did you send us a purchase order?" can help uncover important details more efficiently.

→ **Establish a common ground** by agreeing with the point of concern. A statement like "Yes, a late shipment can certainly upset your company's schedule; let me look into this further…" will let the client know that you are on his side.

→ **Restate the problem** in your own words to make sure that you fully understand it. For example, you could say to Mr. Murdock: "So the problem is that our sales representative promised you this shipment by the end of the month, and it arrived two weeks late. Is that correct?" By restating the problem, you can give your client the opportunity to confirm your understanding—or to clarify what he or she sees as the crux of the problem.

→ **Offer a probable explanation** for the misunderstanding. For example, you could say: "Our shipments are usually all made by the end of the month, Mr. Murdock. We were unaware that you placed your order with this condition. Had we known, you can be assured that your order would have had top priority."

→ **Suggest alternative solutions.** Ask Mr. Murdock, "Would you like us to recall the whole shipment or just a portion of it?"

→ **Thank the client for bringing the problem to your attention,** and offer to help with any problems in the future. Let all your clients know that you appreciate their business and that you look forward to helping them whenever they have a problem.

Beware: Iceberg on the Horizon

Think of a complaint as the tip of an iceberg. One tactless comment or inference on your part could turn a small mishap into a major catastrophe—and a loss of business for your company. That's right—*any complaint that is brought to your attention has the potential to escalate into an emotional confrontation.* Keep communication on an even keel, and avoid this kind of conflict by being respectful and diplomatic. *Don't:*

✓ Blame the customer for misunderstanding or for making extra work for you.

✓ Make personal judgments about the customer. For example, treat a customer whose account is delinquent with the same courtesy you would give any other customer.

✓ Advise customers as to what they should have done.

✓ Shirk responsibility for the problem. Never say, "Susan takes care of the billing. You'll have to come back on Thursday and straighten it out with her." Instead, tell customers what you *can do:* "I'm sure that Susan will be able to straighten this problem out. Let me take all of the information and have her call you on Thursday. What time would be convenient for you?"

The Irate Customer

Customers' confidence in you wavers when problems arise, and each individual reacts to problems differently. Some customers may remain calm and trust you to handle the situation, whereas others may become upset and doubt your ability. Customer service representatives agree that the most difficult situation is one in which a highly emotional person confronts you with a problem. Why? Because emotional customers usually exhibit defensive or offensive attitudes that act as barriers to effective communication and, ultimately, to your problem-solving efforts. An understanding tone and well-phrased questions, however, will help put clients at ease and break down communication barriers.

M. J. Mitchell, a local real estate agent, refers a significant amount of business to the appraisal firm that you work for. The other secretary you work with has been out sick for several days, and the work load is backlogged. This morning, your boss mentioned to you that the appraisal your sick co-worker had been working on for M. J. Mitchell has top priority and is needed today. You are about a third of the way through the report when the telephone rings. Mr. Mitchell answers your greeting with an offensive "Have you finished that report yet? You've been working on it for a week—and I needed it yesterday!"

An offensive comment could catch you off guard and leave you speechless—and the client may become even more angry. How do you respond to this kind of confrontation? Try these helpful tips:

■ **Remain in control.** A Chinese proverb says, "He who angers us controls us." You can be most helpful to your company and to your clients by maintaining control of an emotional situation. When anxiety is on the rise, keep your emotions in check by excusing yourself for a few seconds. For example, say, "Yes, Mr. Mitchell, I have your report right here—can you please hold?" and take a moment to gather composure. Try to identify the source of your anxiety so that you'll be better equipped to manage your own emotions and handle complaints with an even temper and a positive, professional attitude.

■ **Don't be defensive.** Clients may direct their anger at you because you represent the company. Keep in mind, however, that they are really upset about the problem at hand. Your helpful, concerned attitude will defuse their anger.

■ **Don't interrupt.** Irate people need to blow off steam before they will calm down. Give your clients plenty of time to vent their emotions—interrupting or debating their accusations will only prolong and escalate their anger.

■ **Empathize with clients and acknowledge their emotion.** Say something like "I can clearly understand why you are upset, Mr. Mitchell." Attention like this will help dissipate their distress.

■ **Pay close attention to key emotional phrases,** such as "I can't believe you've been typing this report for a week!" Such emotion should be responded to with facts. Say something like "I'm working on the report right now—I can have it ready for you by the end of the day."

■ **Depersonalize the problem.** Focus on the situation and the facts. Phrase statements this way: "The report was assigned this morning as a priority item" rather than "They only gave it to me today."

■ **Ask "feeling" questions.** The answers you receive will help you respond with an appropriate solution. When a customer is visibly upset, try these questions to get the best response:

- What can I do to help you?
- What needs to be done?
- How do you feel about that?
- Can you explain the problem further?

■ **Apologize.** For fear of showing weakness or admitting mistakes, we don't always make apologies when they are needed most. As difficult as those words are, "I'm sorry" can be the glue that mends broken relations—they mollify clients' hard feelings and win over upset patrons. So the next time there is a misunderstanding that causes a client to be inconvenienced, don't hesitate to offer a sincere comment like "I understand that the report is late, and I'm terribly sorry for the inconvenience..." Your customers will appreciate your consideration.

Say No Nicely

"Is Ms. Walshe available for an appointment this week?" "No." "Can I defer payments on my account until after the first of the year?" "No." "Will that order be shipped out on Monday?" "No."

It's easy to understand why clients get annoyed when you deny their request with a flat No, but sometimes your company's policy *requires* that you say no to a customer's request. How can you say no and still maintain the rapport that you worked so hard to establish? There is a way to say no nicely:

➝ Make positive statements, such as "Mr. Roberts, that is a very innovative idea and we appreciate your time. In fact, that may be a system that we will incorporate in the future."

➝ State your denial: "Unfortunately, our cash flow system doesn't allow for deferred payments."

➝ Close with another positive statement: "We can, however, arrange a monthly payment plan that can best meet your needs, and if our policy changes in the near future, we will be sure to notify you."

Whether it comes from an important client or from a one-time business associate, each complaint is valuable to your company: Each is an opportunity for you to improve the customer service that is vital to your company's success. Providing satisfaction can be a challenge, however, since you may not always be equipped to answer questions or to solve problems. By treating customers with the courtesy and respect they deserve, you'll be able to resolve problems in the most effective and professional manner possible. Respond to your clients with sincerity so that you can earn their confidence for a secure and successful business relationship.

- If your boss asked you to help find a temp, would you know where to begin?

- Let us show you how to prepare for a temp in an organized way.

- Discover how you can ease the awkwardness for a temporary worker and encourage teamwork.

A TEMPORARY SOLUTION

If the work load in your office peaks and declines sharply or if your boss suddenly finds himself or herself short-staffed, your boss may ask you to help find a temporary replacement as a solution to the problem. Would you know where to begin looking for help? Would you know how to help the temp settle in? By knowing how to prepare for a temporary employee and being able to make the best use of the temp's time and skills, you can help keep productivity on an even keel.

How to Find the Right Person

To find a temporary employee who can fill the needs of your office, you obviously must know what your office's needs are. So the first thing you've got to do is sit down and do some serious thinking about what this person's role will be. Here's how to go about it:
- Take the time to find out exactly what your boss's needs are.
- Come up with a brief list of the professional skills and personal qualities needed to fulfill that role.
- Outline the specific duties and responsibilities of the job.
- Go over the outline with your boss to see if he or she agrees with this vision of the job.

Once you know what you need, you can start the actual search. But where to begin? You could start looking for a temporary agency, but why go "over the rainbow" when you might be able to find what you need in your own backyard? Find out if you can "borrow" a worker from an area of the company where the work load is temporarily light.

Of course, if your company doesn't have that kind of personnel available, you will have to go to an agency. If your company uses temps a lot, it may work with specific agencies in your area. If that's not the case, be sure to investigate more than one agency; find out how each operates and what its level of professionalism is. The attitude of the agency can tell you a lot about the people it employs.

Once you have settled on an agency, explain what your needs are. By describing just what your office is like and what type of person you're looking for, you'll have a better chance of getting just what you want. Provide the agency with this information:
- The kind of company you work for (for example, a manufacturing plant)
- The nature of the work environment and the size of the regular staff
- A summary of the work assignment and the specific tasks involved
- A description of the equipment that will be used (word processor, fax machine, etc.)
- Relevant company policies, such as dress codes

Preparation: Your Key to Productivity

How productive a temporary employee is depends on how well you have prepared for his or her arrival. Your company can suffer a loss in time and money if you wait until the temp arrives to figure out how and where he or she will work. Your temporary employee will be more productive if you prepare a work schedule and a work area beforehand. Here's what you can do:

- **Reserve a work area.** Shuttling a temp around trying to find a work area each morning can only result in lost time. If you can, have a workspace established for your newcomer for the entire length of his or her stay.

    NOTE: If you don't have the space available, ask the agency if it has provisions for doing outside work on its own premises.

- **Furnish equipment and supplies that the temp will need to do the job effectively.** For example, will a word processor or a typewriter be needed? a dictating machine? a calculator? a telephone? a stapler? pens? pencils? scissors? Be sure that whatever is needed is on the temp's desk the day before he or she arrives.

- **Prioritize the work load.** Which task must be completed and is most important to your department's operations? What must be done but can wait? Prepare an outline for the temp that clearly explains the sequence. For example, suppose there are three reports for the temp to type. One is due to a client this morning, and the other two are due to the boss later on in the week. Be sure that the temp knows which report should be completed immediately and then when the rest are due.

- **Prepare other employees.** Explain to your co-workers in advance why this person has been asked to come in and help, how long the temp is expected to work with you, and what tasks this person will be responsible for. It should be made clear who is "in charge" of the temp—if that is you, be sure that your co-workers know that all work for the temp is funneled through you. That way, you can be sure that the temp is working on priority assignments.

Your Temporary Team Member

Even though temps are skilled, competent workers, they must often contend with two less-than-ideal situations. First, they have little knowledge of your company, your department's operations, and your work procedures. Second, they really aren't a part of the social aspect of your office that helps make hectic conditions easier. What can you do? Make it a point to give the temp the information needed to do the job effectively, and do what you can to build a good working relationship with him or her. Here are some tips:

✔ **Start the day right.** Be there to welcome the temp when he or she arrives, and provide a brief tour of the office showing the temp only what he or she needs to know to work comfortably and efficiently.

✔ **Be specific about work methods.** If there is a specific way that you want things done, be sure to provide written instructions or have samples available. If there is a particular piece of equipment that the temp must operate, spend the extra time it takes to make sure that the temp knows how to operate it properly.

✔ **Limit your demands.** Keep in mind that this is a temporary employee with limited knowledge about your company. Don't ask the temp to work unreasonable hours or to get involved with complex problems, such as office politics. Situations such as this will only distract the temp from the task he or she was hired for.

Although hiring a temporary employee may not offer all the advantages of a full-time employee, it is a great solution to unexpected productivity problems. Take the time to find the right agency and prepare for a temporary worker, and do what you can to help the new person fit in. Your boss, your co-workers, and your customers will be pleased with the productive results.

- **Let us show you how to effectively prepare to train a new employee.**

- **Learn how you can instruct your new hire to get him or her started on the right foot.**

- **Discover how you can encourage polished job skills and high quality standards.**

EFFECTIVE TRAINING FOR AN ACE EMPLOYEE

Some office-support professionals may consider breaking in a new hire as a one-shot deal: Introduce the job to the employee and see what happens. Unfortunately, this kind of hit-or-miss training may not render the best results. When you take an ongoing approach to training, however, a new hire will learn the skills and attitude necessary to develop into a productive co-worker and a true professional.

Compare methods of job training to teaching a game of cards, for example. To make sure the new player understands all angles of the game, you'd use a process that is twofold. First, you would instruct the novice player on the rules and the goals of the game. Then, after playing a practice hand or two to ensure that he or she understand the rules, you would teach and explain the principles of strategy—the subtle variations that make a difference in whether the game is won or lost.

When it's your responsibility to train a new co-worker, use this same two-part procedure. First, explain company policy and the duties of the job—and do what you can to help your co-worker acclimate himself or herself to your department's methods of working and level of productivity. Once these are understood, you can begin the second phase of training: encouraging your co-worker's professional development. Try to impart the value of quality work and a positive attitude. After all, these work habits are the "strategy for success." By helping your new hire to fine-tune skills and adopt a positive, professional work ethic, you'll be able to work together to achieve top-notch efficiency in your office.

Prepare for a Successful Outcome

Your success in training can determine how soon you will have a competent co-worker to rely on; training must be comprehensive to be effective. Do what you can to prepare for your trainee, and arrange your work schedule so that you will be able to devote blocks of time to training.

Preparing for a newcomer goes beyond setting up a work area and ordering office supplies. Although this kind of preparation is necessary, thoughtful preparation—in which you focus on the training process and anticipate possible questions a new employee may have—is equally important. Follow these tips to help you think your training plan through:

➤ Concentrate on presenting the company and the job in a positive light.
➤ Think about the specific tasks this employee will take on and the correct way they should be done. Jot down notes to yourself on specific details of the job, and examine the order in which you will introduce each task.

Organize your training program by preparing lists—especially if you have never trained anyone before. Lists will guide you through your thought-out plan so that you will be sure to cover all the pertinent information. Here are some suggestions to get you started:

➡ Prepare a departmental list of topics that you will discuss with the

new hire. If you work for a smaller firm, you may have to explain general company policies as well. This list should include:
- Working hours and lunch periods
- Policies on tardiness and absences
- Cafeteria facilities
- Vacations and holidays
- Time clock procedures and compensation
- Safety procedures and first-aid facilities
- Petty cash regulations
- Policies unique to your company—for example, a no-smoking policy

➠ It may also be a good idea to give the new hire a brief introduction to the company. For instance, give the history of the company, and if there is a parent company, explain how they fit in with each other "in the grand scheme of things." And describe your department's role in the company.

➠ Make a tip sheet that your new hire can refer to. Tips may include specifications for memo and letter formats as well as extension numbers that he or she will probably use frequently. The tip sheet will enable the new person to work independently on some tasks almost immediately.

Rules and Goals: A Successful Orientation

When the new person arrives on the first day, make the initial introduction to the workplace a positive and welcoming experience. Although this may be an anxious time for both of you, try to relax and think about your first day on the job. Did you know where to hang your coat? Did you feel uncomfortable helping yourself to coffee? Did you have all the supplies you needed? Remember your own fears to help make your new co-worker's first day more comfortable. Here are more ideas:

✔ **Be friendly when the new person is introduced.** Get on a first-name basis and make pleasant comments about your work environment that will put the new employee at ease.

✔ **Tour the office.** Show the new person his or her work area and the surrounding facility. Try to anticipate your co-worker's needs; for example, show him or her where the supply cabinet is located and where to get coffee.

✔ **Introduce your co-workers.** Be sure to mention what each person does and tell them what the new person will be doing. For example, you could say "This is Jane, our new receptionist at the front desk. Jane, this is Daryl, in charge of billing." This will help the new hire understand the different phases of your office operations, and it will help existing co-workers incorporate the new employee into their daily routine.

More often than not, a new person will be excited about the job and eager to learn everything possible about the company and the position. Take advantage of this enthusiasm and begin training as soon as the new employee is comfortably settled. Use the lists that you have prepared ahead of time so that your orientation is complete. It's usually a good idea to give the new employee his or her own copies of the information (such as the tip sheet we mentioned earlier) to review later on. Discuss what the job entails so that your new co-worker will have valuable background information on the job, as well as knowledge of various functions of your office. Here's what you can do:

➤ Introduce company policies and department protocol. Be as candid as possible when discussing what is expected of employees in your department. Clearly explain that tardiness will not be tolerated. Although you may feel a bit uncomfortable, spelling out policies like this can head off problems.

➤ Give a general overview of the job and clearly explain the responsibilities involved. For example, you may explain that typing up reports is a main part of the job. Other responsibilities may include customer correspondence and answering the telephone. Be sure to tell your trainee the reasons for each task so that he or she understands the job in its proper context.

➤ Discuss the scope of responsibilities. If the job requires proofreading and editing the reports as well as just typing them, be sure to mention it. Or let your trainee know that in your office, answering the telephone is a job shared by two other employees.

➤ Give background information so that your new hire has a firm grasp of how your department functions. For example, if part of the job is ordering supplies from the warehouse, explain that some supplies are bought in bulk and held in storage.

➤ Encourage your trainee to ask questions. Answer whatever questions you can; however, some questions will be easier to answer as you demonstrate the tasks. By discussing what the job entails, you'll be giving your new co-worker valuable background information on the job as well as on the various functions of your office.

The time you spend training your new co-worker on office equipment and job skills will largely depend on the tasks involved and the time you have available. Regardless of how simple or complex a job may be, however, refer again to your prepared material and take each job step-by-step. First, show how the job is done. Then, let the trainee practice. Follow up by offering praise and criticism—but be careful not to discourage a new worker with negative comments. This kind of meticulous training is all a part of teaching your co-worker the rules and goals of your organization.

Strategies for Success

Although instruction should include your office's rules and procedures, ending the training at that point won't ensure a top-notch job performance. Why? Because you also need to teach the strategy that will help your new co-worker succeed. Once your new co-worker is familiar with the job, extend the training one step further and encourage a work ethic that includes efficient work habits, sharp job skills, and open lines of communication. For example, if your trainee's job is to type letters or other correspondence, follow up to make sure the job is done in a timely manner and take this opportunity to point out the importance of promptness. If you have noticed that the trainee's phone messages are not complete, reinforce the importance of detailed messages. Following are key suggestions that will improve the new employee's productivity. Instruct the trainee to:

→ Establish a daily routine.
→ Learn to coordinate his or her schedule with that of the boss or other office employees.
→ Refine skills such as typing accuracy and telephone etiquette.

Of course, job skills and accuracy don't go far without a positive attitude to drive them. Watch the new hire's work habits closely and follow up your training to encourage professional development. For a first-rate job performance, emphasize these skills:

• **Concentration.** The ability to focus on the task at hand is essential to completing a job accurately and professionally.

• **Analytical thinking.** Stress the importance of thinking a job through. For example, knowing what steps are necessary, what information is needed, and how information can be obtained efficiently are skills often needed to get a job done.

- Conscientiousness. Consistently maintaining high quality standards and working up to them is characteristic of a top-notch, professional employee.

Refined skills and a conscientious attitude reflect a professional approach to the work involved. By encouraging this kind of professionalism in a trainee, you'll help develop a confident and positive attitude in your co-worker.

▼ ▼ TAKE A TEST ▼ ▼

Take this test to determine how well you would handle any obstacle you might come across when training a new employee.

1. Your company has hired a receptionist to manage the front desk. Her only duties are to answer the telephone and greet visitors. After you have completed orientation and explained the complex telephone system, your new hire quickly masters the task but loses enthusiasm for the job: She is bored and, very often, idle at her desk. You should:
   a. Suggest that she look for a job that is more challenging.
   b. Do nothing—she'll get used to it.
   c. Delegate more work that can be done during slow periods.

2. You have just finished training an office assistant whose job involves customer contact. Although he has a very outgoing personality, you have noticed that his telephone manner is too boisterous for your conservative office, and his recordkeeping is never up-to-date. You should:
   a. Let it go. He'll catch on after a while.
   b. Review with him your company's telephone procedures and reinforce the importance of conscientious recordkeeping.
   c. Reprimand him for inappropriate behavior and shoddy work habits.

3. A trainee in your office has been on the job for a week and is demanding too much of your time and attention. This new person has no initiative to work independently and continues to pester you with questions. You should:
   a. Structure her day with a schedule of assignments. Assign one or two jobs that she will have to think through without your help.
   b. Give her busywork until you can answer all her questions.
   c. Interrupt your own work to answer questions and guide her through her tasks.

ANSWERS

The answer to #1 is c. It's always best to utilize every employee to his or her full potential. If this employee is able to take on more work, take advantage of this ambitious attitude—your whole office can benefit.

The answer to #2 is b. When a trainee begins to stray from your office protocol, address the problem right away. When you firmly establish a code of behavior and quality work standards, your new co-worker will adapt quickly to your office and settle into a promising career with your company.

The answer to #3 is a. A trainee who becomes very dependent on you is one who lacks confidence in his or her own skills. Create a structured environment to provide the guidance she needs without your constant attention. Assignments that require analytical thinking will teach her to work independently.

With an ongoing approach to training and an organized program, you can help a new hire become a reliable co-worker—one who is a highly skilled, competent office professional.

- **Forming office friendships? Weigh the pros and cons for yourself.**

- **What brings people together in friendship at work? More than just likability. Consider these factors.**

- **Don't let your career hit stumbling blocks posed by office alliances. Watch out for common pitfalls.**

OFFICE FRIENDSHIPS: RISKY BUSINESS

In the finance world, high-risk investments are usually the most profitable. The same holds true for office friendships. Though there are a number of risks involved, office friendships can make your job easier and your office a more pleasant place to work. Some of your friendships will grow and mature with you throughout your career. Others won't survive the pressures of the workplace. In this chapter, we will take an in-depth look at how and why office friendships are formed. But since tact and discretion are always factors in successful office alliances, we will also point out the pitfalls—and where you should watch your step.

A Friendship in the Making

When two or more people work together in the same office with the same boss, they often discover that they share a lot of common ground. In time, they may earn each other's professional respect and confidence. More than that, they may genuinely enjoy each other's company. Thus, a friendship is formed. Relationships among co-workers can make for a more interesting workday, and the easy give-and-take among friends makes sharing supplies, information, and even the boss's time a little easier. On a broader scale, the friendships you form now can be key to your career success. After all, co-workers will not only respect your highly skilled work, but they'll get to know you as a good person. Your friends will know that you are a person with integrity—someone they can count on—and they will be there to support you as you climb the corporate ladder.

But there is more to making friends than respect and goodwill. Here are the elements that come into play:

➤ **Proximity.** How much time you physically spend with another person can have a lot to do with forming a friendship. The familiarity that comes with a close work environment can bridge the basic differences you may have with a co-worker. And when this co-worker is transferred to another department or goes to work for another company, the good rapport you established can remain.

➤ **Mutual needs.** People form alliances from which they can benefit. Whether information or special consideration for projects is needed, these friendships exist on a "you scratch my back and I'll scratch yours" basis. People involved in this kind of relationship often phase in and out of friendships as their needs change, causing social factions to shift in response to changing needs. When the boss hires a new secretary, for example, certain ambitious employees will make it a point to get acquainted. But when the priorities of one of these employees changes (for instance, the employee decides to work part-time), she or he may not have the time—or the need—to sustain that friendship.

Whatever the basis for office friendships, office-support professionals agree that common bonds and amiable relationships foster a better work environment. What could come in the way of such ideal working conditions? Success and self-interest.

Proceed With Caution

Since any true-blue friendship requires loyalty to sustain it, you may find yourself caught in the middle trying to serve two masters: your own interests and your friendships. Although it is possible to be successful at both, you must be aware that your relationships at work must withstand the ebb and flow of job pressures to flourish—and these pressures often have their roots in your competitive nature. Indeed, some friendships do not last. Friends may perceive your ambitions as disloyal and as a threat to their own success. Here's how you can move smoothly through your career achievements and preserve amiable office alliances:

➡ *Keep friendships in perspective and your ambitions to yourself.* Keep your career goals in mind and remember that your co-worker may have similar ambitions. Steer clear of any work-related discussions that could work against you in achieving your goals. For example, if your friend has trouble meeting deadlines and blames another co-worker for his or her low level of productivity, don't risk your own good relations with that co-worker by agreeing.

➡ *Overcome obstacles.* Some friendships can hold you back in your career or can pose hurdles that you must clear before you can move ahead. Lunching with someone who is at odds with the boss, for example, may make you "guilty by association" and leave your boss wondering where your loyalty lies. Be sure that your higher-ups know what your goals are and that you are working toward them.

➡ *Clearly establish your priorities.* Don't allow friendships to negatively influence your work habits. For example, if you are dedicated to your job and quality work is your main concern, don't fall into the habit of stretching your lunch period or chatting at length just because your friends do. And don't play down your achievements in an effort to eliminate competition with co-workers. Enjoy your success (but don't flaunt it) and insist that your friends accept you the way you are—you'll form stronger, longer-lasting alliances.

➡ *Don't get too personal.* By sharing the details of your divorce or other personal problems with your co-workers, you'll leave yourself vulnerable to office gossip. Don't overestimate or tempt the loyalties of your office friends.

➡ *Choose your friends wisely.* You will not find a close friend and confidant in everyone, so use your very best judgment before you confide in someone.

Are office friendships worth the risks involved? Absolutely. Despite the risks, long-lasting office alliances founded on mutual professional respect can be a very rewarding part of your career success. But remember, these friendships will shift and change in response to the demands of the job. If you exercise tact and discretion, the friends you make will be the kind who support your success. Hopefully, they too will be successful and you will grow and mature together throughout your respective careers.

- **When you wonder how you are really doing on the job, an in-depth self-appraisal can give you the answer.**

- **Keep your skills and procedures up-to-scale by using these guidelines.**

- **How do you rate? Use this chart to assess your skills in interpersonal relations.**

CHART YOUR COURSE FOR CAREER SUCCESS

Chances are that your responsibilities are always changing with the changing needs of the office. You may start out screening calls and filing, but as you prove your competence on the job, it's likely that you will move on to tasks involving more responsibility and a higher degree of difficulty. Taking on new responsibilities can add an exciting dimension to your job, but it can also foster insecurity. And when you hear familiar voices in the back of your head saying *Am I doing OK?* after a couple of weeks—or months—at the job, you should answer those insecurities by evaluating your own performance.

A self-appraisal system can not only help you target areas in which you need improvement, it can also define your strengths. Find out how you are *really* doing in terms of overall communication, relations with your boss, cooperation with your co-workers, and customer relations through a self-appraisal program. With this helpful tool, you can determine which of your interpersonal skills are strong and which could use some sharpening. While you could get helpful feedback on your strengths and weaknesses from your boss or a co-worker, their comments may be more motivating than critical. To find out what areas you really need to work on, answer specific questions and rate your performance on interpersonal relations.

Keep track of your effectiveness in the office and of your success in interpersonal relations by regularly evaluating procedures. Use the chart provided here to assess your own skills. This way, you can find out which methods and systems work for you and which do not. For example, if you send letters out to delinquent customers requesting payment, and your records indicate that follow-up phone calls are usually necessary to collect the balance, you may want to rethink your system for collection letters.

Of course, an honest evaluation of your own performance isn't easy—most people tend to either overestimate their talents or play them down. What can you do to get an accurate idea of your competence? Observe a top-performing employee in action. Try to get a feel for the kind of work this person produces—the quality of the work as well as the quantity. How does this person interact with customers and clients (in person and on the telephone)? Is he or she organized? relaxed? aware of the functions of other departments? Compare your routine and try to find areas in which you can make improvements.

An Ongoing Process

Investing the time and energy to become a top-notch employee really pays off when you continually work to keep your skills sharp and your procedures up-to-scale. Here are some helpful strategies:

■ **Take advantage of meetings.** The information you get at staff meetings or in meetings with your boss will indicate his or her priorities. Use this information to target those priorities in your own job. For example, if your boss is working on a project and has asked not to be disturbed, apply your skill at deflecting incoming calls and screening visitors.

■ **Discuss problems with your boss.** After finding out the results of your self-appraisal, discuss them with your boss. Talk about what skills you need to work on, and ask for clarification if you think you need it, and ask for any suggestions that he or she may have to help you improve your performance.

Use the Chart

Use this analysis chart to rate the effectiveness of your interpersonal skills in the office. In the spaces allowed along the top of the chart, fill in the date of the appraisal. Then answer the questions in the left column by rating your performance on a scale from 1 to 5—with 5 being the best possible performance. Total your score on each section in the space provided and, whether you review your performance monthly, quarterly, or biannually, you'll be able to compare your progress in sharpening your interpersonal skills.

SELF-APPRAISAL PROGRESS CHART

FILL IN DATES HERE							
SUCCESSFUL COMMUNICATION							
Do you get your message across in a clear and concise manner?							
Do you always listen carefully to others?							
Do you give complete information?							
Do you weigh situations carefully before you respond?							
Are you able to discern the hidden messages revealed through body language?							
TOTAL							
BETTER RELATIONS WITH THE BOSS							
Do you keep your boss fully informed at all times?							
Do you follow established channels of communication with your higher-ups?							
Do you use tact and understanding if you disagree with your boss?							
Do you remain flexible to accommodate your boss's changing priorities?							
Do you understand and accept your boss's basic nature?							
TOTAL							
COOPERATING WITH YOUR CO-WORKERS							
Do you foster teamwork by giving your co-workers a hand when it's needed?							
Do you help make your co-workers feel like valued players on the office team?							
Are you sensitive to underlying feelings of competition in your workplace?							
Do you deal with office disputes in a courteous, professional manner?							
Do you always allow your co-workers to "save face" if you "win" a dispute?							
TOTAL							
CUSTOMER RELATIONS							
Do you greet office visitors in a professional and confident manner?							
Do you come across as interested, alert, and helpful when you answer the telephone?							
Do you take messages willingly and completely—and repeat the information you've taken down to be sure that it's correct?							
Do you welcome complaints as an opportunity to help a loyal customer?							
Are you tactful and positive when speaking to a disgruntled customer?							
TOTAL							

I   II   III   IV

INTRODUCTION

Do you ever feel as if there's never enough time to accomplish all your tasks? If so, you need to take a good hard look at how you're actually *spending* your time on the job. The following section will allow you to examine your work habits—and to identify those that may be preventing you from finishing jobs in an organized, timely manner. In the process, you'll learn steps you can take to change those habits and to do your job in the most efficient way possible.

Would you like some tips on how to manage your office's mail more efficiently? Perhaps your main interest lies in developing a calendar system that will help you organize your time better? If you'd like to research a particular area of organization and time management, glancing at the index below will help you locate the subject you're interested in.

Mini-Index

- **Does your time seem to slip away? Use our sure-fire method to discover where your time goes.**

- **Often, routine jobs get done first, and important ones are finished in haste. Here: working with the boss to set priorities.**

- **Learn how to make up a plan that suits your needs and your work routine.**

DEVELOPING A DAILY ROUTINE

Learning how to use your time efficiently is often a matter of *getting into the habit* of being organized. It's examining what you now do with a block of time against what you'd like to do in the same amount of time. Then it's developing a routine that works—but not one so inflexible that it can't absorb those surprises that come up once in a while.

Think about the jobs that you do daily. Following the example in the chart below, list each job in the "To Do" column. Then write a brief description of it under "Details." Jot down under "Time" how long it takes you to complete the job.

Chart 1

	To Do	Details	Time
	Typing	Daily sales report	45 min
1.	_____	_____	_____
2.	_____	_____	_____
3.	_____	_____	_____
4.	_____	_____	_____
5.	_____	_____	_____

Setting Priorities

After you complete your list, study each job carefully. Look for nonessentials and shortcuts. Ask yourself:

✔ Must this job be done every day?

✔ Could it be done weekly?

✔ Could it be eliminated?

✔ Could it be consolidated with another job?

✔ Could it be done in a shorter, more economical way?

✔ Am I doing this job at the best possible time?

By answering these questions, you will trim any fat from your schedule and be able to set your priorities. Your employer is also a valuable source of information and should be consulted as you set up your new schedule. Discuss your daily tasks with your employer, and find out what his or her priorities are. Examine the goals of your particular business. Show your boss how you could increase your efficiency if you eliminated the red tape from some jobs or rescheduled others. He or she will be glad to cooperate since any time savings on your part will benefit you both.

After you set priorities, you must schedule your tasks into time blocks. Some jobs, such as opening mail, have to be done at specified times. But many jobs can be done at your convenience.

Arrange your work so that you're doing as many similar jobs as possible at one sitting. For instance, if your list of things to do includes several calls to customers, make the calls one right after the other. Also, schedule your most demanding assignments for your peak periods, those times of the day when you normally have more energy and enthusiasm. For example, if you find the drafting and editing of letters to be a demanding job, then schedule this for the period when your energy is greatest, and save filing for times when your energy is low.

Now you're ready to prepare a permanent work planner. Just list all your daily tasks in the sequence you've decided is most efficient. List the time of day you plan to do the job. Of course, interruptions or rush jobs will make it necessary for you to depart from your schedule occasionally. But if you use your work planner faithfully, you will save yourself a lot of time and effort. It will also give your replacement a handy guide when you're on vacation. Use Chart 2 below or fill in your daily work planner on your own calendar.

Chart 2: Daily Planner

8 a.m.	_____
9 a.m.	_____
10 a.m.	_____
11 a.m.	_____
12 noon	_____
1 p.m.	_____
2 p.m.	_____
3 p.m.	_____
4 p.m.	_____
5 p.m.	_____

Remember, this is only a basic outline of your day. Use the following tips to plan each day individually.

➢ Plan your strategy. Decide what you want to accomplish at the beginning of the day. At first it may be difficult to estimate the number of projects you are able to complete in a given amount of time, but soon your list will become more realistic.

➢ Put first things first. Place the most important projects at the top of your list. This will ensure that they get done, and if you don't have time to finish everything, it will be the less important tasks that remain undone.

➢ Aim for the finish line. Don't leave your projects half done. Returning to a job makes you waste time by having to review what has already been done.

➢ Work at a moderate pace. If you work too fast, you will probably make more mistakes. You won't be saving time if you have to correct numerous errors.

➢ Make a separate list of fill-in jobs. Then, when you find yourself with a few minutes to spare, you can finish off these quick jobs. Having a list handy allows you to make the most of the time that you save by being so organized.

- **Your time is too precious to waste. In this chapter: rethinking the way you approach your job.**

- **Simple, effective tips to help you increase your output.**

- **Ways to organize for efficiency.**

ENHANCING YOUR EFFICIENCY

If you're swamped with work all the time, if you find that there just isn't enough time in the week to do all you're supposed to do, or if you can't get ahead on tasks that should be routine, then you need to rethink the way you approach your job. Learn the right way to do a task *and* how to coordinate it with other ones. In short, become an "efficiency expert." Use the following tips to trim time from your routine.

Planning Your Day

➤ Plan your work and set priorities. First thing in the morning, while you're still fresh, make a list of "must do" jobs in the order of their importance. That way, if you can't get everything done, you can at least complete the most important tasks.

➤ Combine tasks when you can. For example, if you are responsible for delivering supplies and routing memos, do both at the same time so that you won't have to travel the same route twice.

➤ Consider changing your routine. Look for shortcuts and ways to modify your duties. While you work, try to think of easier, faster ways to get your work done. When you have the time, experiment a little and improvise on your work scheme. You just may discover a better way to handle that routine job you face every day.

➤ Don't forget your boss. Your employer will certainly appreciate any efforts you expend to make his or her routine more efficient. For example, mark the articles you think your boss should read in the magazines he or she regularly receives. Or when your boss receives an important letter, bring all related correspondence and pertinent papers with it from the files.

Psych Yourself Up

➤ Attack each top-priority job individually. When you're working on one tough assignment, don't worry about the others that still need to be done. That only reduces your efficiency and wastes time. Just start at the top of your list and work down. When each assignment is completed, put it out of your mind. Cross it off your list and move on to the next item.

➤ Stay cool and calm under pressure. If your time schedule gets tight and rush items pile up, relax a bit to relieve the tension. Get a drink of water. Get up and stretch or do some muscle-relaxing exercises. Even changing position for a few minutes might be all you need to ease the tension.

➤ Motivate yourself. Occasionally, unforeseen tasks pop up that can't be put off; they must be done now. If this happens and you don't seem to have the extra energy for the demands of the assignment, think of some incentive to urge you to get the job done.

Arranging Your Work Area

➤ Organize work time by work area. Avoid constantly moving from one workstation to another. If you have several different items that need to be copied, gather them together and do them all at one time.

➤ Arrange your basic work area to ensure a steady output. Use folders, dividers, and trays to organize paperwork and data. Arrange notes and messages so that they can be found easily. Tape special typing instructions, such as margins, tab stops, and style preferences, to your typing stand. Tape frequently called numbers to the pull-out leaf of your desk.

➤ Keep supplies and materials near your desk for the kinds of jobs you do most often. For example, if you use multiples of certain forms, keep a sufficient supply of them in your desk, not in the supply closet down the hall. Also, keep your often-used reference books handy, not across the room.

Paperwork: Efficiency Enemy Number One

Despite efforts to reorganize office procedures, to incorporate word processing systems, and to hire more office workers, the paperwork problem keeps expanding. Take a look at your workday. Do you find more and more reports, forms, and correspondence crossing your desk every day?

Here are some of the shortcuts you can use to slice your paperwork in half:

➤ Use the telephone. As the quickest and easiest means of communication, the telephone should be used more often to relay simple messages and reminders. Save yourself time, and your office the expense of mailing out reminder notices for overdue bills or appointments, by calling. Not only can you save time and money, but you will also be sure your message gets through. Document the call and any information exchanged for further reference by making brief notes.

➤ Limit your use of the photocopier. Because photocopying is so easy, you may be tempted to make unnecessary copies. Beware of the habit of making extra copies "just in case." Always check the control settings to get a good copy the first time. And consider keeping a log of copier use to discourage unnecessary or personal copying.

➤ Keep your files organized and pared down. In your daily filing procedures, use throw-out dates to get rid of any outdated material. Periodically remove unnecessary duplicates of memos, letters, bulletins, and advertising brochures. At the same time, transfer outdated files to storage areas so that they won't take up prime office space. These measures should give you more filing space while trimming the time you have to spend searching through overcrowded files.

➤ Use concise, simple forms to process information. Evaluate those you are now using to see whether they could be combined or whether certain portions are unnecessary. Also, if you often find yourself collecting the same information without any way to organize and process it, you may want to devise your own form to expedite things. Whatever your use of forms, just be sure they are used to cut your paperwork, not increase it.

➤ Use a form letter notebook. By learning to reply to some of the office correspondence with form letters, you can save time for both your boss and yourself. Set up a notebook of basic letters and paragraphs that cover routine correspondence.

- **Do you constantly put things off until "whenever"? Analyze your behavior and find out why you procrastinate.**

- **Learn simple techniques that help you take control of your time.**

- **One key to success: scheduling projects and tasks realistically.**

AVOIDING AVOIDANCE

Do you ever catch yourself putting off some job until the last possible minute just because you don't want to do it? Have you found that your sudden fondness for sharpening pencils just happens to coincide with a challenging project you've just been given?

Everyone avoids or delays doing necessary jobs from time to time. But if you find yourself putting things off regularly, you may have a problem with procrastination.

Analyze Your Behavior

The first step in overcoming self-destructive behavior like procrastination is to recognize and analyze your behavior. In the chart below, list five tasks that you routinely put off. Now, in the space next to each, list a reason why you put off that task. Try to be honest or this exercise won't be beneficial.

	Task	Why I Don't Do It
1.	_____	_____
2.	_____	_____
3.	_____	_____
4.	_____	_____
5.	_____	_____

Excuses, Excuses

There are several common reasons for procrastination. See if your own behavior is related to any of them.

One of the main reasons for all forms of avoidance is fear—fear of success, fear of failure, or fear of having too much responsibility. Instead of facing those fears directly, you procrastinate.

To reduce fear, try to visualize yourself in the situation you fear. Then, use your imagination to figure a way out of it. If you have a project to do or a presentation to make, visualize yourself getting through the situation well. Channel your fear into actions that will help you face whatever it is you fear, instead of allowing fear to paralyze you.

Another reason for procrastination is an inability to say no. You might automatically say yes whenever someone asks you to do something. Before you say yes, think about how long it will take you to complete the project. Then see if it will fit comfortably into your schedule.

If you procrastinate because the job looks too big to handle, break it into small parts. Do one part at a time—starting with the smallest part. Try to view the whole project as a group of small tasks that add up to a larger whole.

You might also be tempted to procrastinate if you are given an unpleasant task. Accept that unwelcome chores do not go away. No one else is going to do the job for you. So the energy you waste worrying about the job could be better spent doing the job. Then it will be finished and you'll be able to relax without guilt.

How Procrastination Hurts You

By procrastinating, you may not be giving yourself the opportunities you deserve to fulfill your potential. Your job may eventually be jeopardized—especially if your procrastination begins to produce extra expenses for your company because of missed deadlines and overtime costs.

Don't judge or criticize yourself if you procrastinate. Bad habits can't be changed overnight. Already you've taken the first step to managing your time more effectively. You have recognized that you procrastinate. Now ask yourself why you're procrastinating and take action.

Defeating the Deadline Creep

We've all been victims of the deadline creep. This is a type of "sneak" procrastination. This happens when your boss hands you a project with a due date of three weeks later and you think, "No problem. This is an eternity away. . ." Suddenly, it's three weeks later and you wonder where the time went.

The best way to lose control of a new project or task is to shuffle it onto the already huge pile of unidentified paper on your desk. Don't tell yourself that you will get to it later. You probably won't.

Instead, take a close look at the new project right away. If you don't understand exactly what your boss wants, ask questions. The best time to clear up any confusion is while the project is still fresh to you and your boss. You may come up with comments or suggestions to make your job easier. This is the time to okay them with your boss. It will save you time in the long run because you won't have to do anything twice.

The best way to keep a project on schedule is to break the work down into small, manageable tasks that can be accomplished in a day or less. Mark on your calendar what is to be accomplished each day . . . and do it!

Always build flexibility into your project plan. If you plan to do a little each day, schedule concrete tasks for only four days of the week. Use one day to accomplish anything that you didn't manage to get done when it was scheduled.

If an emergency comes up, or if for some other reason you feel that it is impossible for you to complete the project by its due date, tell your boss immediately. There is nothing more annoying than being told at the last minute that something can't be done. Your boss is relying on you.

Summary of Time-Making Tips

✔ Know before you start what you want to accomplish.
✔ Use initiative in solving problems. Don't wait to be pushed.
✔ Don't put off making important, thoughtful decisions. Clarify with your supervisor any questions you have.
✔ Allow yourself enough time.
✔ Schedule to keep tasks moving toward completion.
✔ Follow through on every project to bring it to a successful conclusion.

After you finish the project, review how your original planning worked out. Did you need more time for certain tasks? Did you need less time for others? Keep these notes and use them to plan more accurately for your next project.

- Is all that paper pushing building your biceps? If so, follow these two simple steps for streamlining.

- Break down office tasks into necessary steps.

- Then, trim the "fat" from your routine.

STREAMLINING OFFICE JOBS

If you handle a letter so often that it's dog-eared by the time you give it to your boss, you've probably saddled yourself with too many steps in the process of completing the job. How often do you really have to handle a letter? Do you keep putting it down and then later digging it out from under your work pile again?

Every time you pick up a task and then put it down, you are adding a step. To find your peak level of efficiency, you must analyze your office tasks and eliminate all the unnecessary steps.

Start by taking each task listed on your daily work planner and breaking it down into a step-by-step series of operations. You'll be surprised how involved routine jobs become when you put them down on paper. Suppose, for example, your morning mail-handling duties break down like this:

1. Open mail and sort letters according to those that need your employer's attention, those that need someone else's attention, and those that need your attention.
2. Give employer his or her mail.
3. Take action on other letters one by one.
4. Retrieve mail from employer's desk and reread to determine proper filings.

Analysis:

➤ Step 3 is a time-waster. Why not read all of these letters, one after the other, jotting down the necessary actions to take on each? Then, if you needed information from, say, Shipping, on three letters, you'd have to make only one phone call, not three.

➤ Step 4 can be eliminated altogether. Why not jot down filing directions on each letter as you read through all the mail in Step 1?

The Importance of Putting It in Writing

The trick here is to get the task down in writing. The unnecessary or overly complicated parts of any job will come to light when you get them down in black and white. Analyze all the tasks that make up your workday in this manner. And question everything you do, every time you do it.

Here are some suggestions to follow in analyzing your work:

1. Look for outdated processes. A step in a routine, or even a whole routine that was necessary once, may no longer have any value. Are you sending carbon copies of paperwork to people who no longer need them? Are you maintaining files or ledgers that no one has used in a long time?

It pays to recheck all your office routines regularly. Every business is in a constant state of change, and what was necessary one year may be useless the next. Don't waste your efforts on outdated tasks.

2. Examine regular reports. Could a well-designed form be substitut-

ed for a detailed report? Forms can be filled in easily, can be read quickly, and can contain as much information as a long report. Consider asking your supervisor if a form would be a viable option.

3. Go through the proper channels. Each section or division in your company has one person responsible for a certain type of work. Go directly to that person, and not to a rank-and-file employee, to have a job taken care of. This will eliminate friction because it shows respect for other people's schedules. For instance, if you have a report for the word processing department, take it to the supervisor and let him or her assign it to a typist. The supervisor will see that it is done quickly and efficiently. Cooperation and understanding between departments make for efficient business procedures.

Use the sample chart below to get you started and to help you set up a more complete chart.

	Task	Steps	Improvements
1.	_____	_____	_____
2.	_____	_____	_____
3.	_____	_____	_____
4.	_____	_____	_____
5.	_____	_____	_____
6.	_____	_____	_____
7.	_____	_____	_____
8.	_____	_____	_____
9.	_____	_____	_____
10.	_____	_____	_____

Don't Throw These Lists Away!

Once you've decided what steps are essential to each task, keep these written records on file. They'll ensure that your office can operate smoothly if someone else has to fill in for you.

Each time you begin a new routine or change an old one, be sure to make the appropriate changes in your file. Each record should give a step-by-step description of the task and provide information on who (by job title) performs each step and where the task fits into the total office routine. You'll find this file is both a valuable training device for an assistant, when you get too busy to do it yourself, and a handy reference for refreshing your own memory.

- Forgotten how to set up a certain form letter? That's no problem when you have this handy job manual to refer to. Put it together using these simple tips.

- When training a temp, avoid misunderstandings *before* they start—use a job manual. Here's what your sub needs to know.

- Not sure if you've covered everything? Follow these guidelines to make sure your manual is clear and complete.

CREATING A JOB MANUAL

Are the temps in your office tempted to leave? If they are, something's wrong. Take a minute to think about how confused you were during your first days on the job. You probably learned from experience that a job manual would have been a great help in those hectic days. Someone assigned to do your job in your absence could benefit from your experience. Not only will creating a job manual benefit others, but it will provide a handy reference for you whenever you need to look up a standard letter format or an office procedure. And it will prevent the work from piling up while you're away.

Organizing the Info

Keep these tips in mind as you write your job manual.

✔ Think your job through step-by-step. The little task that seems so routine is often the one that causes problems.
✔ Use a loose-leaf notebook so that you'll be able to make changes later if necessary.
✔ If you have any questions about routines or procedures, get all the facts together before you start writing.
✔ Keep it simple. Don't include unnecessary information that might be confusing.
✔ Make sentences short and to the point.
✔ Try to write in a step-by-step list format. It is easier to understand and refer to than the usual paragraph format.

Putting It All Together

First, give a brief summary of a typical day's activities, including your work hours and lunch break. Then give detailed instructions for each task, explaining *who, what, when,* and *where.* Include filled-in samples of company forms and form letters.

Follow this comprehensive list of questions to make sure that you include all relevant information in your job manual.

OFFICE

- What are the jobs in your office and who does them?
- Who are the company officers, department heads, and key employees?
- Will your substitute have to correspond with other departments or branches? What are their locations and telephone numbers?
- What are the names of other secretaries, clerks, etc., with whom the temporary will have contact?
- What policy or instruction memoranda should a temporary see?
- Where are the instruction booklets for all the equipment used in your office?
- What should be known about your reminder systems?

MAIL

- What are the pickup and delivery times?
- What type of information and material do you route to whom?
- Does your employer answer all correspondence personally?
- If you answer some routine letters, where are samples of such correspondence filed?

FILING

- What is your method of filing?
- Who has access to your files?
- Which files contain confidential material?
- What material might your employer want during your absence, and where is it filed?

TELEPHONE

- In answering the phone, should your substitute use a special phrase?
- Do you screen your employer's calls?
- What sort of inquiries do you have to answer?
- How should inquiries be handled?
- Is your telephone book up-to-date?
- Do you have a list of frequently used numbers?
- Is there a certain procedure for making calls?

VISITORS

- What is your routine for receiving callers?
- How do you handle callers who are waiting?
- Do you have a list of frequent visitors to your office?
- Which persons can you refer to other offices?
- Are you responsible for making your boss's appointments, or does he or she make them and then pass that information on to you?
- Do you remind your boss of appointments?

SUPPLIES

- Where are your supplies kept?
- What procedures and forms do you use for ordering and distributing supplies?

OTHER OFFICE DUTIES

- What dictation procedure do you use?
- What procedures do you use for taking minutes at meetings?
- What other duties and tasks should your substitute know about?

When You're Done

Once you've completed the job manual, have someone who is familiar with your job read it through. If it's clear and complete to that person, have someone who is unfamiliar with the job read it through, too. This ensures that what you have written is clear, organized, and informative—not only to you but to others as well.

- When was the last time you saw the top of your desk? If it was last year, use these tips to tackle that desktop.

- Can't find what you need? Discover the ins and outs of organizing.

- Books are necessities for helping you validate information—whether it's current facts or writing style. Here are some essential references.

ORGANIZING YOUR WORKSPACE

If you have no idea whether your desktop is gray, brown, or pink with purple polka dots, now is the time to find out! Wage a campaign against clutter and *win* with some help from this chapter. Remember, your desktop is your workspace, not your junk pile.

Clearing the Clutter

Being organized doesn't happen by accident. All it involves is three simple steps:

1. Look at what you have.
2. Throw away what you *don't* need.
3. Organize what you *do* need.

But it's not that simple, you say. *I've got a mountain of paper on my desk, and if I touch it, I'm likely to cause an avalanche.* Now, now, now—what you have on your desk may seem like a mountain, but if you break it down into a few molehills, you'll be able to get your desk under control in no time.

Step I

During a slow time of day—possibly at lunchtime, or before or after business hours—clear your desk and shelves of everything, including phone messages, trade journals, reports, files, office supplies, and personal possessions.

Then, set aside a work area—a space where you can put these items and pile them into groups. For example, group all current correspondence together. Do the same for old trade journals, reports, etc., until everything has been categorized and placed in neat piles.

Step II

To ensure that important papers—the ones that do belong on your desk—are not lost in the shuffle, mark folders for them in the following way:

Pending—This folder will hold all those things you have yet to do: correspondence to answer, bills to pay, written reminders to yourself about calls to return, appointments to make, and any research you may have to conduct.

To be filed—This folder will contain everything that you have finished working on that must be saved.

To be copied—Anything in this folder must be copied before you can take further action on it.

For signature—This folder should contain anything that requires your boss's signature or approval.

Now take the papers and put them in the appropriate folders. This action will ensure that important documents are not misplaced or discarded and will also prevent you from having to handle each piece of paper more than once.

Step III

When you've sorted through the loose papers and placed in folders the materials that are to stay on your desk, survey the remaining documents. You'll find that many of them are inactive, but perhaps important, records. Ask your employer whether the files that you have to keep, but will rarely use, can be stored in lightweight storage cartons. If the answer is yes, mark each carton clearly to indicate its contents. Then have these cartons put into company storage.

Step IV

Before you become overzealous and discard the remaining clutter in your workspace, learn what things you should keep. (Of course, if the materials are your own, go ahead and do what you want with them. But if they belong to your employer or your company, get your employer's okay before you proceed any further.) To do this, first make a list of the contents of each of the remaining piles. Also include in your list a description of any excess office supplies and equipment in your work area. Here's a sample list that might help you draw up your own:

➢ Unused or obsolete forms

➢ Surplus office equipment, such as cabinets and chairs

➢ Surplus stationery items, such as pens and pads

➢ Outdated reports, manuscripts, and files

➢ Old trade magazines

Once you've completed your list, give a copy of it to your employer, who can decide from there what goes and what stays.

Step V

Follow your employer's recommendations as to what to save and what to throw away. For example, you might discard obsolete trade and professional journals. Return extra office supplies to the supply closet. Notify Maintenance of any extra office furniture so that it can be removed to storage.

Step VI

Once you've arranged your desk to your liking, mark your shelves, file cabinets, and desk drawers with color-coded, easy-to-read labels for quick storage and retrieval. This way even someone unfamiliar with your filing system and desk setup will be able to locate materials when you're not around.

Disastrous Drawers

Follow these tips for putting your desk and drawers to the best possible use:

➥ Place often-used items within easy reach on top of your desk.

➥ Use the center drawer for frequently used supplies such as pens, pencils, rubber bands, scissors, stapler, tape, and paper clips.

➥ Use one bottom side drawer for personal items.

Remember, keep only frequently used items on the top of your desk. Put supplies and materials away immediately after you finish using them. Otherwise, your desk will quickly be on its way to becoming a cluttered mess once again.

Odds and Ends

Here are some tips for finding a place for those things that just don't seem to fit anywhere in particular:

▪ Do you lose notes or messages in the stacks of papers on your desk? After you've weeded out everything that's not necessary, use magnetic clips to hold important notes to the side of a metal desk or to a metal partition.

▪ Does your job manual take up too much room on your desk? Type up the information you refer to most frequently, and attach it to your desk pullout. Or attach typing instructions for margins, tab stops, style preferences, etc., to your typing stand.

▪ Does your index file take up too much space? Place it on a nearby filing cabinet or put the box—without its top—in the stationery drawer of your desk. In fact, if the drawer has a partition and there are enough cards to fill the space, you might be able to get rid of the box altogether.

▪ Is your telephone book in the way? Stow it on top of a neighboring file cabinet, in an empty file drawer, or in a desk drawer.

Best Buys for Your Bookshelf

Take a quick inventory of your desk reference materials to determine if they need to be rounded out. Every well-prepared office worker should have a basic set of reference materials to aid in producing accurate information at a moment's notice. Your office bookshelf should be lined with the following:

✔ *A quality dictionary.* In addition to giving word definitions, a dictionary can help you with spelling, pronunciation, word division, parts of speech, and etymology.

✔ *A thesaurus.* To find just the right word for a particular thought, check this source of synonyms and related words. Some editions also give antonyms.

✔ *A current almanac.* Open your almanac for a wide range of facts and figures on subjects such as business, politics, sports, economics, and education.

✔ *An atlas.* This reference will come in handy for pinpointing the location of cities and towns, for checking the correct spelling of their names, and for planning business travel itineraries.

✔ *A style manual.* Keep this writing tool on hand to answer any questions on grammar, usage, construction, technique, or style.

✔ *A secretarial handbook.* A must when you need at-a-glance information on how to type a business letter, address an envelope, set up a filing system, or format a report.

These reference materials will take up some space. Sort through your current collection of books, and set aside for storage those you never use. If there's no room for the essential references on your desk, store them in one of your desk drawers. Keep them in the front of the drawer, and save space behind for personal items.

Keep It Clean

These tips will help you keep your newly organized workspace clear and free of clutter:

➡ Work on only one task at a time.

➡ File papers according to a consistent system *as they cross your desk.* If this isn't possible, keep all loose papers in a "to be filed" folder.

➡ Keep a set of in- and out-baskets on your desk. This keeps mail and memos from encroaching on your workspace.

➡ Take care of work as it comes in to prevent building up a 2-foot-high in-basket.

➡ Don't write notes on scraps of paper, because this makes it easy to misplace them. Instead, keep notes together in a notebook. This way, your notes will be easy to find and the notebook will provide a permanent record if you need to refer to a specific phone conversation or meeting.

➡ Throw away anything you don't need.

Remember this golden rule of organization: "A place for everything and everything in its place." As long as you put everything where it belongs as you finish with it, you will always know where it is. And if you take care of all those pieces of paper as they cross your desk, you will always be on top of things—instead of letting them pile up on top of your desk.

■ If your shelves are over-
flowing with unused and
unnecessary supplies,
here's how to pare them
down to the essentials.

■ Worried about whether
you're going to order too
many or too few sup-
plies? Follow these
steps and you'll end up
with just the right
amount.

■ Having trouble finding
the supplies you need
when you need them?
Use these tips to orga-
nize and inventory your
supplies.

SIMPLIFYING SUPPLIES

If, the last time you opened your supply closet, 10,000 paper clips showered down on you, it's time to take your supplies in hand. Do you really need enough paper clips to last until the year 3000? Do you really need five dozen pink felt-tip pens? If not, do something about getting those shelves organized. Look at the supplies you have and ask the following questions about each item:

✔ Do you use it regularly?

✔ Is it something that you only occasionally use?

✔ Do you ever use it?

There are certain supplies that you use regularly, and you should keep a ready store of these. Supplies that you use only occasionally should be kept in the back of the supply closet. If you find supplies that you *never* use, get rid of them! Consider exchanging unneeded supplies with other offices in your company. Who knows—someone may actually use those pink felt-tip pens every day!

Supply Savvy

Whether you are requisitioning supplies from an in-house source or ordering directly from a distributor, it's important to organize your ordering procedures. Otherwise, you might run out of something when you least expect to. Follow these tips to make sure that your supply ordering goes as smoothly as possible:

→ Compile a list of all the office supplies that you use on a regular basis.

→ Make sure that only one person is doing all the ordering. You don't want to duplicate orders. Too much of a good thing is still too much—and the extra supplies probably won't fit on your shelves.

→ Before ordering anything, ask your co-workers if there is something specific that they need that isn't on the usual supply order list. They will appreciate this courtesy.

→ If your company doesn't have a standard requisition form or the distributor you are using didn't supply one, make up your own. A complete, well-organized requisition will help speed up orders and prevent errors. This form should include spaces for item numbers, quantities, full descriptions of individual items, colors, and, if necessary, unit prices.

→ Order items in standard sizes and packs. Order a box of pencils, not just one pencil. This approach will save your company a lot of money in the long run.

→ Try to place orders on a regular basis. That way, everyone will know when they have to get their requests in to you. Also, you will be able to save time and money. Because you won't be ordering a legal pad every other day, you'll be making fewer phone calls and you won't have to constantly pay small-order handling charges.

→ Order the right quality for the job. Some jobs require first quality; others can be done with lower quality materials. Don't pay for features that you don't need. For example, do you need *wide* cellophane tape—or will narrow do?

→ Order the right quantity. You may save money by ordering a large amount, especially if something is printed just for you. However, large-quantity ordering may be very expensive when you consider storage space, shelf life, and cash outlay. Be particularly careful when ordering materials or items that deteriorate, such as correction fluid.

→ Don't order too great a variety of items. Big savings can be obtained by buying only a few kinds of things. Do you really need three different lead weights in pencils?

→ Stick to your shopping list. Overstocking, or stocking something you don't really need, cuts into your company's cash flow.

You'd Better Shop Around

Before you place an order through a distributor, you should take a look at what's out there. Shop around. Look through discount supply catalogs, call around to local office supply stores. Some of the items you need may be on sale. You should also ask if there is any business or quantity discount available. Often, mail-order catalogs have the best deals because their overhead is reduced and they sell in quantity. Follow these suggestions to keep your mail-order shopping trouble-free:

➢ Deal only with reliable companies. When in doubt, check out the company with the Better Business Bureau or a consumer protection agency where the company is located. Don't rely on catalog pictures to tell the whole story. Read the advertisements and order information carefully. Are there any missing facts or questionable claims? Are the company's warranty and exchange policies clearly explained? Contact the company with any questions you may have and get satisfactory answers in writing.

➢ Select a proficient vendor—one that offers an extensive line of supplies. Finding a supplier that can offer the convenience of a variety of items and the benefit of technical expertise will help to eliminate unnecessary paperwork, save time otherwise spent on ordering from more than one company, and reduce the headaches of purchasing.

➢ Work with your account representative. Remember, this is your richest source of technical advice and cost-saving suggestions. By establishing a good working relationship, you both stand to benefit.

➢ Keep in mind that it's riskier to shop by telephone than it is to shop by mail. It's tempting to use the phone because so many mail-order companies now offer toll-free numbers. But without any written records of the order, there is more of a chance that a mix-up will occur. So unless you're prepared to wait indefinitely, fill out that mail-order form and send it off without delay.

➤ When ordering by telephone or by mail, make sure to have available all the information you may need, including the item number and quantity, etc. Also have your account number on hand.

Taking Stock

Are your office supplies readily available? Are they stored neatly in a cabinet or closet where everyone can get them? Supplies are tools that help people accomplish their jobs. If the work is to flow smoothly, the proper stores should always be at hand. Use these tips to make sure that you maintain a complete inventory of all the supplies needed:

✔ Make a checklist. List every supply used on the job. Record each item separately and describe it accurately. For example, paper must be broken down by types, paper clips by size, and pencils and pens by color. *The chart on the next page will help you accomplish this task. Simply make a photocopy of it and fill in the blanks for each item.*

✔ Review your inventory of office supplies regularly. Keep an eye on the supplies that go quickly, and be aware of those that are on the shelves forever. When things are running low, don't assume that there is a stock of them elsewhere. Finally, make sure you regularly order the supplies that are used most often.

✔ Insert a "Reorder Now" slip in each pile of supplies. For example, if you use one box of pens per week and your shelves hold a dozen boxes, rubber band the last four boxes with the slip. Then, the person who begins to use the four-box supply should submit the slip to you and you can reorder. This technique keeps supplies from dwindling to nothing before you know it.

Storing Your Supplies

➥ Don't overload the stock area. If you don't have enough room to handle all the supplies needed for a month, order more often. But don't fill every nook and cranny with papers, envelopes, and pens. Soon these supplies will be shoved to one side, dropped on the floor, and finally thrown out because they're torn, crumpled, and dirty.

➥ Organize storage space. Arrange all stock items in a manner that is logical for your office. Limit each area to a particular item. Then paste labels on the front of each shelf to indicate what goes where. Or, if you use file cabinets to hold supplies, tab each file drawer with a description of the contents. Place the most frequently used supplies, such as letterhead and envelopes, in the most accessible places.

➥ Keep paper items covered. Ask your supplier to deliver stationery and other paper products in boxes. This helps to keep out dirt and to keep the paper fresh and uncrumpled.

➥ Make a chart of the supply area. A large, easily read diagram of the storage area will help both new personnel looking for everyday items and other employees searching for seldom-used supplies. Your inventory job will also be made easier.

SUPPLY INVENTORY

Month: _____

Item Description	No. on Hand	No. to Order	Other Information

■ **Does dealing with the
mail consume half your
morning? Trim that time,
using these tips.**

■ **If you have problems
keeping all that incom-
ing correspondence
straight, here's a work-
able sorting system.**

■ **Incoming mail is not the
only challenge to organi-
zation. Here's how to
give outgoing mail an
effective once-over.**

MANAGING THE MAIL

If every morning you are greeted by an avalanche of incoming mail, now is the time to take control of it. Mail represents an important connection between your company and its customers and clients. It connects your office with the outside world. Managing the mail is a job that takes time. But why take more time than you need? Cut your mail-handling time, using these tips:

➤ Tackle the mail all at once if you can. Don't spread the job throughout the day.
➤ Follow a regular sorting procedure. This ensures that you don't miss any steps and that the mail will be handled in an organized and efficient manner.

Smart Sorting

You still have a huge pile of unopened mail on your desk. Now what? Just follow these ten steps. You will end up with several *small* piles—each of which can be easily handled.

Step 1:
Sort all the mail into four stacks: correspondence, bills and statements, advertisements and circulars, and newspapers and periodicals.

Step 2:
Open all the correspondence except those pieces marked "confidential" or "personal." Set those aside for your boss. Then, stack all the envelopes with the flaps up and away from you, and open them all before putting down the letter opener. Remove the contents of each letter, making sure that nothing is left in the envelope.

Step 3:
Attach the contents to the envelopes. Stamp the date on each letter.

Step 4:
Sort the letters into three stacks: those requiring your boss's attention, those requiring the attention of someone outside your office, and those requiring your attention. Read each letter *only once*.

Step 5:
Prepare your boss's mail. If there's a file or previous correspondence relating to the current letter that would be helpful, attach it to the letter before giving it to your employer. Arrange all the mail in order of importance with the most important on top.

Step 6:
Attend to any correspondence requiring someone else's attention. If

necessary, attach the pertinent file or previous correspondence. Keep a daily log of all the mail you send to other offices for action. It will be an invaluable aid when you need to follow up on a particular piece of correspondence. Include: to whom you sent the letter, the date it was sent, the action to be taken, and the deadline date for follow-up.

Step 7:

Go through the newspapers and periodicals. Select the ones that your boss likes to read and put them in a folder on his or her desk. Highlight any articles of interest.

Step 8:

Sort through advertisements and circulars. Don't throw these away until you've looked at them. Put those that you think might be of interest to your boss on his or her desk with the newspapers and periodicals.

Step 9:

Review the bills and statements. If a check is received, make sure that the amount enclosed is the same as the amount mentioned in the letter or on the statement. If your office's practice is to file such mail until a certain time of the month, do so. However, you might want to get a head start if you have the opportunity.

Step 10:

Attend to any correspondence requiring only *your* personal attention.

Outgoing Mail

The first question to ask yourself when you are preparing to write a reply to a letter is whether or not a formal written reply is necessary. Consider these two alternatives:

1. If you can, answer a letter with a phone call. It saves time for you—and for your boss.

2. Consider sending your reply on the original letter. Write your note on the letter you received and then photocopy it. Mail the original letter back to the sender. The sender gets a prompt response and you save time.

If you must send a letter, check these items *before* sealing the envelope:

➤ Is the signature clear and clean and in ink?

➤ Are the correct enclosures included?

➤ Does the address on the letter agree with the address on the envelope?

These may seem obvious, but are easily overlooked. The letters that you send reflect on your professionalism. Taking a few minutes to check these items over is not too much to ask to protect your—and your company's—image.

- Does your boss use his or her desk as a horizontal filing cabinet? Here's how to mesh your working styles.

- Are you confused about your boss's priorities? Now's the time to find out what they are!

- If papers constantly seem to get lost in the shuffle between you and your boss, here's a way to get them organized.

ORGANIZING A DISORGANIZED BOSS

If your boss's idea of being organized is to stack papers into piles 3 feet high on every flat surface available, then you know what it's like to work for a disorganized boss. Your boss might tell you that he or she knows where any document is at any given time, but that doesn't help you. Having so many papers lying around is distracting and decreases efficiency—for both you and your boss.

Do Your Job

As an office-support professional, your role is to aid your boss in reaching his or her goals relating to the company, such as quality and productivity goals. To be able to *be* supportive, however, you must first understand what your boss's goals are, what the goals of the company are, and what the purpose of your job is.

The first step to doing your job is to find out exactly what it entails. Ask your boss to discuss with you how you spend your time. Learn what your boss considers his or her main priorities so that you can keep yourself on track when deciding how to spend time. Write your boss's top five priorities on the lines below. Review these goals regularly so that you don't lose sight of your mission.

GOALS

1. _____

2. _____

3. _____

4. _____

5. _____

Clear Communication Channels

One of the difficulties in working with a disorganized boss is understanding exactly what he or she expects you to do. If you are unclear as to what the instructions for a particular task are, or when that report is due, ask. It's better to make sure that you know what you are supposed to do *before* you do it. Then you won't have to do it again.

Shuffling Paperwork

Here are a few tips to help you help your boss handle paperwork as efficiently as possible:

➡ Take over as much of your boss's paperwork as you reasonably can, especially if he or she has a tendency to mislay papers. There are many letters and pieces of routine correspondence that you already know how to handle. Ask your boss if it is okay for you to handle certain items. After you have taken care of them, simply give your boss a typed list of the items and your responses so that he or she can be sure that each item was handled correctly.

➡ Designate a place for you and your boss to keep current files and documents that are being used by both of you. This way you won't need to spend 5 minutes searching through your boss's clutter for files or a client's letter, and he or she won't have the opportunity to lose these papers among the others strewn across the office.

➡ Consider setting up a system of In and Out boxes just for papers that pass between you and your boss. That way, each of you can pass work along to the other without causing an interruption.

➡ Establish a place for you to put reading materials that are not urgent, but that your boss should read. That way, they won't get mixed up among the more important items on your boss's desk.

➡ Review the list of publications that your boss receives, and ask what subjects he or she is interested in. Instead of giving a pile of magazines to your boss to read, maintain current files on each of the different topics specified by him or her.

➡ Ask your boss if you can check his or her desk routinely—perhaps once a week— for any correspondence or other papers that are no longer current and can be filed. This gives you an opportunity to help your boss out by cleaning off his or her desk.

Keeping Track

Consult with your boss daily to make sure that both of you are aware of what appointments are scheduled and what the priorities are for the day. You might also consider suggesting weekly meetings—Friday afternoon might be best—in order to establish clear goals for the coming week.

If you know, for instance, that your boss tends to procrastinate on projects or reports until the deadline is imminent, you might want to suggest tactfully that he or she get started on it soon. For example, you might say, "And if you can give me that market research report by next Thursday, I'll be able to type it up for the meeting on Monday." You can also ask if there is any way for you to help out—by doing research or by helping construct an outline.

When you work with a disorganized boss, it's important to help him or her as much as possible—but always in a discreet and professional manner. After a while, your work styles will begin to mesh more easily. Through it all, keep in mind your ideal of an organized office, and slowly work toward making it a reality.

- Do you use so many calendars and schedules that you don't know which ones to pay attention to? Learn how to trim them to the bare minimum in this chapter.

- Having trouble knowing what you should keep track of? Here's a list telling you which dates and appointments should be recorded.

- Not only do you need to establish a reminder system, you have to maintain it. Here's how.

KEEPING A CALENDAR

Calendars are the backbone of any reminder system. Without them, both you and your boss would probably be lost forever in a sea of appointments and things to do. Neither of you would be able to accomplish very much. So for you, your boss, and your office to function efficiently, it's important that you keep a comprehensive view of your boss's appointments and tasks by maintaining at least two cross-referenced calendars—one for your desk and one for your boss's.

Types of Calendars

Here are a few examples of calendars that will keep all dates to remember organized:

✔ *Your word processor.* On your computer or word processor you can create a calendar file and keep a daily, weekly, or monthly schedule on a disk—making additions or deletions as they occur. This can be a helpful tool if you call up your calendar at the beginning of each day to remind you of "must do" tasks. You might even want to print it out and place it where you're sure to see it all day. Then you can check off tasks as they're completed.

✔ *Your workstation calendar.* Use either a standard desk calendar or a bound yearbook. When choosing, keep this point in mind: A desk calendar puts the day's activities before your eyes, but it also makes your schedule visible to anyone who glances at your desk. So if confidentiality is required for any reason, a yearbook is your best bet. Whichever calendar you pick, the day pages should be subdivided into half-hour segments so that you can note deadlines, appointments, meetings, and the like at their scheduled times.

✔ *Your boss's desk calendar.* Since your boss may also want to keep appointments under wraps, ask if he or she prefers a yearbook format or a standard desk calendar. If a yearbook is preferred, be sure to use one with enough space to include not only the names of individuals with appointments but also any special problems or information to be discussed during their visits.

✔ *Your boss's pocket calendar.* This portable counterpart of the desk calendar lets your boss see what's going on when he or she is away from the office and ensures that conflicting appointments aren't inadvertently arranged. Check with your boss regularly to find out about plans or appointments that may have been made without your knowledge, and add them to your calendar.

Important Business Dates

When you're making up calendars, it's helpful to have a list of recurring matters that you and your boss must remember. Here's a breakdown of entries frequently included on calendars year after year. Not all of them will apply to your job, and there are likely to be others that you'll want to add, but at least you can use this sample as a jumping-off point for drawing up your own list:

- Staff meetings
- Production meetings
- Business association or service club meetings
- Renewal of subscriptions to professional and/or technical publications
- Payment dates for dues to professional associations
- Legal holidays
- Department vacation schedules
- Annual meetings or conventions

Important Personal Dates

In addition to important business dates, many office-support employees also keep track of numerous personal dates for their bosses. If you don't already do this, your boss would no doubt appreciate your notation of these dates on both sets of calendars. You'll find that this practice is a real time-saver because personal business can often affect your boss's availability. Here is a short list of dates you may want to keep track of:

- Medical and dental appointments
- Alumni meetings and club meetings
- Family birthdays and anniversaries

Once you have drawn up a tentative list of recurring matters, show it to your boss in case additions or changes need to be made.

Calendar Upkeep

Finally, keep these points in mind with regard to entries on your calendar:

➤ When entering a matter that needs advance preparation, such as a meeting or a report, or a task that must allow for mailing time, such as sending dues, include additional reminders well in advance of the actual deadline date. For instance, if a report is due on July 10, enter this date on the calendar, but make additional notes in early June and mid-June to serve as reminders.

➤ Be on the lookout for possible additional entries that may crop up. Pay attention to incoming and outgoing correspondence, and note any commitments that are made on the calendar.

➤ If dates for certain matters have not yet been established, write yourself reminders to keep checking.

➤ Transfer dates from year to year with care. For instance, remember that if staff meetings are held on the last Friday of each month, meetings in the upcoming year will be held on dates different from those of the preceding year.

Why not get a head start on that calendar update right now? Take a few minutes to think of the important dates that should always be on your calendar, and jot them down on a sheet of paper. Then be sure to enter these reminders on your desk or disk calendar.

- Untie those strings from your fingers! A tickler file can set your mind— and your memory—at ease.

- Do you have trouble choosing which tasks to tackle on a certain day? A tickler file can help you decide what to do and when.

- Here: simple steps for setting up and operating a tickler file.

TRACKING TASKS WITH A TICKLER FILE

We all have tasks that sometimes have to be put off until another time. For example, there may be a news release that must go out a month from now but that you've just received today. What do you do with it?

You could leave it on your desk with all your other work and run the risk of losing it. Or you could stash it in a desk drawer and hope that you'll remember it. But either way, you are taking a big chance—the chance that you'll forget to send it out on time.

"I forgot" are two words that your boss should never hear you say. On any given day there might be correspondence awaiting answers, memos to send out, reports or contract renewals coming up for periodic consideration, meetings to attend, or a host of other obligations. Keeping your boss alert to these commitments and helping to prepare for them are important parts of your job. With all these things to remember, you probably need something to help you—and a tickler file is just the tool you need.

What Goes in a Tickler File?

There is no limit to the kinds of things you can put in your tickler file to serve as timely memory joggers. The system should include as many items as you need help remembering. The following list should give you an idea of the kinds of things that usually go into a tickler file:

- Situations referred to your boss's colleagues or an outside source for information or comments

- Correspondence that you or your boss must answer

- Correspondence that you or your boss has sent requesting information or specific action, or promising the same

- Delivery dates on orders

- Administrative issues that periodically come up for consideration

- Reminders of recurring tasks, such as renewal of subscriptions or memberships

- Expiration dates on insurance

- Tax deadlines

- Payment due dates

Setting Up a Tickler File

1. Label 12 folders with the names of each month of the year.

2. Label another 31 folders with the numbers 1 through 31, one for each day of the longest month. If you prefer, an expanding file—one that

folds out like an accordion—can be used instead of individual folders.

3. Label one more folder "Future" for any items to be done beyond 12 months' time.

Put the daily folders in the front of a drawer in numerical order. Behind them place the monthly folders, with the next month's folder first and the current month's folder at the rear, ready to receive any material to be followed up on in the same month of the following year. At the very rear of the drawer place the folder marked "Future."

Insert any follow-up material you now have in the folders according to the date when action must be taken or begun. You may either directly insert the actual material that will require your attention into the reminder file, or insert a note reminding you of this material, while putting the material itself in your regular files. If you put the actual material in the reminder file, be sure to put a charge-out card in the regular file.

Operating Your Tickler File

Each morning remove the papers from that day's reminder file folder and transfer the empty folder to the rear for the coming month. By doing this, you will always have 31 folders for follow-ups—some of them for the remaining days of the current month and some of them for the first part of the forthcoming month.

Examine the material. You'll probably find that much of the correspondence in the file has already been answered. After doing what is called for, destroy any copies or memos and return any originals to their files. If a heavy schedule prevents you from devoting attention to all the material in the daily folder, mark the less important matters for follow-up at a future date.

Place the material that is to be followed up more than 31 days in the future in the proper monthly folder, after labeling each paper with an exact follow-up date whenever possible.

On the first day of each month, transfer the material from that month's folder into the daily folders. You can avoid filing material for follow-up on Saturdays, Sundays, and holidays if you reverse the folder for those days so that the blank side of the label faces the front of the file.

Though setting up a reminder file may seem to be a chore, you'll find that once you get started, it's really quite simple and easy to maintain. You'll also find that using a tickler file will increase your efficiency significantly. Any chance of your failing to perform some task on the right date or to ready your boss for any commitments is practically eliminated. The time you spend setting up and operating your file will more than pay for itself by allowing you to avoid the mistakes the system prevents.

- Are people always "dropping in" on your boss? Follow these tips to screen visitors effectively.

- Here's how to schedule your boss's time efficiently.

- If you have trouble keeping your appointment book straight, here are some guidelines to help you out.

ARRANGING APPOINTMENTS

An important aspect of your job is to help your boss manage his or her time by running the office efficiently. You would be able to manage your boss's schedule most effectively if you could arrange all appointments beforehand. However, in many offices it's the norm to constantly interrupt the boss to announce drop-in visitors or phone calls. If you do this, you are sabotaging your own good work.

Executives rarely have time for all the people who want to see them. They don't even have time for all the people *they* want to see. That means that a lot of people must be "screened out" of the picture—and screening is a double-edged sword for every office worker: It is important that the right people do get appointments to see your boss, but those who don't have a legitimate claim to his or her time must be weeded out.

Screening Callers

There's no way to take all the guesswork out of the screening procedure, but here are four basic rules that can make the screening process a lot easier for you:

➢ First, ask the caller for his or her full name, the name of his or her firm, and the reason for the visit or phone call.

➢ Second, try to make the caller as comfortable as possible while he or she is waiting in the office or is on hold.

➢ Third, judge which callers would be welcomed by your boss, which ones should be seen or spoken to by someone else, and which ones you can take care of yourself.

➢ Last, be tactful in your explanations to those callers to whom your boss does not have the time to speak.

Scheduling Appointments

If you're the one in the office who's in charge of scheduling appointments, you know how confusing that job can get. Because there are so many ways that requests for appointments come to you, you may end up double-booking a date or a time, and that could spell trouble for all parties.

These are some of the ways that you may receive requests for appointments:

- Your boss tells you to schedule one.

- You receive inquiries by mail.

- Someone calls you on the telephone.

- Someone requests an appointment in person.

Once you receive a request for an appointment, there are many factors to keep in mind:

✔ **Avoid overscheduling.** If your boss normally allows an hour for appointments, then stick to that time frame. But if the amount of time that is spent with each person fluctuates, spread the appointments at least a half hour apart. If you think that your boss may need more time with a particular individual, check with your boss and schedule accordingly.

✔ **Schedule according to your boss's preferences.** Some supervisors like to keep Monday mornings and Friday afternoons light, while others prefer a full schedule. Be sure that you stay attuned to what your boss prefers.

✔ **Don't schedule an appointment for first thing in the morning.** Everyone likes a few moments of quiet at the beginning of the day to get settled into the routine. Many supervisors take this time to go over the day's work and to review their schedule.

✔ **Keep late afternoons free.** You boss won't appreciate it if you schedule an appointment at this time and it runs overtime—especially if he or she has made plans for the evening. Additionally, just as your boss may want to get organized at the beginning of the day, he or she may prefer to use the last few minutes of each day for wrapping up loose ends.

✔ **Unless you're absolutely sure that there is an opening for an appointment,** pencil it in and advise the person making the appointment that you will confirm the date after checking with your boss. If you work in a busy office where your boss makes appointments too, this will help you to avoid double bookings.

✔ **Be sure to get the person's telephone number.** That way, if your boss is unable to keep the appointment, you will be able to contact the person, thereby saving a wasted trip. This is important because everyone's time is valuable in today's fast-paced society.

✔ **Use your appointment book as a trigger** to let you know what materials your boss will need for each appointment. You can do this by leaving space near the appointment entry to write down the materials needed.

Also, remember that if your boss asks you to set up an appointment, let the person you're scheduling it with know that you have to confirm it with your boss. Once the appointment is made, be sure to remind your boss to set aside time in his or her schedule in order to keep it.

By using these simple techniques, you will find it easier to keep your boss on schedule, even if he or she sees people by appointment only.

PLANNING MEETINGS EFFECTIVELY

- **Are meetings driving you mad? Here's how to keep track of the details and keep your sanity at the same time.**

- **Taking meticulous minutes the easy way.**

- **Follow this simple format to type up minutes that enhance your image as a professional.**

Being called upon to plan a meeting can give even the most professional and competent employee the jitters. What if you forget to inform a key person of the meeting's time and place? What if the room is unsuitable? What if you bring the wrong agenda? It's enough to make you lose sleep at night. Conquer the "what ifs" by planning for all the variables.

Before the Meeting

➢ **Set the time.** Don't assume that an hour will be enough for every meeting. Some topics are complex and require more time for consideration. Check with your boss to see how long this meeting is expected to last. You may want to schedule the meeting for at least 30 minutes longer than he or she thinks is necessary in order to provide a cushion between the end of the meeting and the rest of the day's appointments.

➢ **Confirm the meeting.** Inform each attendee's secretary of the date, time, and place of the meeting and the topic to be discussed. Give the names of those who will be attending, and indicate whether an agenda or other materials will be distributed before the meeting.

➢ **Distribute the agenda** a few days before the meeting. Include a list of motions, reports, and resolutions that will be presented as well as any other background material your boss decides will help the attendees prepare for the discussion.

➢ **Prepare the meeting room.** Check to see that there are enough chairs and that any audiovisual equipment is set up. If a flip chart and markers are to be used, have them delivered and set up in the right area. Also, put a name card, memo pad, and pencil or pen at each place.

Taking the Minutes

Before the meeting starts, list the names of all those attending—be sure of the accurate spelling of each name—and assign, opposite each name, a number. When you are taking the minutes, after you have used the person's name once, substitute his or her number in future references.

Remember, unless you are told differently, minutes do not need to be verbatim; just the general discussion should be recorded. However, all resolutions or special statements to be entered into the record must be accurate and exact. Sometimes you may be given a list of these ahead of time. If not, and you feel some sections need clarification, don't hesitate to interrupt the speaker to ask for an explanation. You might want to establish a prearranged signal with the chairperson so that he or she can stop the speaker for you. Make sure to sit where you can see and hear every speaker without straining.

When a motion is made, circle the word "motion" in your notes. If, after pages of discussion, the motion is passed, check the circled word. If the motion is defeated, draw a red line through the word. After the meeting, if your boss wants to know how many and what motions were accepted and how many were rejected, you can find out quickly without searching through all your notes.

Immediately after the meeting, make a separate list of actions to be taken.

Typing the Minutes

If you're responsible for typing the minutes of meetings, you have a very important job. After all, one error on your part and a vote could be changed or a decision overturned. The minutes are the official record of the meeting, so accuracy is a primary concern.

Draw up and edit a draft of the minutes before you type them to make certain that your language is precise and understandable. When you are ready to type the final draft, the format you follow depends on your company's policy. To refresh your memory of the proper format, just use the minutes taken at a previous meeting as a guide. Most minutes include the following standard items:

- ✓ Company name and address
- ✓ Type of meeting
- ✓ Date
- ✓ Time (when meeting was called to order)
- ✓ Names of those attending
- ✓ Corrections to and acceptance of minutes of previous meeting
- ✓ Old business
- ✓ New business
- ✓ Announcements

Once you're sure that all of these items are included, you're ready to type the minutes. To make them look professional, follow these guidelines:

1. Maintain a 2-inch margin at the top of the page and a 1-inch margin at the left, the right, and the bottom of the page.
2. Capitalize the title of the meeting and center it.
3. Skip two lines, then type the date and the kind of meeting in capital letters.
4. Double-space the rest of the minutes for easy reading.
5. Use subheads in the margin to indicate different sections.
6. Capitalize any words that refer to the meeting: Board of Directors, Corporation, Company, etc.
7. Sums of money should be both spelled out and typed in figure form when they are mentioned in motions or resolutions.
8. Each page of the minutes should be numbered at the bottom.
9. Include a closing such as "Respectfully submitted by," and type a line for both the signature of the person who took the minutes and the signature of the chairperson.

By following these simple guidelines, your minutes will come out looking professional every time.

- Your boss is going on a trip—but you're still at the office. Here's how to make the work flow smoothly.

- Taking notes for your boss's posttrip debriefing.

- Helping your boss get back into the swing of things as quickly as possible.

TRAVEL MADE EASY

When your boss is away on a trip—whether it's a vacation or a business trip—things tend to pile up. Letters still need to be signed, papers still need to be read, and memos still need to be sent, even when your boss is out of the office. The phones will still ring, and visitors will still arrive. Is there any way to avoid having mountains of paperwork and lines of people waiting for your boss on his or her first day back? Yes, with some astute, pretrip planning. Use the following guidelines:

While Your Boss Is Still in the Office

• A week or so before your boss's trip, notify department heads and any other associates who should know about your boss's absence. They may want to get instructions concerning ongoing projects, or they may want to discuss other important matters that might come up during the trip.

• Find out who, if anyone, is to make decisions in your boss's absence.

• Check all calendars for any appointments or meetings that are scheduled on dates during your boss's absence. Find out if they should be canceled indefinitely or if new ones should be arranged for a date after your boss's return.

• Go through your tickler file for any correspondence or reports coming due; check for instructions on how to handle them.

• Ask for definite information on just what message telephone callers or office visitors should be given. Should you tell them where your boss is and give them a phone number? Should you say that he or she is out of town? Or should you just tell them that your boss will not be available for a while?

• Will there be any important reports or correspondence that must be forwarded? If your boss will be at just one hotel, send them there. But if it is an extended trip with stops at several places, send one copy to the hotel where you expect your boss to be and a duplicate to the next hotel. Your boss's plans might change, and sending two copies will ensure that at least one is received.

• If your boss is delivering a speech during the trip, give him or her a copy to take along—and send a duplicate to the hotel. Briefcases can be lost en route.

• Make one final check to be sure that your boss has all necessary travel tickets, passports, and paperwork. Look over the final itinerary carefully to make sure that it is up-to-date and accurate.

- If you are responsible for your boss's personal financial duties, be sure your boss signs checks for insurance, mortgage, subscriptions, and loan payments that will come due during the period of his or her absence.

While Your Boss Is Away

- Keep a list of all incoming letters, with all pertinent information: Include arrival date, name of sender, brief description of contents, and the action, if any, that you have taken.

- List all telephone calls and all necessary details concerning them: Include caller's name and title, company name, the date the call was made, subject matter of the call, and a phone number where the person can be reached.

- Keep a list of office visitors: Include visitor's name and title, company name, the date of and the reason for the visit, and a phone number where the person can be reached.

These lists will bring your boss up-to-date quickly with what went on in the office during his or her absence. And the details can be handled at a later time after your boss is able to establish priorities.

When Your Boss Returns

- Be sure to review important details pertaining to the trip while they are still fresh in your boss's mind.

- Make a list of any follow-up actions concerning the trip that need to be taken.

- Transcribe all travel and meeting notes for your boss's files.

- If file folders were taken along, check them to be sure that they are complete, and return them to the files.

- Complete the expense accounts as quickly as possible. Be sure that you attach all receipts.

- If your boss was entertained or was someone's guest while on the trip, write thank-you notes as soon as possible.

- If you keep file cards of business associates met on these trips, get all new information on any promotions and changes in company affiliations to keep the file current.

- Do you have trouble keeping your filing under control? Tame the paper monster with these tips.

- If your in-box is lost in a backlog of filing, here's what you should do to sort it out.

- Special materials require special handling. Use these guidelines for proper storage.

FILING FUNDAMENTALS

You've probably seen the cartoon of the secretary madly searching for something in a shower of flying papers—while the boss stands nearby wearing a deep frown. If you're lucky, this has never happened to you. However, if you've ever had to search through an overcrowded file drawer or riffle through a stack of unfiled papers to find what you need, you know how stressful and time-consuming it can be.

If you want to avoid a repeat of this not-so-funny scene, you should sharpen your filing finesse. A good filing system is only as good as the person who keeps it; filing accuracy and efficiency depend on you. The following are a few reminders for fast filing and easy retrieval:

• **File new material regularly.** Few things make a boss more angry than being told, after asking for a particular file, "It must be in that pile on top of the cabinet," or "It's somewhere in that stack on my desk." Filing may not be your favorite task, but it isn't going to get any better if you let it build up into several hours' worth of work. This doesn't mean you have to interrupt your work every time you get one piece of paper to file, however. A better way is to set aside a few minutes each day to take care of that day's filing. A good time is at the end of the day, when you've caught up on the rest of your work and need a break from other tasks.

• **Check the contents of material before you file it.** First, make sure that no further action is required concerning the material. Then, be sure to put the material in the appropriate file, and check to see that all pieces that are clipped together belong in the same file. Also check any material that contains paper clips or staples to be sure that other pieces of filing have not accidentally become attached to the back of the piece you are filing. Because paper clips can come off or catch onto other contents of a file, it's best to use staples wherever possible.

• **Don't overcrowd or overcategorize.** A file folder that's crammed full of material is a sure sign of a file category that's in need of pruning. If you can't break the file down by subject, try breaking it down by date, by sender, or according to some other criterion. At the opposite extreme, a series of file folders each containing one or two pieces of filing is usually a sign that you have created unnecessary work and confusion by dividing your filing into too many subcategories, which makes it harder to find the material at a later date. Try to stick to fairly standard, obvious categories.

• **Keep cross-referencing to a minimum.** It's nice to be able to find every piece of information on a particular topic in one file folder, but cross-referencing can become a real time- and paper-waster if it gets out of hand. So, don't copy one article five times to put it into five different files. It's more efficient to know that a combination of files will yield the required information than to have to deal with redundancy and file cabinets that are bursting their seams due to duplication.

• **Put a throw-out date on all files.** Your boss can help you determine how long various pieces of information should be kept. As you do your daily filing, be on the lookout for expired dates. That way, your files will be cleaned out regularly and automatically, and you'll be able to find what you need when you need it.

NOTE: The first rule of filing is not to fall behind. Suppose, however, that a sizable backlog of unfiled material has accumulated on your desk. How can you avert catastrophe? March to the file cabinets or shelves with the material in disarray? You'd be there for hours agonizing over such a hit-or-miss operation. Instead, organize the materials to be filed before you leave your desk. It will save you a great deal of aggravation in the long run.

Filing Technology

Has there been a change in the type of material you've been filing lately? With the conversion to the automated office, you may be filing computer printouts, audiocassettes and videotapes, and diskettes, in addition to the everyday documents.

Here are some tips to keep in mind:

• **Make files accessible.** When deciding where to put file holders, remember to keep them accessible without placing them in the line of traffic. Material should be easily retrievable, drawers should open and close without banging into anything, and more than one person should be able to use any of the files at the same time.

• **Match the material to the housing.** Word processing and computer materials require special handling. You shouldn't stick computer printouts in a file cabinet drawer. Instead, use holders that are specially made for storing printouts. The same is true for filing diskettes. Diskettes should be stored in a covered file in order to protect them from dust, smoke, or other pollution. There are holders for each type of material you must file. If you use the correct holder, you'll have a better chance of storing your material neatly and keeping it that way.

• **Keep classified material secure.** If some of the work you file has a security rating, then your boss may have a special place for you to store this material. Just be sure that this area stays as organized as the other file areas. When filing security-rated material, remember to lock the holder after removing or returning the material. It only takes a minute of carelessness for an otherwise secure file to be violated.

FILING SYSTEMS

An efficient filing system is essential to any well-run office because, regardless of what type of business your company is in, there is always information that needs to be stored—somewhere, somehow. Stacking everything on a shelf, no matter how tempting that might be, just won't be effective in the long haul. Not only will sheets of paper rain down on your head whenever someone bumps the shelf, but the one piece of paper that you *do* want to find will continue to elude you until it's no longer needed.

Types of Filing Systems

Each of these types of filing systems has its advantages and its draw-backs and is used for a specific purpose. Which do you use?

Decimal. The decimal system, also known as the Dewey Decimal System, is used extensively by large corporations and libraries. Under this system, all records are classified under 10 or fewer principal headings, numbered from 000 to 900. Each heading is divided into subheadings, numbered from 10 to 90, preceded by the applicable hundreds digit. Each subheading can be further subdivided, numbered 1 to 9, preceded by the appropriate hundreds and tens digits. An extensive alphabetical/subject cross-index is usually necessary if you use this system. For large filing systems, however, it is highly effective.

Numerical. This filing system also utilizes numerically arranged filing folders, cross-indexed with alphabetically arranged index cards. One index card is made up for each file folder and filed separately in alphabet-ical order. Numerical filing works best when each job, client, or subject has an identifying number; when confidential records must be filed; or when extensive, permanent cross-referencing is necessary.

The one drawback of both of these sytems is that two searches must be made every time papers are withdrawn or filed: one of the card index and one of the files to locate the material.

Chronological. This type of filing is used in addition to, not in place of, other systems. Copies of all outgoing correspondence, memos, bulletins, and reports are filed by date. This is especially useful when you have a request from your boss for a certain communication and he or she can remember only that it was handled in November and involved a com-plaint about an order. This type of file can also bring your boss quickly up-to-date after an absence. By glancing through the dates covered, he or she can see just what you have taken care of.

Geographical. Companies that have large sales organizations often arrange their files by geographical location because they are more inter-ested in a review of a certain territory than in a particular company or individual.

Docket. The docket file is a method of subject filing that is used mainly in law offices and large construction companies where all papers concern-ing a particular case or job must remain together. Each letter or instrument is placed in chronological order and bound. Thus, papers arranged in pad form don't become separated and can be examined without fear of one being lost. When all material has been collected, the docket is closed and an inscription is placed on its side.

    Alphabetical. By far the most common type of filing system, alphabetical filing is also the easiest—if you follow the rules consistently. Quick filing and retrieval depend on how well you know the rules for indexing files in alphabetical sequence. Otherwise, files may end up in the wrong drawer, lost forever—or until you make the same filing mistake again.

▼ ▼ TAKE A TEST ▼ ▼

Number the entries from 1 to 4 in each group below so that they will be in correct alphabetical order. Answers and explanations follow.

1. David C. Martinson ____
   D. Thomas Martinson ____
   Wilma Martin-Bennett ____
   Claude Martin ____

2. Byron D'Ascenzo ____
   Carol Van Ness ____
   Leroy Vann ____
   Fred Atkins ____

3. Billings' Hardware Store ____
   George Billings ____
   Boyer's Agency ____
   Charles Boyer ____

4. Eveready Co. ____
   Ever-All Co. ____
   Evereasy Inc. ____
   Everett-Irving Inc. ____

5. 60 Second Photo ____
   Westport Eatery ____
   West Port Marina ____
   70 West St. Clothiers ____

ANSWERS:

1.   4, 3, 2, 1. The order for filing the names of individuals is surname; first initial if that's all that's given, first name if spelled out; middle initial if that's all that's given, middle name if spelled out. Hyphenated surnames are treated as a single word.

2.   4, 1, 3, 2. When an individual's name has an attached prefix, treat it as one word when alphabetizing. Also disregard any apostrophes, spacing, or capitalization.

3.   2, 1, 4, 3. When a word ends in "s," treat it as spelled, regardless of whether the "s" denotes a plural or a possessive ending.

4.   2, 1, 3, 4. Separate most firms' names into indexing units as written. Treat words joined by hyphens as one word.

5.   4, 1, 2, 3. Treat numbers as if they were spelled out. Compound geographical names should be treated as separate words.

- You have to do more than just file it: Here's what to do with all the paper that comes across your desk.

- Add a little color to your life with these tips on color coding your filing system.

- Are you overwhelmed by the mere thought of reorganizing the office files? Use this Records Inventory Chart to pin down what files are where.

RECORDS MANAGEMENT

Office automation can present as many pitfalls as promises for companies that rush into the "paperless" office of the future without first developing a formal records management program. Adding word processors and electronic mail systems to departments that have not yet established effective programs for organizing, managing, and disposing of records doesn't bring a long-neglected records system under control. All it can do is add to the paper flow, thus actually *decreasing* office productivity and *increasing* office costs.

What can you do to stem the rising tide of paperwork and control the paper flow? Probably the most effective action you can take is to establish an integrated records management program. Records management involves more than just filing: The systematic controls of such a program automatically resolve the problems of file storage and handling.

How do you set one up? To set up an effective system, you must use a method that follows the life of company information from beginning to end. And that usually involves four steps: record identification, standardization, indexing, and establishing a records retention schedule.

Record Identification

Record identification is essential to your success in setting up a records management program. It familiarizes you with the subject, format, and location of each existing document so that appropriate filing decisions can be made.

When making a records inventory, be sure to identify each file by its subject (what the file contains), format (how the information is stored), location (where the file is stored), and volume (how much space this file takes). Use the sample Records Inventory Chart on page 96 for this task.

Since the purpose of a records management program is not only to simplify filing and retrieval operations but also to restructure and establish a streamlined file system, be sure that you note retention suggestions next to each item you list on your inventory chart. This will save you time later on.

Once you've completed your inventory of records, evaluate your findings by answering these questions:

> Do other departments use your filing system? If so, speak to your boss about the possibility of having it moved to a central location to allow easy access for all who use the system, and to cut down on congestion in your area.

> Does your filing equipment meet file needs? Equipment should be evaluated in terms of cost, use, space requirements, filing ease, and maintenance. For example, an open-shelf arrangement might be better for your office than the file cabinets that are now in use.

➢ Could some of your files be disposed of or placed in inactive storage? Is microfilming an option?

➢ Are documents that must be kept for a specified time destroyed as soon as that time elapses? This is an important part of records management. Court cases have been lost because companies did not have records that should have been available.

Records Standardization

Standardizing file names, listings, and procedures is vital for three reasons: It makes filing and retrieval of information fast and easy; it streamlines paperwork and record storage; and it helps to establish and maintain a records retention schedule.

To standardize your file system, first simplify file names and procedures. Use labels and/or color coding to enable file system users to quickly identify document and folder headings and ensure that information is correctly filed.

Color Coding

In addition to your basic filing system, you might also want to use color coding to maintain your files more accurately. Color coding virtually eliminates misfiling because it makes mistakes obvious. A green dot will stick out like a sore thumb among all the orange dots.

So how can you get started on your own file system? Your reorganization should begin with a visit to your local office supply dealer to become familiar with all of the filing aids on the market. You may be surprised to find that supply manufacturers have complete systems already designed, and your local dealer may have free sales literature you can take back to the office and study.

Your next step should be to evaluate your existing files to determine what kinds of changes you want to make and where to begin. Consider the following suggestions:

• To reorganize existing files, you can apply press-on dots in different sizes and colors without having to remove the folders from drawers or storage units.

• Color-code files by categories. For example: customers, suppliers, branch offices, and so on.

• Use a different color for each current project to prevent notes, sketches, and drawings from going astray.

• Use colored dots for cross-referencing. In equipment files, for instance, a green dot could mean "See manufacturer file for additional information."

If you do decide to use color in your records management strategy, there are two important points to keep in mind. First, you must design a color key to identify the various classifications. Keep one copy of the color key handy at your desk, and another at the front of the filing cabinet for general use.

The second point to remember? Color must *mean* something—a date, a subject, a division of the alphabet, a temporary or permanent file. Attaching different colored labels just because they're available is misleading and inefficient.

Second, standardize placement of documents in folders. For example, file the most recent papers in the front of each folder. This makes sense because most requests are for the most current materials available on a particular topic.

Third, group similar files into units—for example, general correspondence, and statements and bills. When filing these folders, be sure that you allow 3 to 4 inches of workspace in each drawer. This will make the files more easily accessible.

Record Indexing

To be truly effective and efficient, a records management program should include indexing of all records. Indexing is an invaluable tool for file system users and records management personnel. It enables the user to search for information by title, subject, or author, and can be used to maintain close control of record operations.

Records Retention Scheduling

To keep your records system in good working order, you must periodically purge your files of old or outdated material and retain only those records that are necessary. And that's what a records retention schedule is intended to do.

A records retention schedule is a list of the different kinds of records you keep. It notes how long each type of record should be kept. Typically, records retention is divided into two categories: active and inactive. Records that are in current use are classified as "active," and records that are no longer referred to are classified as "inactive." Inactive records can be stored separately, either in an inactive records center or on microfilm.

How long should records be saved before they are destroyed? In order to meet applicable state, federal, and industry regulations, certain records must, by law, be retained permanently—such as tax returns and all supporting papers—while others need only be retained for a specified length of time. Company policy dictates how long other records should be kept.

Therefore, before you put a new records retention schedule into effect, it's essential that you check with your company's legal department to verify all state and federal retention requirements. Rules can change and your company may have particular needs. Certain documents may be relevant to an issue or project of which you are not aware.

Records Inventory Chart				
File Subject	Format	Location	Volume	Retention Period

- **Are you doing all that you can to improve your organizational skills? Find out in this chapter.**

- **Evaluate your efficiency by taking this time management test.**

- **More organizational and time management tips.**

TEST YOUR TIME MANAGEMENT SKILLS

We all start off the year with 365 days ahead of us. We each have exactly 24 hours in a day. How we choose to spend that time is what counts. And the only time to spend it is now.

The following quiz reviews several basic organizational and time management skills discussed in previous chapters of this section. Answer Yes or No to each question and then read the suggestions that follow to learn how to manage your time better. For more comprehensive instructions, you might want to review any chapters related to a particular topic.

▼ ▼ TAKE A TEST ▼ ▼

1. Do you take time on a regular basis to plan your work?
   YES   NO

2. Do you tackle the easy tasks before the important ones?
   YES   NO

3. Do you frequently find yourself without enough time to complete long-range projects?
   YES   NO

4. Do you often leave tasks partially completed?
   YES   NO

5. Do you maintain a good tickler file and follow-up procedure?
   YES   NO

6. Do you think before you act?
   YES   NO

7. Are you interrupted frequently?
   YES   NO

8. Do you look for ways to make your and your boss's job procedures more efficient?
   YES   NO

9. Do you often find yourself overloaded with work?
   YES   NO

ANSWERS: Give yourself two points for each No answer to questions 2, 3, and 4. Eliminate numbers 7 and 9 since those answers can vary from day to day. Give yourself two points for each Yes answer to the rest of the questions. If your score was not between 10 and 14, your time management skills could be improved.

1. Begin planning by doing a personal time study. One of the simplest methods is to write down on your daily calendar, every 30 minutes, exactly how you spent the last half hour. After a week or so, summarize your log. Add up the amount of time you spent on each task—typing, filing,

answering the phone, making calls, consulting with your boss, getting supplies, compiling statistics, etc. Don't forget the interruptions. Not only will you be able to see your work patterns, but you will gain a lot of insight into personal time-wasters.

2.   If you're having trouble getting the important tasks done, you may have a habit of tackling easier jobs first. This is a subtle form of procrastination—and a sure way to fall behind. If you wait until Thursday to type the schedule due on Friday, you may find yourself spending time on unexpected dictation—while the schedule remains unfinished. Don't procrastinate on unpleasant tasks—they won't disappear.

3.   If you frequently find yourself scrambling to meet a deadline for a long-range project, you may be having trouble accurately determining how long a particular task will take. Keep a log of the steps involved in completing a task and the times (both estimated and actual) you assigned to each step. Eventually, your estimated times will become closer to the actual times—and you will be completing your projects on time.

4.   One of the biggest time-wasters is jumping from one task to another. You might be tempted to skim a number of tasks, none of which have pressing deadlines. The result could conceivably be many starts—and no finishes. Switching from a project that is beginning to bore you to a new one is fine—sometimes. In general, though, it is wise to make it a rule to *complete* what you start, unless a higher priority task comes up.

5.   Maintaining a tickler file and follow-up procedure is a good method of keeping track of deadlines and items delegated to other offices. One way to set up a tickler file is to have a card file with 31 dividers, one for each day of the month, and another section of 12 dividers for future months. If your boss sends out a letter requesting information by a certain date, jot this down on a card (with a reference to where the copy is filed) and file it under the due date. Review the tickler file at the beginning of each day to see what is due that day.

6.   Being busy and active doesn't necessarily mean that you are achieving results. Let's say you plunge into typing that speech your boss just finished writing, only to find later that you had misplaced the note telling you to double-space it for easier reading. If you had considered the purpose of the draft before acting, you might have remembered the note. Time spent thinking, whether planning your to-do list or looking for a shortcut in a routine task, is not time wasted.

7.   Some secretaries have found that three to four hours of paperwork can be accomplished in one hour when there are no interruptions. Telephone interruptions are the top time-waster—and they're impossible to avoid. If you are under pressure because of a rush job—and if it's okay with your boss—ask a co-worker to cover the phones for you while you finish the task.

8.   Looking for ways to make your own and your boss's job procedures more efficient will help you make the most of *your* time. There are many shortcuts you and your boss might use. For example: Try to handle each piece of paper only once. Learn speed-reading. Telephone rather than write whenever possible. Work on difficult projects when you are most alert.

9.   By implementing the time management ideas given here and in previous chapters, you can become more productive. Ask your boss to sit down with you periodically to discuss how well time is being used in the office. Explain how you spend your time and bring up any efficiency problems. You may find your boss beginning to appreciate your time as much as you do.

mu·ni·ca·tor *n.* —com·mu·ni·ca·to·ry (kə·myoo'·
nə·kə·tôr'ē, -tō'rē) *adj.*
com·mu·ni·ca·tion
The act of
chang   conveyance o
         pondence. 2 That
       ated; a letter or messag
of communicating, as a highw
also, a telephone, telegraph, or
etc. 4 Eucharistic communion.

interests, etc. 2 A body politic. 3
society at large. 4 A group of p

COMMUNICATING CLEARLY:
Making Words Work

INTRODUCTION

Words are the raw material with which you work, and it's only natural to want the best. A large vocabulary—properly used—is a valuable asset to any professional; in the office, it's almost vital. Your language skills are on display daily. What kind of image do they project of you and your company?

This section is devoted both to increasing the number of words at your disposal and to helping you use them accurately. After you've gone through this section and seen the results, you'll agree that brushing up on your grammatical skills was well worth the effort.

Are you interested in tips that will help you improve your spelling? Or perhaps you'd like some advice on how to keep your participles from dangling? If you're interested in researching a particular area of vocabulary or finding the answer to a single grammatical question, you can find the subject you want by glancing at the index below.

- Are you a superior speller? Test yourself with our spelling skills quizzes, and remember the following hints.

- Rules help, but exceptions are many—and must be memorized.

- An office professional's best friend is still a good dictionary.

SPELLING

The English language is full of pitfalls for those who would perfect their spelling skills. There are almost as many exceptions as there are spelling rules; it is perhaps wiser to treat these rules as general guidelines rather than as laws engraved in stone.

Fortunately, frequent use of tricky words helps us to commit their correct spelling to memory. But sometimes we start to write a perfectly simple word and draw a blank; other times, a word we have written "looks funny." On these occasions, the only recourse is to look it up.

The Perils of Improper Pronunciation

Most of us are guilty of occasionally dropping or adding consonants or vowels to certain words. Casual or lazy pronunciation of some words is so common that their proper pronunciation may sound strange to the ear. But if you make the effort to pronounce difficult words properly and enunciate them clearly, you may find that spelling them correctly becomes simple.

Following is a series of quizzes on some typical problem areas. Write the correct spelling next to the word, then check your answers at the end of the quizzes.

QUIZ 1 Dropped Vowels

1. auxilary _____
2. minature _____
3. temperment _____
4. mathmatics _____
5. labortory _____
6. comprable _____
7. privlege _____
8. incidently _____
9. Niagra _____
10. boundry _____
11. temperture _____
12. sophmore _____
13. maintnance _____
14. treachrous _____

QUIZ 2 Added Vowels

1. disasterous _____
2. mischievious _____
3. rememberance _____
4. umberella _____
5. athaletics _____
6. publically _____
7. burgular _____
8. enterance _____
9. monsterous _____
10. grievious _____
11. hinderance _____
12. laundery _____
13. aluminium _____
14. mayorality _____

Dropped Consonants

1. Artic _____
2. consumtion _____
3. drunkeness _____
4. represenative_____
5. reconize _____
6. canidate _____
7. tenative _____

8. authenic_____
9. kinergarten _____
10. rythm_____
11. lanlord_____
12. quanity _____
13. enviroment _____
14. reumatism_____

Silent Letters

Proper pronunciation won't help you a bit with this group of puzzlers:

1. indeted _____
2. condem_____
3. rasberry _____
4. gastly _____
5. morgage_____
6. rhumatism _____
7. connosseur_____

8. colume_____
9. blite _____
10. forein _____
11. colone_____
12. arial _____
13. maline _____
14. receit_____

ANSWERS

QUIZ 1: **Dropped Vowels**—**1.** auxiliary; **2.** miniature; **3.** temperament; **4.** mathematics; **5.** laboratory; **6.** comparable; **7.** privilege; **8.** incidentally; **9.** Niagara; **10.** boundary; **11.** temperature; **12.** sophomore; **13.** maintenance; **14.** treacherous

QUIZ 2: **Added Vowels**—**1.** disastrous; **2.** mischievous; **3.** remembrance; **4.** umbrella; **5.** athletics; **6.** publicly; **7.** burglar; **8.** entrance; **9.** monstrous; **10.** grievous; **11.** hindrance; **12.** laundry; **13.** aluminum; **14.** mayoralty

QUIZ 3: **Dropped Consonants**—**1.** Arctic; **2.** consumption; **3.** drunkenness; **4.** representative; **5.** recognize; **6.** candidate; **7.** tentative; **8.** authentic; **9.** kindergarten; **10.** rhythm; **11.** landlord; **12.** quantity; **13.** environment; **14.** rheumatism

QUIZ 4: **Silent Letters**—**1.** indebted; **2.** condemn; **3.** raspberry; **4.** ghastly; **5.** mortgage; **6.** rheumatism; **7.** connoisseur; **8.** column; **9.** blight; **10.** foreign; **11.** cologne; **12.** aerial; **13.** malign; **14.** receipt

Are You Sure of That Suffix?

Three groups of suffixes are responsible for more than a fair share of spelling errors. Here are some hints to help you out:

-sede, -ceed, -cede

To keep these sound-alike suffixes straight, remember the following:
• There is only one word in the English language that ends in -sede: *supersede.*
• There are only three words that end in -ceed: *succeed, proceed,* and *exceed.* (Try this tip to remember them by: The first letters of these three words, arranged as shown, are the beginning of the word *spell.)*
• All other words that end in this suffix sound end in -cede.

-able, -ible

Choosing between -able and -ible is not so easy; there are far more exceptions to the rule. However, here's a guideline to go by:
• If the noun from which the adjective is derived has an -ation ending, the adjective takes the suffix -able.

application, applicable　　　　*negotiation, negotiable*　　　　*reputation, reputable*

It's important to note, however, that the rule does not always work in reverse. There are many nouns that do not end in *-ation* whose adjective forms also take the suffix form *-able:*

comfort, comfortable　　　　*love, lovable*　　　　*work, workable*

The hard-and-fast rule applies only to *-ation* words; if you are unsure of others, you will have to look them up in the dictionary.

-ance, -ence

Pronunciation is the clue to choosing an *-ance* or an *-ence* suffix. Here are the rules:

• When the suffix is preceded by a hard *c* or *g*, use *-ance, -ancy,* or *-ant.*

significance　　　　*extravagant*

• When the suffix is preceded by a soft *c* or *g* (that is, a *c* with the sound of an *s*, or a *g* with the sound of a *j)*, use *-ence, -ency,* or *-ent.*

negligence　　　　*convalescent*

Take this quick quiz to test your understanding of the rules for the spelling of suffixes:

QUIZ In each of the following word groups, one word is misspelled. Underline that word, and check your answers below.

1. mendicent, secede, permissible 　　3. proceed, communicible, elegance
2. separable, accede, convergance 　　4. reminiscent, indispensable, receed
5. supersede, collectible, emergance

ANSWERS **1.** mendicant; **2.** convergence; **3.** communicable; **4.** recede; **5.** emergence

I Before E, Except...

There are a great many exceptions to this old schoolroom classic, but it's a rule worth remembering nonetheless. This is the way it goes:

I before *E*, except after *C*,
Or when sounded like *A*
As in *neighbor* or *weigh.*

Examples:

i before e	e before i	a sound
thief	receive	weigh
wield	ceiling	vein
believe	deceive	freight

Some common exceptions: *ancient, caffeine, conscience, efficient, either, financier, height, leisure, neither, proficient, seize, sovereign, surfeit, their, weird.*

QUIZ Is it *ie* or *ei*? In the following quiz, all the words but one in each group are spelled correctly. Underline the misspelled words, then check your answers below.

1.	niece	4.	science	7.	mischeivous	10.	deign
	greivous		reciept		piece		forfiet
	leisure		weird		achieve		eight
2.	friend	5.	seige	8.	counterfeit	11.	neighbor
	recieve		neither		weigh		feirce
	financier		relieve		percieve		conceit
3.	hygeine	6.	lieutenant	9.	believe	12.	frontier
	feint		concieve		freight		sliegh
	ancient		deceit		proficeint		sufficient

ANSWERS **1.** grievous; **2.** receive; **3.** hygiene; **4.** receipt; **5.** siege; **6.** conceive; **7.** mischievous; **8.** perceive; **9.** proficient; **10.** forfeit; **11.** fierce; **12.** sleigh

The Final Exam

Experts tell us that 90 percent of all spelling errors are caused by a relatively small group of words. The following test includes a number of them. Ready? Choose the correct spelling of each word, and check your answers below.

	A	B
1.	absence	absense
2.	accomodate	accommodate
3.	acheive	achieve
4.	arguement	argument
5.	bookkeeping	bookeeping
6.	bulletin	bulettin
7.	category	catagory
8.	changeable	changable
9.	comittee	committee
10.	coolly	cooly
11.	corroborate	coroborate
12.	definitely	definitly
13.	developement	development
14.	dilemma	dilema
15.	dissapoint	disappoint
16.	disatisfaction	dissatisfaction
17.	eligable	eligible
18.	embarass	embarrass
19.	exceed	excede
20.	extrordinary	extraordinary
21.	harassment	harrassment
22.	indispensable	indispensible
23.	irrelevent	irrelevant
24.	irresistible	irresistable
25.	liaison	liason
26.	license	lisence
27.	maintainance	maintenance
28.	misellaneous	miscellaneous
29.	necessary	neccessary
30.	occurrence	occurence
31.	parallel	parallell
32.	perseverance	perserverance
33.	possesses	posseses
34.	preceed	precede
35.	privelege	privilege
36.	proceed	procede
37.	recede	receed
38.	receive	recieve
39.	recommend	reccomend
40.	sieze	seize
41.	seperate	separate
42.	transferred	transfered
43.	vacuum	vaccuum
44.	viscious	vicious
45.	weird	wierd

ANSWERS 1. a; 2. b; 3. b; 4. b; 5. a; 6. a; 7. a; 8. a; 9. b; 10. a; 11. a; 12. a; 13. b; 14. a; 15. b; 16. b; 17. b; 18. b; 19. a; 20. b; 21. a; 22. a; 23. b; 24. a; 25. a; 26. a; 27. b; 28. b; 29. a; 30. a; 31. a; 32. a; 33. a; 34. b; 35. b; 36. a; 37. a; 38. a; 39. a; 40. b; 41. b; 42. a; 43. a; 44. b; 45. a

- **Does word division come easily to you? If not, read on!**

- **Clear-cut rules exist for syllabication, the division of words according to syllable.**

- **Study our examples and learn to save wear and tear on your dictionary.**

WORD DIVISION

Life would be easier if all lines of copy were created equal. Undesirable though the division of a word is, sometimes it's unavoidable. When you must divide a word in order to justify a margin, it's important to divide it correctly according to syllable. (A syllable is a word or a part of a word that is pronounced with one vocal effort. The word *child* has one syllable; *childish* has two syllables, and *childishness* has three.) You can't be expected to know the correct syllabication of every word that you're likely to use, but you can save yourself a lot of time and effort with the dictionary by learning the rules for word division.

Take the following quiz to see how proficient you are at syllabication. Divide each word correctly in the space provided on the right. Answers and the rules that govern them follow.

1. accommodate _____

2. verify _____

3. readable _____

4. about _____

5. weight _____

6. financier _____

7. filing _____

8. running _____

9. handling _____

10. proofread _____

11. bosses _____

12. 35,000 _____

13. conversion _____

14. project _____

ANSWERS

1.   ac-com-mo-date   **RULE:** Divide a word according to pronunciation.

     RULE: Divide a word that has double consonants between the consonants. (*re-*

com-mend, mar-ry)

2. veri-fy   **RULE:** When a vowel alone forms a syllable in the middle of a word, divide the word after it rather than before. *(sepa-rate, ana-lyst)* For the exception to this rule, see number 3.

3. read-able   **RULE:** In words ending in *-able* or *-ible,* the vowel should be carried over to the next line. *(man-age-able, con-vert-ible)* A word that contains a prefix or suffix is normally divided between the root word and the prefix or suffix. *(pre-historic, mis-guided)*

4. about   **RULE:** When a single letter forms the first or last syllable of a word, do not divide it from the word. (Not *e-vict* but *evict;* not *blear-y* but *bleary.*)

5. weight   **RULE:** Never divide words of one syllable.

6. fin-an-cier   **RULE:** There is usually a point of division between two consonants that separate vowels. *(aus-pi-cious, con-cern)*

7. fil-ing   **RULE:** When a present participle must be divided, carry over the *-ing. (typ-ing, dic-tat-ing)*

8. run-ning   **RULE:** When the last consonant of a verb is doubled before adding the *-ing* to form the present participle, the second consonant should be carried over to the next line along with the *-ing* ending. *(bat-ting, swim-ming)* This is an exception to the rule immediately above.

9. han-dling   **RULE:** When three consonants follow one another consecutively in a present participle, the first consonant stays with the root word and the second two are carried over. *(dan-gling, fon-dling)*

10. proof-read   **RULE:** Divide compound words according to their derivation and meaning. *(run-way, heir-loom)*

11. bosses   **RULE:** When a word that ends in an *s* sound adds a syllable to form the plural, avoid dividing on the plural. *(course, courses, base, bases)*

12. 35,-000   **RULE:** A number of five numerals or more may be divided at a comma, and the comma should be retained before the hyphen. *(625,-000; 1,225,-680)*

13. con-ver-sion   **RULE:** Word endings that contain elided vowels and are pronounced as one syllable (such as *-cion, -gion, -sion, -tion, -ceous, -cious, -geous, -cial, -sial,* and *-tial*) should not be divided. *(gor-geous, sub-stan-tial)*

14. pro-ject *or* proj-ect   **RULE:** Words whose pronunciation changes according to their use as different parts of speech should be divided according to correct pronunciation. *(pro-gress, prog-ress, pro-duce, prod-uce)*

A final note: Too many word divisions can spoil the appearance of a letter or other document. If your typewriter or word processor automatically justifies margins, then this consideration is out of your hands. But if the decision to divide a word is yours, be judicious in your use of the hyphen.

- If certain pronouns are not among your favorite relatives, have we got some help for you-know-who(m)!

- Is it *she* or *her*, *he* or *him*? We have some objective advice to offer about these persons.

- Follow these hints and you'll find that pronouns don't have to cause you problems.

POINTERS ON PRONOUNS

A pronoun is a word that can substitute for a noun, either common or proper. It is used, not surprisingly, in the same ways that a noun is used: as the subject of a sentence or as the object of a verb or a preposition.

Personal pronouns come in three cases: the nominative, possessive, and objective. The first two cases seldom cause problems, but the objective can be tricky. Many people choose the wrong pronoun form in this case in a misguided effort to sound educated or erudite. Fortunately, knowledge of a few basic rules can help to prevent this kind of embarrassing error.

Relative pronouns are also notorious troublemakers, but careful consideration of a sentence's structure should help anyone make the correct choice between *who* and *whom*. Before we get to the rules for proper use of pronouns, here is a handy outline of all three cases:

SINGULAR

	Nominative	Possessive	Objective
First Person	I	my, mine	me
Second Person	you	your, yours	you
Third Person	he, she, it	his, her, hers, its	him, her, it

PLURAL

	Nominative	Possessive	Objective
First Person	we	our, ours	us
Second Person	you	your, yours	you
Third Person	they	their, theirs	them

RELATIVE OR INTERROGATIVE PRONOUNS

	Nominative	Possessive	Objective
Singular	who	whose	whom
Plural	who	whose	whom

Knowledge of the following rules will help you to select the correct pronoun form with confidence. Study the examples of each rule to prepare for the short quiz that follows.

➤ Use the nominative case when the pronoun is the subject of a verb in a sentence or a clause.
- *She* typed the letter.
- *He* and *they* met in the conference room.
- *Who* prepared this report?

➤ Use the nominative case whenever a pronoun follows any form of the verb *to be* (am, was, were, is, are, etc.).
- This is *she*.
- Did you think it was *he?*
- John wasn't prepared, and neither were *we.*

➤ Use the possessive case in general when the pronoun immediately precedes a gerund (a verb form used as a noun).
- I appreciate *your* arriving early for the appointment.

- The supervisor approved of *his* going on the trip.
- *Her* moving to Europe made her co-workers jealous.

➤ Use the objective case when a pronoun is the direct object of a verb. (A direct object is the person or thing to which an agent does something.)
- She hired *me.*
- We offended *him.*
- The boss asked *them* to do it.

➤ Use the objective case when a pronoun is the object of a preposition.
- He got the data from *us.*
- Between *you* and *me,* this must remain confidential.
- To *whom* did you send the report?

➤ Identify the position of a relative pronoun in the sentence structure in order to choose the correct form. Let's take, for example, the sentence *I don't know who is coming.* Although the clause *who is coming* is the object of the verb *know, who* is the subject of the verb within the clause and must therefore be in the nominative case. Be especially careful with relative clauses used as objects of prepositions. Although prepositions take the objective case, if the relative pronoun *who* serves as the subject of the verb within the clause, it must be in the nominative.
- Send a copy of this memo to *whomever* it concerns.
                          but
- The honor should go to *whoever* deserves it.

▼ ▼ TAKE A TEST ▼ ▼

In the following quiz, underline the correct pronoun:
1. Between you and (I, me), I don't think either (he, him) or (she, her) knows how to do the job.
2. People like (they, them) get what they deserve.
3. She had dinner with (he, him) and (I, me).
4. Jim is a man (who, whom) hates to be pitied.
5. I was told by the girl (who, whom) knew the woman to (who, whom) the accident occurred.
6. She is the person (who, whom) we should send.
7. I shall welcome (whoever, whomever) wants to attend the meeting.
8. They are no busier than (we, us).
9. Did you give it to (she, her) or (he, him)?
10. Everyone but (I, me) left early.

ANSWERS

1. *Me* is the object of the preposition *between; he* and *she* are both subjects of the verb *knows.*
2. *Them* is the object of the preposition *like.*
3. *Him* and *me* are objects of the preposition *with.*
4. *Who* is the subject of the verb *hates.*
5. *Who* is the subject of *knew; whom* is the object of the preposition *to.*
6. *Whom* is the object of the verb *send.*
7. *Whoever* is the subject of the verb *wants.*
8. *We* is the subject of the verb *are,* which is understood.
9. *Her* and *him* are the objects of the preposition *to.*
10. *Me* is the object of the preposition *but.*

- If you think that Latin is a dead language, this chapter may surprise you.

- Would you believe that you almost certainly use Latin root words daily in the course of your correspondence?

- Read on, and learn how a little knowledge of an ancient tongue can greatly increase your current vocabulary.

OUR LATIN ROOTS

Ours is a living language, growing and changing at an incredible rate in this era of high-tech communication. Latin, on the other hand, ceased to be spoken even before modern English began to evolve, many centuries ago. But Latin proved to be so useful—and English so enterprising—a language that many Latin words found new life in another tongue, which they continue to enrich today. We all use daily words derived from Latin, often without being aware of it. Consider these Latin roots for the numbers one to ten, and then take the quiz that follows to test your familiarity with the many English words derived from them:

1. uni-
2. duo-, bi-, bin-
3. tri-, ter-, tert-, trini-
4. quadr-
5. quin-

6. sex-
7. septem-
8. octo-
9. novem-
10. decem-

QUIZ   Fill in the blanks with the appropriate English word.

1. a person 80 years of age _____

2. a child's three-wheeled vehicular toy _____

3. one of a kind_____

4. one who remarries without first obtaining a divorce _____

5. a formal fight to the death between two antagonists_____

6. the eight keys of a musical scale _____

7. a three-part story _____

8. to multiply by four _____

9. the seventh month of the Julian calendar _____

10. of or based on the number 10 _____

11. five children born at the same time to the same mother _____

12. an eight-tentacled mollusk_____

13. to make one (out of two or more) _____

14. a six-sided navigational instrument _____

15. having the ability to speak two languages _____

ANSWERS   **1.** octogenarian; **2.** tricycle; **3.** unique; **4.** bigamist; **5.** duel; **6.** octave; **7.** trilogy; **8.** quadruple; **9.** September; **10.** decimal; **11.** quintuplets; **12.** octopus; **13.** unite (or unify); **14.** sextant; **15.** bilingual

Abbreviations

Latin abbreviations are commonly used in the footnotes of research papers, but many are also found in the text of formal documents. Even if you seldom have occasion to use them yourself, it's useful to know what they mean when you run across them. The following are some commonly used Latin abbreviations with which you should be familiar:

c.—*circa*—around, about, approximately (used with dates)
e.g.—*exempli gratia*—for example
et al.—*et alii*—and others
etc.—*et cetera*—and so forth, and the rest
ibid.—*ibidem*—in the same place
i.e.—*id est*—that is
loc. cit.—*loco citato*—in the place cited
N.B.—*nota bene*—note or mark well
op. cit.—*opere citato*—in the work cited
Q.E.D.—*quod erat demonstrandum*—which was to be demonstrated or proved
v. or vs.—*versus*—against
viz.—*videlicet*—namely

Common Latin Words and Phrases

Those who work in legal offices are not unaccustomed to dealing with Latin words and phrases that have survived intact and are used routinely in legal documents. But the rest of us are also exposed to a great many of these words and phrases. They appear from time to time in business correspondence, contracts, research articles, and even in general reading. Here are a few such terms that you may find it useful to know:

ad hoc—for a particular or specific purpose
ad infinitum—without end
ad nauseam—to a sickening degree
bona fide—made in good faith or with sincere intent
caveat emptor—let the buyer beware
de facto—actually so; in reality
de jure—legally so; by a lawful title
ergo—therefore
ex post facto—after the fact; retroactive
facsimile—an exact copy
in absentia—in absence
in loco parentis—in the place of a parent
in media res—into the midst of things
ipso facto—by the fact itself; by the very nature of the case
modus operandi—method of operation
ne plus ultra—the highest point capable of being attained
non sequitur—a statement that does not follow logically from what came before it
per annum—in or for each year; by the year
per capita—per unit of population; for each individual
pro bono publico—for the public good
quid pro quo—an even exchange; something for something
sic—intentionally so written; indicates a word or phrase reproduced exactly, complete with errors
sine qua non—an essential characteristic or trait
status quo—the existing state of affairs

Latin as a Rich Relation

We've already established that a great many English words are direct descendants of the Latin language. The ability to recognize just one such word often helps us to decipher the meanings of many related words. Consider the following Latin words and stems and you'll see what a wealth of words we owe to our Latin roots:

Aequus—equal. From *aequus* and its related root words we get *equality, equity, equitable, equable, equation, equilibrium, equivalent.*

Animus—life, breath, soul, spirit, mind. This family of words gives us *animal, animate, inanimate, animadvert, animosity, animism, pusillanimous.*

Bene—well. *Bene* offers us *benefit, beneficent, beneficial, beneficiary, benevolence, benison.*

Credere—to trust, believe, have confidence in. This verb provides us with *credence, credential, credible, credit, creditable, creed, incredible, credulity, credulous, incredulous.*

Confirmare—to establish, to strengthen, to render certain, to ratify. This is another useful verb from which we get *confirm, confirmation, confirmatory.*

Dicere—to say or tell; to call, name, or pronounce. *Dicere* gives us *dictate, dictation, dictator, dictaphone, dictatorial, diction, malediction, predict, edict, indict.*

Ego—I. We are all well acquainted with this one; from it we get *egocentric, egoist, egotistic, egotism, egomaniac.*

Excellere—outstanding. From *excellere* come *excel, excellence, excellency, excellent.*

Facere—to make, create, compose, cause, do. *Facere* provides us with *fact, factual, factor, factory, factotum, faction, satisfaction.*

Illustrare—to explain, make clear; to make famous. To *illustrate* the scope of this word, we have *luster, lustrous, illustrious, illustration.*

Lumen—light, lamp. From *lumen* we get *luminous, luminary, illuminate, illumine.*

Magnus—great, large, big. *Magnus* gives us the stem of *magnanimity, magnate, magnify, magnification, magnificence, magniloquence, magnitude, magnum.*

Male, malus—badly, wrongly; bad, evil, harmful. *Male* and *malus* provide us with the extremely useful prefix found in such words as *maladjusted, malcontent, malediction, maleficent, malfeasance, malformed, malfunction, malign, malnutrition, malodorous, malpractice.*

Manus—hand. From *manus* come *manacle, manage, mandate, maneuver, manicure, manifest, manner, manual, manumit, manuscript.*

Portare—to carry. This family of words includes *import, export, report, reporter, deport, deportment, comport, comportment, port, porter, portable, portfolio, portmanteau.*

Potens—able, capable; strong, powerful. From *potens* we get *potent, potential, impotent, potentate, potency.*

Reflectere—to bend or turn back. This verb gives us *reflect, reflection, reflex, reflective.*

Signum—sign. From *signum* come *sign, signal, insignia, design, signature, signet, significant, insignificant, assign, assignment, assignation.*

Valere—to be strong, able. This useful verb's many descendants include *valid, validity, validate, validation, invalidate, valor, value, valuable, evaluate, devalue, evaluation, devaluation.*

Volens—willing, wishing. This Latin participle comes from the verb *velle*, and gives us *volunteer, voluntary, volition.*

Review

Take the following quizzes to see if your brief course in Latin basics has helped to expand your vocabulary. In the first quiz, the word or phrase on the left describes an English word that is derived from the combination of two Latin root words or stems. Feel free to refer to the previous sections of this chapter if you get stuck. The second quiz is simple matching. Write the appropriate letter in the space provided after each word. Answers follow.

QUIZ 1

1. blessing _____
2. a felon _____
3. an even temper _____
4. one who produces something by hand _____
5. of a single mind _____
6. kindliness _____
7. of equal value _____
8. big hearted; of generous nature _____
9. one who does good _____
10. bearing ill will _____

QUIZ 2

1. credulous
2. magnate
3. equilibrium
4. factotum
5. pusillanimous
6. manacle
7. illustrious
8. comportment
9. benefactor
10. malediction

a. one who does good
b. eminent, famous
c. curse
d. easily deceived
e. a person of power or influence
f. handcuff
g. balance
h. cowardly
i. bearing, demeanor
j. a general servant

ANSWERS

Quiz 1—1. benediction, from *bene*, well, and *dicere*, to speak; **2.** malefactor, literally "evil doer," from *malus* and *facere*; **3.** equanimity, from *aequus*, equal or even, and *animus*, mind; **4.** manufacturer, from *manus*, hand, and *facere*, to make; **5.** unanimous—from *uni-*, one, and *animus*, mind; **6.** benevolence, from *bene*, well, and *volens*, wishing; **7.** equivalent, from *aequus*, equal, and *valere*, to be strong or able; **8.** magnanimous, from *magnus*, large or great, and *animus*, spirit or mind; **9.** benefactor, from *bene*, well, and *facere*, to do or make; **10.** malevolent, from *malus*, evil, and *volens*, wishing.

Quiz 2—1. d; **2.** e; **3.** g; **4.** j; **5.** h; **6.** f; **7.** b; **8.** i; **9.** a; **10.** c

- Introducing the verb, the single part of speech without which no sentence is complete: Ready? Action!

- Are your verbs pallid and passive? You can tone them up and make them active in no time.

- If the very thought of the past perfect makes you tense, this chapter is for you. Here's how to perfect your knowledge of verb tenses.

ALL ABOUT VERBS

The verb is the part of speech that gives your sentence life and makes it move. It's also the only part of speech that can stand alone as a complete sentence. (*Go. Study!*) Your choice of verb can be vital to clear communication, but that choice is not always an easy one. Verbs can be active or passive, indicative, imperative, or subjunctive; they also come in a wide—and sometimes confusing—variety of tenses. In this chapter we'll explore the ways in which verbs can enhance expression—and explain the rules that govern their use.

Voice

Verbs are either active or passive in voice. The active voice indicates action on the part of the subject; the passive voice indicates that the subject of the sentence is acted *upon:*

Active: *Ms. Morris arranged the meeting.*
Passive: *The meeting was arranged by Ms. Morris.*

The passive voice is formed by adding the past participle of a verb to a form of the verb *to be:* She *is instructed, was instructed, has been instructed, will be instructed,* and so forth. Although the passive voice has many legitimate uses, it is not a forceful means of expression. In most business writing, strength of purpose is called for—and the active voice best expresses it:

Passive (weak): *It is intended that we sign the contract this week.*
Active (strong): *We intend to sign the contract this week.*

When you need results fast, or simply want to convey an impression of decisiveness or energy, be sure to use the active voice. Use the passive voice when the subject is either unknown or unimportant. For example:

Vague: *The order was cancelled.*
Forceful: *John cancelled the order.*

QUIZ 1 Rewrite any sentence below that can be improved by a change in voice. Mark sentences that are correct with a C.
1. The interview was conducted by the personnel director.
2. Many people meet their deadlines.
3. The boss has been delayed.
4. The meeting was adjourned.
5. The report was collated by Ben.

ANSWERS **1.** The personnel director conducted the interview; **2.** C; **3.** Something has delayed the boss; **4.** C; **5.** Ben collated the report.

Mood

The mood of a verb indicates the attitude of the writer or speaker on the subject at hand. Is a fact being stated? a request being made? an order given? a supposition being made? The choice of mood answers these questions. The English language has three verb moods: the indicative, the imperative, and the subjunctive. The first two moods seldom cause problems, but the third—the subjunctive—can be tricky.

• The indicative mood is the one we most commonly use; it is a question or a statement of fact:

Is she coming in today?

He is very conscientious.

• The imperative mood makes a request or issues a command:

Take a 10-minute break.

Go to your room!

• The subjunctive mood is not so simple. (Would that it were!) The subjunctive is used to express the following—

✓ **Wishes or desires** (in clauses beginning with *that*):

I wish that I were young again.

Mr. Mitchell strongly desires that you be present.

✓ **Requests, commands, or recommendations** (also in *that* clauses):

She requested that her mother's will be executed promptly.

I recommend that the motion be tabled.

✓**Conditions contrary to fact:**

If he were here, he could give us the answer. (He is not here.)

If I were sure of the facts, I could act on them. (I am not sure.)

It's important to note that not all *if* clauses indicate conditions contrary to fact. Consider these sentences, in which the subjunctive is not required:

If she was there, she didn't speak up. (She may have been there.)

I looked to see if the road was clear. (It may have been.)

Many people are unsure of the subjunctive forms of verbs. The following conjugations of the verb *to be* in the present and past tenses may help:

Present Subjunctive

Singular	*Plural*
(if) I be	(if) we be
(if) you be	(if) you be
(if) he, she, it be	(if) they be

Past Subjunctive

Singular	*Plural*
(if) I were	(if) we were
(if) you were	(if) you were
(if) he, she, it were	(if) they were

As you can see, the subjunctive forms of a verb are a great deal easier to remember than the rules for their usage. A final hint: If a sentence sounds stilted (or incorrect), simply rewrite it in such a way that you can correctly use the indicative.

QUIZ 2   In the following sentences, choose the correct verb form. Answers follow.
1. Sue wishes that she (was, were) at the beach right now.
2. If he (was, were) here, he'd know what is going on.
3. Alex checked to see if the report (was, were) complete.
4. He requested that we all (are, be) prompt in responding.
5. Do you know if she (was, were) going straight home?

ANSWERS   **1.** were; **2.** were; **3.** was; **4.** be; **5.** was

Tense

The tense of a verb indicates the time at which an action takes place. There are six tenses in English:

Present: *I walk*   Present Perfect: *I have walked*
Past: *I walked*   Past Perfect: *I had walked*
Future: *I shall (will) walk*   Future Perfect: *I shall (will) have walked*

➤ The present tense is used for an action that takes place in the present, or one that is ongoing:

This memo *makes* our instructions clear.
He *takes* a walk before dinner.

The present tense is also used colloquially to indicate future action:

He *leaves* for New York next week.

➤ The past tense expresses an action that took place and was completed in the past:

He *moved* to Chicago five years ago.
She *spoke* to the boss yesterday.

➤ The future tense describes an action to come:

We *will start* work on the project next week.
They *will make* a decision by the first of the month.

➤ The present perfect tense expresses action that began in the past but either is completed or continues in the present:

He *has made* his position clear.
I *have* always *given* generously to the charity drive.

➤ The past perfect indicates an action completed before some other action:

He *had* already *graduated* from college when he joined the firm.
We *had agreed* on an apartment before we married.

➤ The future perfect tense describes an action that will be completed before some specific time in the future:

I *will have been* in this job for five years on the first of June.
By the time the guest of honor arrives, we *will have eaten* all the cake.

Tense Sequence

➡ In order for a sentence to make sense, it's important to give careful consideration to exactly *what* happens *when*. Writers most often have difficulty choosing the correct tense in complex sentences that call for the use of a perfect tense:

Incorrect: The company *cancelled* the order after I *paid* for it.
Correct: The company *cancelled* the order after I *had paid* for it.

In the sentence above, one action—paying—definitely took place before the other action—cancelling. Therefore, the verb *pay* must be in the past perfect tense.

➡ Many people mistakenly use *would have* in a conditional situation that actually calls for the past perfect:

Incorrect: If you *would have called* earlier, we *could have fixed* it by now.
Correct: If you *had called* earlier, we *could have fixed* it by now.

To be safe, always avoid the use of *would have* in *if* clauses and use the past perfect instead.

➡ Problems frequently arise when a choice must be made between a present and a past infinitive, and when the word *like* is involved:

Incorrect: We would have liked *to have had* everything in order before the meeting began.
Correct: We would have liked *to have* everything in order before the meeting began.

Because the wish to have everything in order was still intact and true when the meeting began, the present infinitive—to have—is called for.

➡ Problems are also frequently caused by the participle (-ing) form of the verb, which also has both a present and a past tense:

Incorrect: *Finishing* his dinner, he *got up* from the table.
Correct: *Having finished* his dinner, he *got up* from the table.

Since you don't get up from the table while you're still in the act of finishing your meal, the past participle is called for.

QUIZ Choose the correct verb tense in the following sentences. Answers follow.

1. Will she (leave, have left) for the day by the time I return?
2. They realized later that they (made, had made) a mistake.
3. Do you know if they (reached, have reached) a decision yet?
4. I notice that my elbow (hurt, hurts) after playing tennis.
5. He shouldn't have attempted (to complete, to have completed) the project by himself.
6. If I (had known, would have known) about the luncheon, I would have attended.
7. (Rising, Having risen) to the occasion gracefully, he deserved his boss's thanks.
8. She would have liked (to be, to have been) invited.
9. When he went for a haircut, he found that his favorite barber (promised, had promised) to cut three other customers' hair.
10. We (will be, will have been) married 10 years next June.

ANSWERS **1.** have left; **2.** had made; **3.** have reached; **4.** hurts; **5.** to complete; **6.** had known; **7.** Having risen; **8.** to be; **9.** had promised; **10.** will have been

Verb-Subject Agreement

A verb must agree with its subject in person and in number. That's easy enough to remember, but what may not be easy is figuring out exactly what the subject *is*—or whether it's singular or plural. The following guidelines will help solve some common mysteries—

• When two subjects are joined by *and*, they form a compound subject and usually take a plural verb:

The *desk* and the *typewriter are* to be replaced.

• When two parts of a compound subject form a single thought, the verb remains in the singular:

The *wear and tear* on my typewriter *is* considerable.

• Don't be confused by intervening phrases that are not part of the subject:

The *annual report*, as well as a stock prospectus, *is* being mailed today.

• Don't be misled by the subject's position in the sentence:

In this report *are* listed *office expenses*.

• When two subjects of differing number are connected by *either/or* or *neither/nor*, the verb should agree with the subject nearer to it:

Neither the *boss* nor the *typists are* happy with the new office.

• Collective nouns—words such as *committee, jury, audience, majority*—may be singular or plural, depending on whether they refer to individual members of the group or to the group as a unit:

The *committee is* scheduled to meet on Monday.
but
The *committee are arguing* over the wording of the resolution.

THOSE PROBLEM PRONOUNS

■ How intensive are your
pronouns? Only you
yourself can answer that
question!

■ Is it *which* or *that*? The
rule is *relatively* easy to
remember.

■ Are indefinite pronouns
always singular? Read
on for the definitive
answer.

In a previous chapter we examined the purpose and form of the pronoun, a useful little part of speech that can cause problems of major proportions in the hands of a careless writer. In this chapter we'll consider a few of the ways in which misuse of specific pronouns can wreak havoc with the clarity of your copy.

Incomplete Constructions

Choosing the proper pronoun can be especially confusing when the pronoun follows the word *than* or *as* in an incomplete construction. Consider the following sentences:

> Mike admires Laurie more than she.
> Mike admires Laurie more than her.

As you can see, the choice of pronoun in this sentence changes the meaning completely. In the first example, Mike admires Laurie more than someone else admires her; in the second, Mike admires Laurie more than he admires someone else. How can you be sure which pronoun you want? Just complete the sentence mentally:

> Mike admires Laurie more than she (admires Laurie).
> Mike admires Laurie more than (he admires) her.

This is a very simple trick that takes only a second and is foolproof. Try this one:

> They try harder than (we, us).

When you complete the sentence, the correct pronoun becomes obvious:

> They try harder than we (try).

Reflexives and Intensives

Pronouns that end in *-self* or *-selves* are either reflexive or intensive—but whichever they are, they're frequently misused:

> My wife and *myself* prefer our steak rare.
> Could she do it better than *yourself?*

Never use a reflexive pronoun when the simple nominative case is called for. The sentences above should read:

> My wife and *I* prefer our steak rare.
> Could she do it better than *you?*

The reflexive pronoun is properly used to refer to the subject of the sentence:

> *I'd* rather do it *myself.*
> *He* needs to discipline *himself.*

The intensive pronoun is used strictly for emphasis:

> *I myself* don't have an opinion.
> The *committee itself* will tabulate the results.

Relative Confusion

When is it *which,* and when *that?* These relative pronouns are used constantly—and often incorrectly—in business documents. The choice between the two is governed by their use: *Which* is used to introduce a nonrestrictive clause, and *that* introduces a restrictive clause.

A nonrestrictive clause is one that can be eliminated from the sentence without altering its meaning; a restrictive clause, on the other hand, is necessary to complete the thought of the sentence:

> The group's momentum, *which* was never great, began to falter.
> The sense of purpose *that* had sparked them was gone.

A nonrestrictive clause should always be set off by commas, and this provides a good clue to the correct choice of pronoun. If a comma is obviously called for at the beginning of the clause, use *which*.

Indefinites

Because an indefinite pronoun does not refer to a specific person or thing, it's sometimes difficult to decide whether a singular or a plural verb is called for. Some indefinites are obviously singular in nature—*each, one, either, neither,* and usually any indefinite ending in *-one, -body,* or *-thing (someone, anybody, everything)*. Others—*both, few, many, several*—are just as obviously plural. Problems arise when the indefinite pronoun in question can be either singular or plural, depending upon its use. These problem pronouns include *all, most, some, none,* and *any.* Consider these examples:

> All is ready. (All *the food* is ready.)
> All have brown eyes. (All *the puppies* have brown eyes.)
> Some is better than none. (Some *money* is better than none.)
> Some are arriving early. (Some *people* are arriving early.)

The best advice for dealing with these very indefinite pronouns is to think the sentence through and consider exactly what the pronoun refers to. Once you've identified the subject of the sentence, it's easy to make the verb agree.

The following quiz will test your mastery of problem pronouns. Underline the correct pronoun or verb in each sentence. Answers follow.

▼ ▼ TAKE A TEST ▼ ▼

1. She's a better friend than *(he, him)*.
2. Jack and *(I, myself)* were assigned to the project.
3. Neither Ann nor she *(is, are)* going to the party.
4. The file *(that, which)* you mislaid turned up today.
5. I baked brownies for the sale; if any *(is, are)* left, you may have them.
6. We work longer hours than *(they, them)*.
7. Our latest deadline, *(that, which)* we hope to meet, is tomorrow.
8. No one understands that better than *(I, me, myself)*.
9. How many *(is, are)* there?
10. Either Jim or Charlie *(is, are)* going to take care of it.
11. Can anyone in the office type faster than *(you, yourself)*?
12. The ring *(that, which)* he bought her was too small.
13. Each of us *(is, are)* planning to take a class this semester.
14. The Talman project, (that, which) was put on hold last week, is now back on schedule.
15. Preparations are completed; all *(is, are)* ready for the conference.

ANSWERS **1.** he; **2.** I; **3.** is; **4.** that; **5.** are; **6.** they; **7.** which; **8.** I; **9.** are; **10.** is; **11.** you; **12.** that; **13.** is; **14.** which; **15.** is

VERBALS

- When is a verb not a
  verb? When it functions
  as another part of
  speech. Introducing verbals, which may act as
  nouns, adjectives, or
  adverbs.

- Is it wrong to casually
  split an infinitive? The
  answer may surprise
  you.

- Dangling participles can
  be good for a laugh—but
  you want to be sure it's
  not at *your* expense.

Verbals are words that take the form of verbs but that serve the function of other parts of speech. This extremely useful group of words includes infinitives, participles, and gerunds. Although they all look like verbs, none of them, in fact, can stand alone as a predicate. Instead, you will find them modifying the predicate—or its subject or object—or even serving *as* the subject or object.

Confusing? No, not really. You use verbals many times daily, and you probably use them correctly without even thinking about it. Just in case, here is a brief review.

Infinitives

The infinitive is one of the most easily identified verb forms, preceded as it usually is by the word *to*. It's also the most versatile of verbals, able to serve as a noun, an adjective, or an adverb:

- To call *your boss this morning is your top priority.* In this sentence, the infinitive *to call* serves as a noun—in fact, it is the subject of the sentence.

- *If you'll hold one moment, I'll give you the number* to call. The infinitive *to call* is an adjective in this sentence, modifying the noun *number.*

- *This phone is used* to call *our branch offices.* The predicate of this sentence, *is used*, is modified by the infinitive *to call*. In this case, the infinitive is an adverb.

During our school days, most of us had one cardinal rule about infinitives drummed into our heads: *Don't split them.* In other words, never put another word or phrase between *to* and the verb. Most grammarians today feel that it's perfectly acceptable to split an infinitive if the alternative is a construction that is awkward and strange-sounding. For example:

- They attempted *to establish firmly* outposts on the river.

The adverb *firmly* sounds out of place after the infinitive; it breaks the flow of the sentence. In this case, the infinitive should be split:

- They attempted *to firmly establish* outposts on the river.

If, however, the infinitive can be kept intact without awkwardness, it's preferable to do so. *She asked me to read the passage slowly* sounds better than *She asked me to slowly read the passage.* When in doubt, trust your ear.

Participles

Participles have both present and past tense forms. The present participle always ends in *-ing: typing, filing, instructing.* The past participle usually ends in *-ed (typed, filed, instructed),* but in irregular verbs it may end in *-en (given, written, chosen)* or make some other change *(gone, laid, lain).*

One standard feature of all forms of participle is their use—they always function as adjectives. Participles may modify any noun in a sentence, and therein lies the only real difficulty they pose: They are extremely easy modifiers to misplace. Consider the following example:

- *Running* to catch the bus, the books slipped out of her arms and fell to the ground.

Obviously, the books weren't running to catch the bus, but that's what the sentence says. A construction such as this is known as a *dangling participle*. It's a common error, and one to watch for closely. Why? Although it's an easy mistake for a writer to make, it's also an easy one for a reader to spot—and that makes the writer look careless, if not foolish. Unintended humor can easily result from a dangling participle:

- *Sweating* and *whinnying* with fright, she caught the runaway horse.

If you don't want to give readers a good laugh at your expense, always check your participles carefully to be sure they modify the correct noun.

Gerunds

The gerund has the same form as the present participle—it ends in *-ing*. Although the form is identical, the function is entirely different: The gerund acts as a noun.

- *Typing* and *filing* take up most of her time.
- I prefer *swimming* and *running* to most team sports.

In the first example, the gerunds *typing* and *filing* serve as the compound subject of the sentence; in the second, *swimming* and *running* are direct objects of the verb *prefer*.

There is only one small trick to remember about using the gerund properly: It takes the possessive case of personal noun and pronoun.

- She doesn't approve of *his clowning* around.

There are two exceptions to this rule. If the subject of the gerund is a plural noun, it takes the accusative case:

- I don't approve of *people* (not *people's*) swearing.

And if words appear between the noun or pronoun and the gerund, the objective case is used:

- She started to speak without *anyone* (not *anyone's*) in the room acknowledging her.

In order to observe these rules, care must be taken not to confuse a gerund with a participle. Consider this sentence:

- I can't imagine (him, his) *doing* such a thing.

Which is correct, *him* or *his*? They both are, depending upon what you mean. If it's this particular person—*him*—that you can't see undertaking this thing, then *doing* is a participle that modifies *him*. But if it's the act itself that's unimaginable to you, then *doing* is a gerund and requires the possessive, *his*.

WHICH WORD DO YOU WANT?

■ What are homonyms?
They're words that can
wreak havoc with your
correspondence if you're
not careful.

■ Is it *insight* or *incite*,
compliment or *comple-
ment*? It's seldom safe
to trust your ear with
tricksters like these.

■ Herein, a simple guide
to some of those confus-
ing soundalikes.

Homonyms are words that sound alike but have different meanings. Sometimes their spelling is identical, which actually simplifies matters— but more often it's just close enough to add an element of confusion to the correct choice. The English language suffers no shortage of these brain- teasers, and they can make life especially difficult for an office worker who takes or transcribes lots of dictation.

Of the following pairs and groups of words, only some are true homonyms; others are simply close enough in spelling or pronunciation to offer ample opportunity for error. When in doubt, you can use these pages for a handy reference; better yet, commit the spellings and mean- ings of these soundalikes to memory. It will save you untold time and trouble in the future.

● abjure and adjure—*Abjure* means to give up or to renounce: A true vegetarian *abjures* eating any animal product. *Adjure* means to command, charge, or entreat solemnly: The lecturer *adjured* his audience to heed well the lessons of the past.

● accede and exceed—*Accede* means to agree to: The union hoped that management would *accede* to its demands. *Exceed* means to go beyond: If you *exceed* the speed limit, you may be fined.

● acclamation and acclimation—*Acclamation* means loud and enthusias- tic approval: The candidate gratefully acknowledged the crowd's *acclama- tion*. *Acclimation* means to accustom or to become accustomed to a differ- ent climate, environment, or circumstance: Her *acclimation* to Denver's higher altitude took months.

● adapt, adept, and adopt—*Adapt* means to adjust: He *adapted* the pro- gram to suit his department's needs. *Adept* means highly skilled: She's an *adept* typist. And *adopt* means to choose or take up as one's own: We *adopted* a puppy from the pound.

● adverse and averse—*Adverse* means opposed, unfavorable, or harmful: The child suffered an *adverse* reaction to the medication. *Averse* means reluctant or unwilling: Although it made her uncomfortable, she was not *averse* to reporting her co-worker to their supervisor.

● affect and effect—*Affect* means to change or influence: This new dead- line may *affect* our plans to go out tomorrow night. *Effect* means result or outcome: We're waiting to see what *effect* the change in scheduling will have on production.

● allusion, delusion, illusion—*Allusion* means an indirect reference or casual mention: I choose to ignore his *allusion* to my tardiness. *Delusion* means a false belief or opinion: He's suffering from the *delusion* that everyone thinks he's wonderful. And *illusion* means a false perception or interpretation of what one sees: I thought that woman in the restaurant was my sister, but it was just an *illusion*.

- **altar and alter**—*Altar* means a structure used in worship: The couple knelt at the *altar*. *Alter* means to change: I don't want to *alter* my plans at the last minute.

- **appraise and apprise**—*Appraise* means to estimate or to assess the value of something: The boss said she'll *appraise* my proposal this morning. *Apprise* means to inform or to tell: I've been *apprised* that my proposal has merit.

- **ascent and assent**—*Ascent* means the act of climbing, or an upward slope: The *ascent* of the plane was steady, graceful, and incredibly swift. *Assent* means consent or agreement, or to agree: He finally *assented* to his daughter's marriage, even though he loathed his prospective son-in-law.

- **biannual and biennial**—*Biannual* means twice a year: Our *biannual* blood drives are held in January and July. *Biennial* means every two years: The family didn't get together this year—our reunions are *biennial*.

- **capital and capitol**—*Capital* means money invested, or the governing city of a state or country: He invested most of his *capital* in a construction company that's renovating the downtown area of the state *capital*. *Capitol* refers to the building in which a legislature meets: There is some talk of renovating the *capitol* itself.

- **censor and censure**—To *censor* is to delete offensive or sensitive parts of a film, book, article, or other document; also, the person who performs this activity is a *censor*: Many films must be *censored* before they can be shown on television. *Censure* means to condemn, to strongly disapprove of, or to reprimand: The senators *censured* their colleague for unethical conduct.

- **cite and site**—*Cite* means to refer to or to quote, or to summon before a court: He was able to *cite* a precedent for his unusual defense. *Site* means a place or location: There is little doubt that the garage was the *site* of the murder.

- **complement and compliment**—A *complement* is something that completes or brings to perfection: A good white wine would be the perfect *complement* to this meal. A *compliment* is something said in admiration or praise: Our boss is great about giving us *compliments* on a job well done.

- **council and counsel**—A *council* is a group of people that confers, advises, or administers: The city *council* met to discuss the fourth district's sewage problem. *Counsel* means advice, or one who gives advice—especially a lawyer: I thanked her for her wise *counsel*.

- **credible and creditable**—*Credible* means believable: I find her account of the accident to be *credible*. *Creditable* means worthy of praise: She did a *creditable* job of reconstructing the facts.

- **device and devise**—A *device* is a mechanical appliance or invention that fills a specific purpose: He invented a nifty little *device* for wiping rain from eyeglasses. *Devise* is to contrive or plan: Because the gadget was not a success, he was forced to *devise* another use for it.

- **disassemble and dissemble**—To *disassemble* is to take apart: We have to *disassemble* the swing set every time we mow the grass. To *dissemble* is to conceal or disguise facts, feelings, or intentions: When she asked if I liked her new hairdo, I thought it best to *dissemble*.

- **eligible and illegible**—*Eligible* means fit or suitable to be chosen: He's a very *eligible* bachelor—you should accept his invitation. *Illegible* means difficult or impossible to read: His handwriting is totally *illegible*—I'd rather try to decipher hieroglyphics.

• **eminent and imminent**—*Eminent* means distinguished: We are honored to have so *eminent* a scholar address us. *Imminent* means likely to happen without delay: We rushed to the hospital, fearing that the baby's arrival was *imminent*.

• **equable and equitable**—*Equable* means steady, even, tranquil: Jane is easy to work with; she has such an *equable* temperament. *Equitable* means fair and just: The attorney proposed an *equitable* settlement that was acceptable to both parties.

• **formally and formerly**—*Formally* means in a formal manner, or with regard for form: Pierre charms women by bowing *formally* over their hands when introduced. *Formerly* means in the past: He comes from Paris, and was *formerly* an officer in the French army.

• **hypercritical and hypocritical**—*Hypercritical* means overly critical: Mr. Alway is so *hypercritical* that it seems there's no pleasing him. *Hypocritical* means dissembling, insincere, or false: Sometimes Emma is so *hypocritical*—today she lectured me for being five minutes late, but she took an hour and a half for lunch.

• **incite and insight**—*Incite* means to stir up or to arouse: The speaker hoped to *incite* the crowd to action. *Insight* means a clear understanding of the inner nature of things: She had been studying the problem for weeks when a sudden flash of *insight* made the solution clear.

• **ingenious and ingenuous**—*Ingenious* means clever: She came up with an *ingenious* idea for marketing the product. *Ingenuous* means naive, without guile: Unfortunately, she's so *ingenuous* that she'll let someone else present the proposal, and she'll never get credit for it.

• **negligent and negligible**—*Negligent* means careless or remiss: She is too *negligent* to be assigned to important projects. *Negligible* means small, unimportant, or trifling: We took the larger of the two apartments since the difference in rent was *negligible*.

• **official and officious**—*Official* means formally set or prescribed: The *official* opening date is June 25. *Officious* means meddlesome, especially in an overbearing way: I'm fed up with her *officious* advice—she treats me like a child.

• **ordinance and ordnance**—An *ordinance* is a law: The city council passed a new zoning *ordinance*. *Ordnance* is military weapons and supplies: He is officer in charge of *ordnance* at Fort Meade.

• **perquisite and prerequisite**—A *perquisite* (or *perk*) is a privilege or benefit in addition to regular pay, resulting from one's position or job: A private parking space was one of the *perquisites* that came with the job. A *prerequisite* is something required beforehand: Good word processing skills are a *prerequisite* for this position.

• **plaintiff and plaintive**—A *plaintiff* is someone who brings suit in a court of law: The *plaintiff* charges that the defendant assaulted him. *Plaintive* means mournful or sad: Camping on the prairie, we listened nightly for the *plaintive* howl of the coyote.

• **precede and proceed**—*Precede* means to be, come, or go before: I started working here last August, so she *preceded* me by several months. *Proceed* means to advance or go on: *Proceed*, please, or let me pass.

• **prescribe and proscribe**—To *prescribe* is to order or advise: The doctor *prescribed* bed rest and a liquid diet to combat the flu. To *proscribe* is to outlaw or forbid: Our boss has *proscribed* wearing jeans to work.

- **stationary and stationery**—*Stationary* means fixed in one place: I'd like to rearrange my office, but my desk is *stationary*. *Stationery* means letter paper, or materials for writing or typing: We need to reorder letterhead *stationery*.

- **tortuous and torturous**—*Tortuous* means winding or twisted: The road to the summit is narrow and *tortuous*. *Torturous* means cruelly painful: I find waiting in the dentist's office to be almost more *torturous* than the treatment itself.

- **urban and urbane**—*Urban* means of, relating to, or constituting a city: The newspaper ran an award-winning series on *urban* decay. *Urbane* means polished or suave: She was charmed by his *urbane* maturity.

- **venal and venial**—*Venal* means open to corrupt influence or bribery: His escape from prison hinged on finding a *venal* guard to assist him. *Venial* means forgivable or excusable: She's a bit abrupt, but that's a *venial* fault under the circumstances.

- **waiver and waver**—A *waiver* is the intentional relinquishing of a right or privilege: This adoption hearing cannot proceed without a *waiver* from the child's natural mother. To *waver* is to hesitate: It was a big commitment, but he never *wavered*.

▼ ▼ TAKE A TEST ▼ ▼

Underline the proper word in each of the following sentences.

1. The company (prescribes, proscribes) the use of alcohol during work hours.
2. Stop shouting—do you want to (incite, insight) a riot?
3. He was (formally, formerly) inducted into office this morning.
4. Our distinguished guest's arrival is (eminent, imminent).
5. It's better to be the (plaintiff, plaintive) than the defendant.
6. We hope to (precede, proceed) with the hearings as soon as possible.
7. The manuscript got soaked and became totally (eligible, illegible).
8. Management experience is a (perquisite, prerequisite) for the position.
9. Do we have to (disassemble, dissemble) the bookcase to move it?
10. What is the purpose of this silly little (device, devise)?
11. A realtor is coming to (appraise, apprise) the house.
12. I've received lots of (complements, compliments) on this dress.
13. What (affect, effect) will the budget cuts have on our department?
14. Albany is the (capital, capitol) of New York.
15. I hope that just this once you'll (accede, exceed) to my wishes.

ANSWERS

1. proscribes; **2.** incite; **3.** formally; **4.** imminent; **5.** plaintiff; **6.** proceed; **7.** illegible; **8.** prerequisite; **9.** disassemble; **10.** device; **11.** appraise; **12.** compliments; **13.** effect; **14.** capital; **15.** accede

- How well do you understand the building blocks you use to construct a sentence?

- Do you know the difference between a phrase and a clause?

- In this chapter, we'll examine the raw materials needed to produce a polished complex sentence.

BUILDING BLOCKS: PHRASES AND CLAUSES

A sentence, at its most basic level, must contain a subject and a predicate. *(He left. Jane jogs. It figures.)* Few sentences, however, are so uncomplicated in construction. Most must be carefully crafted with phrases and clauses thoughtfully placed for proper fit. It's up to you, the wordsmith, to build your sentence in such a way that the thought you want to convey is expressed explicitly.

Phrases

A phrase is a group of words that does not express a complete thought—that is, it does not contain both a subject and a predicate. Phrases may serve as nouns, verbs, adjectives, or adverbs; they may be classified as prepositional, participial, infinitive, gerund, or verb, depending on the part of speech of the introductory word:

Prepositional: They followed us *into the library*. (The phrase *into the library* modifies the verb *followed*.)

Participial: That woman *leaving the office* was looking for you. (The phrase *leaving the office* modifies the noun *woman*.)

Infinitive: *To own a home* is the goal of many young couples. (The phrase *to own a home* serves as the subject of the sentence.)

Gerund: *Swimming laps* is a good way to stay in shape. (The phrase *swimming laps* is the subject of the sentence.)

Verb: He *can be reached* at home until five. (The phrase *can be reached* is the predicate; verb phrases contain auxiliary or helping verbs.)

Clauses

What's in a clause? A clause is simply a group of words that, unlike a phrase, does contain a subject and a predicate. Clauses fall into either of two major classifications: main (or independent) and subordinate (or dependent).

➤ **A main clause** can stand on its own as a complete sentence:
We worked quickly.

➤ **A subordinate clause**, although it contains both subject and predicate, cannot stand alone as a sentence. It is dependent upon some part of the main clause, which it modifies.
Since time was running out, we worked quickly.

Subordinate clauses, like phrases, can function as various parts of speech:

Noun: *That she is qualified* is not in question.
Adjective: The clerk *who pulled these papers* has an innovative system.
Adverb: *When you come in*, please bring the contract with you.

➤ **Coordinate clauses** are those that carry equal weight within a sentence; they are either both main clauses or both subordinate. They are connected by coordinating conjunctions such as *and*, *but*, and *or*:

  ★ *John walked the dog* and *I fed the cat.*
  ★ I attended the party, *fearing that it would be a disaster* and *praying that it wouldn't.*

Sentences

Phrases and clauses are the building blocks with which we construct a sentence. There are four types of sentence structure: simple, compound, complex, and compound-complex.

➤ **A simple sentence** consists of one main (independent) clause:

  I typed.

➤ **A compound sentence** contains two (or more) main clauses:

  I typed and Jane filed.

➤ **A complex sentence** contains a main (independent) clause and one or more subordinate (dependent) clauses:

  I typed while Jane filed.

➤ **A compound-complex sentence** consists of two (or more) main clauses, at least one of which contains a subordinate clause:

  I typed while Jane filed, and we managed to finish by five.

▼ ▼ TAKE A TEST ▼ ▼

Describe the phrases in italics on the left by matching them to the correct letters on the right. Answers follow both quizzes.

1. *Typing letters* takes up most of my time.	**a.** prepositional
2. That file is *in the desk drawer.*	**b.** participial
3. *To visit Paris* was her dream.	**c.** infinitive
4. She *had been hired* before I came.	**d.** gerund
5. The child *walking the dog* is my niece.	**e.** verb

Identify the clauses in italics as main or subordinate clauses:

1. Although she was late to work, *Marie managed to catch up.* _____
2. She was furious *because her alarm didn't go off.* _____
3. She had to eat breakfast *while she was dressing.* _____
4. *Harried as she was*, she forgot her watch. _____
5. *It's a miracle* that the rest of her day went smoothly.

ANSWERS

Quiz 1: 1. d; **2.** a; **3.** c; **4.** e; **5.** b
Quiz 2: 1. main; **2.** subordinate; **3.** subordinate; **4.** subordinate; **5.** main

■ What single punctuation mark can create more confusion in a sentence than any other? The common comma can!

■ For want of a comma, many a sentence has been misread.

■ Help is at hand, though—this chapter will show you how to put the comma in its place.

PUNCTUATION, PART ONE: THE COMMA

As punctuation marks go, the comma seems fairly unimpressive. It lacks the impact of the exclamation point or the period, and it certainly can't compete with the mysterious aura that surrounds the use of the semicolon. It is the comma's dull duty to indicate a pause, and this it does with great frequency. The comma is, in fact, the most commonly used punctuation mark—*and* the most misused one.

The comma's main function is to clarify a sentence. Used singly, it separates words, phrases, or clauses from other elements in a sentence; used in pairs, it encloses elements that must be set off from the rest of the sentence. The comma is also used in a number of ways that have little to do with clarity but are simply the accepted means of punctuating a specific structure. We'll examine these first.

Standard Comma Use

■ **Use a comma to separate elements in dates:**
> *She was born on July 14, 1955, in New York.*

If only the month and year are given, it is acceptable to omit the comma:
> *The last convention was held in June 1988.*

■ **Use a comma to separate elements in addresses:**
> *Her address is 13 Sutton Place, Brewster, New York.*

Do not, however, use a comma before the ZIP Code when writing addresses:
> *29 High Street, Mystic, CT 06355*

■ **Use a comma to separate elements of geographical proper names:**
> *The firm has offices in Falls Church, Virginia, and Toledo, Ohio.*
> *New Orleans, Louisiana, and San Francisco, California, are famous for their regional cuisines.*

■ **Use a comma in large numbers to separate thousands:**
> *2,500   17,250   125,000   3,465,225*

■ **Use a comma to separate titles from the proper names that precede them:**
> *David Jones, D.D.S.   Alta Collins, Ph.D.   Malcolm Moore, M.D.*

■ **Use a comma after the complimentary close in a letter:**
> *Sincerely,*   *Yours truly,*
> *Emily Ahearn*   *George M. Steele*

Isolating Interruptions

Interrupters are words or phrases that pop up somewhere in a sentence and break up its rhythm or flow. Also sometimes called parenthetical expressions, these words and phrases are unnecessary to the meaning of the sentence; they can be omitted and the sentence will flow smoothly and clearly. Interrupters are set off by a pair of commas if they occur in the middle of a sentence, or by a single comma if they fall at the beginning or end.

■ **Use a comma after such introductory words as** *well, yes, no,* **and** *oh:*
Yes, ma'am.   *No, sir. Oh, all right.*   *Well, if you insist.*

■ **Use a comma to separate a term of address from the body of the sentence:**
What did you say, Doctor?
Sue, are you going out to lunch?

■ **Use a comma or commas to set off transitional words or phrases:**
He was, of course, hired for that purpose.
Nevertheless, I intend to proceed.
That's what this is all about, in fact.
Harris, for example, will be reassigned.

■ **Use a comma or commas to set off contrasting elements in a sentence:**
The war ended in 1945, not 1946.
The black horse, not the bay, is favored to win the race.

Using the Comma for Clarity

Most of us go by ear or by eye when we add a comma to a sentence; we put one in because a slight pause sounds right or the comma itself looks right in that particular spot. This system often works perfectly well for casual correspondence, but business writing demands a degree of precision that can be guaranteed only by a thorough understanding of the rules. Following are some of the more important ones.

■ **Use commas to separate items in a series:**
We had soup, salad, and hard rolls for lunch.
It is acceptable to omit the comma before the conjunction in the series if there is no possibility of the sentence being misread. But consider this example:
Sam, Patrick and Mary are coming to the party.
Are two people coming to the party, or three? Is Sam being told who's coming, or is Sam also a guest? If the latter is the case, the sentence must read: *Sam, Patrick, and Mary are coming to the party.* Since it is always correct to include the comma before the conjunction in a series, it's probably safest to do so routinely.

If all items in a series are connected by conjunctions, *do not* use commas to separate them:
I think that Jean or Michael or Ellie is going to handle that.

■ **Use a comma to set off nonrestrictive modifiers.** A nonrestrictive element is one that is not necessary to the main message of the sentence; a restrictive element, however, is an essential part of the sentence and must not be set off:
Nonrestrictive: *The puppy, which we got at the pound last week, is not housebroken.*
Restrictive: *The puppy that we got at the pound last week is not housebroken, but this one is.*

When a nonrestrictive modifier occurs in the middle of a sentence (as in the example above), be sure to set it off with a pair of commas. If the modifier is restrictive, use no punctuation.

■ **Use commas to set off an appositive.** An appositive is a word or phrase that refers to a noun or pronoun preceding it:
Errol Flynn, the legendary actor, was famous for his swashbuckling roles.
Our receptionist, Julie Mellitis, has a lovely voice.

Do not set off an appositive that has become an accepted part of a name:

Catherine the Great   Bluebeard the Pirate   Richard the Lionhearted

Appositives can also be thought of as restrictive or nonrestrictive. As a general rule, a very short (often one-word) appositive that immediately follows the noun or pronoun it modifies is restrictive:

Tolstoy's novel War and Peace is his most famous work.

This restrictive appositive takes no commas; if the title of the book were removed, the sentence would indicate that Tolstoy wrote only one novel, which is not the case.

Longer appositives tend to be nonrestrictive:

Any kind of dessert, even instant pudding, will make him happy.

In this sentence, the phrase even instant pudding can be removed without altering the meaning; it must be set off.

QUIZ 1

The following sentences contain both restrictive and nonrestrictive modifiers and appositives. Add or remove commas as necessary. If a sentence is correct as written, mark it with a C. Answers follow.

1. Rome the Eternal City is the capital of Italy.
2. The city which is my favorite in all of Europe is built on seven hills.
3. The report, that he left on your desk, is due tomorrow.
4. The report that you and I wrote was widely praised.
5. The child playing hopscotch is my niece.
6. Janie playing hopscotch fell down and skinned her knee.
7. Kevin Daniels offered two jobs in this office will work for Ms. Jones.
8. Applicants, offered more than one job, must choose carefully.
9. My sister Susan is coming to visit.
10. The recent work of Janna Forsythe the impressionist painter will be shown this month at Stoneledge a local art gallery.

ANSWERS

1. Rome, the Eternal City, is the capital of Italy.
2. The city, which is my favorite in all of Europe, is built on seven hills.
3. The report that he left on your desk is due tomorrow.
4. C
5. C
6. Janie, playing hopscotch, fell down and skinned her knee.
7. Kevin Daniels, offered two jobs in this office, will work for Ms. Jones.
8. Applicants offered more than one job must choose carefully.
9. C
10. The recent work of Janna Forsythe, the impressionist painter, will be shown this month at Stoneledge, a local art gallery.

■ **Use a comma to separate an introductory phrase or clause from the main clause:**

Beaming brightly, he told me his good news.

Before she left, she cleaned off her desk.

In the soft light of the early morning, she took her coffee to the garden.

■ **Use a comma to separate main clauses joined by a conjunction:**

I wrote a memo to him, and his secretary responded with a lengthy report.

Without the comma, this sentence could initially be misread to mean that the writer wrote a memo to two persons instead of one.

This rule is especially important to observe when the conjunction used is *for*, in the sense of *because*. Consider this example:

I bought some aspirin on my way home for the day was hot and my head was pounding.

As you can see, the comma is needed before *for* to make the sentence immediately clear.

Note: A comma is *not* needed if you are dealing simply with a compound predicate rather than a compound sentence:

She typed the letters in the morning and mailed them after lunch.

QUIZ 2

Add or remove commas as necessary. Mark correct sentences with a C. Answers follow.
1. I asked him for a decision but he hasn't gotten back to me.
2. She filled out the form and submitted it promptly.
3. Although the report is overdue we can't submit it yet because it hasn't been proofed.
4. The dog howled all night, and slept all day.
5. He's been free all morning but I haven't had time to see him.

ANSWERS

1. I asked him for a decision, but he hasn't gotten back to me.
2. C
3. Although the report is overdue, we can't submit it yet, because it hasn't been proofed.
4. The dog howled all night and slept all day.
5. He's been free all morning, but I haven't had time to see him.

■ **Use a comma to separate a series of two or more adjectives preceding a noun:**

She's an assertive, efficient secretary.
I have a dark, cramped office.

Do *not* use a comma before the last adjective in the series if it may be considered part of the noun:

They bought a small, inexpensive ranch house.
We adopted a big brown dog from the pound.

In the sentences above, *ranch house* and *brown dog* are single thoughts; no comma is needed after the adjective immediately preceding them.

Also do not use a comma after an adjective that modifies another adjective in the series:

I bought a shocking pink T-shirt at the sale.

QUIZ 3

Add commas where needed; mark correct sentences with a C. Answers follow.
1. Sturbridge is a quaint old village.
2. The deep blue placid waters of the lake lapped gently at the shore.
3. The Pacific Northwest enjoys a cool damp climate.
4. Joey is a cheerful witty chubby little boy.
5. He works for the second-largest international airline in the country.

ANSWERS

1. C
2. The deep blue, placid waters of the lake lapped gently at the shore.
3. The Pacific Northwest enjoys a cool, damp climate.
4. Joey is a cheerful, witty, chubby little boy.
5. C

PARALLEL STRUCTURE: A BALANCING ACT

- Do you understand the principle of parallel structure?

- Like a gymnast on the parallel bars, a writer, too, must strive for balance.

- With the help of this chapter, you'll be able to say that you came, you saw, and you conquered the perils of parallel structure.

The writing of a well-balanced sentence is often similar to the performance of a juggling act. What to put where? How to make it flow? How to ensure that it all hangs together?

One skill that can help is a thorough understanding of the principle of parallel construction. The term *parallelism* can be defined as the expression of parallel ideas or concepts in parallel grammatical form or structure. Sound confusing? This example of *un*parallel construction may help make it clear:

> *Your duties are typing, filing, and to answer the telephone.*

In the sentence above, there are three similar elements (the duties), but they are described in two different ways. *Typing* and *filing* are both gerunds, but *to answer* is an infinitive. For the sentence to be parallel in structure, it should read:

> *Your duties are typing, filing, and answering the telephone.*

Coordinate Conjunctions

Note that the series of gerunds in the sentence above is connected by *and*. The sight of a coordinate conjunction (*and, but, or, nor*) connecting a series of similar ideas should act as a flag to indicate to you that parallel construction is called for. Consistency is the key. If the first in a series of similar concepts is expressed as a noun, a verb, an adjective, or a phrase, then the second, third, and fourth ideas should also be presented in the same grammatical form: Adjective must follow adjective, noun must follow noun, active voice must follow active voice, and so on. Following are some examples of faulty constructions followed by constructions using parallel structure:

Not: Problems may arise in the areas of *personnel* (noun), *management* (noun), and *financial* (adjective).
But: Problems may arise in the areas of *personnel* (noun), *management* (noun), and *finance* (noun).

Not: If you *leave* (active voice) early, *catch* (active voice) the bus, and your connection *is made* (passive voice), you should arrive in time.
But: If you *leave* (active voice) early, *catch* (active voice) the bus, and *make* (active voice) your connection, you should arrive in time.

Not: I admire *her sunny disposition* (phrase), *her outlook on life* (phrase), and *that she pays attention to detail* (clause).
But: I admire *her sunny disposition* (phrase), *her outlook on life* (phrase), and *her attention to detail* (phrase).

Sins of Omission

Words that don't need to be repeated in a connected series are sometimes omitted. It's perfectly acceptable to do this—as long as the words that are dropped really aren't required. For example:

He should and could spend more time with his family.

Molly can and will reach her goal very soon.

In the sentences above, the verbs *spend* and *reach* don't need to be used twice, because their form would be identical with both auxiliary verbs. But this isn't always the case:

I never have and never will give her any advice.

I never have give? For a completed parallel construction, this sentence must read:

I never have given and never will give her any advice.

Problems are especially likely to arise when a writer fails to coordinate infinitives or prepositions:

Stacey plans to eat and then bathe her dog.

One can only wonder why Stacey doesn't plan to wash the dog *before* she eats him. In this case, one little omission—the word *to*—completely changes the meaning of the sentence, which should read:

Stacey plans to eat and then to bathe her dog.

The omission of a preposition is fine as long as both words involved take the same preposition and the meaning is clear, but consider this sentence:

She is interested and admiring of his work.

Interested never takes the preposition *of;* in order to be completely parallel, the sentence has to read:

She is interested in and admiring of his work.

Correlative Conjunctions

Words that occur in pairs and are used to connect two phrases, clauses, or other words are known as correlative conjunctions (not only … but also, either … or, neither … nor, both … and, whether … or not). To maintain parallel structure, the second part of the correlative must be the same as the first:

Not: *She both felt elated about her transfer and dejected about leaving her friends.*

But: *She felt both elated about her transfer and dejected about leaving her friends.*

The trick here is to be sure that the correlative conjunction immediately precedes the parallel term. Here's another example:

Not: *He is either depressed or I am.*

But: *Either he is depressed or I am.*

▼ ▼ TAKE A TEST ▼ ▼

Rewrite the following sentences to make them parallel in structure. Answers follow.

1. She shops for shoes in the city, at the mall, and when she gets catalogs.
2. This job requires intelligence, assertiveness, and someone with insight.
3. I always have and always will write personal letters during the holidays.
4. Sharon wants to find clothes that make her look thin and take on a cruise.
5. He not only is president of the company but also chairman of the board.

ANSWERS

1. She shops for shoes in the city, at the mall, and by catalog.
2. This job requires someone with intelligence, assertiveness, and insight.
3. I always have written and always will write personal letters during the holidays.
4. Sharon wants to find clothes that make her look thin and to take on a cruise.
5. He is not only president of the company but also chairman of the board.

PUNCTUATION, PART TWO: POINTERS

- What's stronger than a comma but weaker than a period?

- Does the question mark go inside or outside the quotation marks? Does the period come before or after the final parenthesis?

- In this chapter, we'll try to answer these questions and others on the subject of proper punctuation.

Punctuation marks are as vital to written communication as road signs are to safe driving. The reader needs to know when to slow down, to stop, or to pay attention to a new condition, and telling the reader these things is the function of punctuation.

In Chapter 10, we took an in-depth look at the comma, the most frequently used (and misused) punctuation mark. In this chapter we'll examine the others—their basic uses, their limitations, and the ways in which they, too, are most often misused.

The Question Mark

Everyone understands the function of the question mark, but people sometimes are confused about its proper placement. For review purposes:

➤ **Use a question mark after a direct question.**
Is she planning to attend the seminar?
➤ **Use a question mark at the end of a parenthetical question.**
Sandy (or was it Susan?) was looking for that file.
➤ **Use a question mark after a formal request.**
Will you please reply by this Friday?
➤ **Use a question mark to express doubt about the accuracy of a statement.**
The original building was constructed in 1850(?), and the new wing was added a century later.
➤ **Use a question mark to make a question out of a statement or expression.**
She said that? Really?
➤ **Do not use a question mark after an indirect question.**
He asked whether I could go to dinner.

Whether the question ends the sentence or not, the question mark should always follow the question itself. Keep these rules in mind:

➤ **If the question appears in the middle of a sentence, it isn't necessary to follow the question mark with a capital letter.**
What on earth will happen next? *she wondered.*
➤ **If a question is quoted, place the question mark inside the quotation marks.**
"Have you seen Mark this morning?" the boss asked.
But if the question is not actually part of the quoted material, place the question mark outside the quotes.
Did you hear her say, "I can't take it anymore"?

The Colon

Chances are that you use the colon more frequently than you realize. Consider these common calls for a colon:

➤ **Use a colon after the salutation in a formal letter.**

Dear Sir or Madam: *Dear Ms. Forsythe:*

➤ **Use a colon between hours and minutes expressed as figures.**

6:45 p.m.   *3:15 a.m.*

➤ **Use a colon to separate figures in ratios.**

4 : 1   3 : 2

In addition to these common uses, the colon also functions effectively to indicate a break in the grammatical construction of a sentence. Sometimes referred to as the mark of anticipation, the colon directs the reader's attention to that which follows.

➤ **Use a colon to separate two independent clauses if the second amplifies, illustrates, or explains the first.**

Tom is a wonderful doctor: He's thorough, kind, and compassionate.

When a complete sentence follows a colon, always capitalize the first word of that sentence. If a fragment follows the colon, lowercase the first word.

➤ **Use a colon to introduce a list or series, especially if anticipatory words, such as** *following* **or** *as follows,* **either introduce the list or series or are implied.**

Remember the following pointers: Set your priorities, organize your materials, and manage your time.

Also, do *not* use a colon to introduce a list or series if that list or series serves as the object of a verb or preposition.

Some pointers to remember are the setting of your priorities, the organization of your materials, and the management of your time.

➤ **Use a colon to introduce a formal extract or quote.**

His opening statement read as follows: "Progress implies change, but not all change implies progress."

Do not use a colon, however, before an indirect statement or question.

His opening statement indicated that although progress implies change, not all change implies progress.

The Semicolon

Think of a semicolon as a cross between a period and a comma, and you'll have a good idea of its function. Stronger than a comma but weaker than a period, the semicolon indicates a pause that falls somewhere between the two. These are some of the common ways to use this punctuation mark:

➤ **Use a semicolon to separate two independent clauses** *not* **joined by a conjunction** *(and, or, but).*

The first segment of the project was grueling; the rest was easy.

➤ **Use a semicolon to separate items of a series when those items themselves contain commas.**

The officers elected include Ann Greene, president; Dewey Hicks, vice president; and Erin O'Neil, secretary.

➤ **Use a semicolon to separate two long independent clauses that are joined by a conjunctive adverb** *(moreover, however, nevertheless, consequently, therefore, etc.).*

The candidate seldom had his facts straight or presented his ideas clearly; however, he had great appeal to a certain segment of the population.

Parentheses and Brackets

These two punctuation marks have a great deal in common: They are both used in pairs and they both set off certain words from others. They even look a lot alike, although the curvy parentheses are slightly more graceful than the squared-off, businesslike brackets. Similar though they are, parentheses and brackets are not interchangeable. Rules for the specific uses of both follow.

Parentheses

➤ **Use parentheses to set off nonessential information from the rest of the sentence.**
President's Day was formerly celebrated as two separate holidays (Washington's and Lincoln's birthdays).
Requests for handouts must be received at least a month (30 days) in advance.
Do *not* use parentheses if the word or phrase you want to set off is vital to the structure of the sentence, or if the information is critical to the meaning of the sentence. The following are examples of incorrect use of parentheses.
The director of the (Planning and Zoning) Commission attended the meeting.
The booklet is well researched (but occasionally inaccurate).
➤ **Use parentheses to set off directions, references, dates of a person's life or of an event, and numbers or letters enumerating items in a series or outline.**
Statistics show (see Figure 2) that proper diet can lower the risk of some diseases.
Marcel Proust (1871-1922) was an incredibly prolific author.
We require that you (a) submit a resume, (b) take a typing test, and (c) be available to start work immediately.
The use of other punctuation with parentheses is not very complicated. Normally, no end punctuation is required within parentheses, but occasionally a question mark or an exclamation point may be called for within a parenthetical expression.
Someone said (was it Suzy?) that our deadline has been postponed.
She said (really, she did!) that the project isn't due until next month.
When parentheses fall at the end of a sentence, the period follows the final parenthesis.
The supply cabinet contains an abundance of letterhead (50 boxes or more).
But when an entire sentence is contained within parentheses, its initial word is capitalized and the end punctuation falls within the parentheses.
The measure passed the committee by an overwhelming majority. (Opponents, though vocal, were few.)

Brackets

➤ **Use brackets to set off parenthetical material within parentheses.**
(For more information, see the file for Stanley [formerly Jones] Insurance.)
➤ **Use brackets to set off insertions in quoted material by someone other than the original speaker or writer.** Such insertions usually qualify an ambiguity, identify a missing letter or word, or add an important comment.
"It is noteworthy that those two [Wesson and McCleary] left under a cloud."
➤ **Use brackets to set off the term *sic* in quoted material.** So used, *sic* points out that a preceding error is quoted exactly as it appears in the original material.
My sister wrote to say she'd found work in Conneticut [sic].
➤ **Use the same punctuation rules for brackets as for parentheses.**

Quotation Marks and Italics

Like parentheses and brackets, quotation marks and italics serve a similar function.
Both are used (again, like parentheses and brackets) to set off certain words from others. This pair can be a bit trickier, however—there are situations in which they are rela-

tively interchangeable or in which they serve complementary purposes. We'll look at these circumstances first:

➤ **Direct quotations and direct thoughts.** Quotation marks are always used to set off a direct quotation.

> "We're considering that option," he said.

Direct thoughts are most often set off by italics.

> *Does it have any chance of working?* he wondered.

➤ **Definition of a word or phrase.** Either quotation marks or italics may be used to set off a word or phrase defined within a sentence.

> The word "halcyon" refers to a state of happy tranquillity.
> To *debug* is to remove problems from a computer program.

➤ **Titles.** The rules are very specific here; quotation marks and italics are never interchangeable in these instances, although they are frequently complementary.

Use italics for the titles of:

books	magazines	long poems
works of art	newspapers	plays
movies	television series	radio series

Use quotation marks for the titles of:

songs	magazine articles	short stories
short poems	newspaper articles	lectures
chapters of books	episodes in a TV series	sermons

In other words, titles that represent *parts* of whole works should be set off in quotation marks, whereas the titles of *complete* works should be italicized. For example:

> Please read Chapter 3, "The Price of Freedom," in *The History of the American Colonies.*

➤ **Foreign words and phrases.** Italics are used for any foreign word or phrase not yet adopted into the English language.

> Joel is quite the *enfant terrible;* he drives his parents wild.

But the English translation of such a word or phrase is usually set off in quotation marks.

> The motto of the U.S. Coast Guard is *semper fidelis,* "always faithful."

Using Quotation Marks and Italics With Other Punctuation

➤ **When single or double quotes are used with a comma or a period, the quotes always follow the comma or the period.**

> "Please be patient," said the new clerk, "and I'll catch on."
> "His excuse was 'I don't have enough money.'"

When a quote contains another quote, single quotation marks are used around the quote contained.

> "When he said, 'You're a great secretary,' I was pleased."

➤ **When colons or semicolons are used with quotation marks, they are always placed outside the quotation marks.**

The flier read "Entries must be received no later than Friday"; however, several arrived the following week.

➤ **When either an exclamation point or a question mark is used in a quotation, it should precede the quotation marks if it is part of the quoted material; otherwise, it should follow.**

> He shook me, shouting, "Wake up!"
> Did the man just say, "Please leave the room"?

➤ **When words, phrases, or sentences are italicized, italicize all punctuation.**

PLAYING THE NUMBERS GAME

- Even a math whiz may have trouble typing numbers correctly in documents.

- For instance, should you write *forty-five* or *45*? The answer may depend on the kind of business you're in.

- If you can't tell a cardinal from an ordinal, don't worry—and don't rush out to buy a bird book. Just read on for help.

When to spell out, and when to use numerals? The answer generally depends on the type of document you're preparing. If you work for a legislator, for example, and find yourself drafting a proclamation, you'll be working on a very formal document: All numbers must be spelled out, even years. But if you work in a research lab preparing statistics, you'll use strictly figures in your work.

Most documents that you type will fall somewhere between these two extremes. Unless you *do* work in a specialized field, chances are that most of your routine typing assignments fall into the general business category—and require the use of both numerals and spelled-out numbers. The rules that govern the use of numerals in general text are many, but when you're typing a document with numbers in it, perhaps the most important thing to remember is that consistency of style should be maintained throughout.

When to Spell Out

In general business writing, the following circumstances usually call for numbers to be expressed as words. You should:

➤ Spell out numbers under 101 in general writing.
We have forty-seven phones on this floor.

➤ Spell out round numbers and numbers used in approximations.
They expect an audience of about five hundred.

➤ Spell out a number that begins a sentence, or reword the sentence.
Not: 129 *students attended the lecture.*
But: *One hundred twenty-nine students attended the lecture.*
Or: *The lecture was attended by 129 students.*

➤ Spell out one of two numbers that follow each other consecutively in a sentence. This ensures clarity; it doesn't matter which of the two you choose to spell out.
I'd like six 25-cent stamps.
We need 112 twenty-foot boards for the deck.

➤ Spell out *ordinal* numbers (first, ninth, twenty-second, etc.), which are those used to indicate order. (*Cardinal* numbers are those used for counting, such as one, nine, and twenty-two.)
We'll celebrate his fourth birthday on the sixth of this month.

➤ Spell out the names of months, and also dates of the month when they precede the month in the order given.
February 2 (not 2/2)
the second of February

➤ Spell out fractions except in specifications or tabulations.
  one-half cup of sugar
  two thirds of the vote

➤ Spell out hours except when they are used with minutes.
  See you at ten o'clock tomorrow morning.
  The meeting starts at 10:45 a.m.

➤ Spell out certain common expressions that involve numbers.
  This gadget has a thousand and one uses.
  She looks like a million dollars.

When to Use Numerals

In general business text, numerals are normally used in the following circumstances. Try to remember to:

➤ Use numerals for specific numbers over one hundred.
  We have 432 employees.

➤ Use numerals when a series or a group of numbers is contained in the same sentence. (The style of the larger numbers governs that of the smaller.)
  The audience included 330 men, 276 women, and 54 children under 12.

➤ Use numerals for round numbers when they appear with specific numbers.
  I need 125 copies of this report, but nearly 200 of that one.

➤ Use a cardinal numeral when the day follows the month in a date.
  July 4, 1776
But note that many foreign countries and the military place the cardinal numeral before the month, with no comma preceding the year:
  4 July 1776

➤ Use numerals with abbreviations and symbols.
  3 cc   *25 mph*   *68°F*   *88%*

➤ Use numerals to express scores and statistics.
  The home team won, 21-7.
  This formula has a 3-1 ratio of solids to fluids.
  The measure passed by a vote of 33-29.

➤ Use numerals for specific sums of money.
  She owes $3.65 to petty cash.

➤ Use a combination of numerals and words to express round numbers in the millions and billions.
  As much as $30 billion in additional revenue may be necessary.
  He sold $105 million worth of common stock.

Your employer may have a preferred house style for expressing numbers that differs in some instances from these general rules. Whether you have such a style manual to follow or whether you use the guidelines above as a reference, be sure to be consistent throughout a document in your treatment of numerals.

TO CAP OR NOT TO CAP?

- When to cap and when to lowercase a word? It's a question that stops many of us with annoying frequency.

- Is it Spring or spring, South or south? You don't have to guess—there are rules that apply.

- Here are some guidelines to go by when the question of capping has got you confused.

That is often the question, according to many frustrated office workers. Everyone knows that proper names are capitalized, as well as the first word of a sentence—but that leaves a lot of grammatical territory uncovered, and a lot of people still in doubt about whether to cap or lowercase a word.

Some rules for capitalization are absolutes, and some are apt to change with the times. (A century or so ago, it was not unusual for almost every other word in a sentence to be capped.) There are also situations that are a matter of personal preference; when you make a decision, stick to it—consistency is important. Remember to always cap:

■ Proper names.

In addition to proper names, capitalize all titles, positions, or indications of family relation that precede a proper name or are used in place of a proper noun.
- Dorrie met *Prime Minister* Thatcher at Wimbledon.
- I suggested she talk to *Training Director* Jim Folkes.
- We saw *Mother* at *Aunt Jane's* house last night.

Do not, however, capitalize these words if they are used alone or with possessive pronouns or articles.
- Dorrie met the *prime minister* at Wimbledon.
- I suggested that she talk to the *training director.*
- We saw *my mother* at *my aunt's* house last night.

There is an exception to this rule: Always capitalize the titles *President* and *Vice President* when they refer to the President and Vice President of the United States.
- We saw the *President* on television last night.

■ Nouns that indicate race, nationality, ethnic group, or language.

- She bought a dress made of *Thai* silk.
- Charles is fluent in *French* and *Italian.*

■ Adjectives, nouns, and verbs that are derived from proper nouns, including currently copyrighted trade names.

- That was a *Freudian* slip, Sally!
- Will someone please *Xerox* this memo?

But note that many words derived from proper nouns have become so commonly used that they are no longer capped. For example:
- She has a lovely collection of fine *china* teacups.
- The fruit basket arrived wrapped in *cellophane.*
- The crack was sealed with plaster of *paris.*

If you're in doubt about whether to cap a word that falls into this category, it's best to check the dictionary.

■ Geographical terms.

Capitalize specific addresses and geographic locations.

- While in *Paris,* you must try Chez Hercule on the *Champs Elysée.*
- They have a cottage on *Wood Lane* in *Siasconset* on *Nantucket.*

Do not, however, capitalize words such as *street, lake, city,* or *state* when they are used in the general sense and do not follow a proper name.

- She lives on *Broad Street;* it's a nice *street.*
- I love *Lake Tahoe;* do you like the *lake?*
- *New York State* has some fine vacation spots, and so does the *state* of Connecticut.

■ Compass points.

Capitalize the points of the compass and adjectives derived from them only when they designate specific sections of the country; when they simply indicate direction, they should be lowercased.

- Have you ever been to the *West Coast?*
- I'm a *midwesterner;* he's from the *Midwest,* too.
- We toured the *Middle Atlantic* states for two weeks, then headed *south.*

■ Seasons.

Do *not* capitalize the names of the seasons unless they are personified in the poetic sense.

- If *Winter* comes, can *Spring* be far behind?
- There's nothing like *autumn* in New England.

■ Sums of money.

Capitalize sums of money that are written out in legal or business documents.

- *One Thousand Three Hundred Fifty-Three Dollars*

■ Titles and headings.

Capitalize all words in titles of paintings, songs, and short stories, and in titles and headings of books, magazine and newspaper articles, reports, lectures, etc.—with the following important exceptions:

✓ Do *not* capitalize articles (*a, an, the*) in titles unless they appear at the beginning of the title or follow a colon or a dash. (The first word following a colon or a dash in a title is always capitalized.)

- *A* Room With *a* View
- "Gorbachev: *An* Intimate Portrait of *the* Man"

✓ Do *not* capitalize prepositions or conjunctions of three or fewer letters unless they appear at the beginning of the title or follow a colon or a dash.

- *To* Have *and* Have Not
- *Of* Mice *and* Men
- *The* Taming *of the* Shrew

■ Company preference.

Some companies prefer to capitalize certain words (names of departments or divisions, company titles, local geographic names) that would normally not be capitalized.

- Ms. Farr is *Administrative Assistant* to Edward Ails, *Director of Training.*
- We must ascertain how this proposal will affect the *City.*

If your company has its own style manual, be sure you follow house rules for capitalization.

MISPLACED MODIFIERS

Word order is very important in written English sentence structure, and few parts of speech are as easily misplaced as modifiers. Modifiers are words or phrases that describe other words or phrases, and they have an unfortunate habit of popping up where they don't belong. Usually the result of such an incursion is only mildly confusing—or even amusing: *They bought a puppy from that lady with a kinky tail.*

In some cases, however, the migration of even one small word within a sentence can cause a serious misunderstanding—and there's no room for that in business writing. In a previous chapter we touched upon dangling participles, one especially common form of misplaced modifier. Now we'll consider some of the other likely paths that confusion can take to creep into your writing.

Adverbs

In spoken English it is common to place a limiting adverb—a word such as *only, almost, nearly, just, even,* or *hardly*—before the verb. The speaker's inflection gives the listener the correct interpretation of the information. If you tell someone that "Bill only went to New York last week," the chances are excellent that your listener will understand exactly what you mean to say—because of the vocal emphasis you give to key words in the sentence. But let's consider that same sentence being read as part of a memo:

Bill only went to New York last week.

What does this sentence really mean? It says that Bill only went. Did he not return? Was it a one-way trip? Or, since he only went to New York, does it mean that he took no side trips, made no visits to Newark or New Haven? And since he only went to New York last week, does that mean that he has never been there before? Or does it mean that it was just last week, maybe Wednesday, that Bill went to New York? As you can see, a written sentence such as this is open to interpretation.

In order to prevent misunderstanding, always place the limiting adverb directly before the word or phrase it modifies. Here are some examples that may help to clarify the point. The first sentence of each pair illustrates the way you might say the sentence aloud—and the way it might be misinterpreted if you were to write it that way. The second sentence gives the correct placement of the modifier.

➤ *We only leased that building.* (We didn't buy it.)
We leased only that building. (We didn't lease any others.)

➤ *I almost walked to the park.* (I walked to the mall instead.)
I walked almost to the park. (I stopped a block short.)

Phrases

Prepositional phrases that are used as modifiers should almost always follow as closely as possible the words they modify in order to avoid confusion.

Unclear: *Rumors were heard all over the area of his disease.*
Clear: *Rumors of his disease were heard all over the area.*

Unclear: *I warned him about stealing from petty cash on Friday.*
Clear: *I warned him on Friday about stealing from petty cash.*

An adverb phrase can usually be placed at the beginning or the end of a sentence, or within it near the verb that is modified. Sometimes, however, caution is called for:

Unclear: *He muttered that monsters are coming in his sleep.*
Clear: *He muttered in his sleep that monsters are coming.*

Unclear: *She landed on the ground as I ran after her horse with a thud.*
Clear: *She landed on the ground with a thud as I ran after her horse.*

Clauses

Adjective clauses, which often begin with *who, which,* or *that,* should immediately follow the nouns they modify.

Unclear: *The woman made an apple pie who won the blue ribbon.*
Clear: *The woman who won the blue ribbon made an apple pie.*

Unclear: *The office has a window that I want.*
Clear: *The office that I want has a window.*

Adverb clauses, like adverb phrases, can appear at the beginning or at the end of the sentence, or within it close to the verb that is modified. But, like adverb phrases, adverb clauses also require careful consideration.

Unclear: *He filed the report with his home office after it was approved.*
Clear: *After it was approved, he filed the report with his home office.*

Unclear: *Annie decided to sell the dog because she was pregnant.*
Clear: *Because she was pregnant, Annie decided to sell the dog.*

▼ ▼ TAKE A TEST ▼ ▼

Rewrite the following sentences so that the meaning is clear:
1. Jane just did enough work to get by.
2. We saw the houses through the woods that were designed by Frank Lloyd Wright.
3. The baby didn't want his blanket because it was warm.
4. Did you see that girl wearing the orange dress with blond hair?
5. He registered for the class without enthusiasm.

ANSWERS

1. Jane did just enough work to get by.
2. Through the woods we saw the houses that were designed by Frank Lloyd Wright.
3. Because it was warm, the baby didn't want his blanket.
4. Did you see that girl with blond hair wearing the orange dress?
5. He registered without enthusiasm for the class.

- When does a compound take a hyphen and when does it not?

- Is it one word or two?

- You don't always have to guess—there are rules to help eliminate compound confusion.

COMPOUND CONFUSION

If you find yourself constantly reaching for the dictionary when you confront a compound word, take heart. Even language experts say that consulting a good dictionary is the safest way to sort out the confusion that compounds can cause. The problem lies in the nature of our language, which is both vital and complex.

For example, a compound may take one of three forms: It may be written as two or more separate words (*bank loan, mail order*), as a hyphenated word (*break-in, warm-up*), or as one word (*deadline, letterhead*). Typically, a compound starts out as two words. As the use of the compound increases and it becomes more familiar, it tends to become hyphenated—and finally to become one word. The word *baseball* is one example of a compound that underwent this evolution; *life-style* (or *lifestyle*) is another example. (Although most dictionaries hyphenate this compound, it is increasingly seen in print as one word.)

Compounds tend to be most confusing when they are used as modifiers. Fortunately, there are hard-and-fast rules to follow in this area. Some of the more common follow.

✓ Hyphenate all compound modifiers beginning with *all, self,* or *quasi:*
> *all-encompassing* plan
> *self-made* man
> *quasi-historical* document

✓ Hyphenate a compound modifier that consists of an adjective and a noun. This prevents misreading of the description; you know immediately that the adjective modifies the first noun, not the second.
> *brown-bag* lunch
> *small-town* mayor
> *ancient-history* student

✓ Hyphenate compounds consisting of an adverb and an adjective or a participle *if* the compound precedes the noun that it modifies and could be misread without the hyphen.

long-awaited decision	but	The decision was long awaited.
best-educated candidate	but	This candidate is the best educated.
much-needed support	but	His support was much needed.

✓ Do not hyphenate such compounds if the adverb ends in *-ly* and could not be misread. (To test this, try dropping the adjective or participle to see if the remaining phrase makes sense.)
> *equally interesting* theories
> *newly found* freedom
> *sorely needed* assistance

✓ Hyphenate modifying phrases that express a single thought.

up-to-date records

state-of-the-art design

cut-and-dried decision

✓ Hyphenate expressions of dual nationality.

Sino-Soviet relations

Anglo-Arab stallion

French-Canadian exchange student

✓ Hyphenate two nouns of equal significance.

secretary-treasurer

owner-operator

singer-dancer

✓ Hyphenate modifying fractions that are written as words. Do not, however, hyphenate the fraction if it is used as a noun and followed by *of*.

one-third share	but	*one third* of a share
one-eighth inch	but	*one eight* of an inch
three-fifths majority	but	*three fifths* of the majority

✓ Hyphenate compound numbers from twenty-one to ninety-nine, but don't add a second hyphen when fractions are formed. And if part of a fraction is already hyphenated, don't add a second hyphen.

thirty-nine hundredths

fifty-six thousandths

one forty-fourth

✓ Hyphenate compounds that consist of a cardinal number and a unit of measurement.

four-foot board

two-quart casserole

three-liter jug

▼ ▼ TAKE A TEST ▼ ▼

In each of the pairs below, one sentence contains the correct form of the compound or compounds. Circle the correct version. Answers follow.

1. **(a)** Those copper-bottomed pans were a long awaited addition to my kitchen.
   (b) Those copper-bottomed pans were a long-awaited addition to my kitchen.
2. **(a)** The kind hearted couple took in several poorly-fed children.
   (b) The kind-hearted couple took in several poorly fed children.
3. **(a)** He has an instinct for self preservation.
   (b) He has an instinct for self-preservation.
4. **(a)** John was elected secretary-treasurer of the sports club the year he joined the Greco-Roman wrestling team.
   (b) John was elected secretary treasurer of the sports club the year he joined the Greco Roman wrestling team.
5. **(a)** My two liter bottle is three-fourths empty.
   (b) My two-liter bottle is three-fourths empty.

ANSWERS

1. b; **2.** b; **3.** b; **4.** a; **5.** b

PREPOSITION PRECISION

- **Do you dare to end a sentence with a preposition? There are times when you should.**

- **Are you prone to preposition redundancy? We'll point out the problem.**

- **Is it *differ from* or *differ with*? Some prepositional idioms must be memorized, but most come easily.**

The preposition is an extremely useful little part of speech that seldom causes problems for anyone. Even when a preposition does create a problem, the error tends to be subtle enough so that the writer may easily miss it when proofreading the document—and therein lies the problem. Fortunately, there are a limited number of ways in which prepositions can be misused. We'll consider the more common ones in this chapter.

Preposition Position

We've all been taught not to end a sentence with a preposition, but never was a rule made that so begged to be broken. It's true that a sentence that ends in a preposition may be weak or may sound awkward: *She wants to major in computer science, which she has just taken her first course in.* This sentence is much stronger without the terminal preposition. (*She wants to major in computer science, in which she has just taken her first course.*)

On the other hand, a sentence can sometimes be made stronger by placing the preposition at the end. Consider these examples:

What are you talking about?
I know what I'm getting into.

These sentences would sound silly if they were rearranged to avoid the terminal preposition. Don't ignore the old rule entirely, but learn to trust your ear. If the sentence sounds most natural and forceful with the preposition at the end, then that's where you should place it.

Preposition Redundancy

Writers often get carried away and use more prepositions than are required:

➤ My car gets *from between* 25 *to* 30 miles per gallon of gas. (This sentence should read either *My car gets* from 25 to *30 miles...* or *My car gets* between 25 and *30 miles...* The use of *from* and *between* together is redundant.)
➤ She wondered where the boss was *at.* (*At* is redundant. The sentence should read *She wondered where the boss was.*)
➤ Someone get that spider *off of* me! (*Of* is unnecessary. It's correct to simply say *Get that spider off me!*)

Whenever you find yourself using multiple prepositions in a sentence, take a good look to be sure that they're all necessary.

Prepositional Idiom

Some words in the English language must be followed by specific prepositions; choosing the correct preposition depends on the meaning the word it accompanies is supposed to convey. If you memorize the more commonly used prepositional idioms, you can save yourself a lot of time. For starters, how well can you do with these?

▼ ▼ TAKE A TEST ▼ ▼

Circle the correct prepositional idiom in each sentence. Answers and explanations follow.

1. Is the restaurant convenient (to, for) our meeting?
2. I'm tired of contending (with, about) this proposal.
3. Criticism is easier to take when it's accompanied (by, with) a compliment.
4. I wouldn't entrust these files (to, with) anyone but you.
5. Bob is disappointed (in, with) his new trainee's work.
6. The car-pool members agreed (between, among) themselves on a time to meet.
7. I'm afraid he's angry (at, with) me.
8. These figures aren't bad compared (to, with) last month's.
9. We concur heartily (with, in) your assessment of the situation.
10. Sue and Tom are at it again—do they often differ (from, with) each other?
11. Does the figure you've got correspond (with, to) the one I came up with?
12. Has the boss agreed (on, to, with) the client's terms?

ANSWERS

1. **for.** *Convenient to* means to be nearby, to be easily accessible, as in "The restaurant is convenient to our office building." *Convenient for* means to be suitable for a particular purpose.
2. **about.** To *contend with* means to fight or struggle with an enemy, as in "I'll have to contend with John about this." To *contend about* means to argue or dispute an issue.
3. **with.** Use *by* when referring to a person, as in "She was accompanied by a business associate." Use *with* when referring to a thing.
4. **to.** To *entrust with* means to assign a duty or trust, as in "I'm entrusting you with these files." To *entrust to* means to commit the care of something to somebody.
5. **with.** Use *in* when referring to someone, as in "He is disappointed in his new trainee." Use *with* to refer to a thing—in this case, the trainee's work.
6. **among.** *Between* is used in reference to two people, places, or things, or to two succeeding items in a series, as in "Between them, Alex and Laura agreed on a deadline" or "Please pack those dishes with tissue paper between them." Use *among* when referring to three or more people, places, or things.
7. **with.** Use *at* (or *about*) in reference to a thing, as in "He was angry at what I said." Use *with* in reference to someone.
8. **with.** Use *to* when suggesting a likeness or analogy between things that are essentially unlike: "That's like comparing apples to oranges." Use *with* when making a comparison of quantity or other similarity or difference.
9. **in.** *Concur with* means to agree with a person, as in "I concur with you that the need is urgent." *Concur in* means to be in agreement in thought or opinion.
10. **with.** *Differ from* means to be unlike someone or something, as in "Sue and Tom differ from each other in their taste in books and music." *Differ with* means to be in disagreement with a person.
11. **to.** *Correspond with* means to exchange letters with someone, as in "I correspond with Hattie several times a year." *Correspond to* means to match something or to conform to it.
12. **to.** *Agree on* (or *upon*) means to reach an understanding about something, as in "Are we agreed on the need for a new contract?" *Agree with* means to concur with a person or an idea, as in "I can agree with that philosophy." *Agree to* means to accept another person's suggestion or offer.

- **Review:** To examine or study again; to look back on, to take a retrospective view of.

- **Examination:** An exercise designed to examine progress or test qualification or knowledge.

- Time to test your vocabulary and grammatical skills in communicating clearly!

A REVIEW EXAM

The goal of this section has been to enhance one of the most valuable assets an office-support professional can possess—a strong command of the English language. In this chapter we offer a series of quizzes designed to review what we've covered and to test your progress. Answers follow the final quiz. Good luck!

QUIZ 1 Circle the letter of the word in each pair that is properly spelled or correctly divided.

1. (a) grevious
   (b) grievous
2. (a) percieve
   (b) perceive
3. (a) extravagant
   (b) extravagent
4. (a) supercede
   (b) supersede
5. (a) applicible
   (b) applicable
6. (a) dan-gling
   (b) dang-ling
7. (a) courses
   (b) cours-es
8. (a) an-alyst
   (b) ana-lyst
9. (a) re-com-mend
   (b) rec-om-mend
10. (a) subs-tant-ial
    (b) sub-stan-tial

QUIZ 2 Circle the correct word in each of the following sentences.
1. You couldn't fool him if he weren't so (credulous, incredulous).
2. Doesn't everyone like to receive (compliments, complements)?
3. We need to study the likely (affect, effect) of this proposal.
4. She is a (maleficent, magniloquent) speaker, much in demand.
5. We are fortunate to have so (eminent, imminent) a guest with us.
6. She had the string (quintuplets, quintet) play at her wedding.
7. I wish we could move this table without (dissembling, disassembling) it.
8. She suffered an (adverse, averse) reaction to the medication.
9. Police were called to the (cite, site) of the incident.
10. If you intend to (adopt, adapt) this manual for your own department's use, you're going to have to become more (adapt, adept) at editing.

QUIZ 3 Circle the correct choice of pronoun and/or verb.
1. Between you and (I, me), I would have liked (to be, to have been) asked.
2. We finally realized that we (made, had made) a mistake.
3. I went to the show with (he, him) and (she, her).
4. You shouldn't have tried to (finish, have finished) the job without (they, them) and their staff.
5. Ask (whoever, whomever) you want to join you and (I, me) for lunch; I wish I (had known, would have known) sooner that we could go.

QUIZ 4 Add proper punctuation to the following sentences.
1. The last part of the project went slowly it was completed just last

week
2. Please remit the balance within one month 30 days
3. Paris the City of Light is my favorite place in the world
4. Did you hear the boss say everybody take an early lunch
5. My family motto is ad astra per aspera to the stars through difficulty
6. Her new handbag which is made of imported leather was very expensive
7. John said Janie is my favorite brother but he's awfully drifty sometimes
8. Her grocery list included the following one cucumber two tomatoes five pounds of sugar and a box of dog biscuits
9. Smiling shyly she announced her engagement
10. Dare I try to call him tonight she wondered

QUIZ 5 Each of the sentences below illustrates a grammatical error. To test your skill at spotting each of them, use this letter code to fill in the blank at the end of each sentence with the appropriate letter:

(A) misplaced modifier	**(D)** unparallel construction
(B) dangling participle	**(E)** disagreement of subject and verb
(C) split infinitive	**(F)** improper compound construction

1. I require tact, patience, and someone with energy for this job. ( )
2. Are you enjoying your newly-discovered aptitude for computer science? ( )
3. You should take action on what he said as quickly as possible. ( )
4. Neither of us are taking the class. ( )
5. Swimming across the pond, her strap broke. ( )
6. I want you to thoroughly research this. ( )

ANSWERS

QUIZ 1
1. b; 2. b; 3. a; 4. b; 5. b; 6. a; 7. a; 8 b; 9. b; 10. b
QUIZ 2
1. credulous; 2. compliments; 3. effect; 4. magniloquent; 5. eminent; 6. quintet; 7. disassembling; 8. adverse; 9. site; 10. adapt, adept
QUIZ 3
1. me, to be; 2. had made; 3. him, her; 4. finish, them; 5. whomever, me, had known
QUIZ 4
1. The last part of the project went slowly; it was completed just last week.
2. Please remit the balance within one month (30 days).
3. Paris, the City of Light, is my favorite place in the world.
4. Did you hear the boss say, "Everybody take an early lunch"?
5. My family motto is *ad astra per aspera*, "to the stars through difficulty."
6. Her new handbag, which is made of imported leather, was very expensive.
7. "John," said Janie, "is my favorite brother, but he's awfully drifty sometimes."
8. Her grocery list included the following: one cucumber, two tomatoes, five pounds of sugar, and a box of dog biscuits.
9. Smiling shyly, she announced her engagement.
10. *Dare I try to call him tonight?* she wondered.
QUIZ 5
1. D; 2. F; 3. A; 4. E; 5. B; 6. C

WRITING FOR RESULTS
Better Letters and Reports

INTRODUCTION

Letters, reports, and memos are vehicles of communication. Their intent is to provide helpful information or advice. But often, the intent is lost if these vehicles are not properly organized or well presented—and the results can wreak havoc on customer relations. After all, a badly presented letter or report can reflect poorly not only on you but on your entire company.

An exceptionally clear and well-presented report or memo, on the other hand, says a great deal about how much you know about the relationship between presentation and acceptance, how much attention you pay to detail, and how skillful you are at using the written word to make your boss and your company look good. In this section, you'll learn how to present perfect letters, memos, and reports, and you'll be able to pinpoint the areas where you might need improvement.

Would you like to read about a particular form of business letter? Perhaps you want some pointers on writing the perfect press release? To find information on a specific type of correspondence, simply glance at the index below.

SEVERAL LETTER FORMATS

- In this and the next chapter, six important business letter formats commonly used in today's offices.

- Here: the Official, Semiblock, and Modified Block styles.

- Tips on when to use different formats and how to type them.

If you were to represent your company at a meeting, trade show, seminar, or convention, you would take great care to be properly attired, on your best behavior, well informed about the matters at hand, and sure to speak intelligently and correctly. Sending a letter is another way of representing your company, and you must make the same effort to make a good impression.

When you write a business letter, your first concerns are the subject of the letter (are you seeking information or are you sending it?) and the presentation of the material (is the letter well organized, clearly written, and grammatically correct?). You pay particular attention to these points because you know that when *you receive* a letter that contains factual and grammatical errors, your impression of the person and the company who sent the letter is not a good one. But even if the letter is perfect on these points, there are still several other important considerations—all of which make an impact on readers.

For example, when you take a letter out of its envelope, unfold it, and give it a quick glance, what are the very first things that you notice? Chances are that you first note the letterhead, the color and texture of the paper, and then the style or the format—the way the letter is physically set up on the page. Whether you realize it or not, each of these things will make an impression on you about the content, the writer, and the company from which the letter came. And that could affect the way you respond to the letter as a whole.

Different letter styles are used for different purposes. Here, we will show you three styles, and we will tell you what types of letters they are used for. Your company may have set rules about what format or style it prefers to use for its business letters, and you should always follow company regulations in these matters; however, it would be beneficial for you to know the basic letter formats that are used in business today. The three styles on the following pages are known as …

- Official,
- Semiblock,
- and Modified Block (also called Block style).

These are the more traditional styles of the six that you will see. The three letter styles we'll discuss in the next chapter are…

- Full Block,
- Simplified,
- and Hanging-Indented.

The first two styles are being used by more and more companies that are interested in working faster and more efficiently. The third provides a dramatic look that is often used in advertising.

But first, let's look at the more traditional, tried-and-true styles…

July 16, 19—

Dear Ms. Follett:

Every correspondence manual should include a sample of the Official style. It is used for personal business letters written by executives and other professional people. It is usually typed on Executive size (7 1/4" × 10 1/2") or Monarch (7 1/2" × 10") stationery.

The structural parts of the letter differ from the standard arrangement only in the position of the inside address. It is typed two to five lines <u>below</u> the signature block and flush with the left margin.

The dateline is typed slightly to the right of the center of the page or flush with the right margin. The salutation is typed flush with the left margin. The first line of each paragraph is indented five or six spaces. All lines of the signature block are aligned with the complimentary close.

The identification line should appear only on copies of the letter—not on the original. It is typed two lines below the last line of the inside address. An enclosure notation, if used, appears two lines below that. On personalized executive stationery, it is not necessary to type the dictator's name; however, a handwritten signature is always needed.

Sincerely yours,

Adele Cole
Executive Director

Ms. Barbara Follett
Daimon Secretarial School
142 Huntington Avenue
Rochester, NY 14622

July 16, 19—

Ms. Alicia Handelman
Smythe-Collins School
127 Parkwood Drive
Bethesda, MD 20817

Dear Ms. Handelman:

Most companies have a definite preference as to letter style. Many leading business corporations insist that all letters be typed in Semiblock style. It is one of the more traditional styles—having a more formal appearance than some letter styles commonly used today. Here is a copy to add to your correspondence manual.

If you have a lot of information to send, the Semiblock style can be very effective. The indented paragraphs break up the body of the letter. This creates natural dividing points for the information and gives the reader's eyes a rest.

The first line of each paragraph is indented five or ten spaces. In this sample the paragraphs are indented five spaces. As in all letters, the message is single-spaced with double-spacing between paragraphs.

The dateline is typed slightly to the right of the center of the page or flush with the right margin, two to four lines below the letterhead. The inside address and salutation are typed flush left. The complimentary close begins slightly to the right of the center of the page. All lines of the signature block are aligned with the complimentary close.

No identification line is used in this example. The typist's initials are shown on the file copy.

Very sincerely yours,

Mariel Betham
Administrative Assistant

July 16, 19—
XJ 12:3:1

Ms. Melissa Scott
Bay Business School
1515 Bay Point Drive
Vancouver, WA 98684

Dear Ms. Scott:

You asked me if there is any one style of setting up a letter that is used more than the others. Most businesses probably favor the Modified Block letter over any other letter style because it saves time for the typist. It has a "no nonsense" appearance, and it delivers the message in the most efficient way possible.

The dateline may be centered, slightly off center, or flush with the right margin. The reference line, if used, is typed directly underneath the dateline. The inside address, salutation, and paragraphs are typed flush left. The complimentary close begins slightly to the right of the center of the page. Both lines of the signature block are aligned with the complimentary close.

                              Sincerely yours,

                              Katherine Russell
                              Editorial Assistant

                              mr

- In this chapter, three more business letter styles: Full Block, Simplified, and Hanging-Indented.

- Letter styles that help you get your point across in a no-nonsense way.

- Plus, tips on how to create a balanced look for your letters.

THREE MORE LETTER FORMATS

As we mentioned in the first chapter, even if your letters are technically correct, they won't present a professional image if they're unbalanced and badly arranged. Before we continue with the three other letter styles, we'd like to give you some pointers on how to set up attractive letters.

A Well-Balanced Appearance

Some office personnel can judge how long a letter will be just by glancing at their dictated notes. However, others may have more difficulty in deciding how to set up a letter. Here's how to go about it:

➡ **Estimate the length of the letter.** Count the number of words in three or four lines of your notes to find the average number of words per line. Multiply this number by the total number of lines to give you the approximate number of words in the letter.

➡ **Set margins.** If you're using a typewriter, the chart below can help you determine the pica and elite margin settings for letters of different lengths. (If you're using a word processing program, the margins you need may depend on several factors, i.e., the point size of your characters. Be sure to take these factors into account before printing out your letter.)

	short	average	long
For 8 1/2" x 11" sheet	(50-100 words)	(100-200 words)	(more than 200 words)
Elite 12 characters/inch	25 & 75	20 & 80	15 & 87
Pica 10 characters/inch	22 & 62	17 & 67	12 & 72

➡ **Position letter parts in proper places.** For a short letter, start the address about 22 lines from the top of the page. For an average letter, put the first line of the address on line 19 or 20. For a long letter, start the address about 17 or 18 lines from the top of the page. Subtract one line for each additional 25 words. Allow enough space for any ancillary elements, such as typist's initials, enclosure notation, and postscripts. And remember that you need to include a minimum of six lines of blank space at the bottom of a page.

➡ **Plan continuation sheets as carefully as the first.** If you have to type a multiple-page letter, try to break each page in the middle of the paragraph. The ideal breakpoint allows at least two or three lines of the same paragraph on both pages. Also, if your letter is more than two pages long, try to leave the same amount of space at the bottom of all but the last page of the letter.

➡ **Make a rough draft before you type a long or complicated letter.** That way you can readjust your margins and spacing to make sure the final version looks good.

BUREAU OF BUSINESS PRACTICE • PHONE 203-442-4365
PRENTICE HALL • **24 ROPE FERRY RD.** • **WATERFORD, CT 06386**

July 16, 19—

Ms. Patricia Casey
Gibson Secretarial School
27 Burgett Road
Decatur, IL 62521

Dear Ms. Casey:

This is a sample of the Full Block style letter. Many companies are adopting the Full Block style because it is even quicker and easier to type than the Modified Block style.

The Full Block style has been adopted as the standard letter style for the Bureau of Business Practice. We have reproduced it in our Employee Manual so that everyone will be familiar with the form and the instructions for its use.

As you can see, there are no indentations. Everything, including the date and the complimentary close, begins flush with the left margin.

An optional subject line, typed in all capitals, may be inserted two lines below the salutation.

Our dictation typists always use this form unless the dictator instructs otherwise. The dictator is at liberty to alter the form if a change is desirable for business reasons.

Sincerely,

Nancy Holder
Editorial Secretary

BUREAU OF BUSINESS PRACTICE • **PHONE 203-442-4365**
PRENTICE HALL • **24 ROPE FERRY RD.** • **WATERFORD, CT 06386**

August 24, 19—

Ms. Margaret Harris-Warren
Post Secondary School
121 Boston Post Road
Greenwich, CT 06830

SIMPLIFIED LETTER

As more businesses look for ways to save office costs, many
of them are turning to the Simplified Letter as an effective
format for business correspondence.

What is a Simplified Letter? You're reading a sample. Notice
the general positioning of the letter. The Full Block format
is used, but other modifications are also made. Both the
salutation and the complimentary close are omitted. The
inside address is typed flush left. A subject line is placed
between the address and the body of the letter and is typed
in all capital letters. The subject line gets straight to the
point of the letter and can be used as a filing reference.
The body of the letter is typed without paragraph indenta-
tion. And finally, the dictator's name and business title are
typed flush left on one line in all caps at the close of the
letter.

What does all this add up to? For the executive, a more read-
able piece of correspondence, and for the typist, a reduction
in keystrokes. Thus, the Simplified Letter saves time for
both.

Try the Simplified Letter with its compact style for greater
impact. It will save you time and money.

BELINDA CASE - EDITORIAL SECRETARY

June 24, 19—

Ms. Elizabeth Merrihew
Administrative Assistant
The Honeybee Company
1234 Molino Boulevard
Los Angeles, CA 90745

Dear Ms. Merrihew:

The Hanging-Indented Letter

This is an example of the Hanging-Indented Letter. The
      Hanging-Indented style provides a striking look and is
      most often used for advertising and product promotion
      letters.

The distinctive feature of the Hanging-Indented Letter is the
      paragraph alignment. The first line of each paragraph is
      typed flush with the left margin, but the following
      lines are indented five or six spaces from the left mar-
      gin.

The dateline is typed flush right. The inside address and
      salutation are typed flush left. A subject line is some-
      times placed between the salutation and the body of the
      letter to bring the subject of the letter to the read-
      er's immediate attention.

Unlike most other letter styles, the Hanging-Indented Letter
      was not designed as a time-saver. The format requires
      much tabbing and is not recommended for general corre-
      spondence.

Note that we have used mixed punctuation here; open punctua-
      tion may also be used. The complimentary close is
      aligned under the date, and we have left out the signa-
      ture block to give the letter an appearance of friendly
      informality. If any other notations are used, they are
      typed flush left.

Cordially,

LTP: mlr

ELEMENTS OF A BUSINESS LETTER

- Beginning in this chapter: a review of the basic letter parts.

- Some of the items we will cover: reference line, special mailing notations, and inside address.

- Also: current punctuation styles used in modern business letters.

Typing letters may be almost second nature to you—something you do so often that you don't really think about it. Well, take a minute to think about it. There are many rules to follow and many details to remember. That's what this and the next chapter are all about.

But before we go into the many different letter parts, we would like to discuss the two different styles of punctuation used in business letters today. These are the *open punctuation* and *mixed punctuation* styles.

Open Punctuation. The open punctuation style is always used with the Simplified Letter and may be used with any of the other letter styles we mentioned. Do not punctuate after the following:

- The dateline. But do put a comma between the day and year.
- The ends of the lines of the inside address, except after a company name that contains an abbreviation, such as *Inc.* or *Co.*
- The word *Attention* in the attention line, if one is used.
- The salutation, if one is used.
- The complimentary close, if one is used.
- The signature block.
- The enclosure notation, if one is used.
- The courtesy copy notation, if one is used.

Mixed Punctuation. The mixed punctuation style may be used with any of the Block-style, the Hanging-indented, and the Official letters:

- A colon follows the word *Attention* in the attention line.
- A colon follows the salutation.
- A comma follows the complimentary close.
- A colon or a period follows the enclosure notation, if one is used.
- A colon follows the courtesy copy notation, if one is used.

Do not mix punctuation styles within one letter. Choose one punctuation style and use that style consistently throughout.

DATELINE. The dateline consists of the month, typed in full, and the day and the year in Arabic numerals, separated by a comma.

Example: January 1, 19—

In U.S. military correspondence and in European correspondence, the parts of the dateline are in a different order: The day is first, followed by the month and the year. No punctuation is used.

Example: 1 January 19—

Ordinal numbers (1st, 22nd, 12th, etc.) should never be used in the dateline.

As you have seen in the six letter styles we showed you, the placement of the dateline varies from one letter style to another. Horizontally, it can be typed flush left, centered, slightly to right of center, or flush right. Vertically, the dateline may be placed two to six lines beneath the last line of the printed letterhead, depending on the length of the letter. However, many companies are adopting a standard of three lines between the last line of the letterhead and the dateline.

REFERENCE LINE. A reference line is included in a letter if the addressee requests it. It consists of an invoice, policy, or order number, and aids in the quick filing of a letter. Generally, it is single-spaced directly below the dateline.

Example: February 28, 19—
            V-802-62

SPECIAL MAILING INSTRUCTIONS AND ON-ARRIVAL NOTATIONS. Special mailing instructions, such as AIRMAIL (foreign mail only), SPECIAL DELIVERY, CERTIFIED MAIL, and REGISTERED MAIL, are typed in all capital letters, flush left, about four lines below the dateline and two lines above the first line of the inside address.

On-arrival notations, such as PERSONAL and CONFIDENTIAL, are typed in all capital letters, flush left, about four lines below the dateline and two lines above the first line of the inside address. If a special mailing instruction has been used, the on-arrival notation is typed directly beneath the mailing instruction (single-spaced), with two lines left between the on-arrival notation and the first line of the inside address. PERSONAL means that the letter so marked may be opened and read only by the addressee. CONFIDENTIAL means that the addressee and others authorized may open and read the letter.

Example: July 24, 19—

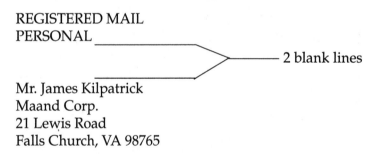

            REGISTERED MAIL
            PERSONAL _____
                                                    > —— 2 blank lines
                           _____

            Mr. James Kilpatrick
            Maand Corp.
            21 Lewis Road
            Falls Church, VA 98765

Vertical spacing may vary, according to the length of the letter.
Note: If special mailing instructions and on-arrival notations appear in the letter, they must also appear on the envelope. (Addressing envelopes will be covered in a later chapter.)

INSIDE ADDRESS. There are two basic stylings for the inside address. The following describe the inside address at its simplest:

When the letter is to an individual, the inside address contains:
   1. The addressee's courtesy title (*Mr., Mrs., Ms.,* or *Miss*) and full name on the first line.
   2. The addressee's business title, such as *Vice President*, on the second line.
   3. The company name on the third line.
   4. The street address, including the suite, apartment, or room number, on the fourth line.
   5. The city, state, and ZIP Code on the fifth line.

When the letter is to be sent to an organization, the inside address contains:
   1. The full company name on the first line.
   2. If necessary, a departmental designation, such as *Research and Development*,

on the second line.
3. The street address on the third line.
4. The city, state, and ZIP Code on the fourth line.

As we mentioned before, the address stylings above describe the inside address at its simplest. There are many details that accompany the inside address. Knowing how to handle these details correctly will distinguish you as a professional.

Placement. The first line of the inside address may be anywhere from three to twelve lines below the dateline, depending on other notations used (as the ones we discussed above) and the length of the letter.

Note: In the Simplified Letter, the inside address begins exactly three lines below the dateline.

Length. The inside address should be no more than five lines long, and none of the lines should extend beyond the middle of the page.

Courtesy Titles. We will restrict the meaning of "courtesy title" to the titles *Mr., Mrs., Ms.,* and *Miss.* The proper way to address people in different occupations is a subject that will be discussed in a later chapter. If the letter is addressed to an individual, that person's courtesy title and full name should appear on the first line of the inside address.

Example: Mr. Scott Handelman   Example: Ms. Susan Oldershaw

Business Titles. The addressee's business title should appear on the second line of the inside address. If the business title extends over the center of the page, it may be continued on the next line, indented two spaces. In this case, it is acceptable to have six lines in the inside address.

Example: Ms. Estrud Gilbert
            Assistant Vice President
                Product Development Group

If the name and business title are short enough to fit on one line without disturbing the balance of the letter, the business title may follow the addressee's name. The name and business title are separated by a comma.

Example: Mr. John Murphy, Dean
            The Rossington School

Company Names. If the letter is addressed to an individual, the name of the company where the addressee works is typed in full on the third line of the inside address. However, if the letter is addressed to the organization itself, the company name appears on the first line of the inside address, followed by a departmental designation (if there is one) on the second line.

Example: Ms. Nicole Russo   Example: Klee Publications
            Supervisory Editor   Art Department
            Klee Publications   1421 Broadway
            1421 Broadway   New York, NY 10019
            New York, NY 10019

Note: Abbreviations should not be used in business titles or in company names. However, if an abbreviation such as *Inc., Corp., Co.,* or *Ltd.* is used in the company's logo, it is acceptable to use it in the address.

Street Address. There is no one way to type a street address. For every secretarial manual that gives the "definitive" way to type a street address, there is another that will give a *different* "definitive" way to type the same address. Because of this, we will not give you any rules that are "carved in stone," but rather, we will suggest guidelines and let you make the decision about what looks best. Your company may have its own preference as to how this should be done. If it does, you should follow its rules.

- Building numbers are typed in numerals unless the building number is *One—*.
  Example: One McMahon Drive   Example: 1580 Surrey Circle

- Numbered street names may be spelled in full, or Arabic numerals may be used. However, to save time and space, authorities suggest that only street names numbered one through twelve should be spelled in full. Arabic numerals should be used for street numbers above twelve. Ordinals may be used.
  Example: 700 West 57th St.   Example: 1356 Seventh Avenue

Note: The words *Street, Avenue, Drive,* etc., are usually typed in full—not abbreviated. However, if the street name is a numbered one and you choose to type it in Arabic numerals, you may also abbreviate the word *Street* or *Avenue* as shown above.

- If a suite, apartment, or room number is necessary, it is typed on the same line as the street address, two spaces after the last word of the address.
  Example: 77 Broadway Suite 4

City, State, and ZIP Code. The city, state, and ZIP Code are typed on the last line of the inside address. City names are typed in full—not abbreviated. Two-part city names, such as *Point Judith* and *Fort Myers,* should also be typed in full. The only exception is for city names with the word *Saint* in them, such as *St. Paul* and *St. Louis.* The name of the state is typed in the capitalized, two-letter abbreviation recommended by the U.S. Postal Service, followed by one space and the ZIP Code.
  Example: Point Judith, RI 02321

ATTENTION LINE. An attention line is used when a letter addressed to an organization or group must be brought to the attention of a particular individual within that group. It is typed two lines below the inside address and two lines above the salutation. In the Full Block and Simplified Letter styles, the attention line must be typed flush left. In the other letter styles, it may be typed flush left or centered. The word *attention* is typed in full—not abbreviated. The first letter of the word *attention* should be capitalized.

Example: D & B Associates
         454 Bayside Drive
         New Haven, CT 06520

         Attention: Mr. Henry Parker

         Gentlemen:

Note: To address letters for use with window envelopes according to the U. S. Postal Service regulations for automated mailing, type the attention line on the *second* line of the inside address. In this case, the entire inside address should be typed in all caps, without any punctuation, and the U.S. Postal Service abbreviations should be used. If a company's mail is delivered to a post office box, the box number is typed on the next-to-last line of the inside address.

Example: D B ASSOCIATES   MR HENRY PARKER
            ATTN MR HENRY PARKER   454 BAYSIDE DRIVE
            454 BAYSIDE DRIVE   PO BOX 101
            NEW HAVEN CT 06520   NEW HAVEN CT 06520

- The rest of what you need to know about the basic parts of a business letter.

- Covered in this chapter: salutation, subject line, body, and continuation sheets.

- Also: complimentary close, signature block, writer's and typist's initials, enclosure and courtesy copy notations, and postscript.

LETTER PARTS

SALUTATION. As we mentioned in the last chapter, determining the correct way to address people in different occupations is a complicated matter. Here, we will give you only the most basic information on salutations. Proper forms of address will be discussed in a later chapter.

The salutation appears in every letter style but the Simplified Letter. It is always typed flush left, two lines below the last line of the inside address or two lines below the attention line if there is one. The first letter of the salutation is capitalized. A comma follows the salutation only in personal, informal correspondence.

If you are not directly addressing the person to whom you are writing, there are several forms of address that are commonly used today:

- *Gentlemen* or *Ladies* if you know that the group you are addressing is all male or all female.
- *Ladies and Gentlemen* if you know that the group you are addressing is both male and female.
- To avoid the dilemma of incorrectly addressing someone whose gender is unknown, many companies now use the addressee's business title in the salutation.
  Example: Dear Sales Manager
  Example: Dear Editor
- The practice of directly addressing a department or a division is also becoming more common.
  Example: Dear Public Relations Department
- Another completely acceptable way of avoiding the problem of how to address an unknown addressee is to use the Simplified Letter, which leaves out the salutation entirely.

Note: Two familiar salutations that are no longer recommended are *Dear Sir* and *To Whom It May Concern. Dear Sir* is archaic, and *To Whom It May Concern* is too impersonal.

SUBJECT LINE. The subject line is used to bring the subject of the letter to the reader's immediate attention. It is typed two lines below the salutation and two lines above the first line of the body of the letter. It is typed flush left in Full Block and Simplified Letters, but it may be centered in Semiblock or Modified Block Letters. The subject line may be introduced by the word *subject*. Even if you're using open punctuation, the word *subject* should be followed by a colon. You can type *subject* in all caps or you can capitalize only the *S*. The words following the colon may also be typed in all caps, or the first letter of each word may be capitalized. If you don't type *subject* in all caps, then you shouldn't type the words that follow in all caps either.

Example: SUBJECT: NEW PRODUCT DEVELOPMENT STRATEGY
Example: Subject: New Product Development Strategy

Note: In the Simplified Letter, the subject line is a mandatory element, typed flush left, four lines below the inside address and four lines above the first line of the body of the letter. It is *not* introduced by the word *subject*. It is typed in all capital letters.

Example: NEW PRODUCT DEVELOPMENT STRATEGY

BODY. The body of the letter begins two lines below the salutation or two lines below the subject line if there is one. The message is single-spaced with double-spacing between paragraphs. However, if a letter is extremely short, the message may be double-spaced. If this is the case, the first line of each paragraph should be indented five or six spaces. In the Full Block, Modified Block, and Simplified Letters, the first line of each paragraph begins flush left. In the Semiblock Letter, the first line of each paragraph is indented five to ten spaces. In the Official Letter, it is indented five or six spaces. In the Hanging-indented Letter, each paragraph begins flush left, with subsequent lines indented five or six spaces. (See Sample Letters in Chapters 1 and 2.)

If the body of the letter contains a table, an enumerated list, or quoted material longer than six lines, set this material off from the rest of the letter by indenting it five to ten spaces from both the left and the right margin. Double-space before and after this material; single-space within it. Double-space between enumerated items.

CONTINUATION SHEETS. If a letter is too long to fit on one page, a continuation sheet must be typed. Use blank paper that matches the letterhead in color, weight, size, and texture. At least three lines of the message must appear on the continuation sheet. Never should the complimentary close and the salutation appear alone. The left and right margins match those used on the first page of the letter. Leave at least six blank lines of space at the top of the continuation sheet. The continuation sheet heading may be typed flush left on three single-spaced lines containing the page number on the first line, the name of the addressee on the second line, and the date on the third line. If a reference line appears on the first page of the letter, it must be typed on the fourth line of the continuation sheet heading.

Example: Page 2
            Mr. Richard Rogers
            July 14, 19—

Note: This style is required with Full Block and Simplified Letters.

The continuation sheet heading may also be typed straight across the top of the page with the addressee's name beginning flush left, the page number in Arabic numerals centered and enclosed by two hyphens, and the date flush right. If a reference line is used, it is typed under the dateline.

Example: Miss Mary Englebreit   -2-   April 29, 19—
                                                      ME CAL 9.87

Note: This style is used with the Modified Block, Semiblock, and Hanging-indented Letters.

For both heading styles, the body of the letter is typed four lines below the heading.

COMPLIMENTARY CLOSE. The complimentary close is used in all letter styles but the Simplified Letter. It appears two lines below the last line of the message. In Official, Semiblock, and Modified Block Letters, the complimentary close is typed slightly to the right of the center of the page. In the Hanging-indented Letter, the complimentary close is aligned under the date. In the Full Block Letter, the complimentary close is typed flush left. (See Sample Letters in Chapters 1 and 2.) Capitalize the first word of the complimentary close. Punctuate the complimentary close according to the punctuation style you have chosen for the entire letter.

Although the complimentary close is one of the shortest elements of the letter, it is an important one. The words with which the writer closes the letter reflect both the tone of the letter and the relationship between the writer and the recipient. Different complimentary closes indicate varying degrees of formality. The following list is a sampling of the kinds of complimentary closes you can use and each one's degree of formality.

Informal/Personal—As ever, Best wishes, Kindest regards
Informal/Friendly—Cordially, Cordially yours
Polite/Neutral—Sincerely, Most sincerely, Sincerely yours
Formal—Respectfully, Very respectfully, Respectfully yours

Note: Over a period of time, a writer may relax his or her style according to the relationship established with the recipient. Thus the writer's first letters might use a more formal complimentary close, whereas later letters may use a more informal one. Once a writer has begun using an informal complimentary close, he or she should not revert to a formal one.

SIGNATURE BLOCK. The signature block contains the writer's name on the first line and his or her business title on the second line (if it doesn't appear in the printed letterhead). The name of the writer should be typed exactly as the writer signs his or her name. The signature block is typed four lines below the complimentary close and is aligned with the complimentary close.

Example: Sincerely yours,

— 3 blank lines

Edward Woodward
Managing Editor

In the Simplified Letter, the signature block takes a different format. It is typed in all capital letters flush left, five lines below the last line of the message. The writer's name and business title appear on one line separated by a hyphen or a comma.
Example: EDWARD WOODWARD - MANAGING EDITOR

Note: In the Official Letter and the Hanging-indented Letter, the signature block may be left out to give a more informal look. A written signature is always necessary.

IDENTIFICATION LINE. The identification line consists of the writer's initials in all capitals followed by the typist's initials in lowercase. The two can be separated by a colon or slash typed flush left, two lines below the signature block.
Example: MAV:mrp   Example: IAZ/rwe

Many companies include the identification line only on the file copy of the letter for use as a filing reference. Others retain the typist's initials on the original letter, but not the writer's, since the writer's name appears in the signature block.

ENCLOSURE NOTATIONS. If enclosures are to accompany the letter, an enclosure notation should appear one or two lines beneath the identification line or the signature block if an identification line is not used. The enclosure notation is typed flush left. The word *enclosure* may be typed in full, with the first letter capitalized. The form of enclosure notation depends on the punctuation style you have chosen for the letter.

Example: *Mixed Punctuation*   *Open Punctuation*
           Enclosure   Enclosure
           Enclosures: 2   2 Enclosures

The word *enclosure* may also be abbreviated and typed in the following ways:

Example:	Mixed Punctuation	Open Punctuation
	enc.	enc
	encl.	encl
	encs.	encs
	2 encs.	2 encs

Note: If the letter contains more than one important enclosure, they should be enumerated and briefly described. In this case, it is not necessary to type the number of enclosures. Make sure each enclosure is clearly identifiable by labeling it with the same description that is in the enclosure list in the letter.

    Example: Enclosures: 1. New Client List
                                2. Profit and Loss Statement

COURTESY COPY NOTATION. The courtesy copy notation is used if copies of the letter are being sent to people other than the addressee. In all letter styles, this notation is typed flush left, two lines under the signature block or two lines under any other notations that are used. The courtesy copy notation may be typed in full or in abbreviated form, using capital or lowercase letters.

    Example: Copies to   Copy to   CC   cc

Punctuate according to the punctuation style you have chosen for the letter.

    There are several ways to identify the recipients of the copies. You may use only the initials typed in all caps, the courtesy title and surname, or the full name. The recipients are listed in alphabetical order, single-spaced.

    Example: cc PMB   cc Ms. Annello   cc Philip Brady
                       DAK   Mr. Cheatham   John T. Oat

A courtesy copy notation may be directed to an entire group.

    Example: cc Editorial   cc Sales Managers

    When the writer chooses to give the copy recipients' addresses as well as their names, type the names and addresses as they would appear on an inside address of a letter. Each name and address is single-spaced, but double-space between different recipients.

    Example: cc Mr. Ryan Hampstead
                    Salmon Brook Road
                    East Hartford, CT 06124

                    Ms. Patricia Quay
                    1450 Madison Avenue Suite 4
                    New York, NY 10012

    If the copy recipient is to receive any enclosures, the number of enclosures should be typed in parentheses after the recipient's name, followed by a description of that enclosure. For several enclosures, follow the multiple enclosure procedure described above.

    Example: cc Laura Harmon (1 copy, New Client List)
                    1 City Place Suite 24
                    Boston, MA 02134

Blind Copy Notation. Sometimes the writer will send copies of a letter to other recipients without revealing this action to the original addressee. In this case, the blind copy notation *bcc* is used. It is typed only on the copies in the same place as the *cc* notation and punctuated according to the punctuation style used for the letter.

Note: Copies are not usually signed by the writer; however, the writer's typed signature does appear preceded by /S/ or /s/, signifying that the original was signed.

POSTSCRIPT. A postscript is typed two to four lines below the last notation. It is single-spaced, and the format follows the overall style of the letter. The letters *PS* may be omitted; the writer should initial the postscript.

- What's just as important as typing a perfect letter? Read on to find out.

- Details, details, details. Find out how good you are at keeping track of them.

- With this quiz, test what you've learned in the first four chapters.

TIME TO TEST YOUR SKILLS

There are so many details to keep track of when you're typing letters. And the more details there are, the more mistakes you can make. Just as important as being able to type a perfect letter is being able to catch your mistakes. In the following quiz, you will have the chance to find out how much you remember about what you've learned in the first four chapters.

▼ ▼ TAKE A TEST ▼ ▼

The following letter is typed in the Semiblock style. Find as many errors as you can, and mark the corrections right here in the chapter. But watch out! There are many kinds of mistakes in this letter—not just "letter specific" ones. Then check your answers against ours.

```
 1                                    September 9th, 19—
 2
 3
 4    Mr. Patrick Seldes, Mgr.
 5    Worldwide Importers Incorporated
 6    29 Phelan Avenue P.O. Box 6504
 7    San Francisco, California, 94112
 8
 9
10    Dear Sir:
11
12    I now have the L.A. figures and am ready to compare the
13    updated lists with those of your organization. I am
14    enclosing a sample copy for your review.
15       I'd like to get together with you to discuss this matter
16    before the end of the month. Either 9/26 or 9/27 is good for
17    me. Please let my secretary know which date is convenient
18    for you. (If you don't have either date aviable, we can
19    make arrangements to meet at another time).
20       There's a trade show at the Palladio Convention Center
21    on Monday. I hope to see you then—if nothing else comes up,
22    and we'll talk more.
23
24    Yours Truly,
25
26
27    Ms. Angela Biedermeyer
28
29
```

CORRECTIONS

Line 1: Ordinal numbers should not be used in the dateline; therefore, "September 9" should not be followed by "th."

Line 4: When using a business title, such as Manager, in an inside address, type it in full; don't abbreviate it. The business title follows the individual's name and is typed on the same line or on the following line, depending on the title's length.

Line 6: The post office box number, when used, should appear on a line by itself. The post office delivers mail to the destination that is on the last two lines of the address. If the addressee's company has mail delivered to the post office, the post office box number should appear on the second-to-last line of the inside address. If the addressee's company has mail delivered to the street address (in this case, 29 Phelan Avenue), the post office box number should be one line above the street address. So, depending on where the addressee's company receives its mail, the post office box number should appear by itself on line 6 or line 7 and the street address should also appear on a line by itself.

Line 7: No comma should appear before the ZIP Code. California should be abbreviated using the USPS two-letter abbreviation CA.

Line 9: The body of the letter is separated from the inside address by only one blank line. Therefore, the body of the letter should start on this line rather than on the next line.

Line 10: When an individual is addressed by name in the inside address, he or she should also be addressed by name in the salutation. In this case, the salutation should read "Dear Mr. Seldes."

Line 12: Because this is a letter in Semiblock style, the first line of the paragraph should be indented five spaces.

Line 12: Avoid abbreviations unless they're obviously preferable to the longer version of the word or words being abbreviated. "L.A." should be typed out as "Los Angeles."

Line 15: One blank line should be left between paragraphs. The paragraph that starts on line 15 should start on line 16. Also, it should be indented five spaces.

Line 16: The month should be typed out as a word, not left as a figure. It should read "September 26 or 27."

Line 18: The word "available" is misspelled. The "a" and the "i" are transposed. The word should be spelled "available."

Line 19: The period belongs inside the closing parenthesis. When an expression is complete and independent of the preceding sentence, the entire expression and its punctuation go inside the parentheses.

Line 20: Again, one blank line should be left between paragraphs. The paragraph that starts on line 20 should start on line 21. Also, it should be indented five spaces.

Line 21: Another dash instead of a comma should be used to end the parenthetical material. The example should read "—if nothing else comes up—." And remember, because this sentence construction falls at the end of the line in the letter, the second dash should end that line, not begin the next one.

Line 24: The complimentary close should begin slightly to the right of the center of the page.

Line 24: The "t" in "Yours truly" should be lowercase.

Line 27: Three blank lines should appear between the complimentary close and the typed signature; therefore, the typed signature should appear on line 28.

Line 29: An enclosure notation should appear on this line, since enclosures were mentioned in the letter.

- Do you know how to address a letter to a rabbi? a professor? a professional engineer? If not, help is here.

- In what part of a letter does a person's professional rating appear? This is where you'll find the answer.

- Some of the titles covered in this chapter are courtesy titles, honorifics, academic degrees, and more.

FORMS OF ADDRESS—PART I

Most people who hold a title, a professional affiliation, or an academic degree are proud to have those titles or affiliations attached to their names. Not being sensitive or knowledgeable enough to know when and where to use these titles can cause offense. Here's a detailed rundown of how to use these titles.

Courtesy Titles: Mr., Mrs., Miss, Ms.

Appear: envelope, inside address, salutation
Precede: full name or surname only
Mr. Jonathan Campbell, Miss Campbell
Separated from name by comma: no
Special Rules: Mr. is never used in the typed or the written signature. Mrs., Miss, and Ms. are optional in the typed signature, but they must be enclosed in parentheses.
(Miss) Adele Johnston
Mrs., Miss, and Ms. are used in the typed signature when the woman has a preference about being addressed as Miss, Mrs., or Ms.
Mrs., Miss, and Ms. are never used in the written signature.
Never use Ms. with a woman's married name.
Ms. Janet Litz, not *Ms. David Arwood*
Plurals: *Mr.—Messrs.   Mrs.—Mesdames*
Miss—Misses   Ms.—Mses., Mss.

Professional Ratings and Affiliations: P.E., C.P.S., A.I.A., etc.

Appear: envelope, inside address, optional in typed signature
Follow: surname
Separated from name by comma: yes
Used with courtesy titles: no
Special Rules: They are never used in the written signature. They are not necessary in the typed signature if they appear in the printed letterhead.

Academic Degrees: M.D., D.D.S., D.V.M., Ph.D., D.D., etc.

Appear: envelope, inside address, typed and written signature
Follow: surname
Separated from name by comma: yes
Used with courtesy titles: no
Jeanne Kelly, Ph.D., not *Mrs. Jeanne Kelly, Ph.D.*
Dr. Kirkpatrick, not *Dr. Kirkpatrick, M.D.*

Professor (Prof.)

Appears: envelope, inside address, salutation
Precedes: full name or surname only
Professor James Wilson, Professor Wilson
Separated from name by comma: no
Used with courtesy titles: no
Professor James Wilson, not *Mr. Wilson, Professor*
Special Rules: Avoid abbreviating when using with surname only.
Professor Brock, not *Prof. Brock*
Use *Professor* in the salutation when it's followed by a surname.
Dear Professor Brock, not *Dear Professor*
Never use *Professor* in the typed or the written signature.
Plural: When addressing more than one professor at once, do not abbreviate the word *professor.*

Professors Brock and Edwards, not *Profs. Brock and Edwards*

The Reverend (The Rev.)

Appears: envelope, inside address, optional in typed signature
Precedes: full name or surname
Separated from name by comma: no
Used with courtesy titles: yes
Special Rules: A first name or a courtesy title *must* intervene between *The Reverend* and the surname.
The Reverend Miss Ward, The Reverend Ann Ward, The Reverend Dr. Ward, not *The Reverend Ward*
Never use *The Reverend* in the written signature.
Do not use *The Reverend* in the salutation.
Use Mrs., Miss, Mr., Dr., Father, Chaplain, etc., in the salutation.
Dear Miss Ward, not *Dear Reverend* or *Dear Reverend Ann Ward*
Plural: *The Reverends, The Revs.*

Rabbi

Appears: envelope, inside address, salutation, typed or written signature
Precedes: full name or surname
Rabbi David Gold, Rabbi Gold
Separated from name by comma: no
Used with courtesy titles: no
Special Rules: It is permissible to use *Rabbi* or *Dr.* in the salutation.
Dear Rabbi Gold, Dear Dr. Gold
Plural: *Rabbis*

Esquire (Esq.)

Who uses: Attorneys, Consular Corps, architects, professional engineers, Justices of the Peace
Appears: envelope, inside address, typed signature
Follows: surname
Separated from name by comma: yes
Used with courtesy titles: no
Marilyn Kapstan, Esq., not *Dr. Marilyn Kapstan, Esq.*, or *Ms. Marilyn Kapstan, Esq.*
Used with business title: yes, the addressee's business title may appear on the next line
Marilyn Kapstan, Esq.
Attorney-at-law
Special Rules: Esq. is never used in the written signature.
Plural: Esqs.

The Honorable (The Hon.)

Who uses: Any high-ranking appointed or elected officials, such as judges, representatives, senators, governors, and the President and the Vice President of the United States
Appears: envelope, inside address
Precedes: full name
Separated from name by comma: no
Used with courtesy titles: yes. But drop the courtesy title when the addressee's full name is used.
The Honorable (Mr., Miss, Ms., Mrs.) Pax
The Honorable Dr. Pax
The Honorable Roberta Pax
Used with business title: yes
Special Rules: A first name, an initial, or a courtesy title *must* intervene between *The Honorable* and the surname.
The Honorable R. Pax, not *The Honorable Pax*
This title is retained even after the person no longer holds the office.
The Honorable is never used in the typed or the written signature.
Plural: The Hons.

FORMS OF ADDRESS—PART II

In the last chapter, we discussed the importance of using proper forms of address in written correspondence. In this chapter, we continue that subject, covering military ranks or ratings and government officials.

Military Ranks or Ratings

The proper use in written correspondence of military ranks and ratings can be mind-boggling. The following rules are organized according to where such titles appear in a letter.

Note: Titles of officers are the same in the Army, the Air Force, and the Marine Corps. (The exception to this rule is the top rank in the Marine Corps. It is *Commandant of the Marine Corps.*)

Envelope, Inside Address
Precede: full name
Followed by: comma and branch of service (abbreviated)
Used with courtesy titles: no
Abbreviations for branches of service:

United States Navy—USN   United States Air Force—USAF
United States Army—USA   United States Coast Guard—USCG
United States Marine Corps—USMC

Note: Abbreviations for branches of service are typed in all capital letters with no punctuation.

Captain Robert Stalle, USAF   Capt Robert Stalle, USAF/USMC
CAPT Robert Stalle, USN/USCG   CPT Robert Stalle, USA

Note: The abbreviations for ranks and ratings vary from one branch of service to another and are too exhaustive to be covered in this chapter. In the examples used here, we have tried to give a balanced representation from each branch. Where slashes and two branches of the service appear, the abbreviations given apply to both. In general, abbreviations for ranks and ratings are used with no punctuation.

Salutation
Precede: surname
General form: Dear (rank/rating) surname

Dear Commander Stalle   Dear Corporal Stalle
Dear General Stalle   Dear Private Stalle

Special Rules: When ranks and ratings appear in the salutation, they are never abbreviated.

For warrant officers and noncommissioned Army officers and for all Navy ranks below commander, the courtesy title and surname are used in the salutation. However, if the addressee is a female, the rank or rating may be used in the salutation.

Chief Warrant Officer USAF/USA—Dear Mr./Ms. Stalle
Ensign USCG/USN—Dear Mr./Ms. Stalle
Cadet (Air Force, Army, Coast Guard Academies)—Dear Cadet Stalle or Dear Mr./Ms. Stalle
Midshipman (Naval Academy)—Dear Midshipman Stalle or Dear Mr./Ms. Stalle

Typed Signature
Follow: full name
Separated from name by comma: yes

Followed by: comma and branch of service (abbreviated)
Used with courtesy titles: no
Special rules: The above rules apply when abbreviations for ranks and ratings are used in the typed signature.

Commander—Robert M. Stalle, CDR, USN/USCG
Warrant Officer—Robert M. Stalle, WO, USAF/USA
Major—Robert M. Stalle, Maj, USAF/USMC   Robert M. Stalle, MAJ, USA

Note: If the rank or rating is spelled out in full, it should appear one line below the full name. In this case, the rank or rating should be followed by a comma and the abbreviation for the branch of service.

Robert M. Stalle
Captain, USAF/USMC/USA/USN/USCG

Federal, State, and Local Government Officials

Senator, U.S. and State
Title: The Honorable
Followed by: If U.S.—*United States Senate*
              If state—*The State Senate* or *The Senate of* _____
Salutation: *Dear Senator Michaels*

Representative, U.S. Congress and State (state includes assemblyman, delegate)
Title: The Honorable
Followed by: If U.S.—*United States House of Representatives*
              If state—*House of Representatives* or *The State Assembly* or *The House of Delegates*
Salutation: *Dear Mr./Ms. Michaels* or *Dear Representative Michaels*

Governor
Title: The Honorable
Followed by: *Governor of* _____ or *The Governor of* _____
Salutation: *Dear Governor Michaels*
Note: In some states, the Governor is referred to as *His/Her Excellency.*

Judge—Federal, State, and Local
Title: The Honorable
Followed by: If federal—*Judge of the United States, District Court for the* _____, *District of* _____
              If state—*Judge of the* _____ *Court* or *Judge of the Court of* _____
              If local—*Judge of the Court of* _____ or *Judge of the* _____ *Court*
Salutation: *Dear Judge Michaels*
Note: The above titles are not used in the written signature. However, they do appear in the typed signature one line below the typed name.

Edward Michaels   *Edward Michaels*
United States Senator   *Governor*

Alderman
Title: The Honorable
Followed by: *Alderman* or *Alderman Edward/Ellen Michaels*
Salutation: *Dear Mr./Ms. Michaels* or *Dear Alderman Michaels*

Mayor
Title: The Honorable
Followed by: Mayor of _____
Salutation: *Dear Mayor Michaels*

- The U.S. Postal Service has an approved format for the address block of an envelope. Find out the details here.

- In this chapter: the answers to such questions as *Should envelope addresses be typed in all capital letters? in uppercase and lowercase? Do you need punctuation?*

- Do you know the proper abbreviations for such words as *expressway*, *junction*, and *memorial*? You will after you read this chapter.

TYPING ENVELOPES

To speed mail processing, the U.S. Postal Service (USPS) has installed Optical Character Readers (OCRs) and Bar Code Sorters (BCSs) in post offices throughout the country. If businesses expect to reap the benefits of this technology, it is important that they cooperate with the USPS to make their address formats as compatible as possible with the Postal Service's electronic equipment.

If you want your mail to be processed quickly, your best bet is to use the addressing format recommended by the U.S. Postal Service. But do you even know what that format looks like?

▼ ▼ TAKE A TEST ▼ ▼

On the envelope below, there are several mistakes. See if you can spot them, and make a note of them on the blank lines below the envelope.

MS MARJORIE JAMES
694 PARK AVE
OAKLAND CA 94611

SAINT THOMAS HOSPITAL
2914 PARK SLOPE HEIGHTS
PHILADELPHIA PN 19123

ATTENTION: GENERAL ADMISSIONS DESK

1. _____
2. _____
3. _____
4. _____

1. The attention line should be in the second line of the address.
2. The word *attention* should be abbreviated to ATTN.
3. Ideally, each line in the address should take up no more than 22 horizontal spaces (including the blanks). The Postal Service offers a list of accepted abbreviations for many commonly used designations. For instance, the words PARK and HEIGHTS can be abbreviated to PK and HTS.
4. The proper abbreviation for Pennsylvania is PA.

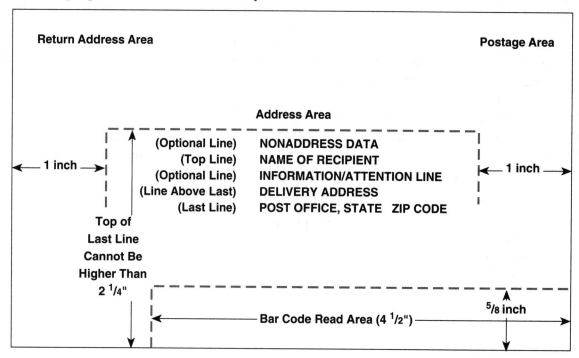

The illustration above shows exactly how an envelope should be typed so that it can be processed by the Postal Service's electronic equipment.

Guidelines for Addressing Envelopes

Envelopes should be no smaller than $3\frac{1}{2}''$ x $5''$ and no bigger than $6\frac{1}{8}''$ x $11\frac{1}{2}''$. The proper positioning of the address block is crucial if the Postal Service's electronic equipment is to be taken advantage of. To make it easy for you to know exactly where to place the address block, the Postal Service has designated a special OCR Read Area on the envelope. The boundaries of this area are shown on the sample envelope above, as are the boundaries of the Bar Code Read Area.

- Nothing may appear within 1 inch of both the left and right edges of the envelope.
- Nothing should appear in the Bar Code Read Area ($4\frac{1}{2}$ inches from the right edge of the envelope and $\frac{5}{8}$ inch up from the bottom edge of the envelope).
- The top of the last line of the address block (post office, state, ZIP Code) must be no higher than $2\frac{1}{4}$ inches from the bottom edge of the envelope.
- The address block must be parallel to the bottom edge of the envelope. (Nothing in the address block should be at a slant.)
- The last two lines of the address block are the most important. The delivery address must be included in the next-to-last line (consisting of either the post office

box number and station, if there is one, or the street address—the actual *place* of delivery). The town or city, state, and ZIP Code must appear in the last line. So that the OCR does not mistake anything else for the last line of the address block, *absolutely* no other printing or marks of any other kind should appear below this line.

• As we mentioned above, the space designated as the Bar Code Read Area must also be clear of all printing or marks. The reason for this is that once the OCR reads the address, it prints a bar code representing that ZIP Code in the Bar Code Read Area. This bar code is then used to further speed up the electronic processing of the mail.

How to Type the Address

Now that you know where to type the address block, you need to know exactly how to type it so that the OCR can read it.

➤ The address block must be typed or machine printed for the OCR to be able to recognize the letters. All capital letters are *preferred* but not required.

➤ Punctuation *may* be left out to save space. This includes leaving out the comma between the city and the state in the last line of the address block.

➤ One or two (horizontal) spaces should be used between elements (numbers and words) in the address. Anything larger than two horizontal spaces will not be read by the OCR.

➤ Use only abbreviations that have been approved by the U.S. Postal Service. (See the next page.)

➤ Single-space (vertically) the lines in the address block. Never type the address block at an angle. (Make sure that the address block is parallel to the top and bottom edges of the envelope.)

➤ The importance of properly typing the last line of the address block cannot be stressed enough. The city or town name, the USPS-approved two-letter state abbreviation, and the ZIP Code must appear in the last line of the address. Use the Postal Service's approved abbreviations for designations, such as *Street, Road, Parkway*, and *Saint*. (See the next page for a list of some of the most commonly used designations.)

➤ The address block format for Canadian addresses is a bit different from the format for United States addresses. The first lines of the address (the addressee's name, company name—if there is one—and street address) are typed in uppercase and lowercase rather than in all capital letters. If you are mailing a letter *to* Canada from *within* Canada, type both the city or town name and the two-letter province abbreviation (see the next page) on the next-to-last line in all capital letters. On the last line, type the six-character Canadian Postal Code.

Note: If you are mailing to Canada from *outside* Canada, type CANADA in all capital letters below the six-character Canadian Postal Code. This will then be the last line of the address block.

Example: *from within Canada*

    Ms. Willa Hempstead
    Edward Robeson, Inc.
    291 Crescent Parkway
    VICTORIA BC
    V8S 1J2

from outside Canada

Ms. Willa Hempstead
Edward Robeson, Inc.
291 Crescent Parkway
VICTORIA BC
V8S 1J2
CANADA

APPROVED U.S. POSTAL SERVICE ABBREVIATIONS

United States and Dependencies

Alabama	AL	Kentucky	KY	Ohio	OH
Alaska	AK	Louisiana	LA	Oklahoma	OK
Arizona	AZ	Maine	ME	Oregon	OR
Arkansas	AR	Maryland	MD	Pennsylvania	PA
California	CA	Massachusetts	MA	Puerto Rico	PR
Colorado	CO	Michigan	MI	Rhode Island	RI
Connecticut	CT	Minnesota	MN	South Carolina	SC
Delaware	DE	Mississippi	MS	South Dakota	SD
District of Columbia	DC	Missouri	MO	Tennessee	TN
Florida	FL	Montana	MT	Texas	TX
Georgia	GA	Nebraska	NE	Utah	UT
Guam	GU	Nevada	NV	Vermont	VT
Hawaii	HI	New Hampshire	NH	Virginia	VA
Idaho	ID	New Jersey	NJ	Virgin Islands	VI
Illinois	IL	New Mexico	NM	Washington	WA
Indiana	IN	New York	NY	West Virginia	WV
Iowa	IA	North Carolina	NC	Wisconsin	WI
Kansas	KS	North Dakota	ND	Wyoming	WY

Canadian Provinces

Alberta	AB	Newfoundland	NF	Quebec	PQ
British Columbia	BC	Northwest Territories	NT	Saskatchewan	SK
Labrador	LB	Nova Scotia	NS	Yukon Territory	YT
Manitoba	MB	Ontario	ON		
New Brunswick	NB	Prince Edward Island	PE		

Often-Used Designations

Academy	ACAD	Freeway	FWY	Plaza	PLZ
Agency	AGNCY	Grand	GRND	Point	PT
Airport	ARPRT	Grove	GRV	Ridge	RDG
Avenue	AVE	Highway	HWY	River	RIV
Boulevard	BLVD	Hill	HL	Road	RD
Branch	BR	Hills	HLS	Rural	R
Bypass	BYP	Hospital	HOSP	Saint	ST
Center	CTR	House	HSE	Santa	SN
Central	CTL	Institute	INST	School	SCH
Church	CHR	Junction	JCT	Seminary	SMNRY
Circle	CIR	Landing	LNDG	South	S
City	CY	Lane	LN	Square	SQ
Club	CLB	Meeting	MTG	State	ST
College	CLG	Memorial	MEM	Station	STA
Corner	COR	Middle	MDL	Street	ST
Corners	CORS	Mile	MLE	Terminal	TERM
Court	CT	Mount	MT	Terrace	TER
Courts	CTS	Mountain	MTN	Tower	TWR
Depot	DPO	National	NAT	Town	TWN
Drive	DR	New	NW	Tunnel	TUNL
East	E	North	N	Turnpike	TPKE
Estates	EST	Park	PK	Union	UN
Expressway	EXPY	Parkway	PKY	University	UNIV
Extension	EXT	Place	PL	Valley	VLY
Fort	FT	Plain	PLN	West	W

MEMORABLE MEMOS

In the preceding chapters, we have stressed how important it is that
your letters be perfect in every way. Your knowledge (or lack of it) makes
a strong impression on others about your company. But a memo is a "letter" that stays within the company. Thus you may be tempted to slack off
a bit. After all, the people who will be receiving the memo work at the
same place you do, so you might think that their impressions are already
formed and your memo won't make a difference in how they feel about
the company.

While a memo may be directed to someone whose opinion of the company is already formed, that person may not yet have an opinion of you
or your boss. Your memo shows others how you feel about your company. A carelessly typed memo can give someone a less than positive
impression of you and your boss.

The memo is a means of sending written communication within an
organization. The memo uses a simple two-part format:

(1) The heading, consisting of the guidewords *TO, FROM, DATE,* and
SUBJECT.

(2) The body or the message.

TO identifies the individuals or groups that will receive the memo.

FROM indicates the name of the writer.

DATE gives the month, day, and year on which the memo was written.

SUBJECT, usually one line, succinctly gives the gist of the message.

A memo is usually typed on standard 8½" x 11" paper, but half-size
paper (8½" x 5½") may also be used. Many companies use preprinted
memo forms. The arrangement of the heading may differ from form to
form and from company to company. If your company does not use
preprinted forms or give any guidelines as to its preferences, you may
have to set up a memo yourself. A standard format for a memo is
described below.

THE HEADING

As we just mentioned, the arrangement of the heading does differ,
depending on your company's preferences or the form you use. In this
chapter, we show you the standard arrangement.

The guidewords should be typed in capital letters and followed by a
colon. Use 1- to 1½-inch margins. You may align the guidewords to the
right and begin the fill-ins three spaces to the right of the colons. Or you
can align the guidewords to the left and begin the fill-ins three spaces to
the right of the longest guideword (in most cases, this is the word *SUB-
JECT*).

TO:	Mariane Connors	TO:	M. Cross
FROM:	Robert Talbott	FROM:	L. Fendi
DATE:	January 5, 19—	DATE:	January 5, 19—
SUBJECT:	Holiday Pay	SUBJECT:	Design Change

TO-Line. A memo may be addressed to one person, to several different people, or to a group of people.

TO: *James Michelin*   TO: *Jan Krieger*
                                        James Michelin
TO: *Sales Department*   *Brett Savoy*

Type the recipients' names in full or use initials and surnames. Be consistent; don't type one person's name in full and another person's name with initials.

TO: *Annette P. Foucher*   TO: *A. P. Foucher*

You may use a job title or a department name in the TO-line:

TO: *James Michelin*   TO: *James Michelin*
      Research Director   *Research and Development*

Note: Courtesy titles are not used in memo headings *unless* the recipient outranks the writer. If the memo is being sent to more than one person and one person in that group outranks the writer, then all recipients' names should have courtesy titles.

If many people are to receive the memo, you may simply type the word *Distribution** followed by an asterisk (as shown) on the TO-line. The distribution list is then typed at the end of the message.

FROM-Line. The FROM-line is typed just like the TO-line.
- One name, several names, or one department may be the sender of the memo.
- Job titles or department names may be used.
- The writer's name may be typed in full or with initials and a surname.
- Courtesy titles are never used in the FROM-line.

DATE-Line. The DATE-line may be typed either in full (January 5, 19—) or in the all numeric form (1/5/—). Use the style that your company prefers.

SUBJECT-Line. The SUBJECT-line may be typed in all capital letters, or you may capitalize the first letter of each word. The SUBJECT-line describes the contents of the memo.

SUBJECT: ORIENTATION FOR NEW HIRES   *SUBJECT: New-Hire Orientation*

BODY or MESSAGE

The content of the message is usually set up with either the main idea presented in the first paragraph and followed by supporting data in the next paragraphs; or with the explanations first, leading up to the main idea. Either way, brevity, clarity, and relevance are the important things to keep in mind when you compose a memo.

The body of the memo should begin four lines below the SUBJECT-line. Single-space the text and type it flush with the left margin. Or paragraphs may be indented five to ten spaces. Double-space between paragraphs.

Short memos may be entirely double-spaced. But if you do this, the first line of each paragraph *must* be indented to set the paragraphs off from one another.

Continuation Sheets—The paper should match the first page in size, color, weight, etc. The margins should match those on the first page. Leave at least one inch of blank space at the top of the page.

Identification Initials—Identification initials may or may not be used. If they are used, they are typed flush left, two lines below the last line of the body.

Distribution Lists—A distribution list, as we mentioned earlier, is typed either two lines below the identification initials or two lines below the last line of the body. The word *Distribution** followed by an asterisk is typed flush left. The list of names is also typed flush left, two lines beneath the word *Distribution*.

PERFECT PRESS RELEASES

- Do you know the purpose of a press release? Do you know what is newsworthy? Find out here.

- Like all the other typing you do, press releases must be error-free. In this chapter: typing perfect press releases.

- *Who did what, where, when, and why?* Learn about the five W's of journalistic writing.

What is newsworthy? Most companies must get information out to the public. Whether it's product or service information aimed at customers or information that will be of interest to the community, information that falls into the "newsworthy" category must fulfill two requirements: It must be timely, and it must be of particular interest to the readers of the publication you're targeting. A list of such information might include physical expansions, high-level personnel promotions and shifts, reorganization, speeches by high-level personnel, participation in or sponsorship of community events, and introduction of new products or services.

Before you put one word on paper, the number-one rule to follow is, *Know the publications you're targeting.* The most interesting and perfect-looking press release in the world won't go anywhere but the circular file if it's not appropriate for the publication you're sending it to. Read the publications before you send anything. When you do find publications that seem to suit your needs, make sure your release suits the needs of the publication. For example, if you're writing for a trade publication, information about the company's involvement in community work may not be appropriate.

Now you're ready to start work on the release. Make sure that all the information you will be using is accurate. Factual errors are the worst possible mistakes you can make. Once you know your facts are straight, here is how to type the release.

The Form. If your company does not have a press release form of its own, you will have to make one. Use a sheet of your company's letterhead or a standard sheet of plain white 8½" x 11" paper. Leave top and side margins of 1 inch and a bottom margin of 1½ inches. The words *P R E S S R E L E A S E* or *N E W S R E L E A S E* should be centered and typed in all capital letters with one space between each letter.

The Heading. The heading contains such information as the company's full name and address (if you're not using letterhead), the date of the release, the names of both the writer of the release and a contact person with whom someone needing additional information can get in touch, and phone numbers of the contact person.

Note: It's very important to date the press release with the date on which the information should be released. When newspapers receive the releases in advance (as they should), they may keep the release on file and use it if they have a small chunk of space to fill. If the release isn't dated, chances are that it will not be used because the editor won't know if the information is current. If the information in the release is effective immediately, type the words *FOR IMMEDIATE RELEASE* in all capital letters at the top of the first page.

PRESS RELEASE

FOR IMMEDIATE RELEASE
Heartland Cards Inc.
357 Mason Plaza
St. Louis, MO 63119

From: Sarah Campbell
Contact: John Parkinson
Day: (555) 001-3298

The Headline. Like the subject line in a memo, the headline is one line that gets right to the point of the story. It shouldn't sound cute or overdone; it should simply tell what the release is about. Use short action words and write in the active voice. Center the headline under the heading, and type it in all capital letters.

The Article. Leave three or four blank lines between the headline and the first line of the article. Type the first line of the first paragraph either indented or flush left. Start with the city (typed in all caps); then type the state (unless the city is well known and reference to it alone is clear), and the date, followed by a dash. Begin typing the story immediately after the dash and double-space all text.

ST. LOUIS, October 26—Heartland Cards Inc. announces the release of a new line

of greeting cards called "Just Write."

The information in a press release should be completely factual and straightforward. Write objectively. The first paragraph of the press release is the most important one. In it, you must answer the questions: Who did What? Where? When? and Why? Information that explains the answers to these questions is then arranged in order of importance in the subsequent paragraphs. This way, if an editor must cut copy, he or she can cut from the end of the story without losing the most important information.

Make your paragraphs short—from three to seven lines each. Use headings to break up your text and emphasize important points. If the press release runs longer than one page, type *-more-* one inch from the bottom of the first page, centered, and set it off with hyphens or parentheses.

Continuation Sheets. Use a blank sheet of paper that matches the first page in size, color, weight, etc. Margins match those used on the first page of the press release. The continuation sheet heading contains a couple of key words from the headline. Type it flush left in all capital letters, immediately followed by a dash and the page number.

"JUST WRITE"—2

End of Story. There are several ways to signal the end of a press release, as shown by the following examples:

-30-   -end-   (END)

Center the end signal two or three lines below the last line of the story.

- Good business writing is sometimes as hard to achieve as the successful finish of an obstacle course. Find out why.

- Redundancy, tautology, and circumlocutions: Learn how to recognize these common writing errors.

- Test your skills at reducing superfluousness in your writing.

WORDS TO WATCH OUT FOR—PART I

In the previous chapters, we have spent a lot of time developing your letter writing skills. We've talked about the look a letter should have and the importance of details, such as forms of address and the proper use of the different letter parts. We've been discussing the medium more than the message. In this chapter, we begin to discuss the message—specifically, some of the problems that may prevent you from putting together a clear, concise, well-written document.

Writing good business documents can be like running an obstacle course. There are many hindrances that can block the path to clear writing. Over the years, business writing has gotten bogged down. It is cluttered with phrases and terms that are now inappropriate in today's business atmosphere. New words and phrases have also come into the language and these too have added to the mess. We are now at a critical point. We realize that we must pare down our writing; we must cut out redundant phrases and obsolete terminology. So here are some hints that will help you clear the path to good business writing.

- **Don't use unnecessary phrases or words.** When you write a phrase to stress a particular point, study it before you move on. You'll often find that substituting a single word will do the trick. In some cases, you may find that you can remove the phrase entirely since it contributes nothing to the meaning of the sentence. For example: *The secretary was busier to a greater degree than most of her co-workers.* (Removing the phrase *to a greater degree* will improve the sentence.)

Repetition is used for emphasis; however, it is often overdone and awkward: *Many drivers in America drive to work every morning.* (Changing *drivers* to *people* improves the sentence.)

- **Remove all redundant expressions.** Although many writers use expressions such as *more expensive in cost* and *necessary essentials*, these expressions are awkward and incorrect. When you catch yourself writing one of these phrases, stop and pare down the expression.

▼ ▼ TAKE A TEST ▼ ▼

Revise the following sentences.

1. The reason why she wasn't in yesterday is because she was sick.
2. The board decided that it was not in a position to come to a decision on that matter yet.
3. The supervisor decided that he should consider firing her because of the fact that she was often late for work.
4. I'd like to refer back to the point I made earlier.
5. The company president was of the opinion that the scientist's new innovation was nothing new.

As we mentioned earlier, superfluity is one of the major obstacles to clear writing. Here is a brief discussion of this problem.

- **Redundancy** is a repetition that results from using two or more words meaning the same thing. For example, *recur again* is redundant because *recur* means *to occur again*.
- **Tautology.** This kind of wordiness is closely related to redundancy. But it refers to the needless repetition of an idea. For example, the phrase "The cause . . . was on account of" is a tautological expression.
- **Circumlocution.** This third type of verbosity literally means "talking around," and it refers to an expression that is unnecessarily wordy.

Here is a list of redundant, overused, or awkward words and phrases that you will probably recognize. From now on, try to eliminate them from your writing and, instead, use the alternatives we've suggested.

Redundancies, Tautological Expressions, and Circumlocutions

absolutely necessary	necessary	joint cooperation	cooperation
actual truth	truth	keep in mind the fact	remember
advance planning	planning	ahead of schedule	early
a large number of	many	let us hear from you	please write or call
and so as a result	thus	made a statement	
a percentage of	some	saying	said
ask the question	ask	never at any time	never
as per instructions	as requested	new innovation	innovation
as yet	still	not in a position to	cannot
at this point in time	now	patently obvious	obvious
call a halt	stop	previous to	before
close proximity	close	persuant to our	
rarely ever	rarely	agreement	as we agreed
due to the fact that	due to	redo again	redo
during the time that	while	refer back to	refer to
enclosed herewith	enclosed	regardless of the fact	
exactly identical	identical	that	regardless
favor us with a reply	please reply	render assistance to	help
first of all	first	results so far achieved	results so far
for the purpose of	to	retain position as	remain
fully cognizant of	aware of	take into consideration	consider
general consensus	consensus	to a greater degree	more
given the fact that	because	still remains	remains
give rise to	cause	until such time as	until
had occasion to be	was	various and sundry	various
in advance of	before	very unique	unique
in connection with	concerning	we are in receipt of	we have received
in order to	to	with reference to	about
in spite of the fact that	although	within the course of	within
in the final analysis	in conclusion	without further delay	immediately

ANSWERS

1. She wasn't in yesterday because she was sick.
2. The board determined that it could not come to a decision on that matter yet.
3. The supervisor considered firing her because she was often late for work.
4. I'd like to refer to the point I made earlier.
5. The company president believed that the scientist's apparent innovation wasn't new.

WORDS TO WATCH OUT FOR—PART II

There has been a lot of talk about sexism in the office today. People everywhere have made great efforts to overcome sexist attitudes. One of the major places where changes have been occurring is in business writing. But sexist writing isn't the only problem. You must also watch out for bias in other areas. In this chapter, we explain how to avoid sexist writing as well as writing that offends people of different age groups and people with disabilities.

Watch Out for Gender Offenders

It was not too long ago that "Dear Sir:" or "Gentlemen:" appeared at the beginning of many business letters. We talked about how much "manpower" we needed to accomplish a particular task and debated about who was "the best man for the job."

Now it is unacceptable to use *he* as a generic. And for some documents, such as job descriptions and policy statements, it is *against the law* to write them in the all-male form. So the question here is, How do you write nonsexist business documents without their becoming awkward? It's really quite simple; it's a matter of changing a few bad habits.

- Use nonpresumptive salutations.
  The only time this is a problem is when you don't know the addressee's name. As we mentioned in Chapter 4, there are several ways to get around this. To restate briefly, your best move when in this situation would be to use a title or a group name in the salutation.
  Dear Colleague: *Dear Supervisor:*   *Dear Data Processing Manager:*
- Avoid gender-specific terms.

Not:		**But:**	
	mankind		*people*
	man-made		*synthetic*
	man-hours		*work-hours*
	manpower		*workforce*
	mothering		*nurturing*
	to man		*to operate*

- Write in the plural.
  Instead of writing *Each employee must hand in his time card*, write *All employees must hand in their time cards*.
- Write in the second person.
  Instead of writing *Each employee must hand in his time card*, write *You must hand in your time card*.
- Use articles instead of third person singular possessives.
  Instead of writing *Each employee must hand in his or her time card*, write *Each employee must hand in a time card*.
- Avoid reference to gender unless it's necessary to the point you're making. When possible, use terms that don't differentiate between the sexes.

Not:	*stewardesses*	**But:**	*flight attendants*

Sidebar:

- Sexist writing is still a problem in many offices. Learn how to avoid this number-one offender.

- Bias in writing is not always obvious. Sometimes the bias comes through more in what you don't say than in what you do say.

- Are you tuned in to subtle bias in writing? Here, a lesson in awareness.

salesmen	*sales representatives*
mailmen	*mail carriers*

- When writing about men and women, refer to each with equal terms.

  Not: *the men and the ladies*   **But:** *the men and the women*

         Mr. Janacek and Katherine   *Mr. Janacek and Ms. White*

- Use the same "common denominator" when making comparisons.

  Not: *Mr. Janacek's aggressiveness and Ms. Ellsworth's powerful physical presence have a formidable impact on clients.*

  But: *Mr. Janacek's aggressiveness and Ms. Ellsworth's determination have a formidable impact on clients.*

Age and Disability Biases

In these categories, the bias is subtle. Statements made about older people and the disabled may seem harmless. But on closer inspection, you'll see that the problem is often not with the exact words but in their implications.

Age. This is a problem that goes both ways. People in a certain age group may have general ideas about people in another age group. And though these ideas might not be mentioned directly, they can come up in writing. For instance, read the following sentence.

> *Hogan, who retired at 62, is still a spry and active individual.*

At first glance, this seems like a complimentary statement. But what does this sentence imply? First, that it's surprising that a person aged 62 or over is active because, second, others at this age are rarely in good physical shape. Both of these inferences are based on stereotypes that don't hold true.

- Avoid patronizing or demeaning words and phrases when discussing people in an age group different from your own. For example, when talking about older people, don't make statements such as:

  > *She is a sweet woman; she unfailingly bakes dozens of cookies to help raise money for the new community center.*

  Instead, write something like:

  > *Through the years, she put in many long hours in her commitment to the betterment of her community.*

  Other words to avoid: senile, crotchety, feeble, wrinkled, eccentric, etc.

  When talking about younger people, don't make statements such as:

  > *Even though he's 16 years old, he has shown a lot of responsibility toward his job.*

  Again, the implications of this statement are based on stereotypes. This sentence implies that most young people are not serious or responsible and that it's noteworthy that there are some young people who *are* responsible.

Disability. This is a subject that you must handle with sensitivity. To be able to do this, you must examine your attitude toward disabled people. Ask yourself these questions:

- In your mind, do you categorize disabled people into a group?
- What are the premises or the criteria that you use to categorize?
- When you think about disabled people, do you think of them in terms of what they can do or what they can't do?

In all these situations, the key rule to remember is this: Don't bring up gender, age, or disability unless it's relevant to the point you're making.

- Are you a legal eagle?
  Typing legal documents
  requires that you be one.

- What do you do with an
  instrument? Where do
  you put a *clause*? Find
  out here.

- Become familiar with
  some legal terms and
  typing tips.

TYPING LEGAL DOCUMENTS

Even though you may not be a legal secretary or work for a lawyer, at some point during your career you will probably be asked to type a legal document. If you've never done this before, the idea may be a daunting one. The style of most legal documents is highly specialized; the language may be unfamiliar to you. But don't worry. As with any other task, you can learn how to type legal documents if only you take your time and practice. We'll start you off on the right foot. There are two categories of legal documents: court documents and legal instruments. Court documents are for the use of the court. These include documents such as complaints, judgments, and petitions. Legal instruments are used by the parties who sign them. Because the rules for typing court documents must be followed explicitly, and because the rules vary widely from state to state, county to county, etc., we cover the typing of legal instruments only. Before you learn these procedures, it will help you to become familiar with some common legal terms. The following definitions are from *Webster's New World Dictionary* (Simon & Schuster, ©1988).

affidavit—a written statement made on oath before a notary public or other person authorized to administer oaths.

brief—a concise statement of the main points of a law case, usually filed by counsel for the information of the court.

contract—an agreement between two or more people to do something, esp. one formally set forth in writing and enforceable by law.

deed—a document under seal that, when delivered, transfers a present interest in property.

lien—a claim on the property of another as security for the payment of a just debt.

mortgage—the pledging of property to a creditor as security for the payment of a debt; also the deed by which this pledge is made.

plaintiff—a person who brings a suit into a court of law.

power of attorney—a written statement legally authorizing a person to act for another.

proxy—a document empowering a person to act for another, as in voting at a stockholder's meeting.

will—the legal statement of a person's wishes concerning the disposal of his or her property after death.

Typing Legal Instruments

Paper. Traditionally, *legal cap*, *a* high-quality white paper, has been used for legal documents. Legal cap is available in two sizes: standard legal size (8$\frac{1}{2}$" x 14") or letter size (8$\frac{1}{2}$" x 11"). Legal cap is also available either ruled or unruled, numbered or unnumbered. The paper size and style you use will depend on your attorney's preferences.

Margins. If you use unruled paper, leave a 1$\frac{1}{2}$" top margin, 1" bottom margin, 1$\frac{1}{4}$" to 1$\frac{1}{2}$" on the left-hand side, and 1" on the right. All typing must be contained within the margins and must never extend over the rules (vertical lines that set off a wide left margin and a narrow right margin).

Dates. Dates may be written in numerals or spelled out; however, always spell out the month. The year may be written in figures even if the date is spelled out—e.g., the twenty-second day of June, 19—.

Spacing. Double-space the body; triple-space between articles or paragraphs with side headings; single-space quotations and land descriptions; triple-space drafts.

Paragraphs. Never use block style on a legal document. Indent 10 spaces for each paragraph. To check against omission of pages, especially in wills, never complete a final paragraph on a page. Always carry over at least one or two lines to the next page. Paragraphs may be numbered. Any of the following ways are acceptable:

1.	Article I.	I.
2.	Article II.	II.
3.	Article III.	III.

Numbering pages. The page number should be centered about three lines below the last typed line on the page. You may or may not number the first page, but numbers must appear on all the following pages.

Numbers and Money. Always spell out numbers and follow them with numerals in parentheses—e.g., five thousand (5,000). Spell out amounts of money, type in all capital letters, and include the word "DOLLARS" followed by the numerals in parentheses—e.g., NINE HUNDRED EIGHTY-SEVEN DOLLARS ($987.00).

Signature. Signature lines are typed slightly to the right of the center of the page. Type one blank line for each signature that will appear on the instrument. The first signature line should be typed four lines below the body of the instrument. Leave enough space between signature lines to let the average-sized signature fit on the line. All signatures must appear on one page. At least two lines of the body of the instrument should appear on the page with the signature, in addition to the witness clause.

When a corporation is one of the parties involved in the instrument, you must type the name of the corporation in all capital letters above the blank signature line. The signature line should be preceded by the word *By:* followed by a colon (as shown here). Underneath the signature line, type the title of the corporate officer who will sign the instrument.

Execution of an Instrument

A legal instrument must be "executed" before it becomes valid. Execution of an instrument includes some or all of the following: testimonium clause, sealing, witness or attestation clause, acknowledgment, and notarization. (The signatures are also part of the execution.)

Testimonium Clause. The testimonium clause closes the instrument. It states that the parties to the instrument have attached their signatures to that instrument. It indicates who will sign the instrument, what officer of a corporation will sign the instrument, and whether the instrument will be sealed and attested.

The testimonium clause is an unnumbered paragraph appearing by itself. It is the last paragraph of the instrument and directly precedes the signatures. A testimonium clause can be worded in the following manner:

IN WITNESS WHEREOF, the parties hereto have set their hands and seals on this third day of July 19—.

OR:

IN TESTIMONY WHEREOF, the parties hereto have duly executed this agreement.

The first three words are typed in capital letters as shown above.

Seal. A seal must appear as part of the execution of the instrument when a corporation is one of the parties to the instrument or when the phrase "hand and seals" is used in the testimonium clause. When a seal is to be used, type the letters *L.S.* (Latin for *locus sigilli,* meaning *place of the seal)* or the word *SEAL* at the end of the signature line. The seal is usually imprinted to the left of the signature. Individual seals are generally not used anymore; the individual's signature serves as the seal.

Witness or Attestation Clause. The witness or attestation clause is included when a corporate seal is part of the execution of the instrument. The secretary of the corporation is usually required to attest to the fact that the seal that is imprinted on the instrument is the actual seal of the corporation. Type the word *ATTEST:* in all capital letters followed by a colon (as shown here) on the left side of the page, opposite and just below the signature lines. Type the word *Secretary* under the word *ATTEST.*

Acknowledgment. The acknowledgment is a separate document that is annexed to the instrument. It states that the person who executes the instrument has declared in front of an officer (such as a notary public) that that person is indeed the person who executed the instrument. (For this example, we have designated the officer as a notary public.) The notary public affirms that the signature is genuine and that the person signing the instrument did so of his or her own free will. Most states require that an instrument be acknowledged before it can be recorded or filed.

The format and the exact wording of acknowledgments vary from state to state. The sample on the next page is a "generic" one that may be used as a guide, but it is not meant to be copied exactly. If you have to type an acknowledgment, the important rule to remember is this: The wording and the format of the acknowledgment should be done in accordance with the statutes of the state in which the acknowledgment will be used, *not* the state in which it is prepared.

The acknowledgment may be either single- or double-spaced, and it must include the following: venue, date of acknowledgment, the name of the person making the acknowledgment, and the notary public's seal, signature, and commission expiration date.

→ *Venue.* Begin the acknowledgment with the venue. The venue shows the political subdivision in which the acknowledgment is made. (Depending on the state, this could be the names of the state and the county, the name of the commonwealth, or the name of the parish.)

Type the venue in the upper left-hand corner in all capital letters. It is double-spaced. Type the name of the state on the first line and that of the county on the second line. Follow both of these with closing parentheses. In the blank line between the state and county names, type a colon, skip a space, then type the letters *ss* (Latin for *scilicet*, meaning *namely* or *to wit)*, followed by a period. Leave three blank lines between the last line of the venue and the body of the acknowledgment.

→ *Date.* The date may appear at the beginning of the acknowledgment as part of the body or at the end of the acknowledgment as a separate statement. The date that is typed on the acknowledgment is the date that the party to the instrument signed the acknowledgment, *not* the date on which the party signed the instrument. An instrument may be dated before the acknowledgment, but the acknowledgment must never be dated *before* the instrument.

→ *Name of person making acknowledgment.* Type this name in all capital letters. If the person making the acknowledgment is acting as a representative of an organization, his or her capacity is typed after the name, but in uppercase and lowercase letters.

→ *Notary's seal, signature, and commission expiration date.* Four lines below the last line of the text and flush with the right margin, type a blank line for the notary public's signature. Underneath the signature line, type the notary's title. Some states also require the name of the officer to appear underneath the signature line. The seal appears to the left of the signature line. Two lines below the title, type *My commission expires _____ , 19—.*

STATE OF CONNECTICUT)

                      : ss.

COUNTY OF NEW LONDON)

    On this the 3rd day of July, 19—, before me, James A. Arnold, the under-

signed officer, personally appeared DEBORAH HARMON, known to me to be the

person whose name is subscribed to the within instrument and acknowledged

that she executed the same for the purpose therein contained.

(seal)   _____

                                           Notary Public

                          My commission expires December 31, 19—

INFORMAL REPORT STYLES

■ Knowing how to present information properly is an important skill. Do you have it?

■ Do you know what your options are when you have to type an informal report?

■ What is a memorandum report? When is a letter report used? Find out here.

We live in an age when information is a very valuable commodity. The person who has the information that he or she needs, and who knows what to do with that information, is in a powerful position.

It is often the office worker's job to present that information in a way that is well organized and consistent with the information that is being presented. We have already talked about letters, memos, and press releases as ways to present small amounts of information. We will now discuss ways in which to present larger amounts of information.

As you well know, reports are an important part of almost every business these days. That's because they are one of the main ways in which information is passed from one person to another. Just as different styles of letters are appropriate for various kinds of greetings, different styles of reports are used to present various kinds of information. In this chapter, we will discuss different report styles and their uses.

The Memorandum Report

For short (2-3 pages), informal reports, many businesses use the memorandum report style. In general, the tone of these reports is informal, as they are usually intended for in-house distribution only. The contents are often of a routine nature—for instance, a weekly sales report or a project progress report.

A memorandum report is typed on the company's printed memorandum paper or, if your company doesn't use preprinted memo paper, on plain bond paper. As with a memo, if the amount of information is small, the report may be double-spaced. When typing a memorandum report, follow the typing guidelines given in Chapter 9 for memos. If you have questions about the placement of subheadings or other questions concerning style, ask the writer what his or her preferences are. A memorandum report may include the writer's typed and handwritten signature.

The Letter Report

A letter report is exactly what it sounds like: a letter (with an address block, a salutation, a complimentary close, etc.) whose format has been slightly altered to present information in an organized and concise manner. Letter reports are generally used for distribution outside the company. For example, they can be from people within the company to off-site company members, or they might be from a consultant who is doing work for the company. The letter report is usually used for informal reports of several pages.

The first page of a letter report is typed on the company's letterhead. As with a letter, the following pages are typed on matching continuation sheets that begin with an applicable heading. Use the block style or the modified block style; both formats are appropriate for the balanced presentation of information that is necessary for a report. Letter reports often include tables or short illustrations. A subject line is often used to draw attention to the report's objective. As with a report, headings and subheadings are used to highlight particularly important information. Here are guidelines for typing headings and subheadings:

Title or Subject Line. Leave three blank lines above the title or subject line (after the salutation) and three blank lines below the subject line (before whatever material follows, whether it is a heading or the body of the letter). Type the title in all capital letters and underline it.

Main Headings. Leave three blank lines above main headings (there may be more than one) and three blank lines after main headings. Type a main heading flush left or centered in all capital letters.

Subheadings. Leave three blank lines above and below subheadings. Type a subheading flush left or centered in uppercase and lowercase letters. Underline a subheading.

Sideheadings. Leave two blank lines between a paragraph beginning with a sideheading and the material that appears before it. Leave two blank lines between the end of a paragraph beginning with a sideheading and another paragraph as long as the next paragraph has no other headings.

The Short Business Report

The last style of informal report is the short business report. With this style, you break away from the letter format and begin to use the formatting techniques of a more formal report. The scope of the subject of a short report is usually limited and can be dealt with in an uncomplicated manner. A short report may be unbound or bound at the top or the side. Short reports include a title page consisting of the title of the report; the name, business title, and address of the recipient of the report; the name, business title, and address of the sender of the report; and the date of the report.

Headings and subheadings (as described in the letter report) will more than likely be used to clarify and separate information. If your company does not have any preferences regarding the styling of a report, you may use the basic guidelines given below:

- Single- or double-space the body of the report.

- Leave one blank line between paragraphs if the report is single-spaced and two blank lines between paragraphs if the report is double-spaced.

- Use a 2" top margin on the first page, a 1½" left margin, a 1" right margin, and a bottom margin of 1" or 1½".

- On continuation sheets, use a 1" top margin. Left, right, and bottom margins should match those used on the first page.

- Center the main heading and type it in all capital letters.

- Center subheadings and type them in uppercase and lowercase letters.

- Side headings should be typed flush left in uppercase and lowercase letters and underlined.

THE CHALLENGE OF FORMAL REPORTS

- Preparing a formal report: Are you up to the challenge?

- There are up to 20 different parts to a formal report. Each one is explained to you here.

- Typing a report can be a bear. But not once you've read this chapter!

Preparing a formal report may be one of the tasks you dread most. Why? Perhaps because you realize the information in the report can have an effect on hundreds of people. The report might be read by hundreds of stockholders or include recommendations that can affect every employee in your company. So every comma, word, and statistic must be perfect.

Therefore, a formal report requires you to use every professional skill you have. Your planning must be perfectly timed, your typing impeccable, and your attention to detail meticulous. And you must know how to work with people to get the information you need when you need it.

The more reports you work on, the less intimidating they will become. And a carefully prepared report is tangible evidence of a job well done. It can draw attention to your thoroughness and creativity. So it only makes sense to seize this fine opportunity to display your talents.

In this chapter, you'll become thoroughly familiar with the formal report. We will explain how it is used, its many different parts, and the complex typing guidelines you'll need to understand. By the time you finish reading, you will be able to tackle a formal report with confidence.

Uses of Formal Reports

Reports provide useful information, put abstract ideas into concrete form, focus attention on problems, and spur people to action. Most reports fall into one of the following categories:

Informational reports are confined to facts and observations. Examples would include companies' quarterly or annual reports, project reports, and evaluation reports concerning attendance, performance, etc.

Analytical reports not only give the facts but also attempt to interpret them, to draw conclusions, or to make recommendations. Examples would include market surveys, time/motion studies, feasibility studies, product analyses, and proposed policy or procedural changes.

An Appropriate Format

If your company has an established format for formal reports, by all means stick to it. If not, you'll want to package your report in a format that is clear, attractive, and convenient for the reader. Most formal reports are organized along the following lines:

FRONT MATTER

Cover: contains the title of the report and the author's name.
Flyleaf: (optional) blank pages at the end and at the beginning of the report that dress up the report and provide space for written comments.
Title Fly: contains only the report title. It is typed in all capital letters, centered horizontally on the page, and placed either in the upper third or in the center of the page.

Title Page: contains the title typed in all capital letters and the subtitle (if there is one) typed in uppercase and lowercase letters. These two elements are centered horizontally, double-spaced, and typed in the top third of the page.

The following information appears on the bottom third of the page: the writer's name (or names if the report has been cowritten) and corporate title, the writer's department name (or writer's address), and the name of the firm. Other information includes name, corporate title, department name, firm name, and address of the recipient of the report, and the report's completion date. If the report is a revision, that should also be noted.

Letter of Authorization: included only if the author received written authorization. A letter of authorization is written by the person who commissioned the report.

Letter of Transmittal: a cover letter used to record the submission of the report. It states briefly the purpose, scope, and contents of the report and sometimes serves as the preface or foreword. If this is the case, it should also include the research methods used for the report, comments, and acknowledgments (if there aren't enough to list separately). The letter of transmittal is typed on letterhead stationery and signed by the writer. It is single-spaced, as for any other letter, and is double-spaced between paragraphs.

Acknowledgments: made to those individuals, institutions, or companies who helped in the preparation of the report. Acknowledgments appear on a separate page only if there are many. This page is single-spaced and is double-spaced between paragraphs. All material is centered on the page. Type the heading ACKNOWLEDGMENTS in all capital letters three lines above the text.

Table of Contents: enumerates, with page references, all the material that follows it, the chapter or section headings of the report itself, and the bibliography, the appendices, and the exhibits at the end.

All material is centered vertically on the page. Type the heading TABLE OF CONTENTS in all capital letters at the top of the page. Double-space between headings and subheadings. Single-space lines that run longer than your margins allow.

If you must use a continuation sheet, center the heading *Table of Contents (Cont'd)* at the top of the page.

List of Charts and Illustrations: If there are only a few charts or illustrations in the report, list them at the end of the table of contents. Otherwise, they should appear on a separate page. You may make separate lists for charts and illustrations if there are many of each. The format should match that of the table of contents.

Summary (also called abstract or synopsis): usually included in long or particularly complex reports. It is a one-page condensation of the report's principal findings. It covers major points, findings, and recommendations. The summary appears on a page by itself, single- or double-spaced. Type the heading SUMMARY or SYNOPSIS, centered at the top of the page.

Foreword: tells why the report was written. A foreword is written by someone other than the writer of the report. It is single-spaced and one page only.

Preface: If a preface is needed, it should explain how the report came about, how it is expected to be used, and who assisted in its preparation.

TEXT

Introduction: The introduction should describe the report's purpose (what the project is supposed to achieve) and scope (the depth of the study); describe what problems were encountered (limitations of project, such as cost or time); give background information (describe circumstances leading up to the situation); and describe the research methods used (tell where and how information was gathered).

Body: In the body of the report, the writer discusses the problem and describes the results of the research or investigation. The way the information in the body of a report is organized depends upon the aim of the report and of the material in the report.

Conclusions: a statement of reasons for recommending action. No new ideas should be introduced in this section. Present conclusions in order of their importance.

Recommendations: recommendations for action based on the research presented in the report. Use active voice. Present recommendations in order of their importance.

REFERENCE MATTER

Appendix: appears before any other reference matter. The appendix can contain graphs, charts, illustrations, and other documents not included in the body of the report. The information may be categorized (Appendix A, B, C, etc.). It is separated from the rest of the report by one page with the heading APPENDIX typed in all capital letters, centered on the page. Half-titles, typed in all capital letters and centered underneath the word APPENDIX, may also be used.

Footnotes or Endnotes: used to document quoted or paraphrased material. Footnotes appear at the bottom of the pages on which the quoted or paraphrased material appears or in a list at the end of each chapter or section of the report. Endnotes appear in a separate list at the end of the report. You can number the footnotes or endnotes consecutively throughout the report. Or, if the report is very long and contains a lot of quoted or paraphrased material, you can renumber the notes at the start of each section. If you do renumber with each section and are using endnotes, be sure to designate clearly which set of notes belongs to each section.

In the body of the report, footnote and endnote references are signaled by a raised numeral typed immediately after the closing quotation mark of the quoted material.

"The footnote number should appear outside quotation marks."[1]

In the footnote or endnote section of the report, these notes are signaled by a raised numeral (corresponding to the one in the body of the report) typed one space before the reference. It is also acceptable to type the numeral on the line, followed by a period and one or two spaces. Indent the first line of each footnote or endnote 2 to 5 spaces from the left margin. Following lines are typed flush with the left margin.

Note: The guidelines for the proper styling of footnotes and bibliographies are very complex and cannot be covered in full here. See Chapter 16 for detailed guidelines on proper footnote and bibliography styling.

Listing of References or Bibliography: Both references and bibliographies list the sources of information a writer used in his or her work. These sources may or may not have appeared in the footnotes. Bibliographies may also contain related works of interest to the reader. Lists of references and bibliographies give credit to the original writers, and they help the reader find additional information.

Bibliographies are usually used in academic or professional journals. Type BIBLIOGRAPHY in all capital letters centered at the top of the page. Entries in a bibliography are unnumbered and alphabetized according to author surname. The first line of each entry is typed flush left. Indent the following lines 1 to 7 spaces.

A list of references is usually used in business and technical reports. Entries are numbered according to the order in which they appeared in the report. The first line of each reference entry is typed flush left, beginning with a number followed by a period and a space. The first word in the entry begins after the space. Following lines are indented and aligned with the first word in the entry.

Index: an alphabetized list of all the major topics and subtopics in the report. Each listing includes page numbers designating where in the report information on those topics can be found. An index is usually found only in very long, detailed reports. An index contains four main elements:

- *main entry*—corresponds to main topics (often represented by a main heading in the text). Type heading flush left; capitalize the first word. Follow entry with a comma only if the page number is given. Follow by a period if a cross-reference is given.
- *subentry*—corresponds to secondary topics. List subentries alphabetically under the main entry. Indent subentry two spaces; type in all lowercase letters unless it is a proper name. Punctuate a subentry the same way as a main entry.
- *sub-subentry*—corresponds to topics of tertiary importance. List sub-subentries alphabetically under the subentries. Indent a sub-subentry two spaces to the right of the subentry. Punctuate a sub-subentry the same way as a subentry.
- *cross-entry* or *cross-reference*—directs the reader to topics related to the main entry. Introduce a cross-reference by the underlined or italicized words "See" or "See also." Capitalize "See." Capitalize the first letter of the first word in the cross-reference.

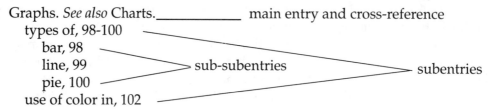

Typing Guidelines

Margins. The margins in a formal report depend on how the report will be bound.

	Unbound or top-bound	Sidebound
Top, first page	2 in.	2 in.
Top, second and ff.	1 in.	1 in.
Bottom	1 in.	1 in.
Left and right	1 in.	Left $1\frac{1}{2}$ in., right 1 in.

Spacing. Single-space or double-space the body of the report. Double-space between paragraphs if the body is single-spaced; triple-space between paragraphs if the body is double-spaced.

Single-space long quotations, tables, and lists. If the copy is very dense, it is sometimes a good idea to leave a blank line of space before and after long passages of quoted material, tables, and lists. If you leave a line before, you must leave one after. Leave one blank line whether you single-space the report or double-space it.

Single-space footnotes, endnotes, and bibliography entries. Double-space between each entry.

Indention. Indent the first line of each paragraph 5 or 6 spaces. Indent long quotations, tables, and lists 5 or 6 spaces from the left and right margins. Indent the first line of each footnote or endnote 2-5 spaces. Type the first line of a bibliography entry flush with the left margin; indent following lines 2-5 spaces.

Pagination. For top-bound reports, center page numbers 3-6 lines from the bottom of the page. For side-bound reports, type page numbers one-half inch to the right of the center of the page or at the right margin, 3-6 lines from the bottom of the page.

Page numbers on all front matter are typed in lowercase roman numerals. Flyleaves are not paginated. The title fly and title page are assigned pages *i* and *ii*, respectively. These numbers do not have to appear on those pages. Pages in the rest of the front matter (letters of transmittal/authorization, table of contents, synopsis, etc.) are assigned numbers *iii* and above.

The first page of the body is arabic numeral *1*. All the following pages, including all reference matter, are numerals *2* and above.

FOOTNOTES, ENDNOTES, AND BIBLIOGRAPHIES

- Footnote form can befuddle even the most fastidious office worker.

- Does the thought of typing bibliographies and footnotes make you cringe? We'll set you straight on styles.

- Bibliographies and footnotes play an important role in the formal report. Do you know what that role is?

The footnote (or endnote) and bibliography sections of the report are last but certainly not least important. Footnotes and bibliographies give credibility to the report, and they document borrowed material.

Footnotes

A footnote or endnote generally includes:
- Footnote number raised above the line or typed on the line followed by a period and one or two blank spaces.
- Author's name followed by a comma.
- Title of the book either underlined or typed in italics followed by one blank space.
- Publication information in parentheses (place of publication—city and state unless the city is sufficiently well known by itself—followed by a colon, publishing company's name followed by a comma, and the year of publication). The closing parenthesis is followed by a comma.
- Page number or numbers followed by a period.

BOOKS

one or two authors

[2] Dr. Wilfred Funk and Norman Lewis, *30 Days to a More Powerful Vocabulary* (New York: Pocket Books, 1971), p. 100.

three or more authors

[3] Leonard Rogoff, et al., *Office Guide to Business Letters, Memos, and Reports* (New York: Arco Publishing, 1984), pp. 151-157.

anthology

[4] Jeanette L. Bely, "Communications," *Webster's New World Secretarial Handbook,* rev. ed. (New York: Simon & Schuster, 1981), p. 139.
Note: If there is one main editor for the anthology, follow the book's title with a comma, the abbreviation *ed.,* and the name of that editor.

later edition

[5] J. A. Van Duyn, *Director's and Officer's Complete Letter Book,* 2nd ed. (Englewood Cliffs, NJ: Prentice-Hall, 1983), p. 74.

corporate author

[6] *How Plain English Works for Business* (Washington, D.C.: U.S. Department of Commerce Office of Consumer Affairs, 1984), p. 87.

anonymous

[7] *Webster's New World Dictionary,* 3rd college ed. (New York: Simon & Schuster, 1988), p. 1372.

ARTICLES

journal paged consecutively

[1] Sally Poncet, "Wildlife Quest to the Icy Seas of South Georgia," *National Geographic,* Vol. 175, No. 3 (Mar. 1989), pp. 340-375.

journal with separate paging each issue

[2] Robin A. Prager, "The Effects of Regulatory Policies on the Cost of Debt for Electric Utilities: An Empirical Investigation," *The Journal of Business,* Vol. 62, No. 1 (Jan. 19—), pp. 33-53.

weekly magazine

[3] Patricia Sellars, "Getting Customers to Love You," *Fortune,* 13 Mar. 19—, pp. 38-49.

monthly magazine

[4] Amanda Lovell, "Control Freaks," *Self,* Jan. 19—, p. 81.

daily newspaper

[5] Peter T. Kilborn, "Mexico Will Seek Debt Relief," *The New York Times,* 13 Apr. 19—, p. D2, col. 6.

letter to the editor

[6] John A. Edwardson, Letter, *The Wall Street Journal* (13 Apr. 19—), p. A23.

Bibliographies

As we mentioned in the last chapter, bibliographies are alphabetized according to authors' last names. Our examples, however, are organized according to type of entry. Note the differences between a bibliography entry and a footnote entry: Bibliography entries are not numbered; a bibliography entry is typed flush left with following lines hanging indented; periods follow author's name, book title, and article title (if appropriate); and page numbers are included for articles but not for books.

BOOKS

one or two authors

Funk, Wilfred and Norman Lewis. *30 Days to a More Powerful Vocabulary.* New York: Pocket Books, 1971.

three or more authors

Rogoff, Leonard, et al. *Office Guide to Business Letters, Memos, and Reports.* New York: Arco Publishing, 1984.

anthology and **later edition**

Bely, Jeanette L. "Communications." *Webster's New World Secretarial Handbook.* Revised ed. New York: Simon & Schuster, 1981.

Note: If there is one main editor for the anthology, follow the book's title with a period, the abbreviation *ed.,* and the name of that editor.

corporate author

How Plain English Works for Business. Washington, D.C.: U.S. Department of Commerce Office of Consumer Affairs, 1984.

anonymous

Webster's New World Dictionary. 3rd college ed. New York: Simon & Schuster, 1988.

ARTICLES

journal paged consecutively

Poncet, Sally. "Wildlife Quest to the Icy Seas of South Georgia." *National Geographic.* Vol. 175, No. 3 (Mar. 1989), pp. 340-375.

journal with separate paging each issue

Prager, Robin A. "The Effects of Regulatory Policies on the Cost of Debt for Electric Utilities: An Empirical Investigation." *The Journal of Business,* Vol. 62, No. 1 (Jan. 19—), pp. 33-53.

weekly magazine

Sellars, Patricia. "Getting Customers to Love You." *Fortune,* 13 Mar. 19—, pp. 38-49.

monthly magazine

Lovell, Amanda. "Control Freaks." *Self,* Jan. 19—, p. 81.

daily newspaper

Kilborn, Peter T. "Mexico Will Seek Debt Relief." *The New York Times,* 13 Apr. 19—, p. D2, col. 6.

letter to the editor

Edwardson, John A. Letter, *The Wall Street Journal,* 13 Apr. 19—, p. A23.

PROOFED TO PERFECTION

- Proofreading puts the final polish on your reports and letters.

- Proofreading has a "shorthand" all its own. Do you know the code?

- Test your proofreading skills with this quiz.

Proofreading your letters before they leave your desk probably comes as second nature to you. Making changes is as simple as putting in a comma here and changing the word order there—a fairly painless task. But what about proofing those long, involved reports—or the copy for a company brochure, which will be typeset? If you've ever had to tackle a major proofreading task, you know how important it is to use the correct proofreading marks. There's nothing worse than having to type from copy that is covered with arrows, scribbles, and cryptic hieroglyphics.

Below is a chart of proofreader's marks. Look it over, then try your hand at the quiz on the next page.

PROOFREADER'S MARKS

∧ Make correction indicated in margin.	tr Transpose words or letters as indicated.	wf Wrong font; change to proper font.	;/ Insert semicolon.
stet Retain crossed-out word or letter; let it stand.	Take out matter indicated; delete.	Qu? Is this right?	:/ Insert colon.
stet Retain words under which dots appear; write "Stet" in margin.	Take out character indicated and close up.	lc Set in lowercase (small letters).	⊙ Insert period.
× Appears battered; examine.	Line drawn through a cap means lowercase.	s.c. Set in small capitals.	/?/ Insert question mark.
= Straighten lines.	Upside down; reverse.	caps Set in capitals.	/!/ Insert exclamation point.
√√√ Unevenly spaced; correct spacing.	Close up; no space.	c&sc. Set in caps and small caps.	=/ Insert hyphen.
‖ Line up; i.e., make lines even with other matter.	# Insert a space here.	rom Change to roman.	Insert apostrophe.
run in Make no break in the reading; no ¶.	Push down this space.	ital Change to italic.	Insert quotation marks.
no ¶ No paragraph; sometimes written "run in."	Indent line one em.	Under letter or word, means caps.	a Insert superior letter or figure.
	Move this to the left.	Under letter or word, means small caps.	Insert inferior letter or figure.
out see copy Here is an omission; see copy.	Move this to the right.	Under letter or word, means italic.	[/] Insert brackets.
	Raise to proper position.		(/) Insert parentheses.
¶ Make a paragraph here.	Lower to proper position.	Under letter or word, means boldface.	1/m One-em dash.
	Hair-space letters.	Insert comma.	2/m Two-em parallel dash.

Before you try your hand at proofing, here are some other proofreading tips:

✓ **Use the buddy system.** When you've been working on a lengthy piece of copy from the rough draft stage through to final clean copy, it's easy to miss mistakes. Your eye tends to see what it expects to see, and common typos are easily overlooked. A co-worker's eye will be fresher. Offer to take on his or her duties in exchange for the favor.

✓ **Read copy line by line from right to left.** It's impossible to skim when you're reading backward; a typo or misspelling will be hard to miss.

✓ **Read aloud against copy.** One person checks the final copy while another reads the original out loud. The reader notes new paragraphs and all punctuation and also spells out any unfamiliar technical terms or proper names.

▼ ▼ TAKE A TEST ▼ ▼

Try out your newly acquired proofreading skills on this copy:

Cleaning out your desk drawers. proofreading a document for the umpteenth time. Filing. These four tsaks have something in common, They are things that people hate to do— and willlgo to nay lengths to avoid. Office workers may let the filing pile up, out and over the edges of their in-boxes, onto their desks and the extra chair in the office. Yes, Everyone has something heor she hates to do.

There is a way to tackle these tasks. It's called getting yourself psyched up. This is not to say that youwill enjoy the task, but you will be able to get over it without cuasing yourself considerable stress.

Don't put the dreaded task on the back burner. You think that if you keep avoiding it , It will go away. Well,it won't. The pile of papers that is slowly creeping over your office should tell you htat. Start th3 jolb as soon as you know it has to be done. otherwise, you'll waste a lot of time thinking about how much you hate to do it, and that won't help at all.

If you are going to think about the job try to think constructively—how you can mke the job go more quickly or how can you make it easier. Don't blwo the job out of proportion. Don't let it turn into a monster lurking around your desk. Taking your concen tra tion away from everything else.

If you can;'t do the whole job right away, break up into sefments and then "layer' it with the ohter jobs you have to do. This way, you have something to look forward to after you've done one part of the no fun job. You'll also have the comfort of knowing that each time you finish a section of the job you don't like, theres less of it to do later. Last, give yourself a reward when the job is done; You deserve it!

- You've come a long way since the first chapter. Now it's time to find out what you remember.

- Are your letter and report writing skills letter perfect? Find out here.

- These quizzes will let you know what you need to brush up on.

THE GRAND FINALE

As you read through the chapters in this section, you took in a lot of information that should improve your performance on the job. Now it's time to find out exactly what you've retained. Even though you know you can always go back to check the previous chapters for information that you may not remember, the more you know off the top of your head, the better.

QUIZ 1   Write the answers on the lines provided below each question. Check your answers on the next page.

1.   Name three types of informal reports.

_____

_____

2.   What is an acknowledgment? What is it used for?

_____

_____

3.   What are three types of superfluity often found in business writing?

_____

_____

4.   What are the five questions to answer in a press release?

_____

_____

5.   Why does the U.S. Postal Service request that addresses on envelopes be typed or machine printed?

_____

_____

6.   What is a letter of authorization used for?

_____

_____

7.   Why are footnotes included in most formal reports?

_____

_____

8.   Name six letter styles that are used in business today.

_____

_____

9.   For whom is the use of the title "the Honorable" reserved?

_____

10. What does the "bcc" notation stand for? When is it used?

_____

_____

QUIZ 2

1. The proofreader's mark for inserting a hyphen is:
   a. $=/$; b. $\overline{\wedge}$; c. $\wedge/=$
2. The letter style in which everything, including the date and the complimentary close, starts at the left margin is:
   a. modified block; b. full block; c. simplified
3. To avoid displaying gender bias in your writing, you can use:
   a. the plural; b. the second person; c. both a and b
4. Which punctuation style uses (in addition to other punctuation) a colon after the salutation and a comma after the complimentary close?
   a. closed; b. open; c. mixed
5. Courtesy titles are used in the "To-" line of a memo when:
   a. the recipient outranks the writer.
   b. the memo is being sent to several people.
   c. both a and b.
6. Abbreviations for branches of the service (army, navy, coast guard, etc.) are typed:
   a. in all capital letters with periods after each letter.
   b. in all capital letters with no punctuation.
   c. with the letters U.S. punctuated and the following letters unpunctuated.
7. Text appearing in the body of a legal instrument is:
   a. double-spaced; b. single-spaced; c. triple-spaced
8. Which of the following is typed with the first line indented?
   a. index; b. bibliography; c. footnote
9. The phrase "are of the opinion that" can be described as a:
   a. redundancy; b. circumlocution; c. tautological expression
10. Which of the following is a mandatory part of a simplified letter?
    a. salutation; b. subject line; c. attention line

ANSWERS

QUIZ 1
1. memorandum, letter, short business report
2. An acknowledgment is part of a legal instrument. It states that the person who executed the instrument has declared in front of a notary public that he or she is the person who executed the instrument.
3. circumlocution, tautology, redundancy
4. who, what, where, when, and why
5. Addresses on envelopes must be typed or machine printed so that the Postal Service's OCR can read the mail and process it quickly.
6. A letter of authorization is a letter sent to the author or the writer of a report giving him or her authorization to do the report.
7. Footnotes give credit to the sources used in a report.
8. full block, semiblock, hanging-indented, official, simplified, modified block
9. The title "the Honorable" is used by any high-ranking appointed or elected official.
10. "Bcc" is the blind copy notation. It is used when copies of letters are sent to other recipients without revealing this action to the original addressee. It appears only on copies of the letter.

QUIZ 2
1. a; 2. b; 3. c; 4. c; 5. a; 6. b; 7. a; 8. c; 9. b; 10. b

WORD PROCESSING AND COMPUTERS
Tackling Office Technology

INTRODUCTION

The high-tech automated office is no longer merely a vision of the future. It's here now, and it's here to stay. Keeping abreast of this new technology isn't easy, but as an office-support professional, you need to stay informed of the changes in office automation. This section is devoted to taking the mystery out of computers and word processing systems and to helping you get the most from this equipment. Not only will you become more confident in your computer and technical expertise, but you'll also learn how office technology can actually make your job easier.

Are you interested in learning about spreadsheets? Perhaps you'd like to know about the different types of computer software? If you'd like to research a particular area concerning word processors or computers, you can find the subject you need by glancing at the index below.

- If you haven't yet been introduced to the automated office, sit down and let us help you get acquainted.

- Can you call yourself an information specialist? Find out in this chapter.

- Tips to help you face the automated office with confidence.

THE AUTOMATED OFFICE

Today's technological advances have altered the way we work. If you aren't working at a word processor or a personal computer now, chances are you will be doing so in the near future. (You've undoubtedly already become accustomed to computers at the bank, the supermarket, and the library.)

A major reason for this rapid growth of computers is the microelectronic revolution that has taken place in computer technology. In the search for faster, smaller, and less expensive means of electronically storing data within a computer, engineers miniaturized the entire circuitry of a computer "brain" to a silicon chip smaller than a fingernail. Today the limits of these tiny devices are being continually expanded. It is doubtful that any business trying to compete in the years ahead will be able to avoid using some form of office automation. This means that you, as a professional, will have to be ready for the automated office.

What Is an Automated Office?

In the early sixties, the automated office was ushered in with computers that could fill an entire room. Today, these same computer functions are handled by dime-sized computer chips. And because chips can be mass-produced, the cost of computers has plummeted. Those computers that used to fill an entire room and cost millions of dollars can now sit on a desktop for a cost of only a few thousand dollars.

As the size of computer installations has shrunk, however, the impact of computers in the business world has mushroomed. Now the "automated office" may mean a single desktop computer with word processing, data processing, telecommunications, electronic mail, graphics, and typesetting capabilities. Such computer equipment can be linked to outside database services, micrographics systems, or a network of other computers within the building or around the world. In fact, the automated office of today is quickly becoming an *integrated* office. Word processing is expanding to *information processing*. And some office workers already identify themselves as *information specialists*. For many, the office of the future is already here—and the smart office professional will start preparing for those future changes now.

What Skills Are Needed for the Automated Office?

Many of the skills needed in the automated office are the same as those in demand in the traditional office. You must still be a language expert, for example, and must still possess strong communication skills and organizational abilities. In the automated office, employees will become familiar with the information resources of an organization and have the ability to organize, analyze, compute, and retrieve information.

The first step you can take to prepare for the office of tomorrow is to begin educating yourself about information technology and electronic office systems. You should read computer books, magazines, newsletters, and ads; visit computer stores; attend workshops or trade shows; and take word processing or computer classes. In addition, if you have a personal computer at home or at your local library, you should get some hands-on experience. And finally, you should learn more about the computer or word processing department in your own company.

Overcoming Automation Fears

Remember—machines can't think. They are simply tools that help to make office work easier and more efficient. However, if you're still harboring doubts about coping with office technology, here are some tips for calming your fears:

1. **Realize that your nervousness is normal.** Any new experience, such as your first day at school or your first day on a new job, is naturally going to be scary. The good news is that, in the end, your fears usually turn out to be unwarranted.
2. **Ask questions.** The more questions you ask, the more answers you'll get and the more confident you'll feel about operating a new office system. Jot down your questions as they occur to you—even if you're at home and begin to wonder, *What if ... ?* The process of putting your fears down on paper will help you view them more realistically.
3. **Imagine the worst possible thing that could happen.** It probably isn't as bad as you think. For example, if you're worried that you'll break a new system—this is extremely unlikely—doing so isn't necessarily a catastrophe. There are repair persons available for new equipment too.
4. **Learn three new skills in addition to the ones you already have.** If you work in a small office, it would be wise to learn other functions, such as word processing. If you already use a word processor, why not stay informed about new developments in telecommunications? The more you update your skills, the less new technology will frighten you.

Forecasts for the Future

What do support workers face in the office of the future? Despite initial fears that automation would eliminate office jobs, the emergence of the automated office has actually created the need for a new breed of office workers—ones who can manipulate and manage advanced office systems. As more managers begin handling their own administrative tasks, such as setting up calendars or sending electronic messages instead of memos, office-support professionals will face increased opportunities to assist their supervisors in areas of greater responsibility.

A welcoming attitude toward change and an interest in working with electronic equipment and computer applications are strong prerequisites for success. With the right outlook, new office technology won't become a burden. In fact, if you look on new technology as exciting, it can be not only educational but also fun. And remember, your success with the latest office technology will reflect a positive image of you and your work. For the employee who is willing to embrace the automated office, the future looks bright indeed.

■ Minis, micros, maxis—
what are we talking
about? Computers, of
course. Read on to find
out more.

■ Learn what differentiates
one type of computer
from another.

■ The basics: how com-
puters operate and what
they can do for you.

START WITH THE BASICS

The world of computers can be confusing, if not downright intimidating, to neophyte computer users. Whether or not you now work with
computers, you probably will in the future. So it's important to know
how computers work and what they are used for. In this chapter, we will
introduce you to the basics of computers.

Computers are truly a miracle of the twentieth century, and they have
come to play an increasingly large role in our lives and our jobs. They can
be used to record, classify, calculate, summarize, communicate, and sort
data, and they do all this faster and more accurately than we could if we
were to do it by hand. That's the major advantage of computers. They can
reduce tedious and time-consuming tasks to the simple act of typing a
few commands on a keyboard.

Computers are often considered intelligent; this is an unfortunate mis-
conception. Always keep in mind that computers are wonderful
machines, but they can't approach the capabilities of the human brain.
They can do only what they have been programmed to do—and if they've been
programmed with the wrong instructions, they will respond by providing
the wrong information.

What Is a Computer?

A *computer* is a machine that performs high-speed computations, using
prewritten instructions. There are many types and sizes of computers,
and they are put to numerous uses or applications, depending on their
capabilities. A computer's "strength" depends mainly on two things: its
memory capacity and the speed with which it is able to do computations.

Traditionally, the larger the computer, the more memory it had and the
faster it worked; however, advances in the computer field have been so
dramatic that that situation is changing. Computers that were once differ-
entiated from one another by certain types of characteristics now may
share those characteristics. Thus, the categories of computers are not as
well defined as they once were.

Different Types of Computers

Ranked according to capability and size, the largest and most powerful
computers are *supercomputers* or *maxicomputers*. They can perform at least
10 million instructions per second. These computers are used mainly in
the fields of weather forecasting, nuclear weapons development, and
energy supply and conservation.

The next rank of computer is the *mainframe.* Mainframes have enormous memory capacity and are often used to support many auxiliary
devices. Traditional users of mainframes have been large universities,
hospitals, and businesses that need large databases.

The third rank of computer is the *minicomputer,* which are smaller than
mainframes and less powerful. One of the advantages of minicomputers

is that they are flexible. They can be expanded as a company's needs expand.

The last rank of computer, and probably the one with which you are most familiar, is the *microcomputer*. Microcomputers are used almost everywhere, from the home to huge corporations. What makes microcomputers different from the other types of computers we've mentioned? The other computers all have one central processing unit (think of it as the brain of the computer) with terminals connected to it. Without the "brain," the terminals will not function. This is not true of microcomputers. Each microcomputer has its own central processing unit, and each microcomputer can function as an independent unit. They differ from minicomputers also in their size and price. As we mentioned earlier, rapid developments in the computer field have given rise to very powerful microcomputers, and the differences, as far as memory capacity and capabilities are concerned, are becoming less well defined.

The Parts of a Computer

A computer has three major components: the *central processing unit,* or *CPU;* the *memory;* and *permanent storage.*

The *central processing unit* is the "brain" of the computer—the place where all calculations are performed.

The *memory* is the part of the computer where programs and data are stored while the computer is in use. When a program is run by a computer, the program and the information needed to run the program are located in the memory area of the computer. There is a constant interplay between the CPU and the memory.

Permanent storage is the part of the computer where information is kept when it's not in memory. The permanent storage device is commonly called the *disk.*

What a Computer Does

There are five categories of computing:
1. Data processing
2. Numerical calculation
3. Logical processing
4. Control processing
5. Word and text processing

Data processing involves the creating, updating, and reporting of information. An example is a program that keeps track of inventory for a grocery store.

Numerical calculations are used to get answers to mathematical problems, such as those found in statistical or engineering applications.

Logical processing systems are those that try to imitate the actions of the brain through logical and predetermined sets of steps. This is still a developmental area of computer technology and includes such things as programs that play chess or translate sentences from one language to another.

Control processing involves the feeding of information into the computer to be used in making determinations of when actions need to be undertaken. For example, the computer could determine what chemicals to add in an ongoing manufacturing process.

Word and text processing is, perhaps, the largest office application of computers. Computers can be used to help in writing, storing, and manipulating information.

If you thought of computers with more than a little trepidation when you began this chapter, we hope that this brief introduction has helped you understand computers better. We also hope that your interest in computers has grown and that you will continue to learn about them.

■ With PC power, the effort
you save may be your
own. Find out why.

■ Here: a special introduction to the powerful per-
sonal computer.

■ Discover how the per-
sonal computer is a
major link between you
and improved word pro-
cessing.

A PC PRIMER

Personal computers (PCs) are now widely used in today's automated offices. This mighty microcomputer plays an important role in helping employees perform their work not only more efficiently but also more creatively. For example, with a PC you can pull complex charts from a spreadsheet program and merge them into the document you are word processing, you can add colorful graphics to your reports, and you can even turn a document into a professional looking masterpiece of near-typeset quality through the use of computerized desktop publishing software.

To reap the benefits of the powerful PC, you'll probably have to develop a slightly higher degree of technical expertise than you use with your trusty typewriter or word processor. You don't have to become a computer programmer or a computer engineer, but you do need to understand basic PC concepts to embrace this new technology with ease and enthusiasm. It's also important to have a clear idea of how the PC works in order to plan, maintain, and carry out its operations.

To help you approach the office PC with confidence, we present the following PC primer. In this chapter you'll be introduced to several basic PC terms and concepts, and you'll find out how PCs work with word processing.

The Hard Facts

Hardware (as you may know) is the name given to the physical units of a computer or word processor. (*Software,* on the other hand, is the term used to describe the programs that make the computer run and perform various functions.) Although many types of hardware devices can be used with a PC, three components make up the essential core: *the system unit, the monitor,* and *the keyboard.*

➤ **The system unit** is the brain center of the computer. It contains the central processing unit (CPU) that directs the system by manipulating the information that flows in and out of the computer. The system unit also holds the computer memory, including floppy and/or hard disk drives. Without the disk drives, you wouldn't be able to run your word processing software or save what you type.

Your PC may have one of several disk drive combinations. It can have one or two disk drives ("single" or "dual unit") or a combination of one or two drives with a hard disk unit. A hard disk offers a more convenient type of storage. The disk itself is essentially part of the PC hardware and has a much larger storage capacity than a diskette. These features allow you to store all your active work in one place, and this reduces the time that would otherwise be spent switching diskettes.

The back of the system unit has "ports," which are metal plugs or outlets that permit you to plug in other hardware devices, such as the monitor, keyboard, and printer. The ports are connected to removable electronic circuit boards inside the box. These boards contain instructions to the PC on how to run the device connected to the external port.

➤ **The monitor** acts as your "window" into the computer by showing your documents or displaying messages on a television-like screen. The monitor is called an "output device" because the computer uses it to send information out to you. If you have a color monitor, you may be able to change the color of the display to suit your preferences.

➤ **The keyboard** is an essential "input device" because it is your primary method for sending information into the computer. Most PC keyboards resemble standard typewriter keyboards, and some also have a series of numbered function keys (F1, F2, etc.). Your software will determine the activity that each function key will perform. For example, in a word processing package, F2 might move the text, F3 might copy the text, and so forth. Some keyboards also have special function keys, named "Alt" or "Control," for example, that, when used with other keys, will perform particular functions. For example, using the "Control" key with the "S" key may tell your computer to save a document.

➤ **The printer** is not part of the core of your PC; the system will run without it. Nonetheless, despite talk that computers will bring about a "paperless office," most offices require a computer with a means of putting information on paper. PCs are generally compatible with a wide variety of printers, and most available software packages support a wide range of printers as well.

Software Talk

Without software, even the most expensive PC configuration will not function. Software is simply a collection of magnetic "files" that are used to either perform tasks or store information. Software may be broken down into three major categories: *the operating system, application programs,* and *data files.*

➡ Every PC relies on an **operating system** (OS)—special software furnished with your PC that controls the operation of the computer. A prescribed set of commands allows you to perform such functions as copying software, viewing a directory of disk contents, displaying the contents of files, and generally maintaining your PC system. The OS also lets you enter special commands that permit access to the program software.

➡ Like the operating system, **application programs** are also supplied on diskettes; however, they do not generally come with your PC. These programs contain special instructions that tell your PC how to perform such applications as word processing, spreadsheets, and desktop publishing. There's a wide variety of program software commercially available for most brands of PCs. You can combine several types of software to take advantage of the strengths of each. For example, you might use a word processing program to create a report, then use an electronic spreadsheet to create, format, and calculate the numerical charts that illustrate the report text.

➡ **Data files** are a collection of stored information generally created when you work with application software. You might be more familiar with data files in the context of data processing in which a data file holds records containing such information as customer names, addresses, and phone numbers for your company's Sales Department. Data files like the customer address list contain a recognizable pattern of information called a "record." For example, the sales file records might comprise a name, an address, and a phone number. Word processing documents are also data files, but each document you create is stored in a format or pattern that is unique to the word processing program you're using. These files are normally not interchangeable between software packages without a conversion process. Nonetheless, your PC still treats each document as if it were just another data file.

The PC and Word Processing

Word processing is one of the PC's major functions in today's office. Document creation usually makes up a large part of an office employee's work load. Because of this, it is often through word processing that the PC comes to play an increasingly important role in the office employee's work. Here, we concentrate on the PC as a word processing tool.

Every word processing system available for use with the PC has a unique way of handling document creation. Each has its own set of keystrokes that you can use to perform certain functions. At the same time, all word processing packages interact with the PC in much the same way. The user manual that accompanies your program will be your constant companion as you learn all the intricacies that make the system special. The instructions will be easier to follow, however, if you know a little about some of the topics that are covered in a user manual.

Setting Up Your System

The first time you use your software, you will need to make it compatible with your PC configuration. This means adjusting your program so that it will interact properly with the various components in your particular system. Specific set-up or "installation" procedures are in the manual that accompanies your software. Follow these procedures carefully. They will tell you how to:

✓ Back up your program disk: No matter how carefully you handle diskettes, they can get damaged. Making backups, or copies, of your program disks will ensure that you always have software available when you need it. Most commonly, the backup disk is used as the working copy, and the original is saved to make a new backup if the first becomes damaged.

✓ Install the program to the hard disk or make your program disk "bootable": Normally, you must power up your PC with an operating system disk in the active disk drive. This is called "booting" the system, and it must be performed before you can use the PC. You can add a portion of the operating system to your word processing program disk, so that you can boot your PC using one disk rather than two. (You do not need to do this if your operating system is on the hard disk.) Many word processing manuals will instruct you in this procedure. Otherwise, check your PC user guide for instructions.

✓ Describe your printer to the word processing system: A multitude of printers are available for use with most PCs. Different printers need different instructions from your software to format and print documents. Your software has a series of special files (sometimes called "printer" or "translate" tables) designed for each of the most popular printers. The manual will tell you how to activate the proper printer table.

✓ Customize your software: You may be able to set up a word processing system to automatically generate your most commonly used format setting for right and left margins, line spacing, tab settings, and so forth. Additionally, you can instruct certain software to watch out for, and automatically correct, "widows," which occur when the last line of a paragraph has been carried over to the top of the next page, and "orphans," occurring when the first line of a paragraph appears alone at the bottom of a page. You can also set printer defaults, or automatic settings, for variables such as number of lines per page, type size, and style.

✓ Customize word processing display and functions: You can also set the display defaults according to your preferences. These options include setting the foreground and background colors (if you have a color monitor), displaying menus and screen graphics, or even setting some or all function keys to your specifications.

Running a Word Processing System

Once the operating system is loaded, your PC is ready to accept commands that you enter from the keyboard. To run a word processing program, the appropriate word processor disk must be placed into the active drive or be installed onto your hard disk so that the PC will have access to the software. Your word processing manual will tell you what command to enter to begin, and it will issue specific instructions about the entire start-up procedure.

Setup for the Printer

Setting up your software to recognize your printer is well explained in most software manuals. If you need to print more than just normal text, however, check the manual for an advanced section that describes how to produce special characters like bullets, copyright, and trademark symbols.

The model of printer you have will determine whether you can print special characters. The set-up procedures can be somewhat complex, but they are done only once. Be sure to read the procedures carefully before you sit down at the keyboard. Next, write down exactly what you want to accomplish (any special codes you will have to enter, for example). If any of the manual's procedures are unclear, call the software company help line (if one is available) for clarification before you begin the conversion process. Finally, be sure to make a backup copy of any diskettes that you will be using for the conversion. This way, if something goes wrong, your software will be protected.

Training for Word Processing on a PC

The largest portion of the word processing manual will be dedicated to the methods and procedures that are necessary to create and edit documents. Some word processing systems have up to three tools to help you learn how the system works:

• **Tutorial diskettes** are supplied with some software packages. A tutorial diskette is a good way to start learning because it's "interactive"; it displays lessons about the various word processing functions, provides exercises for you to practice what you have learned, and notifies you when you have made an error. Tutorials give you a chance to learn the basics as you would in a classroom, using the PC as the instructor.

• **The training manual** is, of course, a second way of learning the system and should be used even if a tutorial diskette is furnished. If no tutorial diskette is furnished, the training manual will be your primary source of education. In some cases, the reference manual (designed for use once your basic training is complete) and the training manual will be provided in one volume. Otherwise, they will be separate volumes. In either case, look for tutorial-type information; you need predesigned exercises with answers, if possible, to learn the software efficiently.

• **Help screens** are the third learning tool, and they are particularly valuable after you have accomplished your basic training. Help screens display summarized information about the available system functions and how to use them. These screens are accessed in various ways, depending on the software package. Generally, you can press a function key while you are working on a document to display the help information you need. In rare cases, the displayed help screens will give you access to an interactive lesson if the help information did not clarify the trouble spot. After you have located and read the information, a single keystroke will redisplay your document.

Once you've mastered the basic concepts, your PC will become a valued tool. As your comfort level rises, have fun—and be inventive! With PC power at your fingertips, the effort you save may well be your own.

■ Get a grip on computer
  basics with this helpful
  overview.

■ Here: Refresh your com-
  puter memory with these
  short review quizzes.

■ Find out what you
  know—and don't
  know—about today's
  office technology.

A WORD PROCESSING & COMPUTER RECAP

In the previous word processing and computer chapters you learned about the automated office, computer basics, and the personal computer. But because the discussion of new office technology can sometimes seem a bit overwhelming, we're going to take time out now to review the information that has been presented so far.

The following quizzes will cover material from each of the earlier word processing and computer chapters. Remember, if you have any trouble with these quizzes, simply refer to the appropriate chapter.

QUIZ 1 Match each of the following definitions with the correct term on the right. Use each letter once. The answers follow.

1._____   A machine that performs high-speed computations using prewritten instructions.   A. Permanent Storage

2._____   Some office workers now identify themselves as this.   B. Data Processing

3._____   The "brain" of the computer.   C. Information Specialists

4._____   The part of the computer where programs and data are stored while in use.   D. Computer

5._____   The part of the computer where information is kept when it's not in memory.   E. Central Processing Unit

6._____   The permanent storage device.   F. Memory

7._____   This involves the creating and reporting of information.   G. Database Services

8._____   Computer equipment can be linked to these.   H. Disk

ANSWERS   1. D; 2. C; 3. E; 4. F; 5. A; 6. H; 7. B; 8. G

The following statements are either true or false. Circle T if the statement is true and F if the statement is false. Then check your answers against those found at the end of the quiz.

1. The personal computer (PC) is widely used in the automated office.   (T/F)

2. To use a PC you must become a programmer or a computer engineer.   (T/F)

3. Software is the name given to the physical units of your computer or word processor.   (T/F)

4. A tutorial diskette is a good way to start learning because it's "interactive."   (T/F)

5. The central processing unit (CPU) directs the system by manipulating the information that flows in and out of the computer. (T/F)

6. The PC has only one disk drive, the "single" diskette unit.   (T/F)

7. You should never make your program disk "bootable."   (T/F)

8. The monitor is the television-like screen that acts as your window into the computer.   (T/F)

9. The keyboard is a nonessential "input device."   (T/F)

10. The printer is the core of your PC.   (T/F)

11. Data files are a collection of stored information generally created when you work with application software.   (T/F)

12. Help screens display summarized information about the available system functions and how to use them.   (T/F)

ANSWERS

1. True
2. False: Although you have to increase your technical expertise, you don't have to become a computer programmer or engineer to use a PC.
3. False: *Hardware* is the name given to the physical units of your computer or word processor.
4. True
5. True
6. False: Your PC may have *one* or *two* disk drives.
7. False: You should make your program disk "bootable" so that your PC will run a program simply as a result of your inserting the program disk and turning the machine on.
8. True
9. False: The keyboard is an *essential* "input device."
10. False: The printer is *not* part of the core. The system can run without it.
11. True
12. True

- Do you spend a large part of your day typing? If so, we've got just what you need: helpful hints to minimize time spent on keyboard tasks.

- Shortcuts to help you do your job as efficiently and speedily as possible.

- Suggestions to simplify your work.

TIPS FOR KEYBOARD TASKS

In the preceding chapters, we've been talking about computers and word processors and how they are such a boon to today's office-support professional. They can reduce time-consuming and boring tasks to quick, effortless ones—enabling the employee to do a more efficient, more professional job. But computers can't solve every problem. You have to know how to make the most of your various jobs. In this chapter, we give you some guidelines for simplifying your keyboard tasks.

1. **Keep troublesome words within sight.** Is spelling a problem for you? If it is, don't forget to use your spell-checking program. Or, if you don't have a spell checker, try keeping a 3 x 5 index card taped somewhere within sight of your keyboard. On the card, you can jot down those words that you look up over and over again (many spell checkers allow you to add words). Gradually, you'll create a timesaving reference of spellings that you can brush up on when you have a spare moment.

2. **Make a note of it.** When your equipment needs repairs, type a note explaining the problems your machine is giving you; then tape the note to the side of your machine. This way the repair people will know what to look for, even if you're not there.

3. **Keep track of good ideas.** When you come across an idea that you might like to incorporate into your work routine, but you don't have the time just then to put the idea into action, start keeping an "idea notebook." In it, write down the idea, its source (publication title, number, date, page), possible action, and other pertinent information. Later, when you have more time, you can easily follow up on the idea by referring to the notebook. Not only will this keep you from forgetting the idea, but it will also save time in locating the source.

4. **Create a "Comment Page."** Some computer programs offer a comment feature that allows you to make notes anywhere in the document. These notes don't appear when you print out the document. If you work on a word processor, consider making a "Comment Page" as the last page of a large-volume document. Comments can really speed up the workflow. You can make notes of any special instructions for margins, spacing, print elements to be used, the type of form to be used, etc. Comments are especially helpful when more than one person will be working on the project.

5. **Use correct terminology.** The use of incorrect terminology can be one of the biggest obstacles to trouble-free training for people who use new automated office equipment. It's easy for the trainer and the new user to fall into the habit of using silly names for particular

parts or operations of the equipment. But "whatchamacallits" and "thingamajigs" are difficult to find when you try to look them up in the operator's manuals. If the trainer isn't nearby when a problem arises on screen, a novice operator is left floundering. Make sure you use the terms that are proper for the equipment. This will make it easier for you when you're trying to troubleshoot problem situations.

6. **Try this setup.** Setting up charts or other specialized keyboarding projects can be a task that makes you see red. But as soon as your blood pressure starts to rise, it's almost impossible to see your way clear to an easy solution. If this sounds familiar, we may have just the suggestion you need.

    Sometimes it's difficult to predict how a printed document will look from what appears on the screen. This can be particularly true when you're working with paper or envelopes of unusual sizes. To solve this problem, make up a chart with character markers across the top of the page and numbers down the left side to indicate the page lines. Now when you need to determine the placement of headings, addresses, or columns, you can pull out your chart, place your paper against it, and use the numbers to determine the correct margin or tab settings.

7. **Create samples.** If you have to set up a lot of keyboarding projects with varying specifications (such as different margin and tab settings), jumping from one project to another can cause real problems. To help you avoid racking your brain to refigure formatting specifications for every project you type, make samples of the different items that you work with. For instance, if you type on different-sized labels, index cards, or letterheads, make a note of the margin settings, tab stops, spacing, and any other helpful information on each of these different items. Keep these samples where you can easily refer to them when you need to.

8. **Rough it.** If you use computer paper, here's a helpful tip. After typing memos and rough drafts, leave the perforated edge of the computer paper on the sheets when you give them to your boss. That way, he or she will know at a glance that they are first copies. Your boss can then either make the necessary corrections or note that the copies are acceptable. When you see the sheets with the perforated edges on your desk, you'll know that something is still in the works.

9. **Systematize your projects.** Keeping documents flowing through various departments in an orderly way is the nuts and bolts of any organization.
    • Put an in-basket in an easily accessible place so that people can drop off their projects even when you're not available.
    • Keep file folders with employee names. Completed projects can go in these folders.

ALL ABOUT DISKETTES

Since most office employees work with computers or word processing equipment every day, it's important for you to know as much as possible about one of the most used storage mediums this equipment uses: the diskette. After all, losing an electronic document can be much more disastrous than simply misplacing a file folder of paper manuscripts.

A diskette is a storage device commonly used with word processing systems and desktop computers. If you're new to either, it will pay to understand what a diskette does and how it should be handled. If you're already familiar with diskettes, remember—the more you know about them, the better you can take care of them and of your company's information.

Dissecting the Diskette

The inside of a diskette looks something like a phonograph record—but without grooves. The diskette stores magnetized bits of information rather than sound and requires a great deal more care than records. The actual disk is less than $\frac{1}{13}$-inch thick and incapable of lying flat without something to support it—which is why the disks are covered by a jacket. The jacket actually does more than just support the disk, however; it also protects the disk from dust, fingerprints, spills, scratches, or other possible sources of damage to the magnetized bits of information.

There are three main *sizes* of diskettes: the $5\frac{1}{4}$-inch, the $3\frac{1}{2}$-inch, and the 8-inch (referring to disk diameter). Most dedicated word processors use the 8-inch version; personal computers use the other two sizes. The $3\frac{1}{2}$-inch "microdiskette" is quickly becoming the most popular size. And because of improved technology, this pocket-sized disk can hold more information than the $5\frac{1}{4}$-inch diskette. The microdiskette, unlike the 8-inch and the $5\frac{1}{4}$-inch diskette, has a hard plastic shell and an "auto shutter," which keep dust and fingerprints off the disks. Many experts believe that in time the microdiskette will be the dominant disk format.

There are two *types* of diskettes: single-sided and double-sided. As the names imply, a single-sided diskette records data on one side only; the double-sided disk stores information on both sides.

Following is a brief look at what you would find if you examined an 8-inch or a $5\frac{1}{4}$-inch diskette closely. The $3\frac{1}{2}$-inch disk has many of the same features on its plastic shell. Examine a disk to familiarize yourself with its features. Although your disk may be somewhat different, the basic elements will be the same.

➤ **Paper envelope:** Eight-inch and $5\frac{1}{4}$-inch diskettes should always be kept in their heavy paper envelopes to protect them from dust, spills, fingerprints, etc., which can damage or destroy the data recorded on the disk. When you've finished using a diskette, always return it to its paper envelope for safekeeping.

➢ **Vinyl sleeve:** If you take an 8-inch or a 5¼-inch disk out of its envelope, you'll find the circular, dull brown or black disk encased in a vinyl sleeve—often called the jacket. The sleeve is a permanent covering for the disk and should never be removed. You'll notice that the sleeve has a circular hole in the middle (as does the disk itself). There is also a smaller hole off to one side and an oblong cutout on another side. You'll notice, too, that the vinyl sleeve contains a couple of notches along one side and a third, larger notch, which is sometimes on a separate side. Each of these cutouts, holes, and notches has a particular purpose. Following is a description of each:

➢ **Centering hole:** The centering hole allows the system's disk drive mechanism to lock onto the disk and spin it inside the sleeve to record commands and typed-in data. Like a phonograph record, the disk must be turned to get at the information stored on it.

➢ **Indexing hole:** The small round indexing hole is the place where the disk drive looks to find the starting sector of each track on the disk. Think of a line being drawn across the radius of the disk. When you add new information to the disk or want to call up material that has already been stored on it, the drive searches out this starting line to find the exact location of the particular information stored on the disk.

➢ **Access hole:** The oblong cutout is the access hole, also called the head window. This is where the head of the disk drive magnetically writes data onto or reads data from the disk. On a microdiskette, the access hole is underneath the auto shutter.

➢ **Alignment notches:** On the edge of the disk sleeve that fits against the inside surface of the disk slot are two alignment notches. These notches insure that the disk is fitted properly into the drive.

➢ **Write-protect notch:** The write-protect notch guards against your recording information over data that is already on a disk. Note that the placement of the notch depends on the size of the disk. The function of the notch also varies with the size of the disk. On 8-inch disks, when the write-protect notch is covered up, you *can* write on the disk, and when the notch is uncovered, you *can't* write on the disk. On the 5¼-inch disks, the opposite is true: When the notch is covered, you can't write on the disk, and when it isn't covered you can. On a 3½-inch disk, the notch can be set to either open or closed position.

Do Diskettes Die?

Do diskettes last indefinitely? This depends on several factors—such as disk quality, frequency of use, and proper care. But generally speaking, a diskette begins to erode after two years of continuous use. About this time, the oxide coating on the disk starts to shed, and that can cause serious read errors. This process may begin sooner if the disk had been stored in a low-humidity area. It is recommended that diskettes be stored in an environment with 40- to 60-percent humidity. Also, diskettes should not be subjected to extremes of temperature. Sudden exposure to radical change in environmental conditions may precipitate dew formation or disk distortion, for example. It's a good idea for a diskette that has been sent through the mail or brought into the office from another location to sit for 30 to 60 minutes. This allows time for the disk to adjust to room temperature before you use it, reducing the risk of losing information.

NOTE: Now that you've had a proper introduction to diskettes, watch for more tips on proper diskette care in the next chapter.

■ Follow these helpful
guidelines for diskette
care.

■ Here: 10 tips on how to
treat your diskette with
tender loving care.

■ Learn proper storage
and handling techniques
for your diskettes.

A DISKETTE FOLLOW-UP

In the last chapter we gave you a close-up look at diskettes. But because diskettes are something most office-support professionals work with every day, it's also important that you understand how to care for them. In this chapter we'll focus on the proper use and care of diskettes.

Following are 10 tips on how to treat your diskettes so that you won't get scrambled data or lose an entire segment of processed material:

1.   **Never touch the surface of a diskette.** Any dirt, dust, oil, or other residue can create real problems on the magnetic surface of the disk, preventing your computer system from reading prerecorded material. That's why it's imperative that you never touch the exposed magnetic surface of the disk. Even the slightest fingerprint smudge can wipe out whole sections of processed material. Always handle the diskette by the vinyl sleeve or plastic shell that contains and protects it.

2.   **Store and use diskettes in a clean environment.** Not only must you be careful how you handle your diskettes, you must take extra care to see that they're kept in as clean an environment as possible. To ensure the best performance from your diskettes, avoid eating, drinking, or smoking around your computer station. Smoke is actually composed of airborne particles that can collect on magnetic surfaces. And food and drink pose obvious problems. For a number of years, cola has been used by filmmakers to erase noise from magnetic sound tracks. A spill, obviously, can destroy hours of hard work. Hot coffee may not demagnetize a disk, but in wiping it off, you may also be wiping off pages and pages of material. So if you want to eat or smoke at break time, do so away from your work area.

3.   **Never bend a diskette.** As many as 1.5 million characters can be stored on the diskette surface. That means that lots of tiny bits of magnetized information are located in a small area. For your computer equipment to be able to read all those characters, the diskette must remain absolutely flat. The slightest crease in the disk may mean that the disk drive of your equipment won't make contact with the surface of the disk. The result: lost information. So handle your disks with care. Always take your time removing them from or inserting them back into their protective jackets. If you must leave one out on your desk, lay it absolutely flat and don't place anything on top of it. And if a diskette must be transported somewhere, make sure the carrier knows not to bend the diskette inside the envelope or package. You want to make sure that the information stored on the disk, as well as the disk itself, reaches its destination.

4.   **Keep your diskettes away from magnets.** Remember that information is *magnetically* recorded on a diskette, so any magnetic or electromagnetic field can scramble or erase any data recorded on a disk. Where should you watch out for magnetic fields? Most of your computer equip-

ment contains magnetic fields. This includes your video terminal, equipment controller, and printer. So be careful not to casually set a disk down on top of your equipment. And because there may be a magnet in the handset of your telephone, always keep disks clear of phones within the office. Your computer system's service representative or your operator's manual may give you additional advice concerning other sources of magnetic and electromagnetic fields in your office.

5. **Don't leave a diskette in the drive when you turn off the power.** Most of the time nothing will happen if you leave a disk in the equipment. But occasionally you may get a power surge, or "spike," when you shut off the power. This can scramble the information already on the disk. The same thing can happen if a disk is in the equipment when it is turned on. So make it a habit to warm up your equipment before inserting a disk. And be sure to remove the disk from the drive before turning the system off.

6. **Store your diskettes properly.** Diskettes should be stored just like phonograph records, horizontally or vertically—especially if they are to be kept in storage for a long time. Disks can't warp like records, but if they stand on a slant for an extended period, they may bend slightly—and that can mean lost information. If your disks are stacked, don't put too many in a pile. In fact, it's best not to stack them more than 10 deep. Also, never use paper clips or rubber bands to hold disks together. Paper clips may be magnetized and rubber bands can bend disks.

7. **Take care when inserting the diskette into, and removing it from, the disk drive.** Most computer systems are designed so that no misalignment can occur when a diskette is inserted into the drive. But to make sure you don't lose processed information just because a disk was miscentered in the drive, take your time when inserting the disk. Likewise, remove a disk slowly and deliberately. Don't handle a diskette hurriedly or sloppily.

8. **Don't let your disks get too full.** If you're processing a long document, be especially wary of trying to store more information on a disk than it can hold. For some machines, disk capacity is determined by the number of individual files stored on it. For these systems, a file containing only one five-letter word may take up as much disk space as a file containing 1,000 characters. So keep track of your disk space, especially if your system doesn't warn you when you're approaching "disk full." A little attention to this can save you a lot of retyping or reconstruction of information.

9. **Label your diskettes carefully.** Before computer systems came on the scene, you could go sifting through your file cabinet to find a particular letter if you weren't quite sure where it was. But when disks become your main information storage medium, labeling is an absolute must. Prepare labels before applying them to disks, and be sure to use a soft felt-tip pen to alter labels already on disks. Using a ballpoint pen or a pencil can damage your disk.

10. **Take care of your computer equipment.** Of course, it should go without saying that you need to take care of your computer equipment, too—for its sake as well as for the sake of your disks. You need all your system components functioning properly to produce clean, accurate copies. Read your operator's manual carefully and talk to your service rep, who should be able to answer a lot of your questions regarding system maintenance and diskette care.

- Keep abreast of modern office technology with this guideline on equipment evaluations.

- Here: keys to selecting new office equipment.

- Find out how to get the equipment information you need.

EQUIPMENT EVALUATIONS

Word processors and computers are part of an evolving technology. That means your company may decide to acquire additional electronic equipment from a different vendor, upgrade its present system, or change systems altogether. Since many businesses begin this process by consulting the end-user (that's you), there's a good chance that you'll be asked for input regarding the selection of new electronic office equipment. The following suggestions will help you make carefully considered, informed recommendations for equipment selections that will best meet your office needs:

> **Start by evaluating your present system.** Even if your company isn't in the market for new equipment right now, it's a good idea to begin documenting what your present system can and can't do and what applications it is used for. Make a checklist of your system's features, using your operator's manual as a guide, and begin collecting sample printouts of the different applications for your system. Then take the time to note on your checklist which features are particularly useful, which ones are rarely used, and which features aren't available that would be helpful in your work. (If you find a function that seems awkward to execute, it may be helpful to mention this to the vendor. Perhaps other users have also expressed this, and the company may develop an improved method.) Your evaluation sheet will come in handy as a means of comparison when you need to evaluate other systems. If another system has a feature or features that you think would be helpful to you, check your list carefully to be sure that a switch to the new system will not sacrifice any of your present system's useful features.

> **Understand your office needs.** To determine whether a system would be cost effective and beneficial for your department, you first need to identify the applications you would have for it. For example, would you use the new system for:

- Word processing?
- Records management?
- Accounting?
- Spreadsheets?

It'll make your job easier if you know what capabilities you need *before* you begin your search.

> **Begin educating yourself now.** The better informed you are, the better the choices you'll make. Familiarize yourself with computer lingo. Read as much as you can about office equipment. Ask marketing representatives to give you some literature on the different types of equipment they offer. Check with your public library for

books on selecting office equipment and for a listing of periodicals that deal with this topic. Read as many computer and software magazines as you can. And don't forget to check the advertisements. They often list important specifications for products. You should also visit equipment manufacturers and computer stores in your area.

➤ **Consult knowledgeable co-workers.** Employees who work on advanced office systems such as word processors or personal computers can offer helpful information even if their job functions are radically different from yours. They'll be able to give you pointers on how efficient or how difficult various systems are to work with.

➤ **Don't be afraid to ask questions.** When the evaluation process does begin in your company, you may be asked to meet with sales representatives or to attend equipment demonstrations. Be sure to take full advantage of these sessions—don't be shy about asking questions. You're there to learn as much as you can, and the sales representative is there to answer any questions you may have. Don't hesitate to interrupt a strong sales pitch by voicing your doubts or asking for more information about the claims being made. If you would like a more detailed demonstration, be sure to request it. It's important for you to base your opinions on as much information as possible.

➤ **Get the details.** Before you make your final decision, request demonstrations of those systems you're considering. Ask specific questions about the features available for each package. Find out which components—such as computer software programs or printers—are compatible with existing systems at your office. If you're purchasing a printer, for instance, you may want to ask:

- What is the quality of the printing?
- Does the printer have graphics capabilities?
- How fast does it operate?
- What features are available?
- Will the printer work with all our software?
- Is the printer compatible with the specific forms our department uses?
- What is the maximum page width?

Remember to find out what services are offered should your new equipment require repairs or maintenance.

➤ **Do a thorough job.** Spend enough time educating yourself and researching the equipment to make intelligent decisions. Absorbing all this technical information is naturally going to take some time, so don't rush through the process.

➤ **Look into the costs.** Do some comparison shopping. You may find that one system offers much more than another for a comparable price. If there's a definite ceiling on how much your company is willing to spend, find out what it is before you make your recommendations.

➤ **State your findings in a positive light.** Once you've made your selection and gathered documentation to support your decision, present your case to your supervisor with confidence. Identify the benefits of the new system for your boss. Attach dollar values to the benefits you'll reap—even to the intangible factors, such as making employees more productive. Your boss is sure to be impressed with your presentation—and with you, too.

- **You have a computer, but do you know how to take care of it? Read on and find out.**

- **Learn what parts of the computer need maintenance and which don't.**

- **Discover the keys to reducing—or eliminating—computer malfunctions.**

EQUIPMENT CARE

Ever wonder how computer glitches got to be called bugs? Believe it or not, it's because an insect caused the first computer breakdown on record. That's right—a moth got into one of the first computers and shorted out the machine when it flew into some wires. Since "a bug in the machine" seemed to be a good way of describing computer problems, the term stuck and it's part of the language today.

It's not hard to see how an insect could get into one of the earliest computers; they were so big that you needed a good-size room to put them in, and so hot that you needed lots of air space for ventilation. Those behemoths used vacuum tubes—which were hot, bulky, and fragile—to do the work; today's computers use integrated circuits (ICs)—fingernail-size chips that contain the equivalent of hundreds or even thousands of separate electronic components. Because of the IC chip, today's personal computer can fit on any desktop and is but a fraction of the price of the first computer, while having considerably more computing power.

Today's computer is also a highly reliable machine—odds are that it will become obsolete long before it becomes unusable. That doesn't mean, however, that computers don't need some kind of care or maintenance. They do, but you can minimize the need for repairs if you're aware of what can go wrong in your computer and what you can do to keep it from happening.

If something does go wrong, the first thing to do is to pick up the manual. Often, what appears to be a breakdown is nothing more than a user oversight; the manual's "troubleshooting" section anticipates these oversights and tells you how to correct them.

The CPU

As we mentioned in Chapter 3, the CPU (central processing unit) is the heart and the brain of the computer, the place where the actual computing takes place. The CPU contains all the chips in the computer, as well as its disk drives and power supply.

Accordingly, the entire CPU—chips, disk drives, and all—is the most fragile component in the computer. Once you put the CPU in place, it should stay there until you have to move it. Here are some other tips to keep your CPU happy:

➤ VENTILATE—Solid-state components run much cooler than tubes, but they are affected by heat and can burn out. Fortunately, most computers include fans that keep the chips and hard disk drive at a comfortable temperature.

Because these fans don't work if their air supply is obstructed, make sure that you leave some space between the fan vent (usually located on the bottom or at the rear of the CPU) and any wall or floor. If you decide to set your desktop-based CPU on its side on the floor, you may need a stand that will raise the CPU to an acceptable height.

➢ KEEP IT CLEAN—Computers will "go down" if their innards get gummed up with dirt and grime. For this reason, it's best to use the computer in an environment where dust or dirt won't be a problem. Keep in mind, too, that cigarette smoke is as dangerous for computers as it is for human beings; try to keep people from smoking around your computer.

➢ KEEP IT CLOSED—Most personal computer CPUs can be easily opened (to add boards or disk drives, replace bad chips, etc.), but if you don't know what you're doing, don't bother. You only risk damaging something inside the CPU or frying yourself. It's better to report a problem or malfunction to your computer service department than to try to fix it yourself.

Diskette Facts

In Chapter 7, we discussed taking care of your diskettes. But what do you do about the disk drive?

Of course, taking care of your disks will help protect the drive, but even before that, the first step you can take is to try to use name-brand disks. If you've ordered supplies before, you know that the best price doesn't always mean the best quality. Beware of generic, cheaper-by-the-caseload disks. Brand-name disk manufacturers take pains to deliver a quality product, one that won't shed magnetic particles that clog up the drive head the way no-name disks can.

If your head does become clogged (you'll know when the computer flashes messages that the drive has trouble reading the disks), take it to your company's service department for a cleaning. Don't do it yourself (unless authorized to); you could damage something inside the drive.

The Monitor

If you've ever called your computer monitor "the television screen," you're not far off the mark. They both use the same technology and they look somewhat alike. And the same precautions must be applied to a computer monitor as are applied to a TV set.

Two things can go wrong with a monitor: a gradual fading of the image, and burn-in. Fading brightness is a fact of life with any monitor, and burn-in—characters or images that are embedded into the screen even after they have been removed—doesn't have to be a problem in the first place. While any monitor will, in time, fade, there are a number of ways to prolong its useful life:

• Keep the monitor at medium brightness and contrast levels while you're working.
• Turn the monitor brightness level down to black when you're not working with it. Not only does this preserve the monitor, but it also keeps people from peeking at your work.
• Use a screen-saver utility program. These programs, or "desk accessories," turn the screen black if you don't press any keys for a certain length of time. Once you resume working, however, the display will come on again.
• An accumulation of dust on the screen is an obvious problem. It can be easily conquered by use of a damp cloth and glass cleaner or a special cloth made for dusting computer screens.

The Keyboard and Other Input Devices

As far as the user is concerned, the keyboard is one of the most important components of the computer. It is the part that he or she uses to communicate with the computer. It is also the part that the user tends to abuse the most. Here are some things to keep in mind while you're using the keyboard:

➤ Don't pound the keys. After constant pounding, the switches inside the keys may wear down and a particular key may not work. (This shouldn't be a problem if you are a touch typist, however.)

➤ Keep the liquids away. One of Murphy's Laws states that the closer a liquid is to an electronic part, the greater the likelihood of its spilling. Whether you believe in Murphy's Law or not, don't take the risk in the first place.

More and more computers are using the mouse as an input device. The mouse usually takes the form of a small box containing a rubber ball that is rolled on the desktop. To keep the mouse in good working condition, keep your desk and the area around your computer dust-free, and periodically take the ball out of the mouse and clean it.

The Power

The only time anyone ever thinks about the power supply in his or her computer is when it goes down. And the main reason a power supply goes down is that it's overloaded from using add-on boards and hard disks that demand more juice than it's capable of giving. If your computer keeps blowing fuses, it may well be because the power supply in your machine is too skimpy. The solution to that is easy enough: Make sure that you get a beefier power supply, one that will meet—and hopefully surpass—all your power requirements.

One other thing—if any component in your system uses a three-prong plug, insert it into a three-prong socket or a properly installed adapter. The third prong is used for grounding—to protect the equipment and the operator from dangerous electrical shocks. Trying to use a three-prong plug in a two-prong socket (without an adapter) is a foolish and needless risk.

The Printer

For a mechanical component, the printer is remarkably trouble-free, requiring little more than occasional maintenance. Still, there are some rules of thumb to go by to keep printer hassles to a minimum.

• **Before you use the printer,** make sure that it can be used with your software. Most software usually includes printer drivers (small programs that translate your data into commands the printer can understand) for most popular printers. The wrong driver for a printer can result in printouts that, at best, will lack the formatting that makes a document visually appealing. At worst, the printouts will contain plenty of garbage along with your text.

If your printer is not among those listed to work with a software package, check to see if your printer is compatible with one that is listed. If it isn't, talk to the software developer or the printer manufacturer about a driver for that particular printer.

• **When you're putting paper into the sprockets** of the tractors, keep the paper taut—but not too taut. You'll know the right degree of tightness as you adjust the feed yourself.

• **After you've adjusted the paper feed,** turn the printer off and on again to set the top of the sheet properly. Do this any time you have to adjust the paper.

• **Don't tamper with any switch or button settings** on the printer if you don't know what you're doing. You could make the printer start spewing out garbage.

• **A lighter than normal printout** is usually a sign that your printer's ribbon is wearing out or its ink cartridge is drying out. This is inevitable. Changing the printer's ribbon or ink cartridge is fairly easy—usually it means popping out the old cartridge and putting in a replacement. Your printer's manual will have instructions on how to do this.

• **Occasionally, the platen (the roller in the printer) may become contaminated** with dirt and paper debris. Since this can lead to paper misfeeds, you may want to clean the platen. Before you do so, however, check to see that you're using the right paper feed setting on the printer. If you're using computer ("fanfold") paper, use the tractor setting. For single sheets, use the friction setting. Bear in mind that the wrong setting can cause a misfeed.

If, as it turns out, you do need to clean the platen, use a specially designed platen cleaner to do the job. Don't use a towel and water or cleaner—you could actually do more harm than good.

If you use a laser printer, there's not much you have to worry about except the occasional paper misfeed or toner cartridge change. Both operations can be done by anyone who is familiar with office copiers (laser printers share the same basic design as office copiers), and neither one takes more than two or three minutes.

Cables

It's easy to take connecting cables for granted—after all, they don't do anything but carry electrical signals back and forth—but a bad cable can cause as many problems as a bad component or chip. Here are some tips for using cables correctly:

➢ **Make sure that you have the right cable for the job,** and don't try to make the wrong one fit. Cables carry not only electrical signals but also the power and grounding that various components need to work. If the cable isn't the right one for the job, find one that is. If you can't, use an approved adapter.

➢ **When detaching a cable from its outlet,** make sure that all clamps or screws that may hold it in place are removed, then grasp the cable by the plug and squeeze the plug as you're pulling. Holding a cable by the cord and yanking it out can damage the cable and/or the computer.

➢ **When inserting a plug into a socket,** turn the equipment off first. Make sure that the plug is all the way in the socket before you turn everything on again.

➢ **Don't use a damaged cable.** If the insulation is frayed or clips or wires are bent, immediately bring this to the attention of your supervisor or Maintenance, who will fix it or issue you another one.

While computer breakdowns are not unheard of, they are still relatively rare. By following these tips, you'll ensure that your computer will be on your desktop all the time, not in the shop.

COMPUTER SECURITY

Before businesses started using computers, people just did their work on paper. If they had any sensitive information—data about a new product or a marketing scheme that they had to keep out of the competition's hands—they just locked it up at night. If someone wanted to see the information illegally, he or she had to physically get to it, which was impossible if the company's security system was good enough.

With computers, however, it's almost impossible to put your work in a safe, unless you want to unplug the entire system and put it in there. Security has become an important issue for anyone using computers. Businesses now find themselves willing to take drastic measures to prevent computer sabotage or tampering, because they need to.

The competition isn't the only security factor a business must pay attention to. Any employee or ex-employee with a grudge can bring a system to its knees without too much work. And hackers—amateur computer users who are particularly skilled at gaining unauthorized access to computer systems—have contributed their own brand of mischief to the computer world. Never has the need for security been greater.

What are the situations that lead to the need for security? Generally, they are:

→ Outright physical theft of printouts or disks.

→ Unauthorized access to local area networks and individual PCs due to employees' careless use of passwords.

→ Outside sources breaking into a company's system via on-line services or electronic mail.

While the first two situations are in-house problems, the third is often beyond a company's direct control. Any company that uses its computer system to communicate with the outside world risks this kind of security breakdown.

Keep Away From My Data

Hard disks are now a standard fixture on computers, for good reason, but they do create security problems. It's easy to take diskettes out of the computer and keep them locked up—but what do you do if your files are on a disk that stays with the machine?

One thing you can do is use your computer's lock to prevent unauthorized use of the machine (many post-1984 computers have key-operated locks somewhere on the outside of the CPU). Another obvious step is to copy work files from the hard disk onto diskettes or tape cartridges at the end of the day, lock up the diskettes or cartridges for the night, erase those files from the hard disk, and then recopy the files back onto the hard disk in the morning. This is a long, arduous procedure, but it's one that many companies have deemed necessary.

Keeping unauthorized eyes away from printouts is easy enough. Don't let the printer go unattended while you're printing out the file, and put the printout in a safe place as soon as you can.

Password Problems

Because computer users often work in groups, and because many peripherals such as printers and large-capacity hard disks can be shared among many users, there is a need for local area networks (LANs) in many offices. Such networks, however, can be a corporate nightmare if the people responsible for controlling them are lax or if there is a mischief-maker within the network.

Most LANs have established gateways whereby only certain employees can get into certain directories. These gateways use a password system whereby an employee enters his or her name (or initials) and a sequence of numbers or letters (which may or may not be a recognizable word). If an employee enters the right information, the network allows the person to begin work; if not, the system stops and the user must reenter the password. Some systems can even report successive wrong entries as attempted break-ins.

If you're part of a network, you will want to keep these steps in mind to minimize security risks:

➡ Don't share your password with anyone—not even a co-worker. Even someone you trust could inadvertently tamper with your data.

➡ Log off the network when you're not going to be at your desk. It might seem silly to go through the log-off and log-on procedures for a 10-minute coffee break, but those 10 minutes are all a saboteur needs to wreak havoc.

A Disease in Your Computer?

Many companies use their computers to communicate with the outside world—to share information with other offices of the company, with other companies, even with other employees within the same office. Needless to say, the potential for security breaches is enormous. Hackers or tailgaters—operators who sneak their way into other people's files—can get into a system and extract or tamper with data, or leave viruses that can crash an entire system.

Viruses are programs that sneak, undetected, into the computer's system files and wreak havoc with the computer. While some viruses are relatively benign (for instance, causing the computer to flash silly messages on the screen), some are vicious, erasing all data on your disks and making the system useless.

Unfortunately, a determined and smart tailgater can get into a system no matter what you do, but there are some things you can do to keep viruses, in particular, from crashing your system:

➢ Avoid software that's been downloaded from electronic bulletin boards or copies from friends' disks. Viruses usually enter a system via these programs or disks containing these programs. Viruses have even appeared in commercial software packages, which gives you an idea of how widespread the problem has become. Even so, there's relatively little chance that commercially purchased programs will harbor viruses.

➢ Use a virus-killing utility. These miniprograms detect peculiarities in a computer's system files (where the viruses usually reside) and restore the system files to "health," in effect killing the virus.

Computer security is necessary precisely because computers are so necessary to businesses these days. Bringing a computer system to its knees often brings a company to its knees. Being lax about security is one way to risk not only your own livelihood but that of your co-workers as well. Is that a risk you really want to take?

- Learn about the three major types of business software and what they can do for you.

- Evaluating software? We've got some questions you should be asking.

- Learning about a new piece of software doesn't have to be painful. Find out how to make it easier.

SOFTWARE

Up to this point, we've concentrated on hardware. But hardware is only one half of the total computing picture; you need software to do anything with the computer. Without the appropriate software, the computer is little more than a high-tech desk ornament, and a pricey and bulky one at that.

The first computer users had to design their own software because the market for software was too small to be commercially viable. However, with so many computers in use today, you don't have to worry about that anymore. There is so much commercial software available that the toughest problem is deciding which package suits your needs.

There are three major kinds of business software. The first, system software, includes the operating system "kernel" (the heart of the system), its shell (the part that "interfaces" with the user), and any device drivers that allow devices such as monitors and keyboards to be used with the computer. System software allows you to manage your disks' files, manage the machine's memory, load applications, and use peripherals such as printers. As you become more skilled with the computer, you'll know more about what these programs do and how to use them effectively.

The second kind of software is utility programs, small programs offering vital features that augment the operating system. You would use a utility when you want to recover a file you accidentally erased from a disk, to print a spreadsheet sideways, or to back up your data.

The third kind of software is application software—the actual programs you use to do your job. There are four major categories of applications. (Other categories, such as desktop publishing or CAD/CAM, tend to be variations of these four or are meant for a specialized market.) Let's look at each category in a little detail:

WORD PROCESSORS: Electronic word processors have two main functions: text editing and document formatting. Text editing is the ability not only to type the words, but to change them at will. This allows you to fine-tune a document without having to retype it in its entirety every time you make a change. This is the great advantage that word processors have over typewriters and handwriting. "Cut and paste," "search and replace," and spell checkers are all examples of text editing functions.

Document formatting features determine how the printed page will look. Margins, tabs, fonts, and spacing are all considered formatting functions. Because text editing in the best word processors is about as good now as it will ever need to be, and because inexpensive, high-quality hard copy is now a reality thanks to the laser printer, developers are working furiously to improve the formatting features of their word processing packages.

DATABASE MANAGERS: Office personnel have been using databases for years; the card file on your desk is a database, as is each manila folder in your filing cabinet. Computerized databases work on the same principle as card files, but they access specified data faster than humans can, and they can cross-reference data easily. Computerized database managers also generate reports quickly.

There are two major types of database managers: "flat file" managers, which work with one file at a time, and relational database managers, which allow you to link different files. Relational databases are a lot more flexible, if somewhat more unwieldy. Programs using relational databases usually include languages that let you design specialized programs around the databases.

SPREADSHEETS: The spreadsheet is to the old-fashioned ledger sheet what the word processor is to pencil and paper. You still enter numbers in rows and columns of cells, but instead of mentally calculating the columns or rows (or using a calculator), you enter a formula in the appropriate cell and the program does the calculating for you. Then, as you make changes in the numbers, the values reflected in the formulas change with them.

The ability to automatically recalculate numbers allows businesses to use spreadsheets to make "what if?" analyses, adjusting variables to see what the future may hold. For instance, let's say that you work in the citrus industry. Since the size of the orange crop can swing wildly, a spreadsheet can help you determine your prices if it's a bumper crop year or if the next year figures to be disastrous.

GRAPHICS: If you have to convey to someone your company's competitive position, how do you think you'd get the message across better: by listing a bunch of numbers or by showing a pie chart that graphically depicted your company's share of the market? Which would *you* rather view?

Until the mid-1980's, computer graphics were rather primitive and unusable in reports or presentations. Thanks to advances in computer and printer technology, however, companies can now create and produce eye-pleasing graphics that can perk up the appearance of any report or presentation.

Deciding whether or not to use graphics isn't as tough as deciding what kind of graphics package to use. If all you plan to make are simple charts and graphs, you might not need anything more than the graphics module of your spreadsheet program. If you want to go beyond that, however, you have four basic choices: paint programs, draw programs, "illustration" programs, and charting programs (which are more comprehensively featured than the spreadsheet graphics module).

Paint programs, which are sometimes called bit-mapped graphics (because essentially, they place bits or dots on a screen or page), are inexpensive, fun, and easy to use. They are rarely used for serious business applications, however, because of the quality of the documents when printed: Unless the paint program has special features that allow high-quality printing, paint documents printed on a high-quality laser printer look like they came from a low-quality dot matrix printer.

Draw and illustration programs are better for business use. Draw programs work with objects; in creating a page with a draw program, discrete objects rather than dots are created and manipulated. Illustration programs take advantage of the best features of both paint and draw programs and are more sophisticated and versatile than either. Both draw and illustration programs generate high-quality images on a laser printer, which make them very suitable for business use.

EVALUATING SOFTWARE

Most software is so good these days that you can live quite happily with a program that isn't necessarily "top of the line." But to prevent making bad choices in the first place, here's a list of questions to ask when you're evaluating a particular program:

* **Will it work with my equipment?** Software tends to be written for whatever hardware is state-of-the-art at the time, so it's quite possible that older machines will not be able to run a program or will run it poorly without extra hardware, such as a mouse or extended memory.

* **Does it have the features I need?** What does the program in question have to do? Can it do everything you ask, or do you have to sacrifice some features? What are your priorities? These are all important questions you'll need to ask during the evaluation process.

It's tempting to buy the program with the most features, but that's often just as silly as buying a program with a limited number of features. Just zero in on the features you need and ignore the features you won't need.

* **Is it easy to learn and use?** You may have to learn the program on your own. If a program is difficult to learn or, worse, hard to use even after you've mastered its basics, you won't get much out of it.

* **How does it perform?** Since computing is supposed to speed up your work, it's very frustrating when you have to wait while a program is completing a task. Speed is most important when you're working with databases and large spreadsheets, which are slowed down by disk searches, and by graphics programs, which make the computer do lots of calculations. (Word processing packages are not nearly as demanding and usually run pretty quickly.)

* **Is the program worth its price?** A piece of software is a good value if it turns out to be less expensive than the cost of not using it. Of course, there are intangibles that have to be factored in here—such as employee satisfaction with a program—but this is still a good yardstick to use to measure a program's potential worth.

USING SOFTWARE

Once you have a piece of software in your computer, the next question is "How do I learn to use it?" Learning new software is often a daunting task, but it doesn't have to be. In fact, it can be easy. Just keep these tips in mind:

The User Interface: Menus Versus Commands

Before you load up a piece of software, look at the manual to see how the developer has designed the program. There are two schools of software design. Programs in the first school use user-entered commands to perform their tasks, while the second school's programs use menus of predefined commands as the primary "user interface."

Which is better? It depends on you. If you're new to a program, you'll prefer menu-driven software. It's much easier to learn: All of the commands are right in front of you or are easily accessible, so you don't have to go through the trouble of learning and remembering commands. The only thing you do have to learn is how to use the menus, and that usually isn't very difficult—most menu formats (and there are several) can usually be deciphered in a very short time.

While command-driven programs are significantly harder to learn than menu-driven programs, some people swear by them, citing their flexibility and speed. If you are going to use a command-driven program, make sure that you have the time to learn it—because you will need that time.

"Where Do I Go for Help?"

Unless your company offers in-house training, you'll usually have to rely on the material the software manufacturer sends with the package. That usually consists of a manual, the bane of computer users. Few users like plowing their way through a thick volume of information, and it's a pain for users to drop what they're doing to go to the manual every time they have questions.

Software developers know how users feel, so they try to accommodate their users by making it easy to solve problems without going to the manual. Many programs have on-line help sections that can be accessed with a few keystrokes, as well as message lines that explain how to carry out a particular operation.

"... But I Have Computerphobia!"

If you're scared of learning a computer program because you think you won't know what you're doing, relax. You probably *won't* know what you're doing, so don't worry about it.

Nobody has ever mastered a new program in an hour. It takes time to learn how to use a program and feel comfortable enough with it to crank out actual work. By setting unrealistic expectations for yourself, you will only doom yourself to failure.

You'll be better off concentrating on the basics first before learning the advanced features.

And don't be afraid to make mistakes! By making mistakes and learning how to get out of them, you'll master a program much more quickly than you would by "playing it safe."

The Future of Software

The software and hardware states of the art are closely related: Look at any popular software package, and you'll see that it is optimized to run on the best equipment available at the time of its development. One classic example of this would be VisiCalc, the first spreadsheet for personal computers. Today's user would find VisiCalc (and the machines it was designed to run on) almost laughably primitive, but it was a very popular program and faded only when better software came along. There is no question that the recent advances in hardware technology will eventually be met by equally impressive software. Voice recognition and speech techniques that permit the user to speak data and commands into the computer are already being used in some special situations.

So what will the software of the future look like? One guess is that software developers will concentrate less on raw performance and more on features that will make their programs easier to use. (Of course, the hardware of the future will be so fast that speed will no longer be an issue in any but the most demanding applications.) Artificial intelligence, a program's ability to "think" for itself and adapt itself to a user's way of working, may become a part of every program. Imagine a word processor that automatically corrects misspelled or misused words, or a graphics program that automatically determines the correct color balance, and you'll have an idea of what artificial intelligence will do.

It's quite likely that tomorrow's software will be the likes of which we've never seen before. Whatever the future of computer software will be, this much is clear: It will enable us to do more work, and do it more easily, than ever before.

PAGE DESIGN BY COMPUTER

The advent of personal computers was supposed to bring about "the paperless office." Needless to say, that hasn't happened; if anything, the ease with which computer users can create reports and letters may have actually increased the flow of paper.

If any one thing is responsible for this, it is the laser printer. First marketed in the mid-1980's, the laser printer is an inexpensive, easy way to generate high-quality hard copy. It has gone from a status symbol to a commonplace business appliance, in much the same manner as fax machines and office copiers.

If there's any problem with the laser printer, it may be that it's too good for many purposes. Handwritten or typewritten communiqués, such as personal business letters or memos, lose some of their intimacy and immediacy if they're printed out on laser printers. It's best, therefore, to save the laser printer for reports, newsletters, ads, and any documents that are intended to go to an extended audience.

Because laser-printed documents go to a large audience and because the type is so visually inviting, if you are using a laser printer, you will have to pay more attention to the design of your documents than you do when you use a dot matrix or daisy wheel printer.

The only real rule in document design is that the style of the document should be visually pleasing (easy on the eyes) and it should be consistent with the message being conveyed. You wouldn't want to design an annual report that looked like a wedding invitation, for example. Realizing that different jobs require different design techniques is the first step toward putting together quality documents.

The second step is remembering to keep things as simple as possible. Too many new computer users try to use every feature of their programs, and the results are usually disasters. Visual gimmicks should be used sparingly, if at all; when the layout of the page calls attention to itself, the message you're trying to convey somehow gets lost.

Fonts

Because the font is usually the strongest visual element on the page, your first decision will probably be about what kind of font to use. There are few situations where a specific font is absolutely necessary, but it will become very clear to you when you've used the wrong font for the document.

(Although we use the term "font" here, since that is standard computer terminology, technically the term "typeface" is more correct. Typefaces are families of fonts, each of which has its own size and style. Therefore, Helvetica 10-point is a different font from Helvetica 12-point or Helvetica 10-point bold, even though they all share the same typeface, Helvetica.)

There are two major styles of fonts. The first is the serifed face. Serifs are short cross strokes at the ends of letters. They improve readability by giving the text a character-to-character flow. Accordingly, they are used in the "body copy" of most documents, where the majority of text is found. Serif faces also convey an impression of dignity, solidity, and strength that says "this is important material." Times Roman, Garamond, and Palatino are all examples of serif faces.

The other kind of face is the sans (without) serif. Sans serif faces give the impression of modernity, progress, and a certain informality. They also tend to be used for captions or headlines since they offer good visual contrast with the serifed body copy. Another application for sans serif faces is when you use small type for body copy—the serifs tend to clutter things up. Other sans serif faces besides Helvetica are Avant Garde, Futura, and Franklin Gothic.

What's Your Style and Size?

Deciding on the correct font is only part of the design process. You have to pick out a style and size as well. There are four different styles—regular (often called roman), bold, italic (or oblique), and bold italic. While most situations call for roman text, bold or italicized text can add a distinctive touch to a document.

Size is an important factor in readability. Too small type will make a paragraph look like one big black block, while too large text forces the reader to break a paragraph into sections, thereby slowing the reader down. Most designers recommend using 9 to 12-point type for body copy (a point is $1/72$ inch), with larger type for headlines and mastheads and smaller copy for fine print.

Columns, Margins, and Line Length

The eye does not read words one at a time, but reads groups of words instead. You should try to make it easier for the eye to read those groups of words in your document. One way of doing this is by using multiple short columns on a page rather than one large column. This technique is often used in newspapers and magazines, which are meant to be read once (and pretty quickly at that).

Just how many columns you'll want on the page also depends on the margins you set. If you plan on using two or three columns on an 8½" by 11" page (the standard page size), you'll want narrow margins on each side of the page since standard margins will make each column look ridiculously small.

Graphics

A graphic can make a page more interesting and more informative. It can also throw the page out of balance if you don't place it correctly. Graphics that can fit into a single column should be placed into that column. If they won't fit into a column, they can be put at the top or bottom of the page. If the graphic doesn't fit "neatly" on the page, "text wrap" (in which the text is arranged around the graphic) can be used. Graphics should ideally be placed near the text they are meant to complement; it's confusing when the text tells you to look for Figure 9 when you're on page 3 and Figure 9 is on page 5.

Experiment, Experiment, Experiment

When you're preparing a document for printing, don't be afraid to try different things before you come to the final design. (With its relatively low cost and easy accessibility, the laser printer, in fact, lends itself to experimentation.) Many successful designs are the result of accidents that ended up looking better than anyone could have predicted. Even if your experiments don't turn out successfully, the knowledge you'll gain by experimenting will help you next time around.

CREATING AND MAINTAINING FILES

One of the most practical things about using a computer is the ability to save and store files for future use. No longer must you type everything perfectly the first time as you had to with a typewriter. You can start out with the germ of an idea the first time you work on a document, and expand on it as time goes on. And you can clean up any spelling or grammatical errors as you catch them.

As great as it is to be able to save documents at will, it also means that you'll have to spend a portion of your time organizing and maintaining the computer files that contain those documents. This is not terribly difficult; once you get the hang of it, maintaining the files on your computer is easier (and faster) than maintaining a file cabinet.

Naming Files

Naming a file is not particularly difficult, but there are some rules that you should follow. The most common method of naming files is to use the *filename.ext* convention. That is, you'll have a filename of up to eight characters (numbers or letters), followed by a period and an optional three-letter extension. However, some systems allow more latitude in naming files.

The filename can be anything you want it to be—any sequence of alphanumeric characters can be used. Generally, you'll want to use a sequence that fairly describes the contents of the file, if only to make it easier for you to remember what is in there when you have to call it up again. If your office has a standard coding system for filenames, you will follow that, of course; but if it doesn't, you may want to name your files by such criteria as the date, the original author, and the department the file was written for. The filename for this article, for example, was COM13 ("Computers, Chapter 13"), but it could have just as easily been 012391 (the date the original manuscript was submitted) or WPRCOMP ("Word Processing and Computers"). The only restrictions that apply when you are naming a file are that some punctuation symbols cannot be used and that a new file should not be given the same name as an old one.

The extension indicates what type of file has been created. Application programs tend to use an *.EXE* (executable) or *.COM* (command) extension (e.g., *SORT.EXE* or *BASIC.COM*); the documents they create have their own extensions. While many programs assign their own extension to the files they create, you can also give a file another extension if you want to. Some of the more common extensions are *.BAT* (batch files), *.BAK* (back-up work files), *.BAS* (BASIC files), and *.TXT* (text files).

While you'll usually want to use the program-assigned extension, sometimes you may use the extension as part of the filename proper, to give you more information about the file in question. If you are typing a number of letters for a particular person all on the same day, you may want to use the filename for that person's initials and the date (e.g., *AB121790*), and use the extension to describe the letter's contents or the order in which it was written (e.g., *.AR* [Accounts Receivable] or *.012).*

Organizing Your Files on Disk

Once you've created a file and saved it onto a disk, the next step is organizing the disk so that you can access the file (and the program used to create it) at will.

Organizing and maintaining a disk of documents involves many of the same techniques that you use to organize and maintain a file cabinet. That is, you'll want everything on the disk to share a common category, you'll want to store a document on the right disk, and you'll want to weed out old and unnecessary files to prevent your disks from filling up unnecessarily. If you save your documents on diskettes, you'll probably want to use one diskette for reports, another for letters written by one person, a third for letters written by another person, and so on. Using diskettes in this manner requires that you label them, of course, and that you store them appropriately so that you can find the file easily.

If you store your documents on a hard disk, computer makers recommend that you use a hierarchy of directories or folders to organize everything on that disk and reduce time spent looking for files. Basically, what this means is that you divide a disk into a number of directories and subdirectories, each of which contains an application and that application's data files. These directories can then be thought of as disks unto themselves. You may want to keep all letters by so-and-so in a subdirectory called SOAND-SO, for example, while someone's else's files go into another subdirectory (see the manual for your computer's operating system for assistance in creating directories and subdirectories). The only drawback in using subdirectories is that you must specify which one you want to send a file to or load one from, unless the file in question is in the "default" directory; if you forget to do this, you'll spend part of your time wondering where your file disappeared to, since it won't be where you expect it to be.

If you're part of a network setup, the file server (the central hard disk) can be thought of as just another disk, albeit one that requires you to enter a password to access. You might have to specify a destination for your files other than the one the program is set for (which will usually be your own directory on the server disk), but for the most part you'll work in pretty much the same fashion as you work with your diskettes or hard disk.

While naming and maintaining computer files entails a little bit of organization and planning on your part, that work will end up saving you time and effort that can be best spent in other areas—on your real work, for instance.

ERGONOMICS: WORKING WITH YOUR COMPUTER

If you think that working in an office isn't hard work, you're wrong. It is; just think of all the times you've gone home feeling tired and sore. *Why should I feel like that?* you ask. *After all, it's not as if I had to stand on my feet or lift heavy boxes all day.*

No, it's because you probably sit in one place for long periods of time. Whether you're standing all day or sitting most of the time, one of the keys to doing your job well is being able to do it comfortably. And you have more control over this than you might think: Over time, you have probably "learned" some bad work habits—slouching, twisting—ignoring signs from your body that it needs a little break. Because you spend so much time sitting, it's important that you learn how to sit properly—and that you "unlearn" those bad habits.

Let's take a look at some areas in which you can make some simple changes—changes that can have a big impact on your productivity and comfort. Remember, the more comfortable you are, the better you will be able to concentrate on doing your job well. Can you make any of the following changes in your work area?

How's Your Chair?

An uncomfortable sitting posture may not bother you at the beginning of the day, but it will soon take its toll on your neck, back, and legs as the day wears on. Here are some suggestions to help you find the position that suits you best:

✓ Adjust the height of your chair so that your thighs are horizontal, your feet rest flat on the floor (if they don't, get a step stool to place under your feet), and your arms and hands are comfortably positioned at the keyboard.

✓ Keep the materials you're working with in front of you so that you don't have to twist your neck to read from them. A stand that will hold papers vertically is a big help in this regard.

✓ Adjust the backrest so that it supports the lumbar (lower) curve of your spine. If you need to, put a lumbar roll (either a premade support or a rolled-up towel) on the backrest or a seat wedge under your buttocks.

✓ Adjust your keyboard to a comfortable level and to an angle that will enable you to keep your wrists in a neutral position—that is, comfortably straight. (Many computers have detached keyboards that will allow you to do this.)

✓ Change your seated position frequently throughout the day.

✓ Make sure that all the tools you need to do your job are easily accessible so that you don't often have to make awkward reaches or twist while you're sitting.

What About Your Eyes?

An hour of reading may not feel like an hour of running or aerobics, but your eyes are getting a workout when you read, and eyestrain is possible. To prevent eye problems:

✓ Have your vision checked regularly.
✓ Advise your vision care specialist of the work you're doing. Glasses suited to one task may not be appropriate for another.
✓ Clean the screen or glare filter of your monitor and your eyeglasses (if you wear them). It does your eyes no good to force them to look through a haze of dirt and dust.

Now for the Display

It's relatively easy to adjust the monitor to suit your needs. Here's what you should be adjusting:

→ **Height.** The top of a standard-sized monitor should be just slightly below eye level when you're sitting at the keyboard. Having it too much lower or higher than that level can lead to neck problems.
→ **Glare.** Since glare is caused by reflected light, position the screen (either by swiveling it or by changing the angle) so that it reflects the least amount of light back at you.
→ **Brightness and contrast.** Too much or too little brightness or contrast can be hard on the eyes. Feel free to experiment with the settings on the monitor until you find a setting that's right for you. If you have a color monitor, you may want to set it at the point where color characters are on the verge of "blooming." At this point, your screen will be at its brightest without any decrease in resolution.

You've Got to Move

There are few better ways to relieve the stress of sitting all day than exercise. Don't worry; the exercises we list below take only a few minutes to complete and can be done in your office in your regular work clothes.

Generally, you need to do only five to ten repetitions of each exercise at a time, several times throughout the day or when you're sore in a particular area. Do each rep slowly, stretching to the maximum extent you can, and breathe properly (inhale during the tension part of the rep, exhale during the release). (*Note:* Before you start this or any exercise regimen, check with your doctor to ensure it's safe for you.)

✓ For your shoulder muscles, do shoulder rotations in both forward and backward directions.
✓ For the middle of your back, rotate one bent arm forward, the other backward. Also, press arms bent at the elbows out behind your back.
✓ For your lower back, stand up, place your hands on your back, throw your chest out, and bend the upper and lower back backward. Also, tighten and release your abdominal (stomach) muscles while you're sitting.
✓ Of course, sitting for long periods of time can affect your mind too. After a while, you begin to get tired and lose concentration. When that happens, take a minute to get up and stretch or walk around. A little break like this doesn't need to be very long, but it will keep you going for a while longer.

It's said that productivity jumps when people "work smarter, not harder." By paying attention to your posture, you'll be able to work more efficiently—and reduce the possibilities of health problems.

COMMUNICATING BY COMPUTER

Most of us are used to thinking of our computers as stand-alone tools, not really connected to the rest of the world. The fact is that, with the proper equipment, any computer can communicate with other computers, no matter if it's a laptop or a mainframe. And it can do so whether it's right next to another machine or halfway around the world from one.

Since computer communication is as varied as human communication, different media have been developed to accommodate the variety of communication needs. There are systems that allow interpersonal communication between users in much the same way as telephone calls, and there are systems that turn the computer into a library. The secret to using the computer as a communication tool is finding the right kind of program for your communication needs.

Networks

You may already be familiar with one method of computer communication. The local area network (LAN), a method of linking a number of computers in a single location, is used in many offices to enable users to share equipment such as hard disks and printers and facilitate machine-to-machine communication. Users can share files, each user adding to the final product, without having to pass disks around.

Working in a networking environment is generally no harder than working with a stand-alone computer—but there are security precautions to be aware of. To prevent unauthorized users from going into private files, networks use a password system that allows certain users access to certain directories.

E-Mail/Computerized Conferencing

The idea of electronic mail *(E-mail)* stems from the ability of computers to process messages in much the same way they process other information. As long as a computer has E-mail software, it can receive and send messages very easily. Many E-mail packages even allow background communication, whereby the computer can process messages while it's doing other work. When the operator is ready to read the messages, all he or she has to do is open up the E-mail program and the messages will be there.

While many networks include E-mail capability in the network software package, E-mail is not limited to network situations. E-mail systems can be used to communicate with computers anywhere, provided both computers doing the communicating have appropriate software, as well as a piece of hardware called a modem.

While E-mail can be sent or received at any time, computerized conferencing is real-time communication where two or more operators are communicating simultaneously. Yes, it is like a telephone conference call, with two important differences: The messages are clearer, and there is less of the chitchat that often goes along with telephone calls.

Other Computer Communications

One popular form of computer communication is the bulletin board system (BBS), a sort of computerized party line with a central operator/administrator. The BBS concept is similar to a regular bulletin board; it is a place where people can exchange information. BBSs can be used to advertise a product, say, or to look for a vendor.

Information utilities and electronic databases are another important part of the computer communication world. These services allow the user to tap into videotext services that can be used to augment an office library as well as monitor current events and stock prices. Public domain software—free programs, games, and utilities—can also be downloaded with these services, but beware of doing this since your computer may catch a virus (See Chapter 10).

Computer Etiquette

Etiquette is etiquette, whether you're communicating in person, by phone—or by computer. And just as there are certain rules you must follow in traditional communication, there are loose social standards that should be followed when using the computer. Some are a matter of common courtesy; others are important security pointers. Users should:

- Consider whether their messages need to be transmitted via computer. In many cases, a simple phone call can convey the same information with a lot less hassle.
- Keep messages as short as possible. There's no reason to use 50 words where five will do nicely. (Just as you would on a letter or memo, edit your messages before you send them.)
- Be properly prepared when making transmissions. Have all the information you need and any additional equipment (diskettes, for instance) at hand before you begin. Also, be prepared to repeat the transmission if problems develop the first time around. Save whatever materials you have until you're sure that the transmission has been successful.
- Respond to any messages that have been received as soon as possible. Otherwise, these parties may interpret your failure to do so as an indication that you did not receive their messages.
- Consider sending messages to all E-mail correspondents saying that their messages have indeed been received and read.
- Make points as clearly and simply as possible. Sarcastic or witty answers or slang may be all right in face-to-face or telephone conversations (where facial expressions or inflections can convey your true meaning), but they could be misunderstood by the person at the other computer.
- Know whatever passwords or access codes the program requires, and don't give them out to anyone but the boss.
- Respect other users' privacy. Don't try to tap into lines or folders you don't have authorized access to.
- Wait for the other party in a conversation to finish before making a response.

Computer Communication: More Than a Game

There are many functions computer communications can fulfill in a business, but they all boil down to the fact that they permit people who are physically separated to share ideas and information. Some companies have instituted telecommuting to allow some employees to work at home; some use networks to link their offices together; some have their own bulletin boards to encourage interemployee communication.

As with any other application, computer communication improves company productivity—if users always keep in mind that they are communicating first.

WORD PROCESSING BASICS

■ If you're just starting with word processing, or if you need a quick refresher, this is the chapter for you!

■ Typing in "antidisestablishmentarianism" every time? Learn how to do it in just two keystrokes—instead of 28!

■ Fix your spelling—in just a few minutes!

Most people think of word processing as something that can only be done with keystrokes. It isn't; handwriting is just as much word processing as typing is. Even talking could be considered word processing, insofar as it involves putting words together to form phrases or sentences.

Computerized word processing is what people have in mind when they hear the phrase "word processing." And word processing on a computer is certainly something much different from composing or editing on a yellow pad with a box of sharpened pencils (and big erasers!) at hand. The main difference is that with computerized word processing, the words are not "carved in stone"—permanent or difficult to change—but can be altered, moved around, and corrected at any time and in any fashion. Drafts and rewrites are quickly and easily produced; revisions are added wherever necessary. Every kind of document—from legal contract to personal correspondence—can be produced with a word processor.

A word processing program has two major functions: text editing and formatting. Editing is the writing/revising process, while formatting is preparing the document for printing. Because Chapter 12 discussed the formatting features available on current word processing packages, we'll concentrate on the text editing functions.

Cut-and-Paste

The ability to mark off a block of text and delete it or move it from its original location to another point in a document is undoubtedly one of the most-used features of word processing. A writer can type out items in no particular order and then reassemble these items into a coherent whole later on.

Search and Replace

There are a number of reasons why you would want to use the search function of your word processor. Some treat it as a sort of database feature, allowing instantaneous access to a word or a phrase, while others use it with the replace feature to make "global" changes within a document. Of course, you may need to change a word, so word processors include the "replace" function to go along with the search function. The process is simple: The word processor finds the string you're looking for and changes it to the string you've specified to go in its place.

Boilerplate

Often, you'll find a recurring word or phrase in your typing. Rather than having to type it in every time, wouldn't it be nice to keep it somewhere where you could find it and insert it into your document whenever you need it? "Scrap" or "glossary" functions allow you to do this. "Scrap" or "clipboard" puts the block in machine memory where you can access it as long as your machine is on. "Glossary" or "library" keeps the block in a disk file, where it can be easily retrieved and placed in any document.

While you will probably use this feature to reduce keystrokes, you will also improve your accuracy. As long as your copy is correct when you put it into the scrap or glossary, it will always be correct whenever you insert it into the document.

Spelling Checkers and Thesauruses

On-line spelling checkers and thesauruses are usually add-on packages to the basic word processor that enhance its functionality and usefulness by electronically doing some of the jobs, such as proofreading and copyediting, that are normally done by humans. They are not infallible, any more than people are, but they can reduce much of the detail-oriented work that can be so time-consuming.

Spelling checkers work by comparing the words in the text against an electronic dictionary. When they spot a word that is not in the dictionary, they point out the word, and allow you to select from a list of possible replacements. Thesauruses take a selected word and present you with synonyms (or antonyms) that can replace it. This is particularly useful if a document uses the same word over and over, or if the original word doesn't quite convey your point.

EXERCISES

The following are some exercises designed to run you through some of the basic features of your word processing program. Since there are so many word processors, each with its own method of working, we cannot explain how to do each command for each word processor, so be sure to consult your user's manual.

1. Type in the following selection:

TO: Mr. Claiborne
FROM: Betty Rodrigues
DATE: April 19, 19—
SUBJECT: New telephones
Mr. Claiborne:

During the last few weeks I've noticed that people in the office have been unhappy with the new telephones. The "flat" headset that comes with the new telephones is less suited for "cradling." A number of users have even complained that the new phones have hurt their productivity, since they now have only one hand free for work.

I've heard two suggestions for solving this problem. One is to install cradling devices on all the headsets. The other suggestion is to give users the kind of headset our phone operators use, so that their hands would be free all the time.

While I favor the second recommendation, I'd like to discuss the problem with you and Ms. Perkins before we present anything to management. I need to know how your people feel about the phones and if they have any of their own recommendations.

Please call me as soon as you can so that we can set up a meeting.

Betty Rodrigues

2. After you're finished typing, mark off the second sentence of the third paragraph and make it the first sentence of the paragraph.
3. Using your program's search and replace feature, change "headset" to "receiver" wherever it appears in the letter.
4. Move the cursor to the word "favor" by using your program's search feature.
5. Type in the word "short," mark it, and put it in the program's scrap or clipboard. Then insert it before "meeting."

SPREADSHEET BASICS: FORMULAS, FUNCTIONS, AND CELLS

For most of the jobs that you do, the computer is merely an extension of what you've already been doing. Word processing, for example, is still typing, and database management is still filing. Nothing new there.

Spreadsheets, however, can add a different kind of challenge to the office worker's job. While you don't have to be a numbers whiz to use a spreadsheet, a certain knowledge of your company's basic accounting practices might be necessary, depending on the complexity of the information you'll be handling in the spreadsheet.

Anyone who has ever worked with a ledger sheet already has a grasp of how a spreadsheet works; the only difference is that the spreadsheet automatically calculates the numbers for you when you tell it to, in the manner you tell it to.

The ability to calculate numbers quickly and without error is, in fact, the spreadsheet's greatest strength. No longer must you manually calculate everything again and again when you change one number in a column; simply tell the program to recalculate the column, and in no time it's done. Spreadsheet programs have made it possible for almost anyone to do sophisticated financial planning.

Formulas, Functions, and Cells: Using a Spreadsheet

When you begin working with a spreadsheet document (called a *worksheet)*, the first thing you notice is a grid of intersecting vertical and horizontal lines, with the cursor at the top left of the grid. That grid is actually a series of *cells,* each of which can contain a number, text, or formula. Each cell has a name that identifies its position in the worksheet, usually an alphanumeric combination, such as A1 (whereby vertical columns are designated by letter, horizontal rows by number) or R1C1 (whereby R indicates the row number, C the column). With the arrow keys on your keyboard, you can move to any cell within the worksheet.

Once you begin working, you enter a column, row, or block of numbers or data into the cells. Then, when you're ready to calculate, you enter a *formula* into an adjacent cell. That formula, which may look something like **"@SUM (A1:A10),"** tells the program to perform the requested calculation upon the designated cells. In the example we've just given, we've told the program to add up the numbers in all the cells from A1 to A10. The command **SUM** is called a *function;* other functions may tell the program to average a series of numbers, multiply them, compare them, and so on.

Macros

There are often circumstances when you need to retype a series of formatting commands (let's say you need a row or column of month names or a block of text in three or four different locations on the worksheet) or formulas that you have already typed into the worksheet. Rather than having to type it in every time, you can store everything in a macro—a "miniprogram" you design and write yourself—that can be called up with only a couple of keystrokes. All you have to do to create a macro is tell the spreadsheet when your "script" begins, when it ends, and what you want to call it.

As you can imagine, macros allow you to automate procedures to the point where anybody can use a worksheet—even those who have never used a spreadsheet program before. In fact, many companies design macro scripts so that newer employees can use a worksheet without too much training.

Graphics

There is no better way to make numbers make sense than to present them in graphical form. For this reason, most spreadsheet programs include graphics sections that allow you to create bar, line, and pie graphs. Some even allow you to integrate the graphic into the worksheet, so the final printed report can show both numbers and graphics.

Making a graphic from a spreadsheet is fairly simple. For the most part, you simply have to specify which column will represent the horizontal "X" axis (which represents a series of dates, offices or branches of a company, or individual people, for example) and which columns represent the vertical "Y" axis (usually the numerical data). Of course, you'll have a fair degree of control (and responsibility) over the formatting of the chart, but the basic steps are very simple and expedient.

EXERCISES

The following are some simple exercises you can do with your spreadsheet program. (Make sure you begin with a clean worksheet.) Because different spreadsheets use different commands, we have not given specific examples of them here. Consult the program's user manual or tutorial for help.

1. Starting with the first cell in the third row (which will be called either A3 or R3C1) and working your way down the column (to A4 [R4C1], and so on), enter each of the 12 months of the year into a cell.

2. Starting with cell C3 (R3C3), enter any numbers you want in the 12 cells from C3 to C14 (R3C3 to R14C3). At the end of the column, skip a cell and, in the next cell (C16 or R16C3), write in the formula that will total all of the numbers you have entered in that column.

3. Follow the same procedure in the next column (D or C4) and for the column after that (E or C5).

4. Skip a column, and in cell G3 (or R3C7) write a formula that will average the numbers in the three cells with numbers in that row. Do the same with the other cells in that column.

5. In cell C1 (R1C3), enter whatever year you want. In the next cell in the row (D1 or R1C4), enter the next year, and in E1 (R1C5), enter the year after that.

6. Next, graph out your worksheet, using data from the first column as your X axis and the numbers from the other columns as Y axis data.

- How much do you know about office technology? Find out here.

- Refresh your memory with this review.

- What do you still have to learn?

A COMPUTER REVIEW

In the previous chapters, we have covered a number of topics. To see how much you have gleaned from these chapters, we have prepared a little quiz for you. The material covered in this quiz was taken from Chapters 5-17. If you have any questions about the material, please refer to the appropriate chapter.

Multiple Choice:

In this section, you are given four possible answers. Pick the one that makes the most sense.

1. The CPU is:
   a. Another name for the monitor.
   b. The part of the computer containing the electronics.
   c. The cable for the printer.
   d. The computer's power supply.

2. How can viruses be transmitted from computer to computer?
   a. Public domain software.
   b. Disks from other computers.
   c. Commercially available software.
   d. All of the above.

3. When you want to change one word to another, you would use what feature?
   a. Cut-and-paste.
   b. Search.
   c. Replace.
   d. Macros.

4. The basic block of a worksheet is called a:
   a. Function.
   b. Cell.
   c. Formula.
   d. Macro.

5. What does the extension of a filename do?
   a. Identifies the type of file you're using.
   b. Makes the file bigger.
   c. Changes the data on the file.
   d. Tells you whose machine the file came from.

6. Which of the following cannot hurt the image on a monitor?
   a. Dirt.
   b. Leaving it on for long periods of time.
   c. Turning the brightness control all the way up.
   d. Bad data.

7. Which of the following is not considered applications software?
   a. Utilities.
   b. Database.
   c. Graphics.
   d. Spreadsheet.

8. How can you prevent back strain?
   a. Make sure that you're not in an awkward sitting position.
   b. Keep the materials you work with in front of you or by your side.
   c. Shift your sitting position every so often.
   d. All of the above.

9. Which of the following determines the appearance of your documents?
   a. Type style.
   b. Line length.
   c. Number of columns.
   d. All of the above.

10. Which of the following should not be considered when evaluating equipment?
    a. Your office's needs.
    b. The equipment's appearance.
    c. Friend's recommendations.
    d. Price.

11. Which of the following is not a standard diskette size?
    a. 8″
    b. 5¼″
    c. 12″
    d. 3½″

12. Which of the following is usually cause for a lighter-than-normal printout?
    a. Bad data.
    b. Clogged platens.
    c. Worn ribbon.
    d. The on-light is not on.

ANSWERS

1. **b.** CPU stands for "central processing unit."
2. **d.** Viruses—short programs that cripple computers in some way—have been known to invade computers through all three methods.
3. **c.** Cut-and-paste allows you to move blocks of text around; search allows you to locate a particular word or phrase. While replace is often used with the search feature to find all instances of the word you wish to replace, it can be used on its own.
4. **b.**
5. **a.** The extension, a three-letter suffix used with the name of the file, tells you the type of file you are working with or some other information about the file.
6. **d.** You may not like what you see on the screen if you have bad data, but it will not degrade the picture.
7. **a.** Applications software allows you to do "productivity" work. Utility software helps you run the computer more smoothly and efficiently.

8. **d.**
9. **d.**
10. **b.** If you consider appearance at all, it should be a minor consideration.
11. **c.**
12. **c.** The others may cause paper misfeeds or may cause the printer not to print at all.

MATCHING

1. Scripts that automate many functions in a spreadsheet program
2. 3½″ diskettes
3. A section of memory where text is stored
4. A section of a disk where files are stored
5. A chain of computers in one location
6. A small box maneuvered on the desktop
7. The part of the disk housing that determines whether or not you can store or change data on the disk
8. Applications that create boxes, circles, etc., that can be changed at will
9. A particular size and style of lettering
10. A box that allows you to transmit and receive computer signals over telephone lines
11. Reflected light from the monitor screen
12. Typefaces without cross strokes at the end of letters

_____ **A.** clipboard	_____ **G.** network
_____ **B.** glare	_____ **H.** write-protect notch
_____ **C.** mouse	_____ **I.** macros
_____ **D.** font	_____ **J.** modem
_____ **E.** directory	_____ **K.** microdiskettes
_____ **F.** sans serif	_____ **L.** "draw" programs

ANSWERS

1. I
2. K
3. A
4. E
5. G
6. C
7. H
8. L
9. D
10. J
11. B
12. F

TRUE OR FALSE:

1. The best posture while sitting in a chair is with your shoulders slightly hunched and your head forward.

2. The first computer bug on record was caused by an insect.

3. Helvetica is a font.

4. You should place your computer away from areas where people will be smoking, eating, and drinking.

5. If your computer has E-mail software, you can communicate with other computers anywhere in the world.

6. Menu-driven software is harder to learn than command-driven software.

7. Confidential data should be stored on diskettes that are secured in a safe place.

8. If you're using a hard disk, you shouldn't create directories and subdirectories to store your files.

9. You cannot alter a document created on a word processing program once you have stored it.

10. It's a good idea to keep a list of frequently misspelled words near your keyboard.

ANSWERS

1. F. This is actually a quick way to get a backache or neckache.
2. T. A moth that flew into an early computer caused the first known computer breakdown.
3. F. Strictly speaking, helvetica is a *typeface*, although it is commonly called a font.
4. T. The dust from smoke and spilled liquids are two of the things that are most damaging to computers.
5. T—as long as you also have a modem and membership with an E-mail network, and the computers with which you want to communicate are similarly outfitted.
6. F. It's usually easier to learn and use a menu-driven program than software that runs on commands.
7. T. Keeping data on a hard disk often means that anyone with access to the computer can tap into your files.
8. F. Directories help you organize all your files into logical blocks that can be found easily.
9. F. You can alter a document at any time.
10. T.

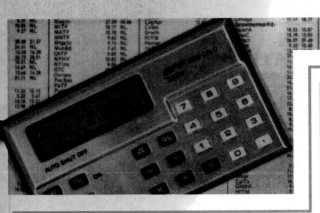

FIGURES AND FINANCE
Mastery of Office Math

INTRODUCTION

As an office-support professional, you have job responsibilities that require more sophisticated math skills than ever before. This section is designed to help you overcome even the worst attack of math anxiety. It will also help you use, improve, and add to the skills you already have. You'll learn how to solve the most common math problems you'll encounter in the office.

You'll find an overview of the fundamentals of business math, complete with explanations, step-by-step instructions, and solutions to problems to help you understand the procedures and calculations involved. You'll also learn by doing, by taking the quizzes and checking the answers provided. In short, the following chapters will help you master the math skills you need to solve your business math problems confidently and correctly.

Would you like to learn how to calculate interest? Does your main interest lie in understanding how to use a balance sheet? If you'd like information on mastering a particular area of office math, using the index below will help you locate the subject you need.

FRACTIONS

Fractions are some of the most basic math tools. A solid knowledge of fractions will allow you to progress to other calculations with ease. Take the following quiz to see what you remember about fractions.

QUIZ 1   Answer the following: *Your Answers*

1. Reduce 24/6.   _____

2. Reduce 10/100.   _____

3. Which is an improper fraction: 13/5 or 45/50?   _____

4. Which is a mixed number: $6^5/_8$ or 25/1?   _____

5. Reduce 36/8 to its lowest terms.   _____

If you had trouble with any of these, you need to review working with fractions. But first, it might be a good idea to reacquaint yourself with some of the terminology used in solving fraction problems.

numerator—the top number of a fraction.

denominator—the bottom number of a fraction.

proper fraction—a fraction in which the numerator is smaller than the denominator.

improper fraction—a fraction in which the numerator is greater than or equal to the denominator.

mixed number—one consisting of a whole number plus a fraction.

to reduce to a fraction—to divide both the numerator and the denominator by one number that divides into both evenly.

lowest terms—the point where you can no longer divide a single number into both the numerator and the denominator. Always reduce fractions to their lowest terms.

RULE 1: An improper fraction may be reduced to a whole number or a mixed number by dividing the denominator into the numerator. For example:

$$24/6 = 24 \div 6 = 4 \qquad\qquad 25/4 = 25 \div 4 = 6^1/_4$$

To turn a mixed number into a fraction, multiply the whole number by the denominator and add the numerator. Put the new numerator over the denominator. For example, to turn $4^3/_5$ into a fraction, multiply 4×5, then add 3. This gives you the improper fraction 23/5.

QUIZ 2 Change the following fractions to mixed or whole numbers:

1. 40/8 = _____	5. 15/3 = _____
2. 41/8 = _____	6. 18/6 = _____
3. 35/5 = _____	7. 9/2 = _____
4. 9/4 = _____	8. 7/2 = _____

RULE 2: When the numerator and the denominator of a fraction both end in zero, you may reduce the fraction by dividing both numbers by ten. This is simply canceling the final zeros. For example: $10/100 = 1\emptyset/10\emptyset = 1/10$.

You can also reduce a fraction if you can divide any number higher than 1 evenly into both the numerator and the denominator. For example: $6/9 = 2/3$, since 3 divides evenly into both 6 and 9.

QUIZ 3   Reduce the following fractions to their lowest terms:

1. $1000/10000 =$ _____
2. $5/10 =$ _____
3. $2/8 =$ _____
4. $6/18 =$ _____
5. $8/20 =$ _____
6. $105/10 =$ _____
7. $9/81 =$ _____
8. $80/10 =$ _____

RULE 3: To multiply one fraction by another, multiply the numerators and then multiply the denominators. Place the new numerator over the new denominator.

For example, to solve the problem $4/7 \times 5/9$, you would do the following:

$$\frac{4 \times 5 = 20}{7 \times 9 = 63}$$

Note: A whole number can be written as a fraction whose denominator is one. For example, 8 is the same as 8/1. And you must change all mixed numbers into improper fractions before multiplying and dividing fractions.

QUIZ 4   Multiply the following and reduce the answers to their lowest terms:

1. $1/4 \times 5/8 =$ _____
2. $3/5 \times 3^{1}/_{3} =$ _____
3. $2/3 \times 3/7 =$ _____
4. $1/3 \times 1/5 =$ _____
5. $4/5 \times 2/3 =$ _____
6. $1/7 \times 1/4 =$ _____
7. $3/8 \times 1/5 =$ _____
8. $7/9 \times 3 =$ _____

RULE 4: Dividing fractions is similar to multiplying fractions, with one major difference. To divide one fraction by another, you must *invert the divisor,* and then multiply. (The divisor is the fraction that you are dividing by.) For example:

$$36 \div \frac{1}{6} = \frac{36 \times 6}{1 \times 1} = \frac{216}{1} = 216$$

QUIZ 5   Divide the following and reduce the answers to their lowest terms:

1. $1/3 \div 2/3 =$ _____
2. $6/7 \div 3/7 =$ _____
3. $6^{1}/_{6} \div 5/3 =$ _____
4. $7/10 \div 6 =$ _____
5. $1/5 \div 3/4 =$ _____
6. $2/3 \div 4^{1}/_{8} =$ _____
7. $4/5 \div 6/5 =$ _____
8. $4^{5}/_{7} \div 7^{1}/_{2} =$ _____

ANSWERS

QUIZ 1	QUIZ 2	QUIZ 3	QUIZ 4	QUIZ 5
1. 4	1. 5	1. 1/10	1. 5/32	1. 1/2
2. 1/10	2. $5^{1}/_{8}$	2. 1/2	2. 2	2. 2
3. 13/5	3. 7	3. 1/4	3. 2/7	3. $3^{7}/_{10}$
4. $6^{5}/_{8}$	4. $2^{1}/_{4}$	4. 1/3	4. 1/15	4. 7/60
5. $4^{1}/_{2}$	5. 5	5. 2/5	5. 8/15	5. 4/15
	6. 3	6. $10^{1}/_{2}$	6. 1/28	6. 16/99
	7. $4^{1}/_{2}$	7. 1/9	7. 3/40	7. 2/3
	8. $3^{1}/_{2}$	8. 8	8. $2^{1}/_{3}$	8. 22/35

FRACTIONS, DECIMALS, AND PERCENTS

- **Finishing the fraction review: addition and subtraction.**

- **More business math basics: converting decimals to percents and vice versa.**

- **Learn how to calculate percents.**

As your secretarial skills increase, you will probably be handling more and more administrative tasks. These could include computing interest and discount rates, creating graphs and charts for reports, and doing statistical work. All of these tasks require a solid knowledge of one subject: business math.

This chapter continues the review of the most common business math tools: fractions, decimals, and percents.

Addition and Subtraction of Fractions

Take this quiz to see what you remember about adding and subtracting fractions. When you're through, check your answers with the ones at the end of the chapter to see how well you did.

QUIZ 1 Perform the following operations and, if necessary, reduce the answers to their lowest terms:

1. $\dfrac{1}{9}$ 2. $4\dfrac{1}{3}$ 3. $\dfrac{2}{9}$ 4. $7\dfrac{1}{3}$

   $+\dfrac{5}{6}$ $+3\dfrac{2}{8}$ $-\dfrac{1}{5}$ $-5\dfrac{4}{7}$

If you had trouble with any of these, use the following tips to refresh your memory about adding and subtracting fractions.

RULE 1: As you probably remember, the processes of adding and subtracting fractions are a bit more involved than multiplication and division. You can multiply or divide any fraction by any other fraction simply by multiplying the numerators and multiplying the denominators. When you add or subtract fractions, you must find a *common denominator*. A common denominator is a number that is divisible by both (or all, if you are performing the operation with more than two fractions) the denominators of the fractions that you are adding or subtracting. (Adding or subtracting fractions with different denominators is like adding or subtracting apples or oranges. It just can't be done.) Let's use this problem as an example: $3/5 + 1/3 = ?$ You must choose the lowest number common to both the denominators, 3 and 5. (This is called the *least common denominator.*) In this case, that number is 15. To arrive at the number 15, you multiply the denominator 5 by 3 and you multiply the denominator 3 by 5. **Note:** In the addition and subtraction of fractions, when you multiply the denominator of a fraction by a number, you must also multiply the numerator of that fraction by the same number. What you are actually doing is *multiplying the fraction by one*, since any fraction with the same numerator and denominator is actually the number 1. This process gives you numbers that you can work with without changing the values of the original fractions. This interim step is shown here in parentheses. In this case, you must multiply the numerator 3 by 3 and you must multiply the numerator 1 by 5, giving you the following fractions:

$$\frac{3\,(\times\,3=)}{5\,(\times\,3=)} \quad \frac{9}{15}$$

$$+\;\frac{1\,(\times\,5=)}{3\,(\times\,5=)} \quad \frac{5}{15}$$

Now that you have a common denominator, you may add the new fractions. Add the numerators (9 + 5 = 14), then put the sum of the numerators over the new denominator, 15. This gives you the fraction 14/15. This cannot be reduced any further; thus it is your answer.

RULE 2: When subtracting fractions, you can proceed in much the same way as you do when you add fractions. You must find the least common denominator, multiply the numerators by the same number by which you multiplied the denominators, subtract the new numerators, and put the resulting number over the least common denominator. Then, if necessary, reduce the answer to its lowest terms.

Note: When adding and subtracting fractions, you should change all mixed numbers. Let's take the following problem as an example: $4^1/_8 - 3^1/_3 = ?$

$$4\frac{1}{8} = \frac{33}{8}\;\frac{(\times 3=)}{(\times 3=)}\;\frac{99}{24}$$

$$-3\frac{1}{3} = \frac{10}{3}\;\frac{(\times 8=)}{(\times 8=)}\;-\frac{80}{24}$$

$$\frac{19}{24}$$

Percents and Decimals

Take the following short quiz to see how much you remember about percents and decimals.

QUIZ 2	Perform the following:	*Your Answers*
	1. Write 10% as a decimal.	_____
	2. Write .045 as a percent.	_____
	3. Find 23% of 60.	_____
	4. 8 is what percent of 40?	_____
	5. $54.45 is 33% of how much?	_____

Now check your answers against the ones at the end of this chapter. If you had trouble with any of these problems, you need to brush up on some math fundamentals. Remember that percents, decimals, and fractions are all ways of saying the same thing:

You can write one half as: 1/2, .50, or 50%
You can write one quarter as: 1/4, .25, or 25%
You can write one fifth as: 1/5, .20, or 20%

The following rules will allow you to solve many basic business math problems by using percents and decimals.

RULE 1: To change a fraction to a decimal, divide the numerator by the denominator.

For example, the fraction 3/8 becomes:

$$8)\overline{3.00} \quad .375$$

RULE 2: To change a decimal, such as .25, to a percent, translate the decimal to a fraction, the denominator of which is understood to be a multiple of ten. In this case, because the decimal point is in the hundredths place, the decimal can be expressed as the fraction 25/100. Now multiply the fraction by 100 and add a percent sign.

$$\frac{25}{100} \times \frac{100}{1} = 25\%$$

Therefore, the decimal .25 is equal to 25%.

You can think of this process more simply as moving the decimal point two places to the right and adding the percent sign. Even if the decimal number goes beyond two places, this rule still applies. For example, .375 becomes 37.5%.

QUIZ 3   Change these decimals to percents:

1.   .335 = _____
2.   .42 = _____
3.   .079 = _____
4.   .0182 = _____

RULE 3: To change a percent to a decimal, take away the percent sign and divide the percent by 100. For example, 3% becomes:

$$3\% = \frac{3}{100} = .03$$

Or you can simply move the decimal point two places to the left. For example:

.3% = .003   3.3% = .033   30% = .30

QUIZ 4   Change these percents to decimals:

1.   1% =   _____
2.   .9% =   _____
3.   .67% =   _____
4.   54% =   _____

RULE 4: When you want to find a certain percent of a number, multiply the number by the equivalent decimal of the percent. For example, find 20% of 30.

$$\begin{array}{r} 30 \\ \times .20 \\ \hline 6.00 \text{ or } 6 \end{array}$$

QUIZ 5   Calculate the following:

1.   Find 15% of 200. _____
2.   Find 12% of 1,000. _____
3.   Find 8% of 50. _____
4.   Find 5% of 40. _____

5. Find 20% of 80. _____

RULE 5: When you want to find what percent one number is of *another*, you divide the first number by the second. For example, 9 is what percent of 90?

$$\frac{.10}{90)9.00} \quad \text{or } 10 \text{ %}$$

In other words, 9 is 10% of 90.

QUIZ 6   Find the following percents:

1. 7 is what percent of 35? _____

2. 12 is what percent of 48? _____

3. 15 is what percent of 75? _____

4. 80 is what percent of 160? _____

5. 3 is what percent of 30? _____

RULE 6: To find the number that something is a percent of, you divide the answer by the percentage. For example, 100 is 40% of what?

$$.40)\overline{100} \quad = \quad 40)\overline{10000}^{\,250}$$

In other words, 100 is 40% of 250.

QUIZ 7   Perform the following:

1. 30 is 15% of what?_____

2. $4.40 is 5% of how much?_____

3. $837.50 is 25% of how much?_____

4. 242 is 22% of what?_____

5. 6 is 20% of what?_____

ANSWERS

QUIZ 1
1. 17/18
2. $7^7/_{12}$
3. 1/45
4. $1^{16}/_{21}$

QUIZ 2
1. .10
2. 4.5%
3. 13.80
4. 20%
5. $165.00

QUIZ 3
1. 33.5%
2. 42%
3. 7.9%
4. 1.82%

QUIZ 4
1. .01
2. .009
3. .0067
4. .54

QUIZ 5
1. 30
2. 120
3. 4
4. 2
5. 16

QUIZ 6
1. 20%
2. 25%
3. 20%
4. 50%
5. 10%

QUIZ 7
1. 200
2. $88.00
3. $3350.00
4. 1100
5. 30

CALCULATING INTEREST

- ■ The numbers may change, but the formula remains the same: P x R x T = Interest.

- ■ Which is the better deal: a 4-year loan at 6% interest or a 5-year loan at 5%? Here's how to find out.

- ■ Confounded by compound interest? This chapter can end your confusion.

Neither a borrower nor a lender be. Good advice—but hard to follow in the business world, where the flow of money depends on borrowing and lending. That's why understanding interest—the price paid for the use of money—and being able to compute it are so important.

Your company takes out a loan to buy equipment and pays interest on the money it borrows. You open a savings account, and the financial institution pays you interest because it "borrows" the money on deposit (to make investments, to lend to other people or businesses, and so on). But whatever the situation, when money is borrowed or loaned, there are three items that determine how much interest is paid:

Principal—The sum of money used (borrowed or lent)

Rate—The percentage of the principal charged as interest (based on one year's use of the money, unless otherwise specified)

Time—The number of periods during which the money is used

But how do you calculate interest—that is, the amount to be paid for using the money? Simply follow this formula: $P \times R \times T = I$, or

$$\text{Principal} \times \text{Rate} \times \text{Time} = \text{Interest}.$$

Here's how it works: Say you borrow $500 at 5% for one year. The Principal is $500. The Rate is 5% (or .05). The Time is one year. And the formula looks like this:

$$\$500 \times .05 \times 1 = \$25.$$

So, with these terms, you would be charged $25 interest. Now let's say you need to borrow $5,000, and naturally, you want more than a year to pay back this larger sum. Being a smart consumer, you do some "comparison shopping" and find that you can get a 4-year loan at 6%, or a 5-year loan at 5%. The 5-year loan offers a lower interest rate, but does that mean you'll pay less interest? Let's compare the two:

$5,000 at 6% for 4 years	**$5,000 at 5% for 5 years**
$5,000 × .06 × 4 = $1,200	$5,000 × .05 × 5 = $1,250

Despite a lower interest rate, the 5-year loan would actually cost more!

How to Measure Time

Computing interest would be cut-and-dried if every loan were issued for one year, 3 years, 5 years, and so on. However, businesses and people borrow for one month, 3 months, 5½ years. It can confuse things, but it just makes good financial sense to borrow only what you need, for the shortest time you'll need to pay it back.

So, how would you calculate the interest if you borrowed $5,000 for a year and a half? You could just follow the formula, using 1½ for Time—but it might not be accurate. You see, in the world of finance, there are two ways to measure time: the Ordinary Method and the Exact Method. And when fractions of years are involved, the interest charged can differ depending on the method used. So you must know which time measurement to use before you compute the interest.

Let's assume you borrow that $5,000 for 1½ years at 5%. Here's how to calculate the interest with the two methods of time measurement:

Ordinary Method: This method gives each month 30 days and a year 360 days (it's like rounding off for easier calculations). For the 1½ years in our example, the "extra" six months would be shown as 180/360. (Since the

Rate is based on one year, shorter periods must be expressed as a fraction of a year.) You can reduce 180/360 to 1/2, so Time would be $1\frac{1}{2}$ in the formula:

$$\$5,000 \times .05 \times 1\frac{1}{2} = \$375$$

Exact Method: With this method, you measure Time using the exact number of days in each month and 365 days in a year. If in our example the "extra" six months run from April 1 to October 1 (183 days), the half-year would be 183/365. Add that to the one year (or 365/365) and Time would be 548/365 in the formula:

$$\$5,000 \times .05 \times 548/365 =$$
$$\$137,000/365 = \$375.34 \text{ (rounded off)}$$

Granted, 34¢ isn't much of a difference. But if you're computing interest on several loans, larger amounts, or longer terms, that little difference between methods can add up.

Conquering Compound Interest

So far, we've been calculating *simple* interest, and the computations have been, well, simple. (Admittedly, you have to work with some rather awkward numbers using the Exact Method, but the formula itself isn't so difficult.) But the financial "powers that be" believe that in certain circumstances, simple interest isn't enough. When money is deposited or lent for extended periods of time, interest is often *compounded*—annually, semiannually, monthly, or even daily. What does that mean to you?

With simple interest, you calculate the interest once and leave it at that. But with compound interest, you *recalculate the interest for each compounding period* over the life of the loan or account. Each time you recalculate, you add the interest from the previous period to the principal, and use this new principal in your computation. In short, you just calculate simple interest … over and over and over. Your calculations will be a bit more involved, but if you remember your formula ($P \times R \times T = I$), you'll be computing compound interest with ease. (And note that since you calculate the interest for each period separately, Time in your formula would be the compounding period, *not* the term of the loan or account.)

Let's try it: Say you deposit $5,000 in an account earning 5% compounded semiannually. How much interest would you be paid after $1\frac{1}{2}$

years? (Hint: There are 3 semiannual compounding periods in $1\frac{1}{2}$ years.) Here are the calculations:

$5,000 \times .05 \times 1/2 = \$125$	1st period interest
$5,000 + 125 = \$5,125$	New principal
$5,125 \times .05 \times 1/2 = \$128.13$	2nd period interest
$5,125 + 128.13 = \$5,253.13$	New principal
$5,253.13 \times .05 \times 1/2 = \$131.33$	3rd period interest
$5,253.13 + 131.33 = \$5,384.46$	Final principal

Now, to find the total interest paid, just subtract the original principal from the final principal ($5,384.46 - $5,000) to get $384.46.

Obviously, these computations can become quite tedious (or overwhelming) when you're dealing with longer terms and frequent compounding. Thankfully, to save time (and lessen the risk of error), financial institutions do have compounding tables available—with most of the calculations already figured in.

▼ ▼ TAKE A TEST ▼ ▼

Find the simple interest (Ordinary Method) on:
1. $7,000 at 6% for 4 years
2. $3,500 at 3% for $2\frac{1}{2}$ years

Find the simple interest (Exact Method) on:
3. $2,000 at 4% from September 1 to December 1
4. $3,000 at 5% from March 1 to December 1

Compute the compound interest in 2 years on:
5. $500 at 7% compounded semiannually
6. $1,500 at 5.5% compounded annually

ANSWERS

1. $\$7,000 \times .06 \times 4 = \$1,680$
2. $\$3,500 \times .03 \times 2\frac{1}{2} = \$262.50$
3. $\$2,000 \times .04 \times 91/365 =$
   $\$7,280/365 = \$19.95$
4. $\$3,000 \times .05 \times 275/365 =$
   $\$41,250/365 = \$113.01$
5. $\$500 \times .07 \times 1/2 = \$17.50$
   $\$500 + \$17.50 = \$517.50$
   $\$517.50 \times .07 \times 1/2 = \$18.11$
   $\$517.50 + \$18.11 = \$535.61$
   $\$535.61 \times .07 \times 1/2 = \$18.75$
   $\$535.61 + \$18.75 = \$554.36$
   $\$554.36 \times .07 \times 1/2 = \$19.40$
   $\$554.36 + \$19.40 = \$573.76$
   $\$573.76 - \$500 = \$73.76$
6. $\$1,500 \times .055 \times 1 = \$82.50$
   $\$1,500 + \$82.50 = \$1,582.50$
   $\$1,582.50 \times .055 \times 1 = \$87.04$
   $\$1,582.50 + \$87.04 = \$1,669.54$
   $\$1,669.54 - \$1,500 = \$169.54$

FIGURING DISCOUNTS

Whether you're paying company bills or purchasing supplies or equipment, you want to be sure that you always get the best price on any item. Comparing prices offered by a variety of suppliers or manufacturers is a good start. But once you've found the best list price, look a little further. Check your invoices or catalogs for notations such as 2/10, net 30. They show that a business discount—a way to lower that great price even more—is yours for the taking.

Cash Discounts

Suppliers are often willing to deduct a certain percentage from the list price of their merchandise if you are willing to pay promptly. To let you know, they use price quotations such as the ones listed below. These are all a form of "suppliers' shorthand" explaining the discount available. And if you can translate it, you can save your company money.

Terms: 5/cash, net 30

Terms: 2/10, net 30

Terms: 10/cash, 5/20, net 30

Breaking the code is actually rather straightforward. Let's assume you buy stationery at $20 a box, and the first quotation—Terms: 5/cash, net 30—appears on the invoice. This means that you can deduct 5% from the list price if you pay immediately—at the time of purchase or upon receipt of the invoice. (So you would save $1 a box: $20 × .05 = $1.) However, you could choose to wait 30 days and pay the full price.

Now what if your invoice reads Terms: 2/10, net 30? In this case, you could deduct 2% (or 40¢ a box) if you paid within 10 days. Or, once again, you could choose to wait 30 days and pay the full price.

Sometimes, however, the price quotations are more involved. With the terms 10/cash, 5/20, net 30, you have three choices: Deduct 10% from the list price ($2 a box) if you pay immediately. Or, take up to 20 days to pay, and deduct 5% ($1 a box). Or, pay full price from the 21st to 30th day.

Note: Don't let the small percentages fool you into thinking the savings aren't worth the trouble. When you consider the number of purchases made by your company (or you) in a year, you'll see that those small discounts can add up to big savings.

Trade Discounts

While a cash discount is a device used to encourage quick payment, a trade discount is a way of coping with changing market conditions. Suppose, for example, an office widget is listed in the catalog for $100, but a drop in market prices forces the manufacturer to bring the price down to $80. The widget would still list at $100, but a trade discount of 20% would be offered. The price quotation would read: $100 each less 20%.

If still another drop in the market forced the price even lower, the manufacturer might have to offer an additional discount, say 5%. Terms would then be quoted this way: $100 less 20% and 5%. However, this doesn't mean you could add the discounts together and deduct 25% off the list price.

Successive Discounts

When two or more trade discounts are offered on an item (as above), they are known as a "series of discounts," or "successive discounts." And as such they must be deducted *successively*, or in order. Apply the first discount to the list price to get a new price. Deduct the second discount from the new price to find your discounted price. (If there are more discounts, continue the procedure, applying each one to the previously discounted price.) The whole process is easier to do than to read about. Let's try it out with the successive discount from above ($100 less 20% and 5%):

$$\$100 \times .20 = \$20$$
$$\$100 - \$20 = \$80$$
$$\$80 \times .05 = \$4$$
$$\$80 - \$4 = \$76 \text{ the final discounted price}$$

▼ ▼ TAKE A TEST ▼ ▼

Calculate the prices you would pay with the following quotations:
1. $50 purchase; Terms: 5/10, net 30
2. $150 purchase; Terms: 10/15, net 30
3. $300 purchase; Terms: 10/cash, 5/20, net 30
4. $600 purchase; Terms: 5/10, 2/20, net 30

Calculate the prices you would pay for items with these trade discounts:
5. $200 each less 15%
6. $300 each less 20%
7. $450 each less 15% and 5%
8. $600 each less 20% and 10% and 5%

ANSWERS

1. $50 × .05 = $2.50; $50 - $2.50 = $47.50 within 10 days
   $50 from 11th to 30th day
2. $150 × .10 = $15; $150 - $15 = $135 within 15 days
   $150 from 16th to 30th day
3. $300 × .10 = $30; $300 - $30 = $270 immediately
   $300 × .05 = $15; $300 - $15 = $285 within 20 days
   $300 from 21st to 30th day
4. $600 × .05 = $30; $600 - $30 = $570 within 10 days
   $600 × .02 = $12; $600 - $12 = $588 from 11th to 20th day
   $600 from 21st to 30th day
5. $200 × .15 = $30; $200 - $30 = $170
6. $300 × .20 = $60; $300 - $60 = $240
7. $450 × .15 = $67.50
   $450 - $67.50 = $382.50
   $382.50 × .05 = $19.13
   $382.50 - $19.13 = $363.37
8. $600 × .20 = $120
   $600 - $120 = $480
   $480 × .10 = $48
   $480 - $48 = $432
   $432 × .05 = $21.60
   $432 - $21.60 = $410.40

BANKING

Money—in a multitude of forms—moves in business. It comes in and goes out—with brief stops or long layovers in banks and other financial institutions. And quite often it crosses your desk on the way. Just as you are responsible for the smooth running of your office, you are responsible for the smooth transfer of money. And a mistake in this area can ruin your reputation. So, whether you're responsible for paying bills, making deposits, bookkeeping, payroll, or handling the office checkbook, it pays to know all you can about banking.

Checks and Checking Accounts

Every year, millions of checks—worth billions of dollars—are written. But each of those checks is just a worthless piece of paper until the proper information appears on it:

1. Date.
2. Amount—written out and in figures.
3. Name of the payee (the party being paid).
4. Signature of payer or drawer.
5. Endorsement (the payee's signature on the back).
6. Name, location, and routing number of the bank on which the check is drawn. (Look for a small imprinted number—usually in the upper right-hand corner—set up like this: 51-116/11. That's the routing number, used by the Federal Reserve to identify the bank.)

All checks must contain these six items. But that doesn't mean all checks are alike. Here are the various kinds of checks available:

Personal: Banks today offer a variety of personal checking accounts—but the differences amount to more than a choice of pictures. Some pay interest on your checking account balance; some don't. Some are "free"; some have certain service charges. Some require monthly minimum balances; some don't. Shop carefully for the checking account that best meets your needs and budget. (And remember that you don't always have to keep your checking account at the same bank as your savings account.)

Company: Every company, large or small, has a checking account to be used for carrying on business. These checks are endorsed with the company name and the name of one person authorized as company representative (who signs the checks).

Voucher: Many businesses use this kind of check because it shows the *purpose* for which the money is paid as well as the information shown on a company check. This saves you the trouble of writing and sending a letter explaining the payment. Voucher checks usually have spaces for recording the date of the invoice being paid, invoice and order numbers, cash discount, and amount of invoice.

Certified: Payment of these checks is guaranteed by the bank on which they are drawn. The bank subtracts the amount from your account and holds it for payment when the payee presents the check. Certified checks are often required for certain types of payment (such as those for large-ticket items, like cars), or where the payer's credit rating is unknown in the payee's area. Getting a check certified is a simple procedure. The cashier or teller will stamp the word "Certified" on your check, and a bank official will sign it—after verifying that you have sufficient funds to cover the check, of course.

Bank, Cashier's, or Treasurer's: For these, the bank draws a check on itself (it is the payer) that is signed by the cashier. These checks are used for large amounts—when customers take out a loan or make a large withdrawal from a checking or savings account, or when a customer has a large payment to make and presents the bank with cash in exchange. (There is a small fee for these, and for certified checks.)

Money orders: These are used when you need to pay by check but don't have a checking account (or don't wish to use your own checks). Money orders have stubs or carbons that can be retained as receipts. The amount is imprinted on the money order; you fill in the date, payee's name, and payer's name and address. You can buy money orders at banks, post offices, and many larger stores. The cost is the amount of the check, plus a small handling fee—and you must pay in cash.

Traveler's checks: These can be used when carrying large amounts of cash would be foolhardy or when personal checks might not be accepted. They may be purchased in denominations of $10 and up, from banks, express companies, and some travel agencies. If your boss needs traveler's checks for a business trip, you can fill in the application form, including the total amount of the checks and the denominations desired, ahead of time. However, to receive the checks, your boss must go to the issuing agency and sign them in the presence of an agency representative. To cash a check on the road, your boss must countersign in the presence of the person doing the cashing. When he or she returns, you can insert your boss's name as payee on the unused checks and have him or her countersign them. Then you can endorse them for deposit as you do regular checks.

Keep Careful Records

You should never trust your memory where office finances are concerned. Record all infor-

mation at the time of the transaction to ensure accuracy. Some checkbooks now come with carbons, so you have an automatic record each time you write a check. (These also have spaces to carry the balance forward and keep a running total.) Other checkbooks have stubs or registers. Fill in the necessary information on these *before* you write a check. Your records should include the date, the number of the check, the person to whom it was paid, the purpose of the payment and, of course, the amount. After you write the check, compare the information on it with the information in your record to be sure they agree. Take care that each entry on your record is complete and detailed enough to satisfy requirements for expense accounts and the accounting or bookkeeping department, as well as for income tax deductions.

Sign Here, Please

A check cannot be presented for cash or accepted for deposit unless it is endorsed. But an endorsement often consists of more than simply signing the back of a check. Here are the types of endorsement you'll see:

Blank endorsement: This *is* just the signature of the payee. But remember, once the check has been endorsed, it can be cashed by anyone. For example, if you endorse a check and then lose it, the person who finds it (if dishonest) can get the check cashed.

Special endorsement: This specifies the person to whom the check is being transferred or to whom the check is being paid. For example, "Pay to the order of James Harris, Art Wills" means that James Harris—and no one else—can cash or deposit the check (originally made out to Art Wills).

Restrictive endorsement: This limits the use of the check and is the type of endorsement most often used by businesses. As an example, "For deposit only, Tri-State Corp." means the check may be deposited but not cashed. Most businesses use rubber stamps to save time when endorsing large numbers of checks this way.

Problems and Solutions

The best solution for problems with checks and checking accounts is *prevention:*

✓ Be familiar with the appearance of company checks. When new checks arrive, be sure the name, address, routing number, and account number (lower left-hand corner) are correct. You can save time, trouble, and embarrassment to the company if you find a mistake before using the checks (especially if the routing or account numbers are wrong, because the bank won't honor the checks).

✓ When writing a check, put the first figure close to the dollar sign so that the amount can't be changed. Fill the unused space after the written amount with a line. Or better yet, see about getting a check protector. This is a machine that imprints the amount of a check to prevent alteration of the amount.

✓ Make it a habit to keep track of outstanding checks (checks that you've sent out but that still haven't been returned to your bank for payment). If a check has been outstanding for an unusual length of time (say, two months), it may be lost. Call the payee to see if it's been received.

✓ Be familiar with your bank's stop-payment and overdraft procedures in case you need these services.

— "*Stop payment*" means you do not want a check honored by the bank—perhaps because of a loss or an error. If your office wants to stop payment on a check, call the bank immediately and give the number, date, amount, and payee. Banks will accept an in-person or telephone request for a stop payment, but it must be verified in writing within a certain time period. There is usually a fee for this service (check with your bank). Note: Payment on certified checks cannot be stopped without a court order.

—*An overdraft* (or overdrawn account) results when the amount of a check exceeds the balance in the payer's account. The bank will send an overdraft notice to the payer or return the payer's check, marked "insufficient funds." A deposit to cover the check—as well as the service charge—must be made, and the check reissued. Be aware: An overdraft on the office account is a sign that your system isn't working. If you're having problems keeping the checkbook up-to-date or reconciling bank statements, call your bank for help. (Note: Chapter 6 contains a step-by-step guide to reconciling bank statements.)

How to Handle Deposits

After seeing the fine points involved in using checks, you may think that making a deposit is a piece of cake. In a way, it's simpler—but you still must take special care to be accurate and keep good records. Here's the information to keep in mind when you're handling deposits:

➤ Always be sure that the name, address, and account number on the deposit slip are correct. If you handle more than one company account, do not substitute the slips of one account for another. The account number is imprinted in magnetic ink for the bank computers to "read," and your deposits could end up in the wrong account.

➤ Before writing up the deposit slip, organize the items to be deposited. Large amounts of change should be sorted into the paper rollers provided by the bank. Turn bills so that they all face in the same direction, and arrange them in order from the largest denomination to the smallest. Count—and recount—the cash, and list it in the space provided on the deposit slip.

➤ Examine each check to be deposited to be sure it is properly drawn. Watch for postdated checks (dated for sometime in the future) and discrepancies between figures and written amounts. If a check is written improperly, contact the payer. Be sure each check carries the proper endorsement. Then list each check separately on the deposit slip. Identify each check by number, payer, or routing number to ensure a good record. (Your bank may require the routing number as identification. Find out before you fill out the deposit slip.)

➤ List other items of currency after the checks. These can include money orders, traveler's checks, share drafts (checks from credit unions) and promissory notes. Money orders and traveler's checks are endorsed as checks. Ask at your bank about how to handle the other items.

➤ After all items have been listed, total them. (Double-check your addition!) Then make a duplicate of the deposit slip for your records, since the bank keeps the original. You will be given a receipt for the deposit, but it won't be itemized.

Credit Cards

Few businesspeople who must entertain or travel for work are without credit cards. After all, they're the handiest form of money transfer to come along since checks. Credit cards not only simplify most purchases or transactions but also provide handy records of business-related expenses. If you're in charge of accounting for your boss's expenses, you'll be interested in the following information.

The benefits. Many credit cards are valid across the country and overseas. They are accepted as payment by airlines, car rental companies, restaurants, hotels, and stores. Mailgrams, telegrams, and cablegrams may be charged. Some credit card companies offer ready cash or traveler's checks at their banks or offices. Some permit the cashing of personal checks; others allow you to get ready cash by directly charging the card account itself.

The terms. Most credit card companies charge an annual fee. Some require that the cardholder pay the entire balance within 30 days—but charge no interest. Others allow partial payments of the balance, with an annual interest charge attached to the unpaid portion. There may be a grace period of 15 to 30 days allowed before the interest is charged. This is usually specified on the billing statement.

You should know the interest rates for each of your boss's company credit cards. Watch for payment due dates, and notify your boss of interest accumulating on unpaid balances.

If your boss has several cards, it might be advisable to pare down to reduce interest charges and recordkeeping. Since most cards offer the same services, you may be able to keep cards to a minimum without losing the convenience factor. Determine your boss's expense needs, and evaluate each card's suitability; then share your information with him or her.

Special care with records. Naturally, you should take as much care with credit card records as you do with other financial matters. But there are a few special steps you should include:

—Keep a list of credit card names and numbers in a safe place in case the cards are lost or stolen.

—Have handy the phone numbers of credit card company offices. Call immediately if a card is lost or stolen so that your company won't be held responsible for illegal charges. The companies are usually prompt in voiding the missing card number and issuing a new one.

—Keep a file of all charge card receipts. If several people in your office use the same charge account, keep the receipts separated by name of charger. (And tell everyone to destroy the carbons of their receipts to help prevent criminals from copying and using the account number.)

—Check each monthly billing against your receipt file, noting the date of the charge and the amount. Research any questionable item—and don't hesitate to call the credit card company should any discrepancy or problem arise.

What You Don't Know...

You've absorbed a lot of information so far—but it's just the tip of the iceberg. Every financial institution provides a different variety of services and products that can offer speed, convenience, security, easier recordkeeping, and lower costs. Here are some examples:

★ Automatic teller machines that handle deposits, withdrawals, credit card payments, and more—day and night.

★ Checking accounts that pay interest or guarantee loans when overdrawn.

★ Lockboxes that speed up the receipt of payments. Your customers can send their checks to the bank rather than to you. This cuts a day or two of waiting time—and saves you from handling the checks and the deposits. (The bank sends you a record of the deposits.)

★ Promissory notes—short-term business loans.

★ Various payroll services, including direct deposit of paychecks into employees' accounts.

★ Retirement plans, such as IRAs, Keoghs, and Simplified Employee Pension plans that your employer can set up at little or no cost, with little or no ongoing paperwork.

Of course, the banking services you need depend on the size of your company and your involvement in office finances. But it couldn't hurt to shop around. Do a little investigating at your company's bank or other banks in your area. You won't know what's available and suitable until you ask. And you may find a way to make your banking easier *and* save your company money.

RECONCILING A STATEMENT

It's a rare occasion indeed when a checking account statement arrives showing the same balance as the one appearing in the checkbook. And that's what sends many people into a state of math anxiety—especially secretaries responsible for handling the boss's or the office's checking account. *How could the balances not agree?* you wonder. *I checked and double-checked my figures as I wrote checks in the checkbook. And the bank's computers are accurate. There's no conceivable reason for the discrepancy.*

But there is at least one good reason—and a simple one at that: a time lapse. Throughout the year, the bank issues statements for set periods of time—say, monthly. Each statement lists the transactions that occurred from the first day (or workday) of that period to the last. It takes a few days to generate and mail the statements to all the bank's customers—and a few days for yours to get to you. Meanwhile, life—and business—goes on, and you continue writing checks and making deposits and recording these in your checkbook. When you receive the statement—say, a week after the date it was issued—the balance in your checkbook reflects these transactions. The bank statement balance does not. (They should appear on the next statement you receive.)

However, having a logical reason for the discrepancy does not mean you can just file the statement away, secure in the feeling that everything will add up in the end. Yes, you checked your figures. Yes, the bank's comput-ers are accurate. But there is always a chance (even if it's a slight one) that a mistake has been made, that the account could become overdrawn. There's always a chance that interest or service charges apply to the account that you haven't figured in. There's always a chance that a check you wrote never made it to its destination. And if an error has been made, the sooner you catch it, the less the cost in time, money, and aggravation. That's why, ideally, you should do a statement reconciliation on the day you receive the statement. (As an added incentive, the sooner you recon-cile, the fewer the calculations involved.)

Granted, the chances of having a problem may be small—but you can't afford to risk it. Nothing will destroy confidence in your work more quickly than mistakes in handling the office checkbook. And the only way to verify your accuracy is statement reconciliation—the ultimate double-check.

The Balancing Act

Following is a bank statement for I. M. Customer, a small-business owner. Rather than take a test in this chapter, you're going to act as Customer's secretary and reconcile this statement with the office check-book. As we take you through the procedure, fill in the Reconciliation Form at the end of the chapter. Check your answers with the ones preced-ing the Reconciliation Form. Pencils and calculators ready? Let's begin:

ABC FEDERAL SAVINGS & LOAN ASSOCIATION

Account Statement

I. M. Customer
12 Third Avenue
Citytown, ST 00000

Account Number
123456789
Statement Date
11/02/00

DATE	DESCRIPTION	DEBITS/CHECKS	CREDITS/DEPOSITS	BALANCE
10/3	Beginning balance			741.80
10/5	Check 1407	50.00		691.80
10/6	Check 1406	30.00		661.80
10/8	Check 1409	48.34		613.46
10/11	Check 1411	50.47		562.99
	Check 1408	40.85		522.14
10/12	Deposit		300.00	822.14
10/14	Check 1412	90.13		732.01
10/15	Check 1413	52.33		679.68
10/19	Check 1410	20.20		659.48
10/20	Deposit		250.00	909.48
10/22	Check 1416	50.00		859.48
10/23	Check 1414	50.50		809.98
10/25	Check 1417	37.85		771.13
10/27	Check 1422	130.00		641.13
10/29	Check 1423	63.00		578.13
10/31	Interest		1.58	579.71
10/31	Service Charge	4.00		575.71
11/01	Check 1420	19.65		556.06

ACCOUNT SUMMARY

Previous Balance	+	Credits/Deposits	-	Debits/Checks	=	Statement Balance
741.80	+	551.58	-	737.32	=	556.06

❶ Take the canceled checks that came with the statement, and arrange them in numerical order if your bank hasn't done so already. (Since it would not be practical to include a batch of sample checks, let's assume that this step and the verifications in steps 2 and 3 have been done.)

❷ Match each canceled check against the entries in the checking account record. (This could be check stubs, check carbons, or listings in a register.) Compare numbers, names, and amounts. If they agree, put a check mark near the corresponding entry in your record. If they do not agree, make the correction in your record, and adjust the checkbook balance.

❸ Match the checks against the descriptions on the bank statement. If they agree, mark them off on the statement. If there is a difference between the amount on a check and the amount listed on the statement, *notify the bank.* (The law requires you to notify the bank of an error on its part within a reasonable time. If you don't, you may lose the right to have it corrected or to have the account credited.)

❹ List any outstanding checks on the Reconciliation Form. These are checks that have been written (and recorded in the checkbook) but have not yet gone through the bank—and so do not appear on the statement. Be sure to include checks that are still outstanding from last month (or the previous statement period). Write the total of the outstanding checks in the appropriate spaces on the form. (For this example, let's say there are four checks outstanding: check 1415 for $21.58; check 1418 for $57.53; check 1419 for $35.42; check 1421 for $30.00.)

Note: If a check is outstanding for two months (or periods), contact the payee and see if it has been received. If it hasn't, it may have been lost, and you should ask your boss about contacting the bank and issuing a stop-payment order. (If you stop payment, note that action in your checkbook, and add the amount of that check to the balance. Write and record a new check, subtract the amount from the balance, and list the new check as outstanding.)

❺ Now go through the checkbook and compare the recorded deposits (and their receipts) with those listed on the statement. Check off those that agree, both on the statement and in the checkbook. (Note: If you made a deposit early in the month and it does not appear on your statement, *notify your bank.*)

If there are deposits in the checkbook that were made after the statement issue date, list them in the appropriate column on the Reconciliation Form. (For this example, let's say Customer made deposits of $325 on 11/1 and $275 on 11/7. The statement arrived on 11/9.) Total these deposits on the form.

(Congratulations! The worst is over.)

❻ Are there any service charges on the statement? Write them in the checkbook, and subtract them from the balance. (For simplicity's sake, the box under the Reconciliation Form will serve as the "checkbook," and the balance is provided.) Note: Work with the last entry in your checkbook, *not* the checkbook balance shown for the date the statement was issued.

❼ Are there any interest payments or credits on the statement? Record them in the checkbook (box), and add them to the balance.

❽ This is it! After adding interest payments and subtracting service charges, you now have a reconciled balance showing for your checkbook (in the box). As your final verification, fill in the blanks on the right-hand side of the Reconciliation Form. The total will be a reconciled balance for your statement. The two balances should—will—now agree. And you will be sure of the amount that is actually available in the checking account.

There now, that wasn't so bad, was it? Granted, it can take a bit of time, and the check comparisons in steps 2 and 3 can be tiresome. But each step is necessary—and doing them conscientiously, in order, can save time and aggravation by preventing errors further down the line.

Final note: Some banks provide reconciliation forms with the statements. You may prefer to use that kind of form, a copy of the one provided here, or one of your own design. Whichever you choose, be sure to put the date of reconciliation on the form, and attach the form to the statement before filing.

Things Don't Add Up?

You've tried to reconcile your statement with your checkbook, and after all that work the balances don't agree. What can you do? Try again.

But first, go over your work carefully. Check your arithmetic. (Helpful hint: If the difference between balances is divisible by 9, the problem is transposed numbers.) Did you add where you should have subtracted, or vice versa? Did you forget to list an outstanding check? Did you miss an interest payment or a service charge on the statement? If after a truly diligent search you still can't find an error, call your bank.

No Checks With Your Statement?

Many banks offer a service known as check "truncation" or "safekeeping." Instead of sending you the canceled checks with each statement, the bank makes microfilms of both the fronts and the backs of the canceled checks—and then destroys the originals. Truncation can be of bene-fit in offices where large numbers of checks are used. Since less filing and storage space is needed, it cuts costs as well as lessens the risk of lost checks. The bank keeps the microfilms for a minimum of seven years. And if you need a copy of a canceled check, you can request that the bank send you one. (The microfilm copies are considered legal proof of payment.)

With check truncation, the bank sends a statement listing the checks in numerical order and indicating which ones have cleared. This means that to reconcile your statement, you have only your own record—check stubs, register, carbons—to use. And that means it is essential that you take special care to enter the proper amount and other information in your checkbook *before* you write out a check.

ANSWERS

"Checkbook"
Service charge: $4.00
Adjusted balance: $1009.95
Interest: $1.58
Reconciled balance: $1011.53

Reconciliation Form
Statement balance: $556.06
Deposits not on statement: $600.00
Outstanding checks: $144.53
Reconciled balance: $1011.53

Reconciliation form

Deposits Not on Statement	Outstanding Checks					
	Number	Amount	Number	Amount		
			Subtotal		Statement Balance _____	
					Deposits Not on Statement + _____	
					Total _____	
					Outstanding Checks -	
					Reconciled Balance _____	
Total Deposits	Subtotal (to next column)		Total Outstanding Checks			

Checkbook Balance	-	Service	=	Adjusted Balance
1013.95	-	_____	=	_____
Adjusted Balance	+	Interest	=	Reconciled Balance
_____	+	_____	=	_____

THE PETTY CASH FUND

As a secretary, your responsibilities may include managing the petty cash fund. That's true whether you work in the only office of a small business or in one department of a large corporation. But don't let the name "petty cash" fool you. Managing the fund is no small task.

The minor expenses covered by petty cash *are* a bookkeeping chore. But at the end of the year, those minor expenses add up to a considerable amount. That's why it's so important to regulate the petty cash flow carefully. In this chapter, we'll show you how to do just that, step-by-step.

How a Petty Cash Fund Works

A petty cash fund is a convenient way to handle small expenses for which drawing a company check would not be practical. (These include all those little bills that pop up in the normal course of business—postage, delivery charges, office supplies, etc.) Here's how it works:

A certain amount of money is set aside in a locked box or drawer. Whenever people need to make a business-related purchase or payment (or have spent money out of their own pocket on such an expense), they go to the petty cash "custodian." They fill out a petty cash voucher, and are either given the money needed or are reimbursed for the money they spent. In either case, they must turn in a receipt as proof of the exact amount spent on the specified purchase or payment. When the fund falls below a set amount, it is replenished.

Where Do You Begin?

If your office does not yet have a petty cash fund, your first step is to decide on the size of the fund. (Note: In some companies, the accounting or bookkeeping department may make this decision for you.) With your boss, estimate the amount of money needed to cover petty cash expenses for a specific period of time. (One month is the usual choice.) List the purchases and payments that typically occur each month and that would qualify as petty cash expenses. Then add $10 to $15 to their total to cover unexpected charges.

Depending on your office or company procedures, it may take one day or several days to get a reimbursement check to replenish the petty cash fund. So you should never allow the fund to dwindle down to nothing. You and your boss should decide beforehand at what point the fund should be replenished—say, when your $100 fund dips to $15 or $20. That way, if there's a delay getting the reimbursement, you won't run short.

Setting Up the Petty Cash Fund

Let's say, for example, it's been determined that your office needs about $100 to cover petty cash fund disbursements. To establish the fund, a check is drawn in that amount and made out to "Petty Cash." The entry in the cash disbursements journal (more on this on the next page) would read:

Petty Cash $100

Cash $100

After you cash the check at your company's bank, place the money in a lockable "petty cash" drawer or box. Put your supply of blank vouchers in the box with the cash. Then lock the box and put it in a lockable desk or file drawer—and lock the drawer. Your petty cash box should be removed only when you receive a request for reimbursement or payment—and it should be promptly returned to the locked drawer when you're through.

Vouchers: The Essential Record

As the custodian or manager of the petty cash fund, you are responsible for your company's money. You will be using petty cash to reimburse and "lend" to co-workers for specified business expenses. With that kind of responsibility, you *must account for every disbursement* (or cash outlay) from the fund. And that's where the petty cash voucher comes in.

Each and every disbursement you make from the fund must be accounted for by a petty cash voucher. Your company may have a standard voucher, or you can buy the forms at any stationery store or even make up your own. Whatever the case, be sure you always have a plentiful supply on hand (say, six months' worth).

A sample voucher appears below. *Your* petty cash vouchers should contain all of the following information:

❶ date
❷ name of the person to whom payment is being made
❸ purpose of the expenditure
❹ amount of payment
❺ authorizing signature
❻ signature of person receiving the money

Date _____ ① _____		No. _____
	PETTY CASH VOUCHER	
$ ④		
Paid to _____ ② _____		
For _____ ③ _____		
Authorized by _____ ⑤ _____		
Received Payment _____ ⑥ _____		

When an expense is to be paid by petty cash, you or the spender must fill out the petty cash voucher, which then must be signed by the authorized person in your office or company (for example, your boss or someone in Accounting). Be sure the information on the form is correct before you give the spender the cash. Count the cash carefully, and have the spender sign the voucher after you pay him or her. Don't forget to get a receipt for the specified expense, and attach it to the voucher.

Where Do the Vouchers and Receipts Go?

Naturally, if your company has a set procedure for keeping vouchers and receipts, that's the one you should follow. But if not, you have a choice. You may keep all the completed vouchers and receipts in the locked box with the petty cash. Or you may wish to group vouchers and their receipts by expense category (for example, Office Supplies, Delivery Charges, Postage, and so on) and keep each group in separate folders in the locked desk or file drawer. Either way is satisfactory—as long as you *keep the vouchers and receipts.*

What About Recordkeeping?

Keeping records organized and simplified is important with a petty cash fund. Otherwise, recordkeeping can become so detailed that it is burdensome. Some companies require that you keep a petty cash journal in addition to the vouchers to keep track of where the money is going. For the journal, there are two basic recordkeeping systems to choose from. (Check to find out if you are required to use a certain system.)

In the first, *at the time each payment is made,* you must enter the amount of and the reason for the payment in the journal, in addition to filling out the voucher. (This can be time-consuming if there is extensive use of the fund.) In the second system, vouchers and receipts are grouped according to category and stored together (in folders or attached to one another). When it is time to replenish the petty cash fund, each category is totaled and the calculator tapes are attached to the groups of vouchers. That way, only one entry is made for all payments for office supplies, all payments for postage, and so on, before replenishing the fund.

Here's how each system works. Let's assume that your $100 petty cash fund was established on August 3. During the month, petty cash was used to pay these expenses: $22 for letterhead, Aug. 4; $12 for diskettes, Aug. 7; $4 for calculator tapes, Aug. 10; $5 for cab fare, Aug. 13; $15 for postage, Aug. 17; $3 for tolls, Aug. 21; $6 for cab fare, Aug. 25; $13 for entertainment, Aug. 26. Here's how your journal would look, using both systems:

Enter at the time of payment				**Group when fund replenished**			
8/3	Petty Cash	$100		8/3	Petty Cash	$100	
	Cash		$100		Cash		$100
8/4	Letterhead	22		8/27	Office Supplies	38	
8/7	Diskettes	12			Cab fare	11	
8/10	Calc. tapes	4			Postage	15	
8/13	Cab fare	5			Tolls	3	
8/17	Postage	15			Entertainment	13	
8/21	Tolls	3					
8/25	Cab fare	6					
8/26	Entertainment	13					

As you can see, the two outlays for cab fare and the three for office supplies were combined to make two entries in the "grouping" journal. Unfortunately, we cannot effectively demonstrate the difference between recording single entries each time a voucher is turned in and recording all the entries at one sitting when the fund is replenished. Only through experience can you determine which system is right for you.

Replenishing the Fund

At the end of the designated accounting period, or whenever your fund has dwindled to the predetermined amount, you must replenish the fund with another check. At this time, if you haven't already, you must group the vouchers and receipts by category. Total each group, and list the expense categories and their totals on a record sheet. (The record sheet should be set up like the sample "grouping" journal page above.) Attach the tapes, vouchers, and receipts to the record sheet (or arrange this package according to company procedure and include your petty cash journal if required).

Now you must "prove" the petty cash. On a separate paper or tape, total *all* the expenses; then add this total to the amount of cash left in your petty cash box. The final total must equal the original amount of the fund. (In our example, there is $20 left in the box and $80 in total expenses—which gives us a grand total of $100, matching our original fund.) If your expenses and remaining cash do not match your original fund amount, go over your calculations, vouchers, and receipts again.

Finally, a check should be drawn up to "Petty Cash" for an amount equaling your total expenses. Then, according to company procedure, bring your record package and check (or check request) to your boss or accounting department. The expenses will be verified; the vouchers marked "Paid"; and the replenishing check issued. After you cash the check, add the money to your cash box and make a journal entry for "Cash" for that amount in the last column on the right (line it up with your first "Cash" entry). Your fund is now back at its original level, and you're all set to begin again.

A Word of Caution

Managing the petty cash fund is a big responsibility. You should be certain of your ability to handle the cash and the records properly. Accuracy and care are essential. We've described the basic methods of efficient fund management. But here are a few extra guidelines for safeguarding your petty cash.

➤ Whether you use vouchers or an expense sheet, keep copies of all the paperwork—receipts, expense records, total tapes, vouchers … everything.

➤ Count the money carefully. Always count it twice: first to yourself and again when you hand it to your co-worker. And never fan the bills like a hand of cards—pull the bills apart and count them out separately.

➤ Once you've chosen (or been given) a system for managing the fund, stick with it. Follow the rules and procedures to the letter, or your records will be impossible to balance at the end of each period. Or even worse, your fund could come up short.

➤ *Never borrow money from the fund*—and never let anyone else borrow from it either. Don't feel that you're being "petty"—taking such care is being *professional*.

▼ ▼ TAKE A TEST ▼ ▼

1. List the five items that must appear on a voucher before the petty cash custodian may pay the bearer.

2. On April 2, a petty cash fund of $75 was established; it is to be replenished at the end of each month, or when it dips to $10. During the fund's first month of activity, the following payments were made: $12 for entertainment, April 4; $3 for pens, April 5; $4 for cab fare, April 7; $10 for business cards, April 11; $3 for cab fare, April 15; $13 for computer paper, April 20; $14 for entertainment, April 22; $5 for postage, April 24; $3 for delivery charges, April 29.

Show how the journal page for this fund would look on April 30, using both the "entry at time of payment" and "entry grouping" systems.

ANSWERS

1. Date; name of person receiving payment; reason for the expenditure; amount of payment; authorized signature. A sixth item, the signature of the person receiving the money from petty cash, is required after payment is made and before the voucher is filed.

2.

Entry at time of payment				Group when fund replenished		
4/2	Petty cash	$75		4/2	Petty cash	$75
	Cash		$75		Cash	$75
4/4	Entertainment	12		4/30	Entertainment	26
4/5	Pens	3			Office Supplies	26
4/7	Cab fare	4			Cab fare	7
4/11	Business cards	10			Postage	5
4/15	Cab fare	3			Delivery charges	3
4/20	Computer paper	13			Cash	67
4/22	Entertainment	14				
4/24	Postage	5				
4/29	Delivery charges	3				
4/30	Cash		67			

EXPENSE ACCOUNT RECORDS

- **Receipts and the right records are all you need for reimbursements or income tax deductions.**

- **Learn the five items that must appear on expense records to ensure a tax deduction.**

- **Here's a checklist of deductible business expenses—and where to find more.**

Few secretaries have the responsibility of making out their employer's federal income tax returns. But many secretaries could help their bosses save tax dollars by maintaining the proper records of deductible business-related expenses.

If you're already keeping your boss's expense account records, you'll learn here what—if any—additional records you'll need to satisfy the IRS as well as your company's accounting department. If you aren't yet handling your boss's company expense account, you'll find some suggestions for setting up an accurate, efficient system. (Note: We realize you may be handling not only your boss's expense account records but also your co-workers', salespeople's, and your own. But for simplicity's sake, we will refer to your boss alone in our explanation. The guidelines discussed, however, do apply to anyone's expense account records.)

Federal Requirements

The IRS requires two types of records to substantiate business expense deductions:
- Receipts—for expenditures of $25 or more; itemized bills or vouchers for all lodging expenses.
- Diary—to record the details of business expenses. The diary may be a small notebook, a purchased account book, or even a set of expense account sheets for the year stapled together.

Note: Expense records should be kept for at least three years after the due date of the federal income tax return they support.

The Five Essentials

In general, companies require certain basic information on their expense account records: the date, the amount, and a description of (or reason for) each expenditure. But to meet federal requirements to support deductions, expense account records must include:

➤ When—the date the expense was incurred
➤ Where—the place the expense was incurred (name and address of business, hotel, restaurant, theater, etc.)
➤ How much—the amount of the business-related expense; the mileage driven (when applicable)
➤ Who—the name of the employee who incurred the expense; the names of those entertained and their business relationship with your employer (when applicable)
➤ Why—the business purpose of or reason for the expense; a description of what the payment was for

Keep these categories in mind when you are purchasing or making expense account forms. Be sure the form you use includes spaces to account for travel away from home, local business travel, meals and entertainment, and miscellaneous business-related expenses. (If you can't adjust your company's form to meet tax record requirements, you may want to record the extra information on a copy of the form.)

One More Important Item

In addition to the five basic items, there is one other thing your records should include: reimbursements or allowances. If your boss is reimbursed for any business-related expenses, the payments must be accounted for on his or her federal income tax return. So, a record of reimbursements received is necessary. If your boss does not get reimbursed for business-related expenses, make a notation of such on the expense account record. That way, all expense-related information will be together at tax time.

A Checklist of Deductible Expenses

Here's a list of the kinds of travel and entertainment expenditures that may be deductible—if they are business related *and* substantiated by records:

- ✓ vehicle expenses (mileage, repairs, parking, tolls, etc.)
- ✓ theater and concert tickets, nightclub bills, etc.
- ✓ gifts for clients, customers
- ✓ telephone and telegraph bills (while away from the office)

- ✓ lodging costs
- ✓ meals and tips
- ✓ transportation (bus, cab, train, and plane fares, car rentals, etc.)
- ✓ cleaning and laundry costs (while traveling on business)

From time to time, federal regulations on what's deductible, or what percentage of expense totals is deductible, may change. However, the IRS offers (free of charge) a publication covering travel and entertainment expenses. If you want a copy for your office reference, you can order one by phone. If your local library has up-to-date IRS publications, you can make your own copy. Or if you have a question regarding the deductibility of an expense, check the Blue Pages of your phone book for your local IRS office or the IRS tax information hotline.

Get That Information!

You yourself should make notations of deductible expenses you handle. For instance, if you make plane reservations for a business trip for your boss, record the cost of the ticket(s) as soon as you hang up the phone.

If your boss accumulates daily expenses, he or she may find that a pocket-size booklet containing an expense-record form for each day of the month is more practical and convenient than a stack of record forms. When your boss goes on a business trip, make sure he or she takes along the record booklet or enough forms. (And give your boss a gentle reminder to fill them out!) If your boss is not one to bother with keeping an orderly record of business expenses, be sure that you get the information orally as soon as possible—before the expenses are forgotten. And whether your boss's deductible business expenses occur daily or only occasionally, *be sure that you get the receipts* that substantiate the expenses.

A Final Thought

By now you've noticed that there have been no actual calculations to do in this chapter. Well, rest assured that you'll be getting plenty of practice in basic addition, subtraction, and multiplication if you keep proper expense account records. And remember, it's better to record "too much" information at the time expenses are incurred than to have too little information at tax time—and risk losing deductions.

A PAYROLL PRIMER

Whether you collect time sheets, pass out paychecks, or actually prepare the payroll, as a secretary you are bound to be involved in payroll procedures to some extent. Of course, many companies—large and small—now use computers to prepare the payroll. But a thorough knowledge of common procedures, forms, and records will give you the background necessary to enhance your capabilities and your worth to your company, no matter what your payroll responsibilities are.

The Basics of Pay

An employee's pay may be classified as commission, salary, wages, or a combination of two or more of these three forms. (Noncash forms of pay, such as stocks, bonds, and cars, are handled in a completely different—and more complicated—manner than monetary payments. Since chances are you will never have to handle the paperwork involved with these forms of pay, they will not be covered in this discussion.)

➤ Commission is pay based on a percentage of the dollar amount of the employee's sales. For example, a salesperson who earns 10% commission would be paid $200 for every 2,000 dollars' worth of sales he or she makes in a set pay period.

➤ Salary is a set amount of compensation that covers a specific period of time. Most administrative-level employees are paid a salary. For example, a supervisor might earn a salary of $25,000 a year, or $480 a week—even if he or she worked more than the "standard" 40 hours in any week. (Some salespeople earn a set salary plus a commission.)

➤ Wages are earnings established on an hourly or piecework basis. For example, a production-line worker could be paid $6 for every hour worked, or 25¢ for every product he or she completes in a pay period. (Piecework rates are carefully established according to industry and area standards of production and pay.)

Payroll Deductions

There's a difference between what you earn each pay period and what you get. That's a lesson we all learned in our youth, with that first hard-earned paycheck. Here's how and why that happens:

■ Gross pay is the total amount of earnings or compensation in the pay period. For those being paid a salary, gross pay would simply be the stated salary amount. For example, the supervisor's gross pay is $25,000, or $480 a week. The salesperson's gross pay (after $2,000 in sales) is $200. The production worker's gross pay takes a bit more calculation, however. If the worker made $6 an hour and worked 40 hours, gross pay would be $240. If the worker were paid 25¢ per piece and produced 1,000 pieces, gross pay would be $250.

Note: According to law, for most hourly workers, any work time over a 40-hour workweek is considered overtime. The pay for overtime must be figured separately at 1½ times the hourly rate. (And in some cases, hourly workers may be paid at twice the hourly rate for working overtime on Sundays or holidays.) For example, if an hourly worker made $6 an hour and worked 44 hours one week, the gross pay would come to $276. Here are the calculations:

$$40 \text{ hr} \times \$6 = \$240 \qquad \$6 \times 1\frac{1}{2} = \$9 \qquad 4 \text{ hr} \times \$9 = \$36 \quad \$240 + \$36 = \$276$$

■ **Net pay** is your take-home pay, or what remains after payroll deductions are subtracted from your gross pay. The number, dollar amounts, and types of deductions can vary from company to company, person to person. But there are two deductions required by law on everyone's paycheck:

- **FICA** is, in effect, your contribution to your future Social Security retirement or disability benefits. (FICA stands for Federal Insurance Contributions Act, which established the system to fund the Social Security and Medicare programs.) The deduction is a set percentage of your wages, up to a set maximum wage amount. (Anything you earn over the set maximum wage is not subject to FICA tax.) The tax rate (or percentage) and the maximum wage amount are set by law and can change from year to year. Call your local Social Security office for the current figures. Note: Your employer matches your contributions to Social Security dollar for dollar when the funds are deposited with the federal government.

- **FWT** stands for Federal Withholding Tax, or your federal income tax deduction. The tax law determines the minimum amount that should be withheld—that is, the amount necessary to pay the employee's annual federal income tax liability. But it's the employee's responsibility to request on his or her W-4 form (see next page) how much tax to withhold. (Some people with higher incomes must also make quarterly estimated tax payments to meet their federal income tax liability. These are not deducted from paychecks, but are paid separately and filed with an estimated tax payment voucher.)

   Note: Whatever an employee receives as payment for work or services—whether it's in the form of cash, property, or services—is subject to FICA and FWT. This includes—but is not limited to—salaries, wages, expense allowances, commissions, bonuses, tips, employee awards, sick pay, vacation pay, severance pay.

There are, of course, many other types of payroll deductions. Some of the most common ones are listed below. Note that in some cases, such as the FICA tax, direct deposits to checking or saving accounts, and pension fund payments, your money is simply routed and held for your future use. And some deductions may be matched by contributions from your employer.

- ✓ state and local taxes
- ✓ accident, health, life insurance
- ✓ union dues
- ✓ direct deposits to bank accounts

- ✓ U.S. Savings Bonds
- ✓ loans, mortgages
- ✓ pension funds, retirement plans
- ✓ charitable contributions

Payroll Record and Forms

Naturally, there's a lot of recordkeeping required to keep track of individual paychecks and the payroll. And much of the recordkeeping is necessary for the preparation of state and federal tax returns. But whatever the reason for the record, *accuracy* is essential. Here are the most common payroll records and forms:

➤ **Form W-2** is the annually issued *Wage and Tax Statement*. This is a summary of an individual's wages, and federal withholding and FICA taxes, and is essential for filing the federal income tax return. The information on the form is taken from the employee's earnings record, and the form is completed in quadruplicate. One copy is for company records, one copy is sent to the Internal Revenue Service, and two copies are sent to the employee. If state income taxes are also withheld, an additional copy is made and sent to the employee. Employers are required by law to send the W-2 form to each employee no later than January 31 each year. (If an individual leaves the company during the year, you may send the W-2 as soon as you want after he or she has left—but still, no later than January 31.)

➤ **Form W-4 (or W-4A)** is the *Employee's Withholding Allowance Certificate*. Companies use this form to determine how much federal withholding tax to deduct from employees' paychecks. That's why it's so important that every employee take the time to fill out his or her W-4 form (or the shorter W-4A) accurately. By completing the worksheets that are part of the form, you estimate your tax liability for the year—and determine the number of withholding allowances you can claim. Each allowance lowers your taxable income (by an amount set by law each year), and therefore lowers your withholding taxes. You can, if you wish, claim fewer allowances than you are entitled to—or even *no* allowances. This results in less take-home pay, but increases your chance of getting a tax refund. But if you claim *more* allowances than you're entitled to, you may have too little withheld for federal income taxes—and face a possible fine and penalties from the government.

Every new employee should fill out a W-4 or W-4A form as soon as possible after beginning work. And note: *Any* employee can fill out a new W-4 whenever he or she feels it's necessary—for example, with a change in marital status, addition of dependent (child or elderly parent), or new eligibility for another deduction (such as mortgage interest). Once the employee completes the worksheets and certificate on the front of the form, he or she turns the certificate in to the employer. The employer, in turn, uses the most recently completed W-4 to compute the employee's withholding deduction.

➤ **Form 1099-R** is the *Statement for Recipients of Total Distributions from Profit-Sharing, Retirement Plans, Individual Retirement Arrangements, Insurance Contracts, etc.* This form summarizes the income an employee received from a retirement plan (and the taxes withheld, if any). Copies are made for the employee, the employer, and the IRS. The form is not filed with the individual's federal income tax return, but the information—or rather, the income—must be reported on the return.

➤ **Federal Tax Deposit Coupon Form 8109** is used by companies when depositing FICA and FUTA (see below) taxes. The form is filed at the commercial bank where the taxes (employees' and employer's contributions) are deposited. The size of the company (and total amount of taxes) determines how often deposits must be made.

➤ **Form 941** is the *Employer's Quarterly Tax Return*. This is a summary of the FICA and federal income taxes deposited with Form 8109, plus the taxes due but not yet remitted. The form also contains all employees' names, Social Security numbers, taxable wages, and FICA and FWT deduction amounts.

➤ **Form 940** is the employer's *Federal Unemployment Insurance Tax Return*. Employers contribute to state unemployment programs by paying this federal tax (under FUTA) annually before January 31. In some states, employees also contribute to the State Unemployment Insurance Tax (under SUTA) through payroll deductions. (The employer files the SUTA return quarterly.) Note: Some states have merit-rating plans that reduce the tax for employers who have stable payrolls or low turnover.

■ **Work attendance record.** The most common form of this record is the time card or time sheet. Some indicate the time spent on specific work assignments, but most simply record the employee's time of arrival at and departure from work. Salaried employees usually don't have to punch in time cards or sign time sheets—but records of their attendance (and vacation and sick time) are kept in some manner.

■ **Payroll register.** This is a compilation of all the information that is on the time cards and sheets or attendance records. Although the design or form (e.g., a journal or a disk) may vary, the register contains columns where you record each employee's name, number of exemptions, hourly rate or salary, hours worked during the pay period, vacation and sick time taken during the period, gross pay (divided into regular and overtime amounts), taxable earnings for FICA and unemployment insurance, deductions, and net pay. The information is broken down by pay periods, and payroll check numbers are listed if payment is made by check.

At the end of each pay period, the totals for each category—for each employee, each day, and the entire pay period—are calculated to close out the period. The figures are then proved to ensure accuracy—and everything *must* balance. For example:

1. The sum of total regular and total overtime hours must equal the sum of all the daily total hours.

2. The figure in the total gross pay column must equal the sum of the total regular and total overtime pay.

3. The figure in the total deductions column must equal the sum of all the deduction columns (i.e., total FICA, total FWT, etc.).

4. The result of total gross pay minus total deductions must equal the figure in the total net pay column.

◼ **Employee earnings record.** This is required by law and is used to prepare the W-2 forms. It contains all the information pertaining to an individual's pay record: the employee's name, address, date of birth, marital status, Social Security number, claimed exemptions, rate of pay, hours worked, gross earnings, deductions, net pay, and paycheck numbers for each pay period and the year-to-date.

Note: While you are required by law to use certain federal tax forms and records, you—or your employer—can purchase or design other payroll-related forms (such as attendance records) that are appropriate for your needs. And not all forms and records must be on paper. There are computer payroll management programs available, and certain federal forms (such as Form 941) can be filed on magnetic tape.

▼ ▼ TAKE A TEST ▼ ▼

Match the following terms with the appropriate description or definition:

1. FICA tax	**a.**	total earnings in pay period
2. commission	**b.**	summary of tax payments deposited or due
3. FWT	**c.**	has all information on attendance and pay
4. W-2 form	**d.**	take-home pay
5. W-4 form	**e.**	shows year's earnings and taxes withheld
6. gross pay	**f.**	amount withheld to pay income tax
7. net pay	**g.**	has year-to-date pay information used for W-2
8. payroll register	**h.**	percentage of sales made
9. employee earnings record	**i.**	amount withheld to fund Social Security
10. Form 941	**j.**	used to figure how much income tax withheld

Joe Brown is paid $12 an hour; last week he put in 44½ hours. With those earnings and the following deductions, what was his net pay?

$84.15 FWT $4.50 health insurance $10.00 Savings Bond
$39.27 FICA $22.44 state income tax $16.83 pension

ANSWERS

1. i;   **2.** h;   **3.** f;   **4.** e;   **5.** j;   **6.** a;   **7.** d;   **8.** c;   **9.** g;   **10.** b

Joe Brown's net, or take-home, pay was $383.81. Here are the calculations:
$40 \times \$12 = \$480$ $\$12 \times 1\frac{1}{2} = \$18$ $4\frac{1}{2} \times \$18 = \$81$ $\$480 + \$81 = \$561$ gross pay
total deductions = $177.19 $\$561 - \$177.19 = \$383.81$

- In this chapter: guide-lines and guides to end your confusion about conversions.

- Learn how the metric and U.S. systems measure up to each other.

- Compare or convert with our easy-to-use guides.

CONVERT WITH CONFIDENCE

Break out your calculator! In this chapter you'll be learning to convert units of measurement within and between the metric and U.S. (also known as the British, or English) systems of linear measurement.

Now don't panic. Being able to convert with confidence requires nothing more than a knowledge of the basics, some practice, and the right tables. And that's exactly what you'll get in the next few pages. So let's get started:

Check the tables on the next page and you'll see that the metric system is far easier to work with. All measurements are some type of *meter*—and the system is based only on the number 10. To convert from one denomination to another, you simply use a multiple of 10. For example, multiply centimeters by 10 to get millimeters:

> 1 centimeter = 10 millimeters   20 cm = 200 mm   25 cm = 250 mm

If you were converting to a denomination two steps down on the scale (say, from meters to centimeters), you'd multiply by 100 (10×10); three steps down, multiply by 1,000 ($10 \times 10 \times 10$), and so on.

On the other hand, to convert to a larger denomination, you must *divide* by a multiple of 10 (or move the decimal point to the left):

> 100 millimeters = 10 centimeters 10 mm = 1 cm 1 mm = 0.1 cm
> 100 millimeters = 1 decimeter 10 mm = 0.1 dm 1 mm = 0.01 dm

The U.S. system, however, has no uniform multiple for conversions. The scale starts with 12 inches to a foot—then 3 feet to a yard; 5.5 yards to a rod, and so on. You still multiply to convert to a smaller denomination and divide to convert to a larger. But you must either memorize the ratios or keep your chart handy. For example, to convert 1 rod to inches, you must go from rods to feet to inches:

> 1 rod = 16.5 feet 1 ft = 12 in. $16.5 \text{ ft} \times 12 = 198 \text{ in.}$

And what about converting between the two systems? Check the table of metric-U.S. equivalents (on the next page)—then multiply or divide. For example, to convert 5 centimeters to inches:

> 1 centimeter = 0.3937 in. $5 \times 0.3937 = 1.9685 \text{ in.}$

To convert 5 inches to decimeters (a larger value, so divide):

> 1 decimeter = 3.937 in. $5 \div 3.937 = 1.27 \text{ dm}$

To convert 1/2 kilometer to miles:

> 1 kilometer = 0.6214 mile $.5 \times 0.6214 = 0.3107 \text{ mile}$

Note: On the next page, we've included a "size guide," which can save you time and energy when you just need to know "Which is bigger?" While it's not drawn to scale, the size guide does display the various units of measurement in order of size. So you can quickly see which is bigger—or smaller—without having to wade through tables or calculate equivalents. And on page 279 is the table you will probably find most useful—the conversion guide. This guide has many of the calculations involved in conversions already figured in—and puts an end to the question "Do I divide or multiply for the answer?"

U.S. Linear Measures

1 foot (ft or ')	=	12 inches (in. or ")
1 yard (yd)	=	3 feet = 36 inches
1 rod (rd)	=	5.5 yards = 16.5 feet
1 furlong	=	40 rods = 220 yards = 660 feet
1 mile (mi)	=	8 furlongs = 320 rods = 1,760 yards = 5,280 feet

Metric Linear Measures

1 centimeter (cm)	=	10 millimeters (mm)
1 decimeter (dm)	=	10 centimeters = 100 millimeters
1 meter (m)	=	10 decimeters = 100 cm = 1000 mm
1 dekameter (dam)	=	10 meters = 100 dm = 1000 cm
1 hectometer (hm)	=	10 dekameters = 100 m
1 kilometer (km)	=	10 hm = 100 dam = 1000 m
1 myriameter (mym)	=	10 km = 1000 dam = 10,000 m

Table of Equivalents

1 centimeter	=	0.3937 inch
1 decimeter	=	3.937 inches
1 dekameter	=	32.808 feet
1 furlong	=	201.168 meters
1 inch	=	2.54 centimeters
1 kilometer	=	0.6214 mile
1 meter	=	39.37 inches; 1.1 yards
1 mile	=	1.609 kilometers
1 millimeter	=	0.03937 inch
1 myriameter	=	6.214 miles
1 yard	=	0.9144 meter

Size Guide

- **millimeter** (0.039 in.)
- **centimeter** (0.3937 in.)
- **inch** (2.54 cm)
- **decimeter** (3.937 in.)
- **foot** (3.048 dm)
- **yard** (0.9144 m)
- **meter** (1.1 yd) (3.281 ft)
- **rod** (5.0292 m) (0.50292 dam)
- **dekameter** (1.989 rd) (32.81 ft)
- **hectometer** (19.89 rd) (109.395 yd)
- **furlong** (201.168 m) (2.01 hm)
- **kilometer** (0.6214 mi) (1,093.66 yd) (3,280.99 ft)
- **mile** (1.609 km) (16.09 hm) (1609 m)
- **6.214 miles** (10 km) **myriameter**

On the next page is a chart that will help you speed through even the most confusing conversion problems. Simply scan the left column to find the form of measurement you have or need to change, and find the corresponding "conversion factor" in the right column. Then, just multiply. For example, if you need to know how many feet there are in 4.5 meters, go down the left column to "meters." Moving to the right, you'll see that the conversion factor in the "meters to feet" row is 3.281. Multiply 4.5 meters by 3.281 to get 14.7645 feet.

What if there is no matching conversion factor for your problem? All you have to do is add a step. Let's say you need to know how many dekameters are in a furlong. There's no conversion factor for "furlongs to dekameters"— but there is one for "furlongs to meters," so start there. One furlong converts to 201.168 meters. Now find the "meters to dekameters" factor: 0.1. Multiply 201.168 meters by 0.1, and you get 20.117 dekameters in a furlong. There now, that isn't so hard, is it?

CONVERSION GUIDE

To Convert	Into	Multiply By
Centimeters	decimeters	0.1
centimeters	dekameters	0.001
centimeters	feet	0.03281
centimeters	hectometers	0.0001
centimeters	inches	0.3937
centimeters	kilometers	0.00001
centimeters	meters	0.01
centimeters	millimeters	10
Feet	centimeters	30.48
feet	decimeters	3.048
feet	inches	12
feet	meters	0.3048
feet	miles	0.0001894
feet	yards	0.333
Furlongs	feet	660
furlongs	meters	201.168
furlongs	miles	0.125
furlongs	rods	40
furlongs	yards	220
Inches	centimeters	2.54
inches	decimeters	0.254
inches	feet	0.0833
inches	yards	0.0278
inches	meters	0.0254
inches	miles	0.00001578
inches	millimeters	25.4
Kilometers	feet	3,281
kilometers	yards	1,093.67
kilometers	meters	1,000
kilometers	miles	0.6214
Meters	centimeters	100
meters	decimeters	10
meters	dekameters	0.1
meters	feet	3.281
meters	hectometers	0.01
meters	kilometers	0.001
meters	miles	0.0006214
meters	millimeters	1,000
Miles	feet	5,280
miles	kilometers	1.609
miles	meters	1,609
miles	yards	1,760
Rods	feet	16.5
rods	dekameters	0.50292
rods	meters	5.0292
rods	yards	5.5
rods	miles	0.003125
Yards	feet	3
yards	inches	36
yards	meters	0.9144
yards	miles	0.0005682
yards	rods	0.1818

Using either equivalents or conversion factors, try the following problems:

1. How many centimeters in a foot? (No checking your ruler!) In a yard? How many decimeters in a yard?

2. How many feet long is a 600″ roll of correction tape? How many yards in that roll? How many centimeters? meters?

3. How many feet must you walk if your car is parked .25 km from your office?

4. What are the dimensions in centimeters of a 3″ by 5″ index card? of a 5¼″ by 5¼″ diskette? What are the dimensions in decimeters of an 8½″ by 11″ piece of paper?

5. Your boss's expense account record shows she drove a total of 372 kilometers last week; 300 kilometers were on business. What was her total mileage? business mileage? personal mileage?

6. Your company is moving to a new building, and your boss has his choice of two offices. Assuming he would prefer the larger office, which should he choose: the one that measures 9 feet by 11 feet or the one that measures 3 meters by 3½ meters?

ANSWERS

1. 30.48 cm in a foot; 91.44 cm in a yard; 9.144 dm in a yard

equiv.:	1 ft = 12 in.	1 yd = 3 ft	or	1 yd = .9144 m
	1 in. = 2.54 cm	1 ft = 30.48 cm		.9144 × 100 = 91.44 cm
	12 × 2.54 = 30.48 cm	3 × 30.48 = 91.44 cm		91.44 × 0.1 = 9.144 dm

conv.: feet to centimeters: 30.48
1 ft × 30.48 = 30.48 cm in a foot
3 ft × 30.48 = 91.44 cm in a yard
91.44 cm × 0.1 = 9.144 dm in a yard

2. 50 ft; 16.67 yd; 1,524 cm; 15.24 m

equiv.: 1 ft = 12 in.; 3 ft = 1 yd
600 in. ÷ 12 = 50 ft   1 in. = 2.54 cm; 600 in. × 2.54 = 1524 cm
50 ÷ 3 = 16.67 yd   100 cm = 1 m; 1,524 ÷ 100 = 15.24 m

3. 820.25 ft

conv.: kilometers to feet: 3,281
.25 k × 3,281 = 820.25 ft

equiv.: 1 km = 0.6214 mi; 1 mi = 5,280 ft
0.6214 × 5,280 = 3,280.992
.25 × 3,280.992 = 820.25 ft

4. 7.62 cm by 12.7 cm; 13.34 cm by 13.34 cm; 2.16 dm by 2.79 dm

conv.: inches to centimeters: 2.54 and **equiv.:** 1 in. = 2.54 cm
3 × 2.54 = 7.62 cm; 5 × 2.54 = 12.7 cm
5.25 × 2.54 = 13.335 cm

conv.: inches to decimeters: 0.254
8.5 × 0.254 = 2.159 dm; 11 × 0.254 = 2.794 dm

equiv.: 1 dm = 3.937 in.   or   1 in. = 2.54 cm; 10 cm = 1 dm
8.5 ÷ 3.937 = 2.16 dm   8.5 × 2.54 = 21.59 cm = 2.159 dm
11 ÷ 3.937 = 2.79 dm   11 × 2.54 = 27.94 cm = 2.794 dm

5. 231.16 total miles; 186.42 business miles; 44.74 personal miles

equiv.: 1 km = 0.6214 mi and **conv.:** kilometers to miles: 0.6214
372 × 0.6214 = 231.16 mi
300 × 0.6214 = 186.42 mi
72 × 0.6214 = 44.74 mi or 231.16 mi - 186.42 mi = 44.74 mi

6. The office measuring 3 m by 3½ m (or 9.8 ft by 11.5 ft) is larger.

conv.: feet to meters: 0.3048
9 × 0.3048 = 2.74 m; 11 × 0.3048 = 3.35 m

conv.: meters to feet: 3.281
3 × 3.281 = 9.84 ft; 3.5 × 3.281 = 11.48 ft

MORE ON MEASUREMENTS

- Gallons and liters; kilograms and pounds … compare or convert quickly with the tables inside.

- You can add, subtract, divide or multiply measurements—once you have a common unit.

- One is not enough: There are different standards for weight, liquid, and dry measurements.

Once again, you're about to learn to convert with confidence. But this time, you'll be working with metric and U.S. *weight* measurements. We'll finish up this "measurement miniseries" with an explanation of how to add, subtract, multiply and divide *denominate numbers* (numbers that specify a given measurement). There will be a test at the end, of course, since practice makes perfect. So you'll need your calculator again—as well as the tables from your last chapter.

Working With Weights

The tables on the next page show the similarities and differences between the two systems. Both systems apply different standards for liquid and dry weight measurements. And although some denominations appear in both sections (e.g., pints, quarts and liters), these "same-name" units do differ, depending on their application. (You cannot convert, say, liquid pints to dry liters.) Metric or U.S., however, conversions of weight measurements are handled the same way as linear measurements: Multiply to convert to a smaller denomination; divide to convert to a larger one. Here are a few examples:

1 gram = 10 decigrams = 100 milligrams [× 10]
10 liters = 1 dekaliter = 0.1 hectoliter [÷ 10]

1 quart = 2 pints	4 quarts = 8 pints [4 × 2]
1 gallon = 4 quarts	2 quarts = 1/2 gallon [2 ÷ 4]
1 kilogram = 2.205 lb	5 kilograms = 11.025 lb [5 × 2.205]
1 hectoliter = 26.418 gallons	10 gal = 0.379 hl [10 ÷ 26.418]

Measurement Mathematics

Sooner or later, you'll have to add, subtract, multiply, or divide measurements. Adding simple denominate numbers such as 6 inches and 4 inches may not faze you. And you should be confident enough to work with different units, such as centimeters and millimeters. (That's right, you convert so that they are both expressed in the same denomination, and then add.) But what about adding, say, 8 lb 4 oz and 3 lb 13 oz? Don't know where to put all the numbers? Arrange them in columns of like units, add each column, and simplify your answer. Here's how:

```
   8 lb   4 oz
 + 3 lb  13 oz
  11 lb  17 oz  =   12 lb 1 oz [17 oz = 1 lb 1 oz]
```

Subtraction works the same way. And you can "borrow" units:

```
   8 lb   4 oz  =    7 lb  20 oz [borrow 1 lb, or 16 oz, from the 8 lb]
 - 3 lb  13 oz  =  - 3 lb  13 oz
                     4 lb   7 oz
```

U.S. Weights & Measures

(Weight)

1 pound (lb)	= 16 ounces (oz)
1 hundredweight (cwt)[1]	= 100 lb
1 ton (T)[2]	= 2,000 lb
1 long ton	= 2,240 lb

(Dry)

1 quart (qt)	= 2 pints (pt)
1 peck (pk)	= 8 qt = 16 pt
1 bushel (bu)	= 4 pk = 32 qt

(Liquid)

1 gill (gi)	= 4 fluid ounces (fl oz)
1 cup (c)	= 8 fl oz
1 pint (pt)[3]	= 2 c = 16 fl oz
1 quart (qt)[3]	= 2 pt = 4 c = 32 fl oz
1 gallon (gal)	= 4 qt = 8 pt = 16 c
1 barrel (bl)[4]	= $31\frac{1}{2}$ gal = 126 qt

Metric Weights & Measures

(Weight/Dry)

1 centigram (cg)	= 10 milligrams (mg)
1 decigram (dg)	= 10 cg = 100 mg
1 gram (g)	= 10 dg = 1,000 mg
1 dekagram (dag)	= 10 g = 1,000 cg
1 hectogram (hg)	= 10 dag = 100 g
1 kilogram (kg)	= 10 hg = 1,000 g
1 quintal (q)	= 100 kg = 1,000 hg
1 metric ton (MT)	= 1,000 kg

(Liquid/Dry)

1 centiliter (cl)	= 10 milliliters (ml)
1 deciliter (dl)	= 10 cl = 100 ml
1 liter (l)	= 10 dl = 1,000 ml
1 dekaliter (dal)	= 10 l = 100 dl
1 hectoliter (hl)	= 10 dal = 100 l
1 kiloliter (kl)	= 10 hl = 1,000 l

Table of Equivalents

1 dekaliter = 1.135 pk/2.642 gal	1 liq. quart = 0.9463 l
1 fluid ounce = 29.573 ml	1 long ton = 1.12 T
1 gallon = 3.785 liters	1 long ton = 1.016 MT
1 gill = 118 ml	1 metric ton = 2,204.623 lb
1 hectoliter = 26.418 gal	1 metric ton = 1.1025 T
1 hundredweight = 45.359 kg	1 metric ton = 0.984 long ton
1 kilogram = 2.205 lb	1 peck = 8.810 l
1 liter = 0.908 qt	1 pint = 0.551 l
1 liter = 1.057 liq. qt	1 quart = 1.101 l
1 liq. pint = 0.473 l	1 ton = 0.9072 MT

[1]"Hundredweight" and "long ton" are used only in certain industrial fields.
[2]Also known as short ton or net ton.
[3]Add the word "liquid" or the abbreviation "liq." to distinguish between liquid and dry pints and quarts.
[4]Depending on contents and/or state law, a barrel can contain 31-42 gallons. Barrels may also be used as dry measures (again, equivalent varies).
Note: The metric and U.S. systems are the two used most often in business. But there are other standards of weight measurement used in certain industries and sciences: for example, apothecaries', troy, and avoirdupois.

➡ On the next page is a guide that will save you time and trouble with conversion problems. Simply scan the left column to find the denomination you have or wish to change, and find the corresponding "conversion factor" in the right column. Then, just multiply. For example, to convert 5 gallons to liters, find the "gallons to liters" row. Multiply 5 gallons by 3.785 to get 18.925 liters. Can't find the conversion factor you need? Just add a step: For example, to convert 3 gallons to cups, find the "gallons to pints" row. Multiply 3 gallons by 8 to get 24 pints. Then go to the "pints to cups" row. Multiply 24 pints by 2 to get 48 cups = 3 gallons.

Conversion Guide

To Convert	Into	Multiply By
Fluid ounces	cups	0.125
fluid ounces	milliliters	29.573
fluid ounces	pints (liq.)	0.0625
Gallons	hectoliters	0.03785
gallons	liters	3.785
gallons	milliliters	3,785
gallons	pints	8
gallons	quarts	4
Grams	centigrams	100
grams	kilograms	0.001
grams	ounces	0.03528
grams	pounds	0.002205
Kilograms	grams	1,000
kilograms	metric ton	0.001
kilograms	pounds	2.205
kilograms	ton	0.0009
Liters	gallons	0.264
liters	kiloliters	0.001
liters	milliliters	1,000
liters	gallons	0.2642
liters	pints (liq.)	2.114
liters	quarts (liq.)	1.057
liters	pints (dry)	1.816
liters	quarts (dry)	0.9083
Long tons	kilograms	1,016
long tons	metric tons	1.016
long tons	pounds	2,240
long tons	tons	1.12
Metric tons	kilograms	1,000
metric tons	long tons	0.984
metric tons	pounds	2,205
metric tons	tons	1.1025
Milliliters	fluid ounces	0.0338
milliliters	liters	0.001
Ounces	grams	28.3495
ounces	pounds	0.0625
Pints	gallons	0.125
pints (liq. + dry)	quarts (liq. + dry)	0.5
pints (liq.)	cups	2
pints (liq.)	liters	0.473
Pints (dry)	liters	0.551
Pounds	grams	453.6
pounds	kilograms	0.4536
pounds	ounces	16
Quarts	gallons	0.25
quarts (dry)	liters	1.101
quarts (liq.)	liters	0.9463
quarts	pecks	0.125
quarts (liq. + dry)	pints (liq. + dry)	2
Tons	kilograms	907.1848
tons	long tons	0.89286
tons	metric tons	0.9072
tons	pounds	2,000

To multiply, arrange the units in columns, and multiply each separately:

$$\begin{array}{rrr} 3 \text{ yd} & 2 \text{ ft} & 5 \text{ in.} \\ \times & & 2 \\ \hline 6 \text{ yd} & 4 \text{ ft} & 10 \text{ in.} \end{array} = 7 \text{ yd } 1 \text{ ft } 10 \text{ in.} \quad [4 \text{ ft} = 1 \text{ yd } 1 \text{ ft}]$$

Even division is manageable if you take it one step at a time. Convert any multiunit denominate numbers to common units, divide, and simplify your answer (that is, convert to the next largest unit). If you have a remainder, express it in terms of the smaller unit. For example, 6 lb 9 oz divided by 2 works out this way:

$$6 \text{ lb } 9 \text{ oz} = 96 \text{ oz} + 9 \text{ oz} = 105 \text{ oz} \quad 105 \text{ oz} \div 2 = 52.5 \text{ oz}$$

$$\begin{array}{r} 3 \text{ lb } 4.5 \text{ oz} \\ 16 \overline{)52.5} \\ \underline{48} \\ 4.5 \end{array}$$

Note: Metric denominate numbers are expressed as decimals (for example, 4.3 km rather than 4 km 300 m). So adding, subtracting, multiplying, or dividing metrics is straightforward (once you convert to common units, of course).

▼ ▼ TAKE A TEST ▼ ▼

1. Which costs more to mail: an 8-oz package or one that weighs 200 grams?
2. The airline allows 20 kg of luggage. Your boss has 40 lb of presentation materials to take on her flight. Will she have to pay extra charges?
3. You ordered ten 25-gallon drums, and got ten l0-dekaliter drums. Is that enough?
4. Add: **a.** 1.75 m and 20 cm **b.** 3 ft 4 in. and 1 ft 9 in.
5. Subtract: **a.** 750 g from 2.5 kg **b.** 1½ lb from 5 lb 3 oz
6. Multiply: **a.** 7.5 cm by 3 **b.** 2 gal 3 qt by 3
7. Divide: **a.** 2.4 kl by 6 **b.** 5 yd 2 ft 7 in. by 2

ANSWERS

1. The 8-oz package. Use 28.3495 to convert oz to g: $8 \times 28.3495 = 226.796$ g
2. No: 1 kg = 2.205 lb $20 \times 2.205 = 44.1$ lb
or use 0.4536 to convert lb to kg: $40 \times 0.4536 = 18.144$ kg
3. Yes: 1 gal = 3.785 l $25 \times 3.785 = 94.625$ l $94.625 \text{ l} \div 10 = 9.4625$ dal
or use 0.264 to convert l to gal (10 dal = 100 l) $100 \times 0.264 = 26.4$ gal

4. a.
$$\begin{array}{l} 1.75 \text{ m} = 175 \text{ cm} \\ \phantom{1.75 \text{ m} =} 175 \text{ cm} \\ + \phantom{1.75 \text{ m} =} 20 \text{ cm} \\ \hline \phantom{1.75 \text{ m} =} 195 \text{ cm} = 1.95 \text{ m} \end{array}$$

b.
$$\begin{array}{rr} 3 \text{ ft} & 4 \text{ in.} \\ +1 \text{ ft} & 9 \text{ in.} \\ \hline 4 \text{ ft} & 13 \text{ in.} = 5 \text{ ft } 1 \text{ in.} \end{array}$$

5 a.
$$\begin{array}{l} 2.5 \text{ kg} = 2{,}500 \text{ g} \\ \phantom{2.5 \text{ kg} =} 2{,}500 \text{ g} \\ - \phantom{2.5 \text{ kg} =} 750 \text{ g} \\ \hline 1{,}750 \text{ g} = 1.75 \text{ kg} \end{array}$$

or
$$\begin{array}{l} 750 \text{ g} = .75 \text{ kg} \\ \phantom{750 \text{ g} =} 2.50 \text{ kg} \\ - \phantom{750 \text{ g} =} .75 \text{ kg} \\ \hline \phantom{750 \text{ g} =} 1.75 \text{ kg} \end{array}$$

b.
$$\begin{array}{rll} 1\frac{1}{2} \text{ lb} & = 1 \text{ lb} & 8 \text{ oz} \\ 5 \text{ lb } 3 \text{ oz} & = 4 \text{ lb} & 19 \text{ oz} \\ - \quad 1 \text{ lb } 8 \text{ oz} & = 1 \text{ lb} & 8 \text{ oz} \\ \hline & 3 \text{ lb} & 11 \text{ oz} \end{array}$$

6. a.
$$\begin{array}{r} 7.5 \text{ cm} \\ \times \quad 3 \\ \hline 22.5 \text{ cm} \end{array}$$

b.
$$\begin{array}{r} 2 \text{ gal } 3 \text{ qt} \\ \times \quad 3 \\ \hline 6 \text{ gal } 9 \text{ qt} = 8 \text{ gal } 1 \text{ qt} \end{array}$$

7. a. $2.4 \div 6 = .4$ kl

b.   5 yd = 15 ft = 180 in.; 2 ft = 24 in.
so   5 yd 2 ft 7 in. = 180 + 24 + 7 = 211 in.
$211 \div 2 = 105.5$ in.

$$\begin{array}{r} 8 \text{ ft } 9.5 \text{ in.} = 2 \text{ yd } 2 \text{ ft } 9.5 \text{ in.} \\ 12 \overline{)105.5} \\ \underline{96} \\ 9.5 \end{array}$$

ALL ABOUT AVERAGES

- **Averages are a better-than-average way to spotlight important data.**

- **Simple mean, weighted, median and mode: There's more than one "average" in any group—and we'll explain the differences.**

- **Learn how to choose the right kind of average—and how to calculate it—in this chapter.**

How do you feel when faced with large groups—or entire pages—of numbers? Frustrated? Annoyed? Discouraged? Confused? Obviously, someone (perhaps you) has gone to a lot of trouble researching and gathering all the data in front of you. It's apparent that a lot of work went into that page or report—and all those numbers are pretty darn impressive. But what good are all those figures if you (or your boss) can't tell what they mean?

The Advantage of Averages

Preparing and working with sales reports, inventories, time-studies, and cost and price calculations … these are just a few examples of business situations where you're confronted with large masses—even thousands—of numbers. To handle such reports and calculations efficiently, you need to find a way to summarize these numbers and reveal the important facts behind them. And the most basic device you can use is the *average*.

The Simple Mean

When a group of numbers all represent units of the same value (inches, meters, dollars, etc.) or the same things (boxes, houses, people, cars, etc.), it's easy enough to find their *simple mean,* or arithmetic, average. In fact, the simple mean was probably the first type of average you learned about in grade school. But let's try a quick review. Here's how to calculate the average length of three reports—one 14 pages, one 10 pages, and one 15 pages:

1. Add the figures together. $14 + 10 + 15 = 39$ pages

2. Divide the sum by the number of figures in the group (3). $39 \div 3 = 13$ pages

In this example, the simple mean, or average length, is 13 pages. Let's try another problem: Find the average number of workers in a department if there are 6 people in the first one, 8 in the second, 10 in the third, and 7 in the fourth.

1. $6 + 8 + 10 + 7 = 31$ workers
2. $31 \div 4 = 7.75$, or 8, workers per department

Weighted Averages

As you can see, finding the average is (pardon the pun) simple when you're dealing with units that are the same or that have the same value. However, there will be times when the numbers you must average represent units of different values. A good example would be when you need to find the average cost per pound of all the raw material on hand, and the inventory report shows the following:

Grade 1: 400 lb costing 25¢ per lb
Grade 2: 600 lb costing 30¢ per lb
Grade 3: 800 lb costing 40¢ per lb

Since each grade has a different cost, you cannot find the average cost per pound simply by adding and dividing. You must find what is known as the *weighted average*. Here's how it works:

1. Find the cost of each grade. (Multiply the weight on hand of each grade by its cost per pound.)

$$400 \times \$.25 = \$100$$
$$600 \times \$.30 = \$180$$
$$800 \times \$.40 = \$320$$

2. Find the total cost of all the material on hand.

$$\$100 + \$180 + \$320 = \$600$$

3. Find the total weight of all the material on hand.

$$400 \text{ lb} + 600 \text{ lb} + 800 \text{ lb} = 1,800 \text{ lb}$$

4. Find the average cost per pound. (Divide total cost by total weight.)

$$\$600 \div 1,800 = .333 = 33¢ \text{ average cost per pound}$$

Note: Although it's known as the weighted average, its use is not limited to problems involving weight (that is, pounds, grams, ounces, etc.). This type of average is used whenever you want to recognize the different values involved and take into account that some figures have more importance (or *weight*) than others. Here's another example to demonstrate:

Find the average score on a test given to 25 job applicants last year, when 3 scored 77; 4 scored 80; 2 scored 83; 4 scored 86; 5 scored 88; 3 scored 91; 2 scored 94; and 2 scored 96.

Hint: When calculating weighted averages, set up a table listing the figures to be averaged and their respective weights (pounds and costs, above; scores and number of applicants getting them, in this example).

1. Score	×	Number of Applicants	=	Weighted Score
77		3		231
80		4		320
83		2		166
86		4		344
88		5		440
91		3		273
94		2		188
96		2		192

2. Total (weighted) scores: 2,154
3. Total applicants taking test: 25
4. Divide total scores by total applicants:

2,154 ÷ 25 = 86.16 weighted average score

Medians and Modes

Along with the simple mean and the weighted average, there are two other kinds of averages used in business: the *median* and the *mode*. Here's a discussion of each to help you choose the appropriate average for the kind of information you're seeking.

Suppose that you want to determine the average sales made this week, and your sales report shows the following:

Salesperson A	$ 800	Salesperson F	$ 770
Salesperson B	$ 420	Salesperson G	$ 820
Salesperson C	$ 950	Salesperson H	$ 1,110
Salesperson D	$ 2,600	Salesperson I	$ 810
Salesperson E	$ 850	Salesperson J	$ 650

Your first impulse might be to find the simple mean (total sales divided by number of sales): $9,780 ÷ 10 = $978. But a closer look at the list of sales shows that in this case, the simple mean is misleading—after all, only two out of the ten sales are $978 or more. That's because the mean is distorted by the unusually large $2,600 sale. You must therefore try a different method of computing the average—either the median or the mode.

The median is the exact midpoint between the highest and lowest numbers in a series arranged in order of size. For example, in the series

$$2 \quad 5 \quad 6 \quad 8 \quad 9 \quad 12 \quad 15$$

the median would be 8, since there are an equal number of figures (3) above and below it. Of course, finding the midpoint is easy when your series consists of an odd number of figures. But what about when your series has an even number, as in our sales example? Just add one to the number of figures and divide by 2: 11 ÷ 2 = 5½. Then find the #5 and #6 figures in the series, and compute their simple average. Take a look at the sales figures arranged in order, and you'll see how this works:

$$420 \quad 650 \quad 770 \quad 800 \quad \underline{810 \quad 820} \quad 850 \quad 950 \quad 1,110 \quad 2,600$$

The two middle sales figures are $810 and $820; their midpoint is $815, the median average sale for the week. So if your goal was to show the size of the average weekly sale, the median would be the correct choice of average. On the other hand, if your goal was to show what size sale occurred most often, or the size at which sales tend to cluster, your choice should be the mode.

The mode is the figure that appears most often in a series. For example, in the series
$$24 \quad 33 \quad 28 \quad 27 \quad 33 \quad 36 \quad 39 \quad 34$$
the mode is 33, since it appears twice. (To find the mode, you don't have to put series in order.) But what if more than one figure appears frequently, as in this series:

$$3 \quad 9 \quad 5 \quad 9 \quad 7 \quad 11 \quad 10 \quad 5 \quad 4$$

In cases such as this, you report all the modes (5 and 9 here). Of course, more than one mode may be a signal that you should use a different average. Now, what if *no* figure appears more than any other, as in our sales example? In those cases, you should group the figures in convenient brackets (we use groups of $100 below). Then find the midpoint of the bracket containing the most figures. Here's how it works:

Sales in Dollars	401 500	501 600	601 700	701 800	801 900	901 1,000	1,001 1,100	1,101 1,200	...	2,501 2,600
Number of Sales	1	0	1	2	3	1	0	1		1

The most sales (3) fall into the $801-$900 bracket, so the mode is $850, the size at which sales tend to cluster.

Final note: Before you find the average of any group of numbers, take a second and decide exactly what your data should be verifying or proving. If your figures are not already in a table format, list them in appropriate columns. Seeing them arranged like that may make it easier to decide on the type of average to calculate. Remember—simple mean, weighted average, median, or mode—an average is useful only if you have chosen the kind that is best suited to summarize the information at hand.

▼ ▼ TAKE A TEST ▼ ▼

1. The methods department wants to know how much time you spend filing on a typical day. After keeping track for a week, you come up with these figures:

   30 minutes 45 minutes 40 minutes 33 minutes 37 minutes

   How much time do you spend filing, on the average?

2. Your boss wants to know the average number of sick days taken in your department. Your payroll records for last year show these figures:

   2 3 5 3 6 4 2 4 2 1

   a. How many sick days are taken by most employees?

   b. What's the average sick time overall?

3. The methods department is doing an efficiency study and needs to know how many customer calls you handle in a day. You keep track for a week, with these results:

   10 3 5 4 6

4. Management is trying out a new production process and wants to compare the new process's reject rate to the one from the old method. As you gather the figures, you notice that some workers have the same number of rejects as others. Calculate the average number of rejects with the new process, using this information:

   2 workers had 11 rejects; 3 workers had 12; 1 worker had 10; 1 worker had 9; and 4 workers had 14.

ANSWERS

1. Use the simple mean:
   30 + 45 + 40 + 33 + 37 = 185   185 ÷ 5 = 37 minutes a day

2. a. Find the mode: More employees (3) take 2 sick days a year.
   b. Find the simple mean:
   2 + 3 + 5 + 3 + 6 + 4 + 2 + 4 + 2 + 1 = 32
   32 ÷ 10 = 3.2, or 3 days is the average sick time

3. Find the median (no figure appears enough for mode, high 10 throws off mean):
   3 4 5 6 10; average number of customer calls is 5.

4. Find the weighted average:

Workers	×	Rejects	=	Weighted rejects
2		11		22
3		12		36
1		10		10
1		9		9
4		14		56

   Total weighted rejects = 133; Total workers = 11
   133 ÷ 11 = 12.09, or 12, is the average reject rate.

GRAPHS AND GRAPHING

A picture's worth a thousand words—a good graph, even more. Few businesspeople have the time or the inclination to pore over pages of explanations or wade through large quantities of numbers or data in search of the
bottom line. And why should they? In a report, letter, or presentation, the
right graph can make a point, sell an idea, illustrate the reasoning behind
a proposal, or show the performance of a procedure, program, product, or
company ... almost at a glance. In fact, a graph is one of the most powerful and impressive communication tools at your disposal.

Of course, your computer may have software that enables you to print
out impressive graphs (in color!). But even the flashiest video effects
won't help if you don't understand graphs. And the best way to learn is
to see them in action:

➡ *Bar graphs* **compare items at a single point in time, or show one
item's status or performance over time.** In a *single-bar graph*, one bar is
divided to show the breakdown of parts in a whole. In a *multiple-bar
graph*, each bar represents a single item, but at different points in time.
The size of each bar reflects the amount or status.

This graph shows
Company X's annual per-
formance. (Data: $300,000
sales, $175,000 materials,
$75,000 operating exp.,
$50,000 net profit.)
Scale: 1" = $100,000.

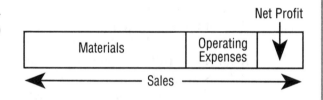

The size of each section is determined by the ratio of each item to total
sales. For example, the calculations for the materials section are:

$$175,000 / 300,000 = 7/12; \, 7/12 \times 3" = 21/12 = 1^3/_4"$$

This graph shows the
annual sales of each mem-
ber of Company Y's sales
force (scale: 1" = $100,000).
Bars are hatched to make
them stand out.

The graph on the next page shows Company Z's annual sales by quarter:
1st = $200,000; 2nd = $250,000; 3rd = $215,000; 4th = $175,000. The vertical
axis marks the amount; the horizontal shows time intervals. The text that
would accompany this graph could provide the exact figures, or you
could write them at the top of each bar. Note: The graph gives the impression that sales are seasonal.

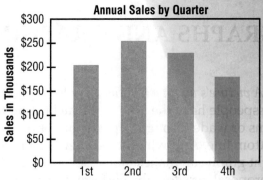

Annual Sales by Quarter

The graph below provides even more information by breaking down Company Z's sales by division. This graph shows that the high sales in the 2nd quarter and the low sales in the 4th can be traced to Division A's performance. The accompanying text should elaborate, giving exact dollar amounts and reasons for the high and low sales.

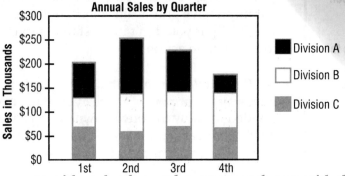

Annual Sales by Quarter

➡ *Pie graphs* compare parts with each other *and* compare each part with the whole. Each wedge shows the percentage of each item of the whole quantity.

Here we break down Company X's sales income in a different way (using the same data as for the first bar graph on the previous page). The calculations to construct this graph work like this: Sales $300,000 = 100\% = 360°$ (degrees in a circle). So the wedge for net profit is:

$50,000 \div 300,000 = 16.7\%; 360° \times .167 = 60°.$

(You can round off decimals—but the sum of all the wedges must equal 360°.) Operating expenses get a 90° sector; materials, 210°.

Annual Performance

○ Operating Expenses
● Materials
● Net Profit

Sales Breakdown

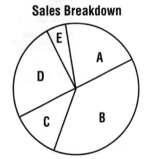

Key	
Product A	$50,000
Product B	$90,000
Product C	$30,000
Product D	$60,000
Product E	$10,000
Total Sales	**$240,000**

This graph shows the sales breakdown by product for Company M. The key is included, but you could put the exact figures in the accompanying text instead.

→ *Line graphs* show trends or fluctuations over a period of time. The setup is similar to that of bar graphs, but points, rather than bars, are used to plot the data. The points are then connected with a line to illustrate a trend. (The line may be "smoothed out" into a curve.) Multiple-line graphs chart trends of related items.

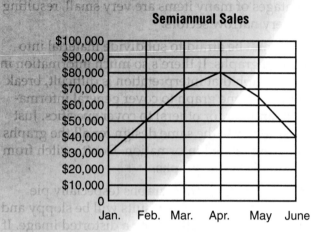

Semiannual Sales

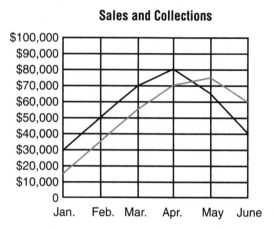

Sales and Collections

The graph on the left charts six months' worth of sales for Company L. (Data: January, $30,000 in sales; February, $50,000; March, $70,000; April, $80,000; May, $65,000; and June, $40,000.) Note: The points plotted on the graph represent sales as of the last day of each month. The connecting line shows the trend of sales from month to month, but it *does not* tell you anything about sales on specific days during the months.

The graph on the right shows both the monthly sales *and* collection records for Company L. (Collection data: January, $15,000 received; February, $35,000; March, $55,000; April, $70,000; May, $75,000; and June, $60,000.) As you can see, in multiple-line graphs, different lines (dotted, solid) or different-colored lines are used to distinguish between data.

**Foreign
40%**

**Domestic
60%**

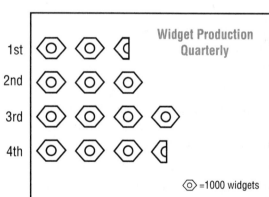

→ *Pictographs* use symbols to compare quantities. They are an interesting way to present your data, but are not as precise as line or bar graphs.

The graph on the left uses symbols of different sizes to illustrate the composition of Ice Cream Chain U's franchises. Note: When using graphs of this style, be sure that the proportions are true.

The graph on the right uses symbols of uniform size to show an item's performance over time. Partial symbols represent appropriate portions of the standard. (So in the first quarter, the company produced 2,500 widgets.) Note that in pictographs, the *vertical* axis represents time; amounts run horizontally.

✓ **Do** check and double-check calculations and measurements. Accuracy is essential. Measurements and spacing must be exact and uniform throughout the graph, so that differences and similarities are precisely reflected.

✓ **Do** remember that appearances count. An attractive graph makes a good impression on your audience and is easier to comprehend. Use color, hatching, solid lines, and dashes to set off sections, bars, and lines to make trends and relationships apparent.

✓ **Do** make a rough draft of your graph. Check it for clarity, thoroughness, aesthetics, and accuracy. Show it to a co-worker and ask for his or her reaction and interpretation. If the graph's not right, consider using another style, adding or eliminating details, changing your scale. Revise until it's perfect.

✓ **Do** make appropriate connections and distinctions if you are using more than one graph. For example, keep the same scales in related graphs, and use the same color bar or wedge for an item that appears in more than one graph. Try to avoid using the same color for unrelated items—the reader may make unconscious connections.

✓ **Do** use *horizontal* bars for a more striking impression when comparing only two or three items or quantities.

✓ **Do** use solid colors or shadings if there are many bars in your graph. Too many bars with hatching (diagonal lines) or dots can have a flashing or strobing effect.

✓ **Do** use a pie graph or a single-bar graph if it suits your needs even if your titles are too long to fit in the sections. You can use arrows to connect the titles to the sections, or color each part differently and include a key to explain the color code.

✓ **Do** use hatching, dots, and gray screens rather than solid colors if your graph will be reproduced on a noncolor copier.

✓ **Do** identify all data and title the graph. Use a key if labels clutter up the graph.

■ **Don't** use a pie graph if your material covers many parts (say, more than eight) or if the percentages of many items are very small, resulting in very narrow sectors.

■ **Don't** be afraid to subdivide material into several graphs. If there's so much information in your graph that interpretation is difficult, break it up. Use one graph to cover general information, another (or others) to cover specifics. Just be sure to use the same design for all the graphs covering related information. Don't switch from bar to pie to line graphs.

■ **Don't** try to draw graphs (especially pie graphs) freehand. The results will be sloppy and inaccurate, and will convey a distorted image. If you don't have a computer that can handle graphs, use a ruler, graph paper, compass, and protractor for neat, accurate results. (Office supply stores have special stick-on tapes of solid, dotted, and dashed lines you can use for more impressive line graphs.)

■ **Don't** use a "suppressed zero" design in bar and line graphs if at all possible. Starting the vertical axis at a number higher than zero distorts the information and casts doubt on your credibility.

■ **Don't** go overboard on special effects. Flashy state-of-the-art graphics, such as a 3-D effect, are often more distracting than effective. They can overwhelm the information you're trying to present, making interpretation difficult and annoying for the reader.

■ **Don't** forget the point you're trying to express. The style of your graph and the details you include must match the idea or information you are presenting. If you must be precise, pictographs, pie graphs, and curve graphs may not be enough. A carefully plotted line graph would be more appropriate. Multiple-bar graphs and line graphs should be used to depict trends—pictographs and pie graphs (even series of pie graphs) won't do the trick.

■ **Don't** separate bars by equal distances if they actually represent amounts at unequal intervals. Keep spacing and scales uniform throughout your graph.

UNDERSTANDING THE
BALANCE SHEET

In this chapter you'll learn about all the numbers and terms that lead to "the bottom line." We'll show you how to interpret a company's balance sheet—one of the most basic and informative financial statements you'll encounter on the job—and walk you through the fundamentals of financial analysis.

The Balance Sheet

Essentially, a balance sheet summarizes the financial condition of a company as of a certain date. (Most businesses prepare their balance sheets on a quarterly or a yearly basis.) Quite simply, this financial statement lists a company's assets, liabilities, and owner's equity (or net worth) and their corresponding dollar values. In fact, a balance sheet could be called a statement of ownership, since it shows what is *owned* and what is *owed*.

On every balance sheet you'll find that assets and liabilities (including owner's equity) *balance* each other. In fact, a balance sheet illustrates the most fundamental bookkeeping equation:

$$\text{Assets} = \text{Liabilities} + \text{Owner's Equity}$$

Note, however, that a balance sheet is accurate only on the day it is prepared. That's because businesses operate under dynamic conditions: Sales are made, materials bought, loans taken, payments received, and so on. But you can monitor a company's performance by comparing balance sheets from year to year or quarter to quarter. (Annual reports often show two balance sheets—for the current and the previous accounting periods—side by side for easy comparison.)

Once you understand the terms used on a balance sheet, the numbers make sense. And if you understand the numbers, you can gain valuable insight into the operations and the financial condition of a company. So on the next few pages we've provided a sample balance sheet, along with explanations of the listings.

Remember, however, that you can't value a business solely on the basis of the information appearing in the balance sheet. Net worth does *not* indicate the market value of a company. Many other factors come into play—reputation, goodwill, past performance, standing in the industry, and so on. The numbers may be "off" because of recent expansion or downsizing, building or buying a new plant, taking on or paying off a large note. But by examining a balance sheet you *can* learn much of what you or your boss will need to know. And by using a few simple formulas (which you'll find at the end of this chapter) you can uncover specific areas of financial strength or weakness and determine whether it's worth the effort—or necessary—for you, your boss, or Accounting to do a more in-depth investigation.

CONSOLIDATED CORPORATION
Balance Sheet April 30, 19___
(in thousands)

ASSETS

LIABILITIES AND STOCKHOLDERS' EQUITY

Current Assets

Cash and cash equivalents.........$522.6	
Accounts receivable 630.4	
Inventories 316.0	
Prepaid expenses, income taxes..401.1	
Total Current Assets....................$1,870.1	

Current Liabilities

Current payable long-term debt..$61.7	
Accounts payable 98.1	
Accrued expenses..........................785.8	
Income taxes payable......................33.8	
Total Current Liabilities...............$979.4	

Fixed Assets

Land 96.2	
Buildings 246.4	
Machinery, equipment, other 187.6	
	530.2
Less depreciation allowance........150.9	
Total Fixed Assets..........................$379.3	

Deferred Liabilities..........................511.1
Long-Term Debt............................1,349.5
Total Liabilities............................$2,840.0

Other Assets

Investment in affiliates..............1,277.8	
Noncurrent receivables 329.5	
Intangible assets 884.9	
Deferred costs 192.3	
	$2,684.5
Total Assets...................................$4,933.9	

Stockholders' Equity

Common stock.................................47.5	
Preferred stock...............................11.9	
Paid-in surplus 521.9	
Retained earnings.......................1,512.6	
Total Stockholders' Equity $2,093.9	

**Total Liabilities and
Stockholders' Equity............$4,933.9**

Every balance sheet *must* list assets, liabilities, and net worth, and have the proper head (name of company, the title "Balance Sheet," and date completed). But beyond that, the sections and listings are up to the particular company. The information may be presented in only a few lines (for a sole proprietorship) or a full page of copy (for a corporation). The particular items listed, and the way they are listed, depend on the size of the business and the industry it's in.

Balance sheets can be set up with assets and liabilities side by side or in one column, with assets over liabilities. (The one-column setup is often used when figures from two consecutive periods are listed, to make comparison easier.) Single-rule lines indicate addition or subtraction; double-rule lines appear below final totals. Also, figures are often expressed in thousands (or millions)—that is, the last three (or six) zeros are omitted for easier reading. (For example, Consolidated has $522,600 in cash and cash equivalents.)

Any information required by state or federal law, if not shown on the balance sheet, must be included in a footnote section. Footnotes should provide specifics, supporting figures, methods of computation, and so on. They are also used to explain significant accounting adjustments, inconsistency with figures in previous statements, and business commitments. The footnote section can range from a few lines to a few pages of copy. (Space restrictions prevent our including footnotes for the sample.)

ASSETS are things of value that are owned by, or owed to, the company. They are listed in order of their "liquidity"—that is, the ease with which they may be turned into cash. The most common types of assets are *current, fixed,* and *other.* Some companies provide a more detailed breakdown of assets than others.

✓ **Current Assets** constantly flow in and out of the company without causing a major change in its basic makeup. The most liquid, and so the first listed, is *cash* (on hand and in bank accounts). *Cash equivalents* (interest-earning securities, stocks, and notes and bonds the company buys to avoid large amounts of cash lying idle) may be included on the same line. *Accounts receivable,* funds owed to the company for goods or services it has already delivered, usually appear next. Some companies also list a deduction (they subtract a set percentage of the receivables total) on their balance sheet in anticipation of some customers' failure to pay their bills. *Inventories* are generally listed at cost. Some companies will break down their inventory listing into raw materials, work in progress, and finished goods. *Prepaid expenses, policies, and taxes* should also appear under current assets. These are payments (such as insurance premiums) already made for benefits or items the company will enjoy or use during the year.

✓ **Fixed Assets** are land, buildings, furniture, machinery, and equipment essential for everyday operation of the business. Since some of these assets wear out or become obsolete over time, a *depreciation allowance* is taken each year over the working life of the property. This is a way to account for the loss in value as well as to show the reserve funds set aside for replacement. Various formulas to compute the amount are used, but basically, depreciation is spreading the difference between the purchase price and the disposal value (or resale price) over the average life of the item.

✓ **Other Assets** is a catchall term to cover items (such as *investments in affiliates*) that do not fit in the first two sections. *Long-term* (or noncurrent) *receivables* are bills, notes, and loans to be paid to the company in the future. *Intangible assets* are things of value, yet are not tangible property—e.g., patents, trademarks, copyrights, and goodwill. (Valuation depends on the industry and the economic climate, among other things.) *Deferred costs* are long-term prepayments, chargeable to operations over several years. Examples are bonus payments under long-term leases, costs of moving to a new location, and certain R&D costs.

LIABILITIES are debts or obligations. They are classified according to when they come due.

✓ **Current Liabilities** are obligations that must be paid during the current accounting year—usually within 12 months. Here are the most common examples: *Current payable long-term debt is* the portion of long-term debt that is due within the coming year. *Accounts payable* are funds owed for merchandise bought. A listing of *notes payable* would include funds owed to banks or creditors (through notes or loans) and payable within one year. *Accrued expenses* are wages, interest, property taxes, insurance premiums, etc.—items that are earned or that add up (accrue) over time, but are not yet paid. *Income taxes payable* are those due in the coming year (they may be included under accrued expenses).

✓ **Deferred Liabilities** (or *deferred revenues* or *charges*) include such hard-to-classify items as funds collected in advance, deferred income on installment sales, premiums on bonds payable, income taxes payable in future years, allowances for moving costs, and equities of minor company divisions.

✓ **Long-Term Debt** covers notes, bank debts or loans, and bonds issued by the company that are payable in more than one year.

STOCKHOLDERS' EQUITY, or NET WORTH, shows what is owned, free of liabilities, by the owners or the stockholders of the company. For a sole proprietorship (one owner), this section might be limited to *capital* (money put into the company by owner). For a partnership (two or more owners), the capital would be broken down into each owner's share. For a corporation (owned by stockholders), equity would be *stock, paid-in surplus,* and *retained earnings.*

✓ **Stock** represents shares of ownership in the company. Holders of *preferred stock* receive dividends before holders of *common stock.* The dollar value appearing on the balance sheet equals the number of shares multiplied by the par, or the stated, value of each share. For example, 100 shares of common stock with a par value of $50 would be listed as $5,000. Details (par value, number of shares issued, titles, conversion features, etc.) about each class of stock should appear on the balance sheet or in the footnotes.

✓ **Paid-in surplus** (or *paid-in capital* or *contributions in excess of par value*) is the amount paid for shares of stock that exceeds the par value of the shares. For example, if stock with a par value of $100 sells on the market for $125 a share, that extra $25 per share is included as paid-in surplus.

✓ **Retained earnings** covers the profit remaining after all taxes and stockholders' dividends have been paid.

■ **Net Working Capital.** A company should have enough net working capital (the difference between Current Assets and Current Liabilities) to meet its current obligations, handle emergencies, and take advantage of opportunities. Just how much is enough, however, depends on the size of the company and the industry it's in. Net working capital for our sample company, Consolidated, comes to $890,700 ($1,870,100 - $979,400). This is a good sign— but not just because the dollar figure is high. What's really important is that current assets would have to shrink a good *50%* before the company would have trouble meeting liabilities (paying off debts and expenses).

■ **Current Ratio.** This ratio (also known as the working capital ratio) is determined by dividing Current Assets by Current Liabilities. It tells potential creditors the degree of safety with which they can extend short-term credit to a company. It also shows how much assets can shrink, or liabilities can increase, without jeopardizing a return of their funds. For Consolidated, the current ratio works out to be a respectable 1.91($1,870,100/$979,400). (Note that this ratio and the ones that follow are expressed in decimal form.) Traditionally, the acceptable cutoff point has been two. But while a result of less than two is considered inadequate for many businesses, a company with a higher ratio is not necessarily in a strong working capital position. Liquidity of assets can come into play. For example, a company with current assets concentrated in inventory is less liquid (and probably in a weaker working capital position) than a company with current assets concentrated in accounts receivable or cash.

■ **Quick Ratio.** Since the current ratio does not reveal the liquidity of current assets, you need another ratio to determine a company's ability to withstand immediate demands on its working capital: the "acid test," "quick current ratio," or simply the "quick ratio." This is found by dividing "quick" assets (Cash and Accounts Receivable) by Current Liabilities. A ratio of at least one to one (i.e., the company has enough quick assets to pay off all current liabilities) is considered desirable. And as you can see, Consolidated's ratio of 1.18 ([$522,600 + $630,400] ÷ $979,400) is adequate. Note, however, that a ratio is not a guarantee: Accounts receivable might not be easily converted to cash before

current liabilities fall due. A substantial lag between sales and collections, or a significant number of overdue accounts, could present a problem. And in seasonal industries, a company in good financial health could have a *low* ratio at the start of the season when inventory is high.

Important as working capital analysis is, it tells only part of what you need to know to evaluate a company's overall financial strength. There may be hidden weaknesses in the firm's permanent capital structure—weaknesses that make it a poor credit or investment risk. The ratios below can reveal them.

➤ **Percentage of Total Liabilities to Total Assets.** From a creditor's viewpoint, the lower the proportion of liabilities to assets, the greater the security for his or her loan. So a low percentage here is a sign of strength. But just how low a ratio is desirable depends on the particular industry. (Precise figures can be found in appropriate trade journals.) Consolidated's ratio of total liabilities to total assets works out to .58 ($2,840,000/$4,933,900).

➤ **Percentage of Net Worth to Total Assets.** Here, a *high* ratio is a good sign. Creditors generally prefer net worth (or owner's equity) to be at least 50 percent of assets. Consolidated's net worth-to-total assets ratio comes to .42 ($2,093,900/$4,933,900).

➤ **Percentage of Net Worth to Total Liabilities.** Unless net worth exceeds liabilities, creditors are taking more of a risk on a business than the owners are. So here, a high ratio (of over one) indicates a strong position. Consolidated's ratio of .74 ($2,093,900/$2,840,000) could indicate a problem.

As you've discovered, while Consolidated is in a strong working capital position, there are apparent weaknesses in its permanent capital structure. More in-depth analysis (by your boss, Accounting, or consultants) may be warranted, depending on the potential relationship between your company and Consolidated.

Note: The relationship between owner's equity (net worth) and assets and liabilities is your primary concern in permanent capital analysis. But—depending on the type of industry and capital structure—the relationships between certain other figures on the balance sheet may come into play. To determine which ratios are most important—and what figures are considered the norm—for your particular business, consult trade journals and pertinent state and federal government reports.

PERIMETER AND AREA

Think back to those hours you spent in geometry class, struggling to memorize measurement formulas for strange-sounding shapes: the perimeter of trapezoids and isosceles triangles; the surface area of spheres and cylinders. Now, be honest: With final exams long gone, how many of those formulas do you recall?

Most of us would be hard-pressed to come up with formulas beyond those for the perimeter or area of basic squares and rectangles. And that's understandable, since most of us rarely need to use many other formulas. But when you *do* need to know how to calculate, say, the area of a trapezoid, guesswork is not enough. You've got to use a specific formula—and that's where this chapter comes in. Here you'll find perimeter and area formulas for a variety of shapes and figures. After you've studied the explanations and practiced using the formulas, you can keep this chapter handy as a reference. But first, let's get started with one of the simplest measurements.

Perimeters

The perimeter of a plane (i.e., two-dimensional or flat) figure is simply the distance around the figure. So to calculate the perimeter of any plane figure, all you have to do is add up the lengths of all its sides. For example, the formula for the perimeter (p) of a square with a side length of a is $p = a + a + a + a$, or simply $p = 4a$ in mathematical shorthand. You'll find the formulas easier to follow if you plug in numbers, as shown in the calculations below. (Note: When you see letters and/or numbers set together, multiply—e.g., $4a = 4 \times a$; $bh = b \times h$. Parentheses also indicate multiplication.)

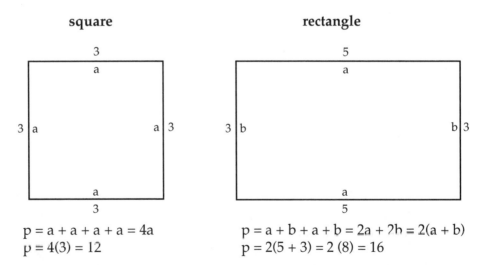

square

rectangle

$p = a + a + a + a = 4a$
$p = 4(3) = 12$

$p = a + b + a + b = 2a + 2b = 2(a + b)$
$p = 2(5 + 3) = 2 (8) = 16$

These formulas also apply to rhombuses and parallelograms ("skewed" squares and rectangles). Trapezoids (only two parallel sides, none equal) have a down-to-basics perimeter formula.

rhombus	parallelogram	trapezoid

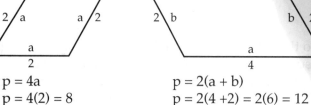
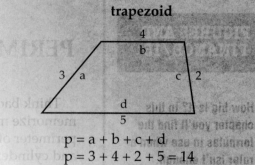

$p = 4a$
$p = 4(2) = 8$

$p = 2(a + b)$
$p = 2(4 + 2) = 2(6) = 12$

$p = a + b + c + d$
$p = 3 + 4 + 2 + 5 = 14$

It would seem to follow, then, that the formula for the perimeter of a triangle would be $p = a + b + c$. And that is the formula for a *scalene* triangle (with three *un*equal sides). But mathematical shorthand comes into play again with the formulas for *isosceles* (*two* equal sides) and *equilateral* (*three* equal sides) triangles.

scalene	isosceles	equilateral

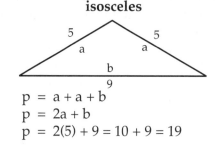
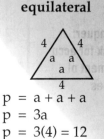

$p = a + b + c$
$p = 4 + 6 + 8 = 18$

$p = a + a + b$
$p = 2a + b$
$p = 2(5) + 9 = 10 + 9 = 19$

$p = a + a + a$
$p = 3a$
$p = 3(4) = 12$

Circumference

Obviously, you can't use a ruler to measure *around* a circle. But you can use a ruler to measure a circle's radius or diameter. Armed with either of those lengths, you can easily find the "perimeter" of a circle, called its *circumference*. All you need to complete your calculations is the number π, or *pi*. (Pi is approximately equal to 3.14 or 3.1416. When the value of pi you should use is not specified, express the answer in terms of pi—for example, 6π.) The two circumference formulas are shown below, with *r* being the radius and *d* the diameter. Values of π are assigned in two examples.

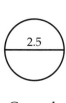
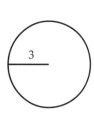
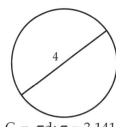

$C = \pi d$
$C = 2.5\pi$

$C = 2\pi r$
$C = 2(3)\pi = 6\pi$

$C = \pi d; \pi = 3.1416$
$C = 4\pi = 4(3.1416)$
$C = 12.57$

$C = 2\pi r; \pi = 3.14$
$C = 2(3.5)\pi = 7\pi$
$C = 7(3.14) = 21.98$

Area Formulas

Now that you've learned how to measure the distance around plane figures, it's time to move on to measuring the space within a figure's borders. Except in the case of circles (where π is involved again), a plane figure's area is found by using its base and height (also known as length and width) measurements. Note: Area is always expressed in *square* denominations—e.g., square feet, square centimeters.

On the next page you'll find the area formulas for all the plane figures covered so far. Here's the key to the formula code:

A = area   s = side   h = height
b = base or shorter base   B = longer base   r = radius

Note: In figures without right angles or perpendicular lines, the *height* must be supplied. For these figures, we've drawn in the height using a dotted line.

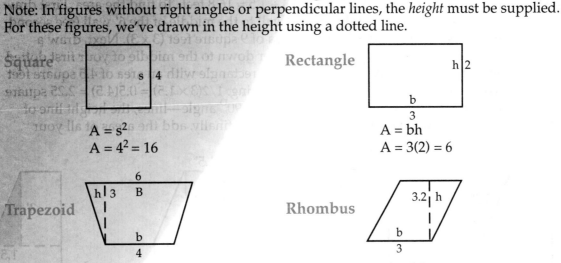

Square

$A = s^2$
$A = 4^2 = 16$

Rectangle

$A = bh$
$A = 3(2) = 6$

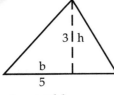

Trapezoid

$A = 1/2 h(B + b)$
$A = 1/2(3)(6 + 4)$
$A = 1\frac{1}{2}(10) = 15$

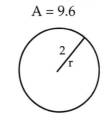

Rhombus

$A = bh$
$A = 3(3.2)$
$A = 9.6$

Triangle

$A = 1/2 bh$
$A = 1/2(5)(3)$
$A = 1/2(15) = 7\frac{1}{2}$

Circle

$A = \pi r^2$
$A = \pi(2^2)$
$A = 4\pi$

What Else Can You Measure?

You've learned a lot of formulas in this chapter. But will these formulas help you measure the floorspace of, say, an L-shaped office or that almost-but-not-quite-rectangular empty space in the warehouse? Sure—all you have to do is break the figure down into recognizable, workable sections and measure them one piece at a time. This simple "divide and conquer" method can help you find the perimeter or area of just about any shape.

Let's start with the diagram of the L-shaped office on the left below. Finding the perimeter is easy enough—just add the sides (12 + 6 + 7 + 4 + 5 +10) to get 44 feet. To find the area: Draw a straight line from the inner corner to the 12' side (middle diagram) to make a small 6' by 7' rectangle on top. That leaves a large 10' by 5' rectangle on the bottom. (Because you're dealing with parallel lines, any perpendicular line you draw from one side to the other will be equal to the "wall" opposite it. So the dotted line represents 6'.) Find the area of each rectangle and add the two areas: 10 × 5 = 50; 6 × 7 = 42; 50 + 42 = 92 square feet.

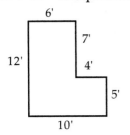
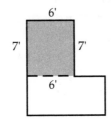
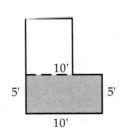

Now, what about that odd corner in the warehouse? (See first figure below.) Again, just add to find the perimeter: 6 + 3 + 3 + 3.3 + 1.5 = 16.8 feet. To find the area: First draw a straight line from the corner of the "bent" wall to the middle of the 6' wall (see second figure). This gives you a 3' square with an area of 9 square feet (3 x 3). Next, draw a straight vertical line from the upper right corner down to the middle of your first dotted line (see third figure). This gives you a 3' by 1.5' rectangle with an area of 4.5 square feet (3 × 1.5). Now find the area of the triangle remaining: $1/2(3 × 1.5) = 0.5(4.5) = 2.25$ square feet. (Note: Since you drew in perpendicular—at a 90° angle—lines, the height line of this "right angle" triangle is the 3' dotted line.) And finally, add the areas of all your pieces: 9 + 4.5 + 2.25 = 15.75 square feet.

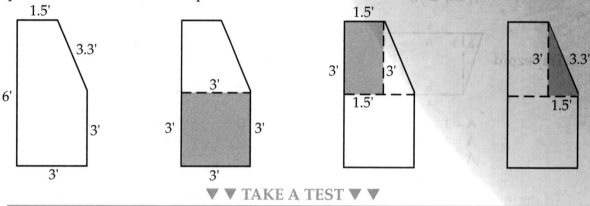

▼ ▼ TAKE A TEST ▼ ▼

1. Find the perimeter (p) or circumference (C) of these figures:
   a. 7" square   b. circle with 3 cm radius   c. 5' by 9' rectangle

2. Find the area (A) of these figures:

   a. 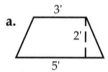   b. 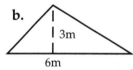   c. (π = 3.14)

3. Find the perimeter *and* area of this figure: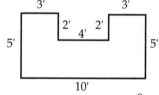

Bonus question: Find the area of this figure (π = 3.14):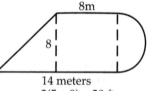

ANSWERS

1. a. p = 4 × 7 = 28 in.   b. C = 2(3)π = 6π cm   c. p = 2(5 + 9) = 28 ft
2. a. A = 1/2(2)(5 + 3) = (1)(8) = 8 sq ft   b. A = 1/2(6)(3) = 1/2(18) = 9 sq m   c. A = $\pi4^2$ = 16π = 3.14(16) = 50.24 sq in.

3. p = 34 ft
   Area x: 15 sq ft
   Area y: 12 sq ft
   Area z: 15 sq ft

   [figure: 3 ... 3 / 5 x 5 ... 4 ... 5 z 5 / 3 y 3 / 3 ... 4 ... 3]

   Total Area: 15 + 12 + 15 = 42 sq ft

Bonus question: The total area of the figure is 113.12 sq m
(Hint: radius = 1/2 diameter; area of semicircle is 1/2 area of circle with same radius)

SURFACE AREA AND VOLUME

In the last chapter, we concentrated on measuring two-dimensional—plane, or flat—figures. And in the next few pages we'll go one step (or one dimension, as it were) further. This chapter explores and explains measurement of three-dimensional figures. We'll start on the "outside," or surface area, and then move to measuring the "inside," or volume. (You may want to have Chapter 15 handy, since some of the formulas there will be used again here—and a calculator will be helpful.)

Surface Area

There are two sets of formulas available for measuring the surface area of a solid figure. The type you choose depends on what portion of the surface you wish to measure. *Lateral area* (L) formulas will give you the area of all the sides on the figure—without the top and bottom. *Total surface area* (T) formulas deliver what they promise—the area of all the sides *plus* the area of the top and bottom.

Now, since experience is often the best teacher, let's calculate the lateral and total surface areas of the rectangular prism drawn below:

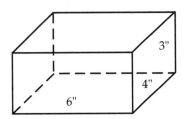

The formula for the lateral area (sides only) of a rectangular prism is L = ph, or the perimeter of the base (p) multiplied by the height (h). Here's how it works:

L = ph   p = 2(6 + 4) = 20   ph = 20 × 3 = 60 sq in. lateral area

Note: You may be wondering why the perimeter of the *base* is involved in this formula, if the top and bottom are not supposed to be included in lateral area. Well, that's just mathematical shorthand at work again. If you compute the lateral area the long way (adding up the areas of all four sides), you'll find you get the same results:

area of front = 6 × 3   area of back = 6 × 3
area of left side = 4 × 3   area of right side = 4 × 3
area of all four sides = (6 × 3) + (6 × 3) + (4 × 3) + (4 × 3) =
3 × (6 + 6 + 4 + 4), or the *height* (3) × the *perimeter* (20)

The formula for the total surface area of a rectangular prism is T = ph + 2A, or simply the lateral area plus the areas of both the top (A) and bottom (A). Here's how this formula works out:

T = ph + 2A   ph = 60 (from above)   A = 6 × 4 = 24   2A = 2 × 24 = 48
ph + 2A = 60 + 48 = 108 sq in. total surface area

Following you'll find the area formulas for four more solid or hollow three-dimensional shapes. Sample measurements are provided to illustrate the calculations involved. The formulas are easier to follow if you remember these two rules: Lateral area equals the perimeter of the base times the height of the figure. Total surface area is always the sum of the lateral area and the area of the base(s).

Key to the symbols used:

L   = lateral area   T = total surface area   r = radius
A   = area of base   h = height (altitude)   s = slant height

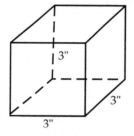

$L = 4h^2$
$h^2 = 3 \times 3 = 9$
$L = 4(9) = 36$ sq in.

$T = 6h^2$
$h^2 = 9$
$T = 6(9) = 54$ sq in.

Cube: Since all sides of a cube are equal, *h* is used to designate length and width as well as height. And if you break down the lateral area formula, you'll see that (as promised on the previous page) it is actually the perimeter of the base (4h) times the height (h), since $h \times h = h^2$. Also, the total surface area breaks down into the lateral area ($4h^2$) plus the area of the top and bottom ($h^2 + h^2$, or $2h^2$).

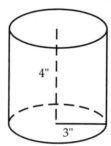

$L = 2\pi rh$
$rh = 3(4) = 12$
$L = 2\pi(12) = $
     24π sq in.

$T = 2\pi rh + 2\pi r^2$
$rh = 3(4) = 12$
$2\pi rh = 24\pi$
$2\pi r^2 = 2\pi(9) = 18\pi$
$T = 24\pi + 18\pi = 42\pi$ sq in.

Cylinder: Don't let the term *height* confuse you when working with cylinders. The height line can run *horizontally* if a cylindrical object, such as a pipe, is on its "side." Area measurements should be expressed in terms of pi (as above), unless the value of pi is specified (as below).

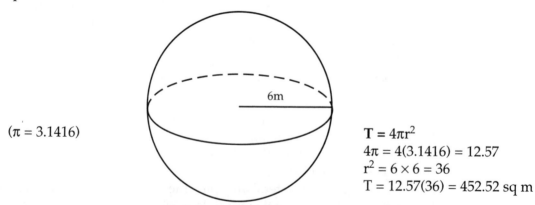

($\pi = 3.1416$)

$T = 4\pi r^2$
$4\pi = 4(3.1416) = 12.57$
$r^2 = 6 \times 6 = 36$
$T = 12.57(36) = 452.52$ sq m

Sphere: Being round, a sphere has no sides, technically, to measure for lateral area. However, being solid or hollow, a sphere does have an "outside," or total surface area, that can be measured—with the formula above.

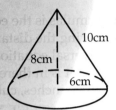

$$L = \pi r \sqrt{r^2 + h^2}$$
or $L = \pi rs$
$rs = 6(10) = 60$
$L = 60\pi$ sq cm

$$T = \pi r \sqrt{r^2 + h^2} + \pi r^2$$
or $T = \pi rs + \pi r^2$
$\pi rs = \pi(6)(10) = 60\pi$
$\pi r^2 = \pi(6 \times 6) = 36\pi$
$T = 60\pi + 36\pi = 96\pi$ sq cm

Cone: Don't panic. The extra formulas are for those instances you aren't given the slant height. You see, since the radius and height form a right triangle with the slant line, $r^2 + h^2 = s^2$ and s equals the square root of $r^2 + h^2$, or $\sqrt{r^2 + h^2}$. (Remember the Pythagorean theorem from geometry class?) Naturally, using the long formula will be easier if your calculator has a $\sqrt{}$ key.

Volume

Whether an object is hollow or solid doesn't matter when you're calculating lateral and total surface areas. And that makes sense, since you're measuring only the outside of the figure. But what about when you're calculating the *volume* of a figure … does it matter then whether you're dealing with a hollow object (like a box) or a solid one (like a block of wood)? Actually, no. Does that surprise you?

To most people, *volume* means capacity, or the space to be filled within a hollow figure. But volume can also refer to the space taken up by a solid figure. The bottom line: The same formula applies whether a specific figure is hollow (a box) or solid (a block).

To see a volume formula in action, let's start again with a rectangular prism. (*Key:* V = volume, l = length, w = width, h = height, r = radius)

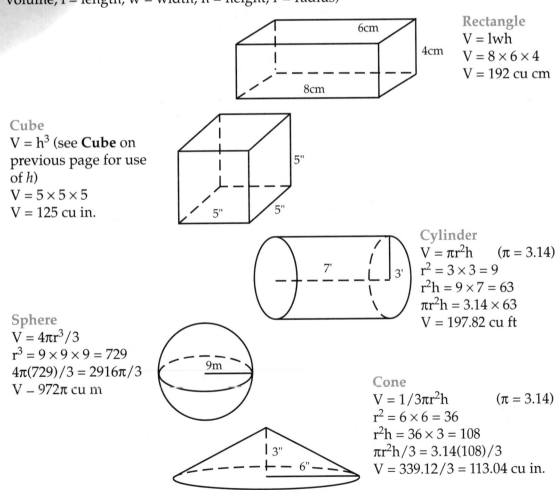

Rectangle
V = lwh
$V = 8 \times 6 \times 4$
V = 192 cu cm

Cube
$V = h^3$ (see **Cube** on previous page for use of *h*)
$V = 5 \times 5 \times 5$
V = 125 cu in.

Cylinder
$V = \pi r^2 h$ ($\pi = 3.14$)
$r^2 = 3 \times 3 = 9$
$r^2 h = 9 \times 7 = 63$
$\pi r^2 h = 3.14 \times 63$
V = 197.82 cu ft

Sphere
$V = 4\pi r^3 / 3$
$r^3 = 9 \times 9 \times 9 = 729$
$4\pi(729)/3 = 2916\pi/3$
V – 972π cu m

Cone
$V = 1/3\pi r^2 h$ ($\pi = 3.14$)
$r^2 = 6 \times 6 = 36$
$r^2 h = 36 \times 3 = 108$
$\pi r^2 h / 3 = 3.14(108)/3$
$V = 339.12/3 = 113.04$ cu in.

Remember: At the heart of all volume formulas is the equation *length times width times height* (or depth). This basically is multiplying the distances the figure spans in three directions or dimensions. (True, this "universal equation" may not jump out at you from, say, the sphere volume formula—but it *is* in there.) Also, volume is always expressed in *cubic* denominations, e.g., cubic inches, cubic meters.

▼ ▼ TAKE A TEST ▼ ▼

1. Find the *lateral area* of each of the figures below:

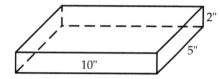

($\pi = 3.14$)

2. Find the *total surface area* of each of the figures below:

 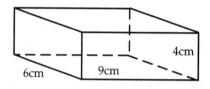

($\pi = 3.14$)

3. Find the *volume* of each of the figures below:

  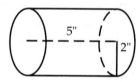

($\pi = 3.14$)

Bonus question: Can a storage bin 6′ by 4′ by 8′ hold 6 cubic yards of loam?

ANSWERS

1. **rectangle**
   $L = ph$
   $p = 2(10 + 5) = 30$
   $h = 2$
   $L = 30(2) = 60$ sq in.

   cube
   $L = 4 h^2$
   $h^2 = 7^2 = 49$
   $L = 4(49) = 196$ sq ft

   cylinder
   $L = 2\pi rh; \pi = 3.14$
   $2\pi = 2(3.14) = 6.28$
   $rh = 2(10) = 20$
   $L = 6.28(20) = 125.6$ sq m

2. **cone**
   $T = \pi rs + \pi r^2$
   $rs = 3(5) = 15$
   $r^2 = 3^2 = 9$
   $\pi rs + \pi r^2 = 15\pi + 9\pi$
   $T = 24\pi$ sq dm

   rectangle
   $T = ph + 2A$
   $p = 2(9 + 6) = 30$
   $h = 4; ph = 30(4) = 120$
   $2A = 2(9 \times 6) = 108$
   $T = 120 + 108 = 228$ sq cm

   sphere
   $T = 4\pi r^2; \pi = 3.14$
   $r^2 = 5^2 = 25$
   $4\pi = 4(3.14) = 12.56$
   $T = 12.56(25) = 314$ sq m

3. **sphere**
   $V = 4\pi r^3/3$
   $r^3 = 4^3 = 64$
   $4\pi(64) = 256\pi$
   $V = 256 \pi/3 =$
      $85\ 1/3\pi$ cu m

   cube
   $V = h^3$
   $h^3 = 6 \times 6 \times 6 = 216$
   $V = 216$ cu ft

   cylinder
   $V = \pi r^2 h; \pi = 3.14$
   $r^2 = 2^2 = 4; h = 5$
   $r^2 h = 4(5) = 20$
   $20\pi = 20(3.14)$
   $V = 62.80$ cu in.

Bonus Question: Yes, with 1.10 cu yd of space to spare.
Step 1. Convert bin dimensions: 6 ft = 2 yd 4 ft = 1.33 yd 8 ft = 2.67 yd
Step 2. Find volume of bin: $2 \times 1.33 \times 2.67 = 7.10$ cu yd
Step 3: Subtract volume of loam from volume of bin: 7.10 - 6 = 1.10 cu yd

BASIC BOOKKEEPING I

If you're responsible for a petty cash fund or monthly bank statement reconciliations, you've already handled bookkeeping on a small scale. That experience with elementary accounting procedures gives you something of a head start. (If you don't handle petty cash or reconciliations, now's a good time for a quick review of Chapters 6 and 7.) In this and the next chapter, we'll show you how to organize and keep a simple set of books. You'll find accounting rules and terminology, examine samples of journals and ledgers (the *books* in bookkeeping), and learn how to record various financial transactions and balance the books.

The System

An accounting system is made up of all the business papers and procedures used to record or report financial transactions. These transactions may range from the purchase of office supplies to sales receipts to lease payments for land, buildings, or equipment. In short, an accounting system is just a financial data processing system. *Bookkeeping* is the maintenance portion of that system—or the actual recording of the data. There are three ways to "keep the books":

Manually: Figures and information are written by hand in ledgers and journals.

Mechanically: Posting machines, calculators, and cash registers handle volumes of repetitive transactions (e.g., sales).

Electronically: Computers of varying sizes (microcomputers to desktops to large mainframes) store, recall, compare, and manipulate information quickly (and often inexpensively).

Using any one of these methods does not rule out using any of the others. In fact, most companies use a combination of all three.

Bookkeeping Basics

Whether you work in a two-person office or a conglomerate, the basics of bookkeeping remain the same. Your process must be an efficient means of recording and summarizing financial information, designed to meet the needs of your company's managers and/or owners. And accuracy, of course, is essential. You'll be recording information necessary for business decisions and financial statements such as the balance sheet. So, your books must show any and all changes that occur in assets, liabilities, or owner's equity. Or to put it in less technical terms: Your books must account for every cent that comes into or goes out of your department or company.

Where do you put all this information? Office supply stores offer all manner of bookkeeping forms, from special pads to hardcover books. You can select from a variety of page setups—two-column, four-column, even twelve-column books. (The number of columns you need depends on the complexity and frequency of transactions you must record.) And computer software is available that displays "pages" similar to those in actual bookkeeping books.

Your books must show where the money "went" and where it "came from." As a barebones example, let's say you paid an outstanding $150 bill from ABC Supplies. Your receipt would serve as a *source document*—evidence of the transaction that provides the information you must record. (Other source documents: canceled check, check stub, voucher, numbered invoice or bill, etc.) With this source document, you are ready to begin the two-step recording procedure:

Step One: The Journal

Write up the $150 as "going to" ABC Supplies' account and "coming from" Cash in a *journal* (a columnar book that serves as a company's financial diary). All journal entries are made in chronological order and include all pertinent information about the transactions. (Your checkbook record is a good example of a simple journal.) The journal is also called the *book of original entry*, since that is where transactions are first recorded.

The Key to Bookkeeping

The first stumbling block most people encounter when learning bookkeeping is confusion about *debits* and *credits*. Many of us have preconceived notions about these terms—that they stand for good and bad, plus and minus. The fact is, however, that in bookkeeping *debit* and *credit* refer to nothing more than the left and right columns of the accounting forms where you record the dollar amounts for each transaction. That's the simple part. The tricky part is learning which kinds of financial activity are considered debits and which are credits:

• Under *debits* you record increases in assets and expenses, and decreases in income, liabilities, and owner's equity (or capital).

• Under *credits* you record increases in income, liabilities, and owner's equity, and decreases in assets and expenses.

Confused? The following lists can help you memorize the debit/credit rules:

Debit	
	increase in assets
	increase in expenses
	decrease in income
	decrease in liabilities
	decrease in owner's

Credit	equity/capital
	decrease in assets
	decrease in expenses
	increase in income
	increase in liabilities
	increase in owner's equity/capital

Now let's see how the system works. Betty Brown, owner of a consulting service, would like to drum up some new business, so she decides to buy some radio time. Paying the $250 ad fee *increased her expenses* and *decreased her assets*. Here's a simple record of the transaction:

	Debit	Credit
Radio Advertisement	$250	
Cash		$250

After Ms. Brown's company car broke down, the repair bill *increased expenses* and payment *decreased assets*:

	Debit	Credit
Car repairs	$500	
Cash		$500

Now you've probably noticed that in both transactions there was an *increase* and a corresponding *decrease*. Don't be fooled by this coincidence.

Sure, all business transactions cause at least two changes in accounts. But while one account (or more) may increase as another (or others) decreases, there are also transactions in which two accounts increase at the same time, or two decrease at the same time. However, the system is designed to handle all sorts of increase/decrease combinations and still have everything add up in the end. Remember: The rule is that *debits and credits*, not increases and decreases, must offset each other in every transaction.

Here are examples of how it works:

The radio ad brings in extra business for Ms. Brown's firm. The first new customer pays a retainer at their first consultation. The $5,000 payment increases both Assets (cash) and Income (paid retainer).

	Debit	Credit
Cash	$5,000	
Retainer income		$5,000

Remember that asset increases are debits, and income increases are credits. So while there are two increases in this transaction, the debit and credit balance each other. Now let's move on to a more involved entry:

The consulting business is booming—and in need of larger quarters. Ms. Brown buys a new building: The building increases assets, the cash down payment decreases assets, and the mortgage she takes on increases liabilities.

	Debit	Credit
Building $100,000		
Cash paid..............................		$25,000
Mortgage payable		$75,000

This is an example of a *compound entry*, where more than one debit and one credit appear. Note that in this type of entry, as well as in the *simple entries* above, the total credited amount does equal the debited amount.

At the top of the next page you'll see these transactions as they would appear in the firm's journal (assuming they were the only transactions for that period). Notice that all the required information is included:

Date of transaction. Include the year and month only on the first entry of each page.

Names of accounts involved. Include the name of the person or company involved when listing Accounts Receivable, Notes Payable, etc.

Amounts debited and credited. Be sure to always enter *debits* first. (Note that zeros, not dashes, are used when amounts have no cents.)

Brief explanation and/or the source document.

Step Two: The Ledger

On a regular basis, each amount debited or credited in the journal must be transferred, or *posted*, to the appropriate ledger account. This can be done daily, weekly, or monthly, depending mainly on the frequency of transactions. Banks, for example, post transactions each day; small companies may post only once a month—or every day immediately after the journal entry is made. Your posting schedule should be set up to meet the needs of your company.

There are two guidelines to follow when setting up your ledger. First, every ledger account must appear separately—on its own card or page (or, if transaction volume dictates, its own section or even its own ledger book). Your breakdown of ledger accounts can be general (Assets, Expenses, Income, Liabilities) or specific (Cash Receipts, Cash Disbursements, Loans Payable, Creditor A—Account Payable, Customer B—

Account Receivable, etc.). In short, you can design your system to be as simple or as complex as necessary to accurately and efficiently record your company's financial transactions.

Second, each account must be assigned a number according to its classification:

Assets: 11 to 19	Revenue: 40 to 49
Liabilities: 20 to 29	Expenses: 50 to 59
Owner's equity: 30 to 39	

Note: If you'll need to list more than ten accounts in any classification, *all the accounts* must be renumbered. Assets would be numbered 111 to 199; Liabilities, 200 to 299; and so on. So choose your numbering system carefully when you set up your books to avoid having to renumber the entire ledger later on.

How to post: Find the account debited in the journal entry; turn to the ledger page or card for that account. Then …

1. Enter the *amount* debited on the first available line.

2. Enter the *date* (include year and month for first entry on page or card).

3. Enter the *journal page number* (on which the transaction appears) in the posting reference (PR) column.

4. Return to the *journal*, and enter the debited *account's number* in the PR column.

5. *Repeat* the procedure for the *account credited*. Move on to the next journal entry and begin again.

The PR numbers provide a cross-reference for anyone double-checking the records or searching for the debits and credits for a particular transaction. They also help you find your place quickly should you be interrupted while posting: Just start again after the last PR number listed in the journal.

Note: Be sure to post *all* amounts debited for a particular transaction before posting the amount(s) credited.

At the bottom of the next page, you'll find partial ledger accounts of Ms. Brown's consulting firm as they would appear after posting our sample transactions from the journal above. (We've assumed certain balances from the previous month and included them on the appropriate lines.)

Date		Account Title	PR	Debit	Credit
199– OCT.	5	Radio Advertisement	51	250 00	
		Cash	11		250 00
		Check no. 173			
	9	Car Repairs	51	500 00	
		Cash	11		500 00
		Check no. 174			
	11	Cash	11	5000 00	
		Retainer Income	41		5000 00
		N.W. Customer consultation			
	23	Building	12	100000 00	
		Cash Paid	11		25000 00
		Mortgage Payable	21		75000 00
		ABC National Bank, loan no. 5572			

Cash   No. 11

199– OCT.	1	Balance	✓	27750 00	199– OCT.	5		8	250 00
	11		8	5000 00		9		8	500 00
						23		8	25000 00

Assets   No. 12

199– OCT.	1	Balance	✓	3000 00					
	23		8	100000 00					

Accounts Payable   No. 21

					199– OCT.	1	Balance	✓	15000 00
						23		8	75000 00

Income   No. 41

					199– OCT.	11		8	5000 00

Expenses   No. 51

199– OCT.	5		8	250 00					
	9		8	500 00					

BASIC BOOKKEEPING II

■ In this chapter: the end
of the cycle, from check-
ing your work to closing
the books.

■ It takes accurate footing
to balance in bookkeep-
ing—so here are tips on
tracking your errors.

■ Learn how to set up a
worksheet: a three-for-
one rough draft of your
formal financial state-
ments.

In the last chapter, you learned about the first portion of bookkeeping—recording the financial information. You saw how the data on the
source document is recorded in the journal, using debits and credits.
From there the amounts are posted to the individual ledger accounts.
Now we'll move on to the second portion of bookkeeping—checking the
recorded information.

The Trial Balance

At set intervals—end of each month, fiscal period, or year—you must
check the accuracy of your books to date. To do that, you must prove that
the debit and credit balances in your ledger are equal. You then prepare a
trial balance—which is basically a list summarizing all the ledger accounts
and their balances.

There are three simple steps involved in preparing for a trial balance:

1. Add (or *foot)* the debit column of each account, and enter each total
—in *pencil*—in small figures at the bottom of each column.

2. Add (or foot) the credit column of each account, and enter each
total (in pencil) in small figures at the bottom of each column. (Note:
These two steps are called *footing the ledger.)*

3. For each account, subtract the smaller footing from the larger one
(on a piece of scrap paper or on your calculator—*not* on the ledger). Then
write the difference, or balance, for each account on the *larger* side—in
pencil, in the account title/explanation space.

The Cash ledger account below (from Chapter 17) shows how footing
the ledger works and looks:

As you can see, this account has a debit balance of $7,000 ($32,750 debit
minus $25,750 credit). Try your hand at footing the ledger on the sample
accounts at the end of Chapter 17. (You can check your results on the
sample trial balance on the next page of this chapter.)

Once you've completed your footing, draw up the trial balance form.
At the top of the page write a heading that tells "who," "what," and
"when." Then simply list your ledger accounts (in numerical order), enter
their balances (your footings), total and double-rule each column.

Following is the trial balance for Betty Brown's firm. (See Chapter 17
for ledger accounts.) Note: The Capital account for Ms. Brown (representing her investment in the firm) was not needed to illustrate the use of

debits and credits in the last chapter. However, it is included below because *all* ledger accounts with a balance—active or not—should appear in the trial balance.

BB Consulting
Trial Balance
October 31, 199—

	PR	DEBIT	CREDIT
Cash	11	7,000 00	
Assets	12	103,000 00	
Accounts Payable	21		9,000 00
B. Brown, Capital	31		15,750 00
Income	41		5,000 00
Expenses	51	750 00	
		110,750 00	110,750 00

Notice that here again, debits equal credits, making the trial balance *in balance*.

This, of course, is your ultimate goal—but unfortunately, it seldom happens on the first try. So, just in case, here are some error-locating tips:

- Add the columns again—in reverse. If you added down the column, add up to check, and vice versa.
- Divide the difference between the debit and credit columns by nine. If the result is a whole number, the problem is transposed numbers—for example, $8,648 was recorded as $8,684.
- Divide the difference by two. If the result is a whole number, look for that number in the trial balance and verify its debit or credit status with the ledger. (A difference evenly divisible by two usually means an amount was posted to the wrong column.)
- Make sure ledger balances were correctly copied on the trial balance.
- Double-check each ledger account balance by re-footing.
- Check that ledger amounts match the journal entries, and that debits and credits for each journal entry are equal.

Note: Never correct errors by writing over figures or erasing numbers written in ink. Such alterations could cause legal problems. Instead, neatly cross out the figure in error and write the correction above it.

How Was Business?

Owners want to know what the net income (or net loss) was at the end of each fiscal period—and a *worksheet* can help you tell them.

The worksheet is done in pencil on a six-column page, and it is basically an extended trial balance. While it is not part of your permanent records, the information on it will be used to complete the company's formal financial statements. The Income Statement section is merely the debits and credits from Revenue and Expenses accounts carried over from the trial balance. The Balance Sheet section contains amounts from Assets (including Cash), Liabilities, and Owner's Equity. A sample worksheet, and the steps to complete it, appear on the next page.

BB Consulting
Worksheet
For the month ending October 31, 199-

Account Title	PR	Trial Balance Debit	Trial Balance Credit	Income Statement Debit	Income Statement Credit	Balance Sheet Debit	Balance Sheet Credit
Cash	11	7000.00				7000.00	
Assets	12	10300.00				10300.00	
Accounts Payable	21		9000.00				9000.00
B. Brown, Capital	31		15750.00				15750.00
Income	41		5000.00		5000.00		
Expenses	51	750.00		750.00			
		11075.00	11075.00	750.00	5000.00	11000.00	10575.00
Net Income				4250.00			4250.00 *
				5000.00	5000.00	11000.00	11000.00

1. Total each column in the Income Statement and Balance Sheet sections.
2. Find the difference between the debit and credit columns in the Income Statement (on scrap paper). If *credits* (revenue) *are greater than debits* (expenses), write "Net Income" at the bottom of the accounts list. (See * line.) If debits are larger, write "Net Loss."
3. Find the difference between debits and credits on the Balance Sheet. (The column differences on the Income Statement and Balance Sheet should be *equal.)*
4. Write the difference amounts in the *smaller* columns in both the Income Statement and Balance Sheet sections (see *).
5. Total and double-rule the last four columns.

Along with a formal balance sheet and income statement, you should also prepare a *capital statement* at the end of each fiscal period. This lists the beginning Capital account balance, any changes (or "activity"), and the ending Capital balance to show how Owner's Equity has changed. (Note that Net Income and Net Loss constitute changes in Owner's Equity.) The capital statement for BB Consulting would be just three lines—Beginning Balance, Net Income, and Ending Balance of $20,000.00—and the proper "who, what, when" heading.

The "headless" sample below shows how to set up a statement when there have been additional investments and withdrawals:

Beginning Balance, Nov. 1, 199-		15750.00
Plus: Additional Investment	10000.00	
Net Income	9750.00	
	19750.00	
Less: Withdrawals	5000.00	
Net Increase in Capital		14750.00
Ending Balance, Nov. 30, 199-		30500.00

Closing the Books

The Revenue and Expense accounts list activity that applies to a specific fiscal period, so they must be closed at the end of each period. That way, you can use them in the next period, starting fresh with a zero balance. However, these accounts *do* show the changes in owner's equity, so you must transfer their balances to the Capital account to keep it up-to-date. *Closing entries* can do both:

1. Starting with Revenue, enter an amount equal to the account balance *in the opposite column*. Since revenue accounts have credit balances, your closing journal entry would be a debit. (See sample below.) You would then post a credit to the Revenue and Expense Summary ledger account (which, as a special Owner's Equity account, is numbered in the 30's).

2. Zero out Expenses by journalizing a credit equal to the account's balance. Then debit that amount to the Revenue and Expense Summary account.

3. Close out the Revenue and Expense Summary. If there was *net income* for the fiscal period, *credit* that amount to Revenue and Expense Summary and debit it to *Capital*. If there was *net loss*, debit Revenue and Expense Summary and credit Capital.

4. Close out owner's withdrawals, if any, with a *credit* to the Drawing account. Then debit *Capital*.

Date		Account Title	PR	Debit	Credit
		Closing Entries			
199- OCT.	31	Income	41	5000 00	
		Revenue and Expense Summary	32		5000 00
		to close Income account			
	31	Revenue and Expense Summary	32	750 00	
		Expenses	51		750 00
		to close Expenses account			
	31	Revenue and Expense Summary	32	4250 00	
		B. Brown, Capital	31		4250 00
		to close Net Income			

In the ledger, total both columns of closed accounts and double-rule them. Accounts that are not closed (with balances that should be carried over to the next fiscal period) must be *balanced and ruled*:

1. Add in the balance amount (in ink) on the *smaller* side, and put a checkmark in the PR column. (See * line.)

2. Enter the total amount on both sides, on the same line. Double-rule across the date and amount columns.

3. On the *larger* side, write the date of the first day of the next fiscal period. Then enter the balance amount and a checkmark. (See ** line.)

Cash No. 11

			PR				PR		
199- OCT.	1	Balance	✓	27750 00	199- OCT.	5	8	250 00	
	11		8	5000 00		9	8	500 00	
		7000.00		32750 00		23	8	25000 00	
						31	Balance ✓	25750 00 7000 00	*
				32750 00				32750 00	
**	199- NOV.	1	Balance	✓	7000 00				

After balancing and ruling, a *post-closing trial balance* is done to prove the equality of ledger debits and credits. The difference between this and the "regular" trial balance? The post-closing balance *does not* list the closed revenue and expense accounts, and it does list the *updated* capital balance.

NOTES